LEARN GENRE FILM SECRETS

From 11 Genres in 22 Films With 24 Concepts To In-depth Romance

By

Sally J. Walker

WRITE NOW WORKSHOPS

Printed in the United States of America

Published by Author Academy Elite
P.O. Box 43, Powell, OH 43035

www.AuthorAcademyElite.com

Paperback ISBN: 978-1-64085-732-2

Hardback ISBN: 978-1-64085-733-9

eBook ISBN: 978-1-64085-734-6

Library of Congress Control Number: 2019907483

AUTHOR ACADEMY elite

Other Books by Author:

Nonfiction

A Writer's Year

Learn Screenwriting*, From Start to Adaptation to Pro Advice*

Learn Fiction Tools*, From Grammar & Literary Skills to Expand/Reduce & Self-Editing to Research & Story Ideas*

Learn Novel Basics*, From Perspectives & Titling to Scene Writing & Anxiety Concepts to Prose Elements & Genres*

Learn Vivid Characterization*, From Fundamentals & In-Depth to Profiling & Life Sources to Dialogue*

Learn Plotting Strategies*, From Fundamentals & Challenges to Never-Ending Resources to Holidays & Synopsis*

Fiction

Desert Time

Letting Go of Sacred Things

The Seduction of Temperance (a novella collection)

Bikes and Badges

TABLE OF CONTENTS

APPENDICES

DEDICATION

I humbly dedicate this book to eight people who contributed to my knowledge of screenwriting and the enjoyment of the subtle and blatant complexities of genre storytelling.

My late father, **Paul Warner**, was a simple Iowa farmer who devoutly loved his TV westerns of the '50's and '60's. His joy infected me. At the age of 16 I noted the name of the writer of one episode of BONANZA and wrote to him in care of Paramount studios. The late **N.B. Stone Jr.** wrote back then mentored my spec teleplay during the summer he was on the shooting set for his film, RIDE THE HIGH COUNTRY, directed by the iconic Sam Peckinpah and destined to be one of the 100 best westerns of all time. To this day westerns hold a special place in my heart. I have been a member of Western Writers of America since 1988.

In 1990 I connected with TV producer **Joe B. Wallenstein** (Knot's Landing, 7th Heaven) who fell in love with my western screenplay STORM MAKER and kindly sent it around to several of his industry friends. Via long distance phone calls, he mentored my subsequent efforts until 1997 when I came under the direct influence of UCLA's Film Chair Emeritus **Lew Hunter** who had retired home to Nebraska. With Lew's encouragement and nudges I wrote 25 more screenplays and worked my way through several tenuous agents. Having been an accomplished writer before becoming NBC Program Director for seven years prior to his "professing years," Lew's opinions and suggestions have always been golden to me.

I fell in love with romance novels and films in the '90's just when that genre was evolving more sophisticated storytelling tenants. I became one of the 10,000 members of Romance Writers of America and subsequently had a romantic novella, *The Healing Touch*, purchased in 1994 as an audio book. Commentator **Bennet Pomerantz** nominated that book for the audio industry's highest award, but it came in second to *Star Wars*—Go figure. Bennet has been a good friend ever since. After I was hired in 2000 by the ever supportive **Ray Hoy** as the Editorial Director for his small publishing company, The Fiction Works, I had the honor of editing a book by one of the founders of RWA, **Parris Afton Bonds**. She also remained a close friend and industry confidante.

Finally, I want to give a backhanded acknowledgement to my fiction writing professor at the University of Nebraska at Omaha, **Richard Duggin**. Toward the end of my studies for my 1985 BFA in creative writing, I proposed an independent study of genre storytelling with the intension of expanding my knowledge base while convincing him that genre fiction could be fine art. I did not succeed in enticing him to step over to the dark side, but that semester's reading, writing, and defending in five genres drove respect for the tenants of genre fiction deep into my creative soul. Concluding he was wrong and I was right, I have been a devout fan, critic, and writer of genre literature and film ever since.

REVIEWS

"I wish I had had material like this for those hungry young minds who moved beyond screenwriting fundamentals in my previous years at UCLA. Sally has struck upon a very unique process of presenting both concepts and the essence of specific genres then actually pointing them out in exemplary films. She presents both the why and the how in a most insightful manner. The whole book motivates the writer who truly wants to create more than one script. There is not one course or book out there like this, including my own *Screenwriting 434*. Not only new writers, but the entire film industry needs this book."

—Lew Hunter, Chair-Emeritus and Professor at UCLA's Film Department, Former NBC Program Director

"Sally Walker's textbook is a comprehensive, valuable resource that can benefit writers of many different levels. There are useful tips, strategies, examples, and recommendations throughout."

—Stephanie Palmer, Former MGM Executive, CEO of Good in a Room (goodinaroom.com)

"I plan to keep *Romantic Screenplays 101* within reach on my desk at all times. *Romantic Screenplays 101* should be a requirement in all writing classes and for all writers, both the novice and the professional. Ms. Walker's manual demonstrates step by step not only *How* to construct a romantic screenplay but, more importantly, *Why* the writer constructs a romantic screenplay in this fashion. (The man who knows how will always have a job; the man who knows why will always be the boss.) I plan to source back to *Romantic Screenplays 101* not only when I am caught in a quagmire of writing but also in my personal relationships—the book is just that downright invaluable in all areas."

—Parris Afton Bonds, best selling author and one of seven founding members of RWA

PREFACE

I present to you material I have learned and skills I have developed in my own writing process over the past 30+ years. Herein are concepts I use, not just think about. As a writer first and a teacher second, I practice the philosophy of teaching practical concepts rather than abstract principles. Ever heard academics described as instructors who "talk the talk, but can't walk the walk" or "Those who can't do, teach"? You will not be able to say either about any of my "Write Now Workshop" materials, including what is here in *Learn Genre Film Secrets*.

Think about using the following principles every time you sit down to write a screenplay. Fundamentals never get outdated. They are what they are: essential to a writing process to create stories that connect with an audience. You must pull from the following pages what works for *you*. Each of us should accept that we are not an all-knowing god thus are perpetually learning, growing, changing as we identify what works and ignore what doesn't. Is that how you approach your learning?

You may be wondering how I evolved the concepts for this particular book. After teaching a number of "Intro to Screenwriting" classes, I had students who wanted more depth, more information to continue their learning process. I pulled notes from numerous articles and screenwriting books, as well as from that study of various genres in my undergraduate days. I discovered a correlation between certain genres and particular aspects of all genres that also applied to film. I simply and logically melded the two storytelling processes of fiction and cinema to create this book, these courses. Finally, I worked to identify specific films that depict the key concepts I choose to explain. Some films are more recent, some are "old." They were not chosen as representative of the "best of the best" but because they demonstrate the concepts I have explained. The challenge I put to you is watch any new film for the concepts you learn here.

Throughout the entire book there are structure and character concepts I repeatedly point out in the various genres. My purpose is not to imply you don't "get it," but rather to demonstrate the importance of fundamentals in all kinds of stories.

My analysis of film examples are purely *my opinion*, based on my timing of the films and my own research.

Note: I also use upper case to emphasize (not to yell at you).

Book Objectives

By the end of this book (and completion of the suggested Exercises) you will be able to:

1. Use the paradigm to analyze any story or film and plan your own screenplay.
2. Identify essential story elements, characterization, and plot types for each of eleven genres.
3. Demonstrate how elements of one genre can be mixed with another to improve your story.
4. Analyze ANY film on your own, identifying what works and what doesn't.

OTHER Book Recommendations

I suggest the following texts because I have pulled and tweaked material from many of them to formulate my own process. I present the list in the order I consider the most helpful to gradually enhance your craft knowledge.

THE IDIOT'S GUIDE TO SCREENWRITING, Skip Press
(A fundamentals-type text with lots of insider questions answered)

THE WRITER'S JOURNEY, Christopher Vogler
(A storytelling construct applying Joseph Campbell's concepts)

SCREENPLAY, FOUNDATIONS OF SCREENWRITING, Syd Field
(Another fundamentals-type textbook)

THE SCREENWRITER'S WORKBOOK, Syd Field
(An applications-type textbook)

THE ART OF DRAMATIC WRITING, Lajos Egri
(A fundamentals concept book for stage & film writers)

THE 1-3-5 STORY STRUCTURE SYSTEM, Donna Michelle Anderson
(A little handbook written by a Studio Reader applying BASICS)
(http://www.movieinabox.com/135/)

Others (in progressively more complex-concept order):
SCREENWRITING 434, Lew Hunter
SAVE THE CAT, Blake Snyder
MAKING THE GOOD SCRIPT GREAT, Linda Seger (And any other Seger books...)
STEALING FIRE FROM THE GODS, James Bonnet
WRITING SCREENPLAYS THAT SELL, Michael Hauge
STORY, Robert McKee
THE ANATOMY OF STORY, John Truby
WRITING FOR EMOTIONAL IMPACT, Karl Iglesias
WHICH LIE DID I TELL? William Goldman
SCREENWRITING IS REWRITING, Jack Epps, Jr.
YOUR SCREEPLAY SUCKS, William M. Akers

And my own:
LEARN SCREENWRITING From Start to Adapation to Pro Advice, Sally J. Walker

Throughout the chapters I will also suggest various other specific books that I have utilized in growing my own storytelling, characterization, and writing skills.

REQUIREMENTS & RATIONALE

Readers will need to use assigned criteria to analyze the following films (two for each genre) to completely understand the genres. Film is a visual medium you cannot understand without seeing it. If you choose not to view any of the films, that is your loss, your choice. Each film has relevance to other specific points in that chapter's lesson. You will find an analysis of each film to guide you, *but* believe that *you* are the one who needs to comprehend how it all works together. If you choose not to watch a particular movie looking for the specified material, you are only short-changing yourself and perhaps compromising complete understanding of the material. And get over the idea that only the most recent examples can demonstrate what is "good" in the film industry. The point is for you to understand the concepts of the industry and the tenants of the genre.

All of these can be ordered on DVD from Amazon.

Mystery
WITNESS (1985)............................ LETHAL WEAPON (1987)

Science Fiction
STAR WARS IV (1977) .... STAR TREK (2009)

Fantasy
LADYHAWKE (1985) .... HARRY POTTER (2001)

Comedy
MRS. DOUBTFIRE (1993) .... National Lampoon's CHRISTMAS VACATION (1989)

Juvenile
THE LION KING (1994) .... SHREK (2001)

Horror
LAST BREATH (2010) .... THE GHOST & THE DARKNESS (1996)

Romance
AVATAR (2009) .... ROMANCING THE STONE (1984)

Western
THE COWBOYS (1972) .... THE MAN FROM SNOWY RIVER (1982)

Historical
THE LAST OF THE MOHICANS (1992) .... BRAVEHEART (1995)

Action-Adventure
GLADIATOR (2000) .... HUNT FOR RED OCTOBER (1990)

Inspirational
KINGDOM OF HEAVEN (2005) .... SMOKE SIGNALS (1998)

After the two-chapter review of fundamental, generalized storytelling concepts, each subsequent chapter will begin with a discussion of in-depth concepts then move into the examination of the needs of a specific genre. The genre sections will address 1) fundamentals of the genre (as gleaned from numerous resources about that genre), 2) character requirements of Protagonist and Antagonist, and 3) PLOT types. The genre criteria will be followed by the analysis of the two example films. The chapter will then end with exercises for you to put the concepts to work in your own work-in-progress.

Let us begin the journey!

LEARN GENRE FILM SECRETS

PART ONE

GENRE FILM SECRETS

24 Cinematic Concepts

found in

11 GENRES' 22 FILMS

CHAPTER 1

Review of Fundamentals: Plot, Character, Format

Every single project that pours out of a writer is hard work, whether it is the 400th poem, a short story in high school, a first novel or the 28th screenplay. Believing that statement puts all writers on an even playing field. We understand and appreciate one another without hubris or ego giving anyone superiority. We are all slaving away to create, some more knowledgeable or more experienced than others, but all working hard.

The creation--the writing--also involves a bit of magic. Each project teaches the writer more about his or her own process and stimulates a growth in confidence. The flip side is the discovery of the adage "The more I know, the more I discover I don't know." For the obsessed professional writer that leads to reading industry magazines and books by the experts then perpetually tweaking the writing process, improving some areas and uncovering what has been taken for granted. The attentive and hungry writer will consistently seek more knowledge from the experts while writing. The belief becomes "You cannot write without learning along the way." Accept it. Get used to it. It's okay!

Most people who love storytelling devoutly read books and watch movies to feed their imaginations. With many it is not escapism, but a need. Routinely wallowing in the make-believe, they develop preferences in genre or types of stories. Some take that taste for granted, but others are very aware of the criteria that satisfies them. The types of plots and characters in genre/category fiction are not necessarily rigid, but the aficionados evolve expectations. Misinterpret or skew something and the devout will eat you alive!

That is why the writer who takes on a genre needs to understand its guidelines and expectations. Floundering ignorance will result in disappointing stories. So, the astute writer must examine and understand each category of fiction to plan plot events, character and nuance that will satisfy the lover of that genre.

Here's the kicker, though: careful consideration can also result in mixing in elements from other categories to create a story with cross-genre appeal that is unique and far beyond stereotyping. That means a bigger audience and ultimately bigger box office which everybody wants.

The world of entertainment competes for the consumer's time. Books, TV, music, movies, gaming, electronic media. The more unique the stories and characters the better a screenwriter's chances are to sell. The wise screenwriter appeals to as many people as possible. Creativity grows, the writer is challenged, the audience is satisfied and the production bean counters are ecstatic.

So this book is intended to move you beyond fundamentals to in-depth concepts, from the examination of each of eleven genres into identifying concepts and genre in two exemplary films for each category, and, ultimately motivate you to apply the lessons learned. You will get the how and the why then the reinforcement of that knowledge at work in cinema. The application part is up to you.

GETTING STARTED

Let's assume you come to this book with a fundamental grasp of screenwriting, a review of sound principles of storytelling in general--and screenwriting in particular--will drive those concepts deep into your mind so you can habitually recall them when needed. You must never take them for granted because they are the skeleton to the muscle and blood of your story. Not only is habitual recall vital when revising, it is also necessary when pouring words on the paper.

These first two chapters are intended to be an abbreviated review. They are not intended as an in-depth explanation of everything but merely reminders of information you should already know. Perhaps you heard the terminology and explanations in a previous class or book, nodded, then promptly shoved it into a corner of your mind. Well, a bright light is about to shine on those corners to callout those terms and concepts to dance at the front your mind's stage while you write.

ALL STORIES HAVE SIX ELEMENTS

Whether it is a short story, a novel, a stage play or a screenplay, ALL narrative forms of fiction's lies have six basic identifiable elements for them to qualify as "stories":

1. **Main Character/Protagonist** to care about
   - Unique, multifaceted, motivated, activist
2. **Environment/Physical Setting** of time & place to feel
   - Credible, effects character, depicts era, sets tone
3. **Objective/Goal** . . . immediately apparent quest based on desire/want
   - Vital to Protagonist, highly personal, intimate awareness, provides tension
4. **Obstacles/Opposition** to Goal THUS Conflict
   - Powerful effect on Protagonist's psyche/response & relationships

5. **Chain of EVENTS/Logical Causality** of stimulus-response
   - Specific, effects character actions-reactions & option awareness
6. **Unity** wherein every element & word contributes to the WHOLE
   - Every word/scene CONCISE, meaningful (or out!)

ALL STORIES HAVE STRUCTURE

A cinematic story is still . . . a story. Even around the caveman's fire, the storyteller had to begin the story, keep the listeners enthralled with a series of events and end the story. If the telling was not interesting and believable, do you think the caveman got any attention when he wanted to tell another? Aristotle discussed the concepts of Beginning, Middle, and Ending in his "Poetics." (If you haven't read the essay, find a copy and do so as part of your fundamental education.) He provided the rock on which modern culture has built its stories.

ARISTOTLE DISCUSSED THE CONCEPTS OF BEGINNING, MIDDLE, AND ENDING IN HIS "POETICS."

Beginning's Set-up and Questions

Approximately one-fourth of any story is the "Set-up of the Ordinary Life" the Main Character is living. In that "Set-up" you must establish your ability to ignite curiosity and tell a credible tale with characters the audience can care about. You have to establish the five W's of 1) Who the story is about, 2) Where the story is taking place, 3) When the story is happening, 3) What is happening to the Main Character and 5) Why that "What" is important to the Main Character. The audience must immediately be asking questions they want answered, that HAVE to be answered in the balance of the story.

Just as the opening sentence of a novel acts as the hook to capture the reader's interest demanding that person read on, the **very first image** on the screen sets the mood for a film . . . be it the uplifting sense of the carefree girl singing in an Alpine meadow of THE SOUND OF MUSIC, the urgency of frontier survival depicted in the race through a forest for the deer-kill in THE LAST OF THE MOHICANS or the overwhelming threat of that huge ship sliding onto the screen in STAR WARS, Episode IV. The impact must be immediate and visual. It helps to have it paired with sound effects and music to hit as many of the senses as possible . . . but those are not the screenwriter's area of expertise. The screenplay is merely a blueprint for all the other collaborators, which this book will repeatedly emphasize.

Of course, the Main Character--the Who of the story--is introduced early in a situation that depicts his or her fundamental personality in the midst of life's complications. The scene must showcase the dominant characteristic that will be vital to the evolution of the story. Yes, that personality can be under-developed or even immature, but **implication** plants the seed of expectation in the audience. Both Ferris Bueller (FERRIS BUELLER'S DAY OFF) and Marty McFly (BACK TO THE FUTURE) are youthful, rather arrogant risk-takers, so you know the stories are not going to be somber and edgy like THE DARK KNIGHT.

Ultimately, at the end of Beginning's sequence, the Ordinary World will be abandoned by the Main Character who must go questing in a New World and prove worthy of survival.

Middle's Confrontations for Empathy and Involvement

Half of any story will be the Middle where the Main Character encounters confrontations and problems. The Middle's purpose is to depict the character's testing, learning and growing in order to triumph over the negative forces working against him or her. Brainstorming anything and everything that could cause stress, stress, stress can easily give you a series of obstacles that must be overcome on the character's journey toward an important goal. The challenge of an enthralling Middle is to be unpredictable yet logical in the cause-effect series of events.

A perpetual rise-and-fall structure of the Middle maintains the audience's concern about the well-being of the Main Character. Tension intensifies as the Middle progresses and the audience is led to ask more emotional questions about the success or failure of the Main Character. Focusing on worsening circumstances which the Main Character must actively attack keeps the middle from "sagging." Every event, every scene must demand the audience's attention to maintain the vicarious experience of the journey with the Main Character.

Not only must the events create jeopardy, but they must also **trigger emotions** in the audience. The audience must vicariously invest attention and internalized commiseration with the experiences of the characters. A successful film plays on the emotional responses of the audience.

Ending's Satisfaction and Insight

The last one-fourth of the story is the culmination or resolution (not a rehashing) of all that has gone before. The Main Character prepares for the "battle" of the Climax. The Ending can be relatively predictable. However, the tension of the risks and the price of the battle should always remain in question right up to the VERY end when one side or the other of positive or negative forces is victorious. Time and again the triumph of "evil" has created "cautionary tales" meant to leave the audience thinking of consequences. The story closer or final scene must be a definitive lasting impression the audience can feel is logical. That ending should trigger the imaginations of the audience, picturing how the characters lived on into the "after-story" world.

THE MYTHIC STORY CONSTRUCT

Joseph Campbell (and Chris Vogler's *THE WRITER'S JOURNEY*) proposed the concept of Beginning-Middle-Ending as "The Hero's Journey" of discovery and conquest, a reliably consistent story model for planning any story, including a cinematic story:

Beginning's Act I/Set-up, ¼ of the entire story

- - Intro the Hero's Ordinary World (out of back-story)
- - Herald's "Call to Adventure"/change
- - Hero's Refusal of the Call (known world safer)
- - Meeting the Mentor (who convinces Hero)
- - Cross the Threshold, Plot Point I event where life changes 180 degrees

Middle's Act II/Confrontation, ½ of entire story

- - First half REACTIONS to Tests, Allies, Enemies/Learning
- - Approach Inmost Cave (Worst Fear glimpsed), Pinch I
- - Supreme Ordeal/Epiphany Experience at Mid-Point & Signal Hero now taking ACTION
- - Reward for Seizing Sword, Acknowledgement/Savoring Accomplishment, Pinch II
- - Road Block/Black Moment of Superior Antagonist defeating of Hero, Plot Point II

Ending's Act III/Resolution, ¼ of story

- - Resurrection when "Mouse Roars" toward Climactic Battle
- - Return with Elixir, Triumphant & Committed into After-story

This pattern repetition of what was just explained is intended to reinforce the structure! You must learn to think in this structure, especially in the planning stage in order to execute it in the writing stage and eventually analyze in revision to identify any aberrations or missed points in the story flow.

Many screenwriting and fiction instructors have dissected the above structure into different parts and assigned their own names to those parts. If it works for them (or you) to look at it differently, that's fine. Remember one thing: the underlying Beginning-Middle-Ending structure is the same in all of them. "A rose is a rose. By any other name it will smell as sweet." Shakespeare's comment applies here as well. Different names merely mean analysis is a matter of semantics and not of significantly different framework.

PARADIGM FORM

In Appendix A you will find the actual plotting form I refer to frequently, a form many screenwriting professionals utilize in both the planning stage and in writing. Various experts have tweaked it with their own terminology or structure, but they basically still adhere to principles proposed by both Aristotle and Joseph Campbell. Appendix B provides the Definitions of the various parts of the form.

This Paradigm can be enlarged, laminated, or copied over and over as a tool for plotting and monitoring tight story progression to assure all the bases are covered in logical manner. The tool is useful to plan and execute the writing of any short story, novel, stage play or screen play. Doing it in pencil allows the writer to erase and revise. Ultimately, the visual tool keeps story structure organized, logical, comprehensive, inclusive of needed material and moving forward from Beginning's Set-up to Ending's Resolution.

FILM ANALYSIS

The representative films of each genre will be analyzed using the Paradigm format. The repetitive dramatic concepts will also be identified in the films. The consistency and reliance on the form will enhance your scripts.

IMPORTANCE OF CHARACTER PROFILING

Some people like getting to know their characters as they write, but in most instances this approach ultimately slows the writing and can lead to wandering plots and illogical, inconsistent characterization. Profiling allows the writer to know who the characters are before actually writing about their current situation. True, writers can always learn more about them as their dialogue and actions are created in the evolving story. It is also known that secrets can erupt to deepen or change the initial character profile. Some writers ask "If that's so, why go to all the trouble of documenting a Character Profile in the first place?" The answer is simply "to project predictable reactions and motivations that keep the story moving forward." A written profile provides four things:

PROFILING ALLOWS THE WRITER TO KNOW WHO THE CHARACTERS ARE BEFORE ACTUALLY WRITING ABOUT THEIR CURRENT SITUATION.

1) **Consistency** that allows the writer to predict reactions and puts the writer in control thus preventing writer's block, a wandering storyline, and inconsistent details,
2) **Complexity** that allows the writer to provide meaningful motivation, avoid stereotyping, and create audience questions
3) **Individuality** that allows the writer to demonstrate unique characteristics relevant to this story from unseen past to quirks or habits,
4) **Exaggeration** that is credible, interesting, powerful, yet arouses audience concern.

The profiling form I propose you use has the three parts of Personal History, Psychological Profile, and Roles in Story's Conflict. Look over the "36-Step Character Profile" in Appendix C. This form gives you the opportunity to "birth" your characters and mentally relate to them intimately. They come alive in your imagination. You see them moving and hear them speaking. An in-depth explanation of the form is provided in Appendix D, an excerpt "On Character Profiling" from my textbook *LEARN SCREENWRITING From Start to Adaptation to Pro Advice.*

The second form in Appendix E, "A Cinematic Character Worksheet," specifically focuses on what you need to pull from the Profile in a screenplay. Key Point: A cinematic character is inherently **dramatic**, a person who makes things happen just by being who they are. In a novel a character can evolve because of events, but in a screenplay the dramatic character creates **drama** in every single scene. The Worksheet allows a writer to perceive how the same character might be portrayed in novel vs. cinematic portrayal.

CHARACTER CONTROL

Character profiling focused on each character with an understanding of that persona's goal, placement and importance to the plot. It also provides insights to what kinds of opposition will frustrate the achievement of the character's goal. Again, understanding each character's goal, placement, and opposition gives the writer the power of natural selection and eliminates other possibilities of story events for that character. The writer controls the scope of the story and the casting.

"Each character" means exactly that. Any and every character in a script is there to impact the main plot. If you are going to depict an imaginary person, have the courage to give each character an underlying drive, right down to the briefest of speaking roles. This is how to avoid stereotyping and how to please actors of every level who will ultimately be depicting these characters.

UNDERSTANDING = MOTIVATION

The essence of "Character Profiling" is creating a realistic, credible fictional character . . . or making fictional suppositions about a real-life person. The only person you can truly "Profile" is yourself. Even then you probably will not be 100% truthful or even totally knowledgeable. After all, don't we learn more about ourselves every day we live? Don't we change throughout each decade, each stage of life? Don't our experiences AND education change how we cope, how we think, what we value?

Documenting the back-story and personal data of a character can certainly be as flexible as our own self-awareness. Watching TOP GUN, we understood a boy's dream to be a fighter pilot like his old man. But why did he have to overcome the bad reputation? How crucial was back-story to the character's motivation? Aw, therein is the subtle need of both character and writer to overcome stereotyping. That one element gave the "Maverick" character consistency, complexity, individuality, and exaggeration that carried the story forward.

> HOW CRUCIAL WAS BACK-STORY TO THE CHARACTER'S MOTIVATION?

CHARACTER ARC: INTERNAL IMPACTING EXTERNAL

Most writers are intrigued by personalities and the why's of actions. They become amateur psychologists, if you will. Storytelling allows a writer the luxury of manipulation. The writer makes the story's characters do what the writer dictates. The chain of events and effects turn out like the writer wants. Of course, in the collaborative effort of movie-making, said writer's visions and intentions can be twisted and subverted . . . but the foundation script must be true to the writer's vision of these characters or the writer fails the most important critic, one's self.

That critic dictates the major players demonstrate some point, some lesson about their life as they experience the story. Driven to understand **why** the characters are motivated, the writer starts from both the Personal History and the Psychological Profile to identify where these people are in their lives when this story begins. What does this character want out of life in general? Then what does he/she want at this very moment? What options does this character perceive that will allow the achievement of these goals? These are **internal motivators.**

Taking it one step further, the writer is also able to identify what could provide the most dramatic **external opposition** to achieving those goals. Voila! The writer has a logical basis for where and how to challenge the character in the story!

The major players need to grow and change, the Protagonists moving in a positive direction, while the majority of the Antagonists suffer defeat. Good over Evil, you might say. Therefore, always demonstrate the internal change. That internal Character Arc must impact the external events in a visual, active demonstration of the change. That active demonstration must be integral to the Main Plot of the story! How did Dustin Hoffman's character in TOOTSIE change and demonstrate that change? And wasn't that demonstration also the Climax of the story? In this instance, the movie was character driven.

The character makes a conscious choice and proceeds to act in a different manner than seen before the motivating event. The change doesn't work if it is sudden, unpredictable, coincidental. The challenges of the stressors in the plot and the character's subsequent actions or reactions must set-up the internal growth. Blatant hints don't work either. That's melodrama. Paying attention to the character's Psychological Profile will prevent that mistake.

Adage: People don't change overnight. (Adages are out there because they are some form of truth.)

Does a Character Arc work in an Action-Adventure plot-driven script? It does if the Arc is integral to the plot. Sometimes the reluctant warrior merely proves his metal as in the warrior-trained Ryan coldly shooting the cook in HUNT FOR RED OCTOBER. Before that, the audience saw an intellectual man who willingly took on physically dangerous challenges inherent to circumstances. We learned his personal history of surviving a helicopter crash yet graduating from the Naval Academy. When he came face to face with the enemy, he did the deed and slept on the plane ride home. There was the visual though subtle evidence of his internal motivation grown to the point of calmly accepting the personal consequences of a life-and-death decision. The Captain of the Dallas changed from distrust to acceptance of Sean Connery's character, Ramius, and willingly played submarine "chicken." Oversimplification perhaps, but both demonstrate subtle Character Arcs all the same.

CHARACTER SPECIFICS IN EACH GENRE

These fundamentals provide points for each of the subsequent genre discussions. Be ready to refer BACK to this lesson point in future chapters. Some will emphasize one area and others will draw from many aspects. You must command:

- Profiling fundamentals of complex personalities to avoid stereotyping

- NINE Character Points in Plotting

1) Action that characterizes
2) Hint of background's influence thru showing, not telling
3) Contrast of characters off characters
4) Names that memorably characterize
5) Conflict, internal & external
6) Reveal character in intense moments
7) Role placement for optimal consequence
8) Circumstance that plays Alpha (physically dominant) vs. Beta (intellectually observant)
9) Routine-Gone-Awry triggers

- Six types of important cast members
(besides Protagonist & Antagonist)

1. Supporting (Speaking Parts)
2. Place-holder (Few Speaking Parts)

3. Children
4. Animals
5. Comic
6. Cowards

- Antagonists who are intense & powerful, both as major & minor opposition
- Plotting Factors from the psyche: Anxiety, Motivation, Challenge

ELEVEN RULES OF CINEMATIC DIALOGUE

Always remind yourself that fictional dialogue is meant to be exaggerated, NOT mimic real life with its "um" type hesitations and mundane exchanges. Keep it condensed, purposeful, powerful!

1. Avoid "on-the-nose" dialogue that announces the obvious or precedes the visually obvious, unless it is meant to be humorous or demonstrate the ignorance of the character.

2. Delete too many direct references (speaker names) in sequential dialogue, especially if there are only two people. Each should have a unique voice so the reader KNOWS who is speaking!

3. DO NOT use speech directives or "said-isms" as parentheticals below the character's name to tell the actor how to say the line, like "Responds crisply," "Whispers," "Roars" "Snaps." Instead, make certain the speech honestly delivers the "said-ism" tone. Leave the inflection to the actor and the director . . . It is acceptable to break up longer speeches with SIGNIFICANT physical action, but ONLY if significant. Otherwise the action is the "business" of the actor and director to decide.

4. Avoid describing dialogue's nuances with parenthetical adverbs, those nasty -ly words. Diction should stand alone. Use ONLY those that will indicate how a sentence or phrase is said DIFFERENTLY than it is written, for example "Sarcastically" or "Sputtering embarrassment." It is needed if the context of the dialogue is not obvious, otherwise the inflection is the realm of the actor and director.

5. Reword heavy-handed (intellectual) dialogue containing too much information. Break it up. More importantly, ask yourself if it is really necessary AND if you can abbreviate it and have the same effect. Think "Five Line Rule." The more succinct the dialogue, the more fast paced the scene. Lecturing or long-winded explanation SLOWS the action, focusing on ONE character. You are writing a movie, not a talkie!

6. Eliminate unnecessary/trivial dialogue, the great time waster, such as "Good morning, Miss Hughes." "And to you, Mr. Evans. Can I get you some coffee?" "Of course and bring the paper back, too." <Yawn> Greetings are greetings are greetings. You may think you are setting the tone of relationship but there are MORE VISUAL ways of doing it than wasting precious space with this inane back and forth.

7. Think about occasional use of tension-building multi-layered dialogue that has the nuance of another message being delivered beyond the obvious meaning of the speech. Develop an ear for "something else is going on here." Have a character say one thing, but by reaction, the listening character realizes there is a meaning beyond these words. The short, innuendo-filed speeches of stoic characters are ripe with humor or dark messages.

8. Pay attention to brevity of speeches and impact of content. Every single speech given should move the story forward in some way. One way to check this is ask yourself "Would a stranger want to eavesdrop on this conversation?" How interesting is the exchange? What will be the consequence of the exchange? Delete if the words are not important.

9. Check for repetitive information, not only in sequential exchanges but throughout the entire work. You can do this by reading JUST the dialogue of each character throughout the work. Yes, one at a time checking for consistency of speech patterns and unique speeches, for repetition of information. Emphasis is fine but saying it three or four times is down-right tiresome and sloppy writing.

10. Let the character's unique syntax and diction flow. Render replicating a particular dialect ONLY if you are an expert. Instead use authentic idioms or phrases like a native Latino or a Scot would use. If you are going to delve into jargon, you had better be an expert or seek the advice of someone familiar with it. Think professional, regional or era. As a historical reader I feel there is nothing more annoying than someone speaking a 19th century phrase in the 13th century or lay terminology coming out of the mouths of two medical personnel exchanging opinions.

PLEASE DEVOTE YOURSELF TO MAKING YOUR MALES SOUND MALE AND YOUR FEMALES SOUND FEMALE.

PLEASE devote yourself to making your males sound male and your females sound female. (Read *Men are From Mars, Women are from Venus* by Psychologist John Grey AND *You Just Don't Understand* by Linguist Deborah Tannen). A basic concept is that women tend to be more verbose and MOST men (except for attorneys and con artists) respond like the Eastwood character in ESCAPE FROM ALCATRAZ when he was asked "How was your childhood?" "Short." Most men are not into baring their souls and explaining themselves.

11. Finally, READ ALOUD facing a mirror, preferably in an enclosed space like a bathroom. Ask "Is it awkward? Does it logically flow? Are the sentences too long? Is the tone of each speech credible? Is the arguing too long-winded instead of accusatory snapping? Does the child sound like a child of that age?" You get the idea. Bottom line: Is it credible?

INVEST IN THE PROPER SOFTWARE

Many people will use "freeware" and that is their choice. Professionals use professional software.

Lew Hunter's most important advice has been "Invest in a good screenwriting software program like Final Draft or Screenwriter's Movie Magic . . . and spend the money on the updates when they come out. Ignore the 'freeware' because their programs may not 'work' with the Final Draft and Screenwriter programs used by the professionals you submit to. Rely on the current software to format your work correctly. If it doesn't look right on the page, the readers and other pros you submit to won't CARE if the story and characters are unique and memorable. They will only see the unprofessionalism of the script and won't bother reading it."

Electronic script submissions are saved in Adobe Acrobat pdf that can be opened and analyzed by the professional. When using Final Draft or Movie Magic, the script data can be quickly program-accessed noting cast size and number of speeches each cast member has. The locations data will list interior and exterior slug lines. And on and on. Bottom line: The professional programs are designed to create an industry standard format that results in guesstimating the budget for that script. An actor reading the script can even count the number of his character's speeches and how many scenes he appears in, thus identifying how important that role is and how much money to ask for.

Of course, the pro software has many of the bells-and-whistles of regular word processing programs, but has them configured to work for the specialized world of screenwriting. Learn them and use them to make your end product as polished as possible.

The competition is stiff out there, so you want your "look" to not be an issue. Remember, these people are so busy with so many scripts to read and analyze, one excuse is all they need to set a script aside and go on to the next one. Don't give them that excuse.

COMMON CONVENTIONS OF A SCREENPLAY

Courier New, 12 pt font
Single spaced
Left margin 1.75 "
Right margin 1.25"
Top & bottom margins 1.25"
Header: (dot).Page #, upper right corner (.46)
UPPER CASE Dialogue Names, centered
Dialogue margin 15 spaces in from left & 10 spaces in from right
Parentheticals 20 spaces in under NAME, enclosed by parenthesis
Single space after parenthetical
Double space after:
- Slug Line
- Each narrative paragraph
- Last line of Dialogue
- Right-hand Transition like CUT TO:

FADE IN: top left of first page
FADE OUT: right margin after centered "THE END"
No longer use CONTINUED (bottom right) if a Scene goes onto next page
Do use MORE if dialogue runs onto next page

Title Page
Title centered about down 1/3 from top
Double-space
"By" centered
Double-space
Your name

If your scripts is an adaptation that information needs to appear next, even if adapting your own material.

If unrepresented, ALL of your contact info in right lower corner of Title Page. DO NOT include your Copyright # or WGA Reg. #. Readers don't care if you protected yourself or not. The number has ZERO to do with the quality of the script. That number is for your use, not theirs.

Covers
Pastel card-stock cover, 2-hole punched with same as "Title Page" (minus contact info)
Bound by #6 Brass Fasteners (1.5" long with larger than "norm" head)—Can order from Amazon

Dialogue

1. If action more than three-word parenthetical, break to narrative, then return to Dialogue:

```
                    JANE
       You won't miss me, Frank.

She grips knife harder, steps to his back, then rams
it up under his left shoulder blade.

                    JANE (Cont'd)
       Because I'm not leaving. You are.
```

2. Because actors need to note the continuation, if dialogue runs to next page:

```
                    RUPERT
       One chance to run, baby. I catch you,
       you are mine. Until death or hell freezes
       over. Your
                    (MORE)
-----------------------------------------------------
                    RUPERT (CONT'D)
       choice. I ain't training another woman.
       Why are you standing there?
```

3. Use upper case or italics for emphasis as little as possible as that is Actor's domain.

4. Use ellipsis sparingly, as well, but use at end of line if fade away and a dash if cut off as in interrupted.

```
                    LINDA
       Let me hold her one more time. Please.
       Just a last cuddle—

                    JAKE
       (Interrupting)
       Move again and I will shoot, witch!

                    LINDA
       Ever the hero. You know I'll come back
       when you're not here.
```

```
                    JAKE
      Go. Now. Before I . . .

He straight-arms the pistol at her face. She squares
her shoulders, turns and exits into the night.
```

5. Use proper capitalization of titles such as Mom or Captain and don't forget to set addresses off with a comma.

```
                    RICHARD
      You hold that title, Mom.

                    BETTY
      I'm grateful she birthed you. So, there!
      Out the door, Ensign. Leave-time's up.
```

6. If a cliché is appropriate to characterize region or personality, use it in dialogue but NEVER in narrative. Even in screenplays narrative clichés are lazy writing.

```
                 AUNT MATILDA
      Boy, you are slower than a turtle in
      molasses.

He mimics her words. She barks a laugh. He grins,
dodges her grasp and scoops cookies off the counter
on his way out the porch door.
```

7. Note foreign language speeches in parenthetical. From my script WHEN EAGLES SCREAM:

She hands the phone to Vance.

```
                    VANCE
      Hola, Emile Alesandro.
           (Beat . In Arabic, subtitled)
      Yes. Your obnoxious friend has
      returned. A woman and I need mountain
      transportation. Tomorrow.
           (Beat. Grinning)
      Reuniting lovers and paying debts.
      It doesn't get any better, does it?
```

BASIC CONCEPTS OF SCREENPLAY NARRATIVE

1. One Page of Courier 12-pt in proper format = One minute of screen time

2. Write present tense SIMPLE noun-action verb sentences. Make it READ and flow . . . like a journalistic short story!

3. Write a movie not a talkie . . . What action could depict these words?

4. Grammar, spelling, punctuation count! (Those are the Writer's Tools)

5. First time a character appears name is in all UPPER CASE with (age) and short characterizing description and/or significant costuming, if necessary. Short means 2-3 phrases, not a paragraph. Descriptions that make the character "pop" without mundane, common factors.

6. Don't micro-choreograph every movement, especially in action sequences (That's a Director's call and an Actor's choice). Just "Chase scene" or "They make love" or "Fight scene" since Director, actors and stunt coordinators will choreograph. Here's a little more detail summarized in climax of PAYING THE PIPER

```
A military-trained killing machine, Jess takes Pete
apart, piece by bloody piece. Despite his size and
bull-headed street fighting, Pete's face and body
turn to hamburger.
```

Mesmerized, not quite believing what she sees, Sherri stands nearby.

7. New paragraph for EVERY new shot. (Hint: Write it out then break it up into paragraphs of five or less sentences.) Be logical but not anal or obtuse . . . Let your audience deduce connections. Many production companies will do "Storyboarding" with an artist rendering a cartoon-like visual image the director can "tweak" before actually doing the expensive shooting with cast and crew. If you think in these kinds of "still" shots, it can help to identify where to have a new paragraph or even a single line.

8. Narrative breaks allow for Special Effects needs to be identified more easily than if they are embedded in the middle of a lengthy narrative paragraph.

9. Slug Lines are either INT. or EXT. and NIGHT or DAY. Your subsequent narrative below the slug line can indicate if "Just before sunrise" or "In the burning heat of the afternoon." Remember to use succinct descriptive terms.

You are NOT writing a novel, merely "setting scene." The more general your location descriptions, the easier it will be for the Location Scout and Director to decide on **where** to shoot the scene.

10. If it can't be seen, it's not on the page! (Thoughts are NOT visual, only reactions are!) It is not necessary for the writer to describe specific reactions. "Actors act; Writers write."

11. Sounds need no longer be put in uppercase in a Spec Script . . . though they will be in a Shooting Script for the Sound Effects people to note.

12. V.O. is "Voice Over" meaning speaking done over the visual. (Examples: THE GHOST & THE DARKNESS, A RIVER RUNS THROUGH IT and DUNE.) **O.S. is "Off Screen" meaning the speaker is in another room** or on the telephone, etc. and "could" appear on screen.

13. Do not use camera angles in Spec Script since this is only "The Story Idea" and Director and Cinematographer make those decisions. You are writing in macro-scenes, not dictating camera movement or what is framed in the camera's lens.

14. Can use POV (Point of View) indicating what a character is looking at.

15. INSERT will indicate an object that needs to be filmed in a close-up manner to be "inserted" at this point. Early film-makers used a lot of inserts, but the more recent trend is minimal usage.

16. SERIES OF SHOTS or MONTAGE in one location can be done, but if the series requires different locations you need to make each brief scene its own Slug Line shot because these must be located and set-up in different locations, maybe even at different times.

17 Do not suggest music, titling or credit placement as that is Post Production jobs of very talented others. Your script is merely a blue-print. The Post-Production work is a melding of Director, Film Editor, Sound Effects and Orchestration and relies heavily on budget . . . which, of course, the writer has zero say.

* * * * *

CHAPTER 2

Expectations of Genre Film & Beating "No New Stories"

Basically, you will find explanations of how to analyze then mix and match plot elements and character qualities, pulling concepts from one genre to fill out and enhance your favored genre of story. So, let's start with "Why do you like a particular genre or kind of story?"

CROSS-GENRE APPEAL

Whether via novel or screenplay, storytellers, like their audience, develop a preference for "kinds" or genres of stories. These stories give them comfort and satisfy a portion of their imagination that craves a particular kind of story. There is no right or wrong of it; it simply is. And thank God, for diversity makes the world interesting and unpredictable. As creative storytellers we in turn seek differences, new twists to people problems and their solutions, new challenges for characters to meet. We will write what we like to read or watch. Yet many a writer cannot identify requirements of their genre and even more have no idea how combining certain elements from another genre will broaden a story's audience appeal and make their story more appealing and more marketable.

WHETHER VIA NOVEL OR SCREENPLAY, STORYTELLERS, LIKE THEIR AUDIENCE, DEVELOP A PREFERENCE FOR "KINDS" OR GENRES OF STORIES.

EXPERIENCED WRITERS UNDERSTAND THE STRUCTURAL NEED FOR BEGINNING'S SET-UP, MIDDLE'S CONFRONTATIONS, AND ENDING'S RESOLUTION.

Experienced writers understand the structural need for Beginning's set-up, Middle's confrontations, and Ending's resolution. They know every satisfying story has to have characters to care about, credible setting, character goals encountering antagonistic elements, and unity of every element taking the audience on a journey for a specific purpose.

So, how do these fundamentals apply to the prescribed structure of screenplays? How does a writer create "fresh" concepts out of genre formula? How does a craftsman become an innovative artist? You must learn the rules of both storytelling and a genre before you can successfully break them.

First, the structure needs to become disciplined habit. This book will explain the storytelling paradigm with an innovative one-page schematic. Designed for screenplays, it can be applied to any kind of fiction. As each of eleven genres are examined, you will expand your expertise in the requirements of that genre. If you choose to do the exercises you will be asked to demonstrate something of the genre and the paradigm element under discussion . . . as well as write a few more pages of a screenplay-in-progress. In other words, you can read then apply the principles in a progressive manner that will drive the concepts home.

Each genre will be presented in terms of audience expectation of main story events, characterization, and plot types. To truly get the most of the material you will need to watch two recommended film examples of each genre to look for both genre expectations and the in-depth concepts discussed in that section.

Not only will you discover a deeper appreciation for a favored genre, but also a critical eye for others. As the paradigm's elements are practiced, the writer can overcome reluctance or even distaste for those other genres. Ultimately, you will understand how to weave cross-genre stories, powerful stories that move beyond formula to imprint themselves on audience memory.

GENRE EXPECTATONS

Why do readers purchase a particular book or choose to see a particular kind of movie? Something piques their interest, be it the cover, the known author's or creator's name, the advertising hype, the lead actors. Expectations are established before the targeted audience dives into the make-believe world the storyteller has created. The deliberate, careful craftsman knows those expectations and intentionally meets and exceeds them.

Aficionados of specific genres seek escapism in stories that meet basic genre expectations. The writer who wants to challenge innate storytelling ability looks for genre elements appropriate to their fundamental story and characters that will have an appeal to more than one genre or category of fiction. The story structure will meet the requirements of another genre but the main thrust of plot and character follows the "guideline" expectations of one.

Let us start with the fundamentals of each genre.

GENRE ESSENCE

1. Mystery: "Crime" committed and solved
2. Juvenile: Children discovering life-lessons
3. Inspirational: Spiritual lessons learned (not just Christian)
4. Historical: Fiction based on actual events and/or people before author's time
5. Western: Humans carving life in rugged frontier (not always American West)
6. Action-Adventure/Thriller: Alpha humans challenged to the ultimate
7. Science Fiction: Humans vs. technology, commonly futuristic or other worlds
8. Fantasy: Incredible society with credible problems
9. Horror: Nightmares made sensually credible
10. Romance: Couple (male-female or same sex) struggle toward commitment
11. Humor: Expectations established then reversed

Note: there are other classifications like the grittiness of Film Noir that could be compared to "literary novels" and the gratuitous film-making of the porn industry or erotica in the publishing world. I personally do not choose to analyze either of these extremes.

A truly good writer with a creative conscience incorporates and follows the guidelines of their main genre yet stuns or excites the audience with:

1) Memorable characters with complex, worthy motivations
2) Realistic, suspenseful causality of Beginning-Middle-Ending structure
3) Adherence to universal, worthwhile Statement of Purpose

LEVELS OF CRAFTSMANSHIP

Don't ever confuse formula guidelines with "hack" or "lack of creative initiative" as some will encounter through category bashing by "elitist critics." Those people have not thoroughly examined the nuances of each and every genre or category to form an appreciation for them.

Well versed, attention-to-detail movie goers will first critique the writer's ability to meet the main genre's guidelines then look for the twists and turns provided by their cross-genre efforts. They will innately look for craftsmanship. Here are the recognized levels applicable to any and all forms of art::

1. Poorly Crafted: Either created by a raw beginner or a person who carelessly throws something into the world with little understanding of the art form's fundamentals. School children being introduced to visual art and hack storytelling are two examples.

2. Simply Crafted: With a basic knowledge of an art form's rudiments, the creative person works to create a simple, basic example that is appreciated by an audience who appreciates direct simplicity. Generally, sit com television shows, children's cartoons and high school essays can be seen as examples.

3. Well-Crafted: The craftsman who studies the art form, utilizes fundamentals smoothly and works on nuance and meaning is the one who finds satisfaction, marketability and recognition for excellence. Commercial advertising, majority of modern music and instrumentalists, as well as repeated best-selling novelists are examples.

4. Fine Art: The highest level of creativity is the one that touches the heart, spirit, soul of the beholder and makes that person aware of a quality of life unrecognized until that moment. Most artists KNOW they strive for well-crafted, but rarely will they achieve the magic that is fine art. Why? Because a power, an unexplainable force contributes to the piece of art which will connect with another human being. Not all pieces of art, mind you, just some. There are folks who may say only educated elitists, academics or qualified critics can identify fine art. Each of us is the judge of fine art that touches our own humanity and it has nothing to do with longevity or mass consensus about the artist! Yes, art, music and literature classes have taught us the names of those creative artists who came before and achieved this level of excellence, like Mozart, Van Gogh, Cather and on and on. It is NOT longevity that identifies their work as fine art; it is the fact that their work continues to move our souls and makes us more attentive to our place in this life.

PROBLEM OF PREDICTABILITY

So, you have practiced and practiced, studied and studied, revised and revised . . . yet how on earth do you avoid the predictability that is inherent to genre/category fiction? Ah, it is not the knowing what will evolve but how the writer will evolve the story that is key. So, yes, there will be a touch of predictability for that is inherent to any genre's expectations.

Look back at the essence of any above category. Mystery. So you know some kind of crime will be committed, be it a crime within a culture, a family, or a society. Thus there will be a perpetrator who will avoid detection and a detective who will investigate. And so on. We will examine each in more detail in subsequent chapters. This is pointed out here to get you over the fearful hurdle of predictability.

THERE ARE NO NEW STORIES

Let's pop another bubble that follows right after "predictability." Truly, there are no new stories. A Frenchman named Polti examined the Greek classics and all of Shakespeare. He came up with a list of 36 basic dramatic situations. You may attempt to prove it wrong, but will not succeed. Examine books, movies, episodic TV, comic books, ballads. Polti is only proven to be correct. Polti's list is in Appendix E.

Literary study has examined another basic element to storytelling: The types of Conflict.

FIVE BASIC CONFLICTS

1. Man against Nature
2. Man against Man
3. Man against Society
4. Man against Himself
5. Man against Fate

Note: *THE OLD MAN & THE SEA* and *TO KILL A MOCKINGBIRD* are classic stories that incredibly utilized ALL of these conflicts in both the novels and the films. Go for simplicity to begin with and identify the MAIN conflict driving your story.

CREATING YOUR OWN MAGIC

What triggers creative images in an artist's mind or awareness of totally new problem solutions in a scientist's mind? Many books and essays on this topic have been written proposing a vast array of opinions. The bottom line seems to be each artist, each researcher who has contemplated their own creativity has come to their own conclusion about how and why an original idea pops into the mind. Though some answers can be categorized as similar, the only important concept you need to know is that You are unique, a creative miracle unto yourself. Being aware of your creative passion that produces original thought will empower you to channel it productively, especially as a storyteller.

Here is a new platitude for you: "There are no new stories, just new characters in fascinating circumstances." Aristotle's "Poetics," Polti's 36 Plot Lines, the Five Essential Conflicts, and the specialized expectations of each of eleven genres provide developmental guidelines, restrictions if you want to be an artistic purest. How you thought-associate these

"THERE ARE NO NEW STORIES, JUST NEW CHARACTERS IN FASCINATING CIRCUMSTANCES."

fundamentals into story is your ability to create. Your thought associations traveling through your brain's neurological pathways allow you to be that creative miracle called a storyteller.

How? More than verbal communication, creative problem solving is what separates us from the lower animals. Humans process concepts as they relate to life experience. At this time in research, neurological science tells us impulses quickly travel familiar or similar neurological pathways already used in the brain. These are thought associations. Some pathways are well-used as in repetitive learning. Others are new branches off the "well-beaten" path, becoming new thoughts or awareness, even a creative image. This is one theory how humans build or expand life experience and knowledge. We can create new concepts, new ideas. We can imagine.

A prime example of creating new concepts is the first FANTASIA from Disney. Music provided the foundation for animated stories and characters, from hippo ballerinas teasing the alligator dancer to the bat-like figure occupying the top one third of the mountain sweeping open his wings and personifying evil. Who could forget the orchestration translated into the splashes and flow of color? The images taught the audience to translate music from mere sound into visual concepts.

Some of us imagine or create effortlessly. Others have to work or struggle to get those thought associations to stretch into a new, untried territory of the brain. Some of us demand that a new idea be connected to the logical, real world. Others race with wild imaginings that challenge sanity. Most successful, marketable storytellers can find themselves safely in between those extremes. We just need to know when to race and when to relax.

ATTITUDE TOWARD PROFESSIONAL DEMANDS

The creative mind asks "What if..." Viola! New characters, a challenging set of events, a series of vivid images blossom in your imagination. The story becomes words that others can read to vicariously share your fictional adventure. In the prose market you need to relate to an editor or literary agent. In the film industry you need to trigger the collaborative imaginations of people who can put their own skills to work to enhance the story. Think of how George Lucas's scripts challenged and forever changed the special effects field. Think of how James Cameron bridged the world between live actors and animation in AVATAR.

Hopefully, as a professional writer, you have formatted the story for your market, be it screen, novel, juvenile lit, whatever. If the project does not appear as the industry rules prescribe, your creative work will never relate to that market. Your words will never connect with the industry professional who knows the rules. Why not? Simply because that person does not have time or mental energy to waste. They pay attention to material presented to them as expected.

This is a pretty hefty responsibility and sometimes a damper on the joy of your imaginative efforts. Get over it! Store that baggage and wildly pursue those images, characters, stories that explode in your mind and posses your soul, that excite your passion to communicate. Tapping into that power will motivate you to create your own magic, a magic that will send shivers down the audience member's back and imprint your story and characters on the audience/script reader's mind.

That's the physiologic or mechanical essence of a writer's imagination.

UNLEASHING YOUR MAGIC

You must differentiate between the retelling of an old story and what is truly innovative. That step is the singular most important choice you must make. Why? Because this is where you race your creative thought. Let go. Forget restrictions. That was done in the perpetual back tracking memories rendered in MEMENTO. Force your thoughts off the well-used pathway into that untried mental territory. "What if..." until you connect with an image, a character, an event that excites you. Thought associate until you are sucked into a story and vicariously live a dynamic character's experiences. This is also how "Writer's Block" can be conquered.

Pay attention to your own passions as you develop this creative process. Have you ever listed those things you feel strongly about? What behaviors especially annoy you? What memories do you cherish? What makes you cry? What makes you spitting mad? Dig deep into your experiences for those events that created your strong opinions. These passions within your heart and mind are the fuel for your racing imagination.

Think about one of your passions. Follow that well-used pathway then "What if..." onto a new pathway. Race with possibility. Let your character face this challenge to the passion you have felt. Push the envelope. Don't play it safe or logical. Both Cameron's and Tarantino's reputations were built on defying the ordinary. Safe storytelling means predictability of the same old story lived by boring characters. Sure, the audience member will understand, but wouldn't you rather that person be stunned into a new awareness?

Race along that creative pathway until you are panting. Truly innovative story, truly passion-driven character, truly magical experience will result in that first draft. Now, it's time to relax.

LET YOUR LOGIC BREATHE

Many a neophyte will argue that revision spoils a story. Bull manure! "Are you so perfect that you can't make it better?"

Racing through first draft magic normally produces holes in logic. How does a character know how to do this? Isn't this too coincidental? How many neurotics does it take to screw in a light bulb? Is it possible or even necessary that every problem be solved by this climax? Did this moment last too long, as in beating a dead horse or use of on-the-nose dialogue? How can all the positive forces possibly be in agreement? Are the dark elements too intense or too weak to challenge the protagonist to jeopardize himself with a greater risk? Will every single scene cause the script reader to thought associate?

You must discipline your mind to relax long enough to analyze every word, every sentence, every speech, every scene. Your logical analysis needs to cut, condense, hone your words until the story is succinctly exciting. Careful crafting does not spoil a passionate story. That edit makes it shiver with diamond-bright possibility.

When the editor, agent or producer reads your story, your passion MUST connect with that person's mind. Carefully crafted story magically pulls them down well-used mental pathways then shoves them into uncharted territory they want to understand, they HAVE to vicariously experience.

That is how a writer creates magic that sells

SEEKING THE UNIQUE "FRESHNESS"

Some writers and literary elitists would argue such deliberate attention to tried-and-true plot and conflict destroys creativity, innovation and audience appeal. Jung, Campbell and Vogler refute that. Modern film making proves them right. It is a vital, pulsating art form that gives the writer the opportunity to create enthralling stories. Hit the audience in their "Collective Unconscious" by playing off their expectations with characters willing to take risks, willing to do more than what is expected. Period. Their histories, their motivations, their capabilities in whatever circumstances you place them create the unique freshness Hollywood is looking for.

The only way to accomplish such a creative feat is to examine what You-the-Writer wants to say about the human condition in this plot, with these conflicts challenging these characters. What experiences will demonstrate your point? Demonstrate, not lecture.

The "freshness" comes from your writing perspective, from your soul. This is not a vague, abstract concept.

LOG LINE

First, you start with an intention to tell such-and-such a story. This is the Log Line, your story in 25 words or less. At this point you look at Polti-s 36 and the Main Plot's main conflict. You state the essence of your Main Character and story in 25 words or less. Your Log Line allows you to focus on what you need in your story and what you can ignore. A Log Line prevents you from wandering off into someone else's experience of the story with a subplot or supporting character that is not essential to your story. Thus the Log Line provides you a thumbnail sketch of what you include and what you exclude.

Through that selection you a) limit the scope of your story, time line, and necessary cast, b) identify where you need to research, and c) provide the foundation for your Beginning-Middle-Ending story structure. A Log Line is absolutely necessary for marking to agents, editors or producers who have the attention span of a gnat.

ATTITUDE

Before moving ahead, you need to examine where your heart and soul is in this project. In other words, how do you feel about what this story is saying? What is this story saying about your attitude about life issues? Lew Hunter Chair Emeritus of UCLA's Film Department and Program Director for NBC for seven years, says "Don't start a story from your imagination and your research. Rip open your heart! Find the story in the burning asphalt of your own life!" By stating your attitude you a) identify what ignites your fire about this story's cause-effect, b) forces you to choose events and characters that will prove your attitude is right, and c) colors your characters' attitudes and perceptions when you put them in motion.

FIND THE STORY IN THE BURNING ASPHALT OF YOUR OWN LIFE!

STATEMENT OF PURPOSE

Finally, what is this story trying to **prove**? This statement requires the use of the phrase "I want to prove." This singular statement will guide the direction of the entire story and each of its contributing subplots. Period. None of your characters or plotting will wander when you have that statement before you and constantly write toward that statement in every scene, every speech. In the Statement of Purpose you find the positives and negatives you inherently want to emphasize in your story. You-the-Writer must assess how "socially beneficial" the Main Character is in comparison to the Opposition. Awareness of that will help you select qualities you are going to depict in your script. . . . so consider these concepts:

1) Principle/Character vs. Society/Environment
2) Principle GOOD then Society EVIL
3) Society GOOD then Principle EVIL
4) Vacillation frequently contributes to story
5) Reader satisfaction results when ONE triumphs

Statement of Purpose: I want to prove war is hell. Those who are forced to participate (Good Society) suffer the manipulations of the planners and commanders (Evil Principle). If a head of state or a commander is guilt-stricken (Abe Lincoln), the story gains more depth and angst.

Statement of Purpose: I want to prove true love can overcome misunderstandings despite family loyalties. Love (Good Principle) strengthens the lovers to seek commitment despite familial social pressures (Evil Society).

A definitive Statement of Purpose provides the foundation for a unique Log Line based on the passionate attitude of the author.

Bottom Line? Freshness comes from your perceptions of life. That's why SMOKE SIGNALS is so very different from the Native American perceptions portrayed in THE LAST OF THE MOHICANS. That's why the surrealism of THE MATRIX is so different from WHAT DREAMS MAY COME. And on and on. The universal appeal lies in the audience grasping the basic story plot and conflicts. The characters living the story have enough common humanity for the audience to empathize. Freshness, that unique quality the entertainment industry so desperately wants, comes from you, your ability to weave a story that will reflect your attitude and prove your point. There are no new stories . . . but there are new writers creating their own versions.

WORK ON A LOG LINE

The art of building a synopsis (summary of a story into 300-650 words) starts from the foundation up . . . . Using the logic of starting simple, you must look to your Log Line first. The story told in this one sentence of 25 words or less is essential to both the mental and the written process. Why?

Saying the story in one sentence focuses the writer on the bare bones of this story, thus automatically eliminating other concepts. The Log Line identifies the main character, the story's driving force and the main obstacle (or antagonist) to be overcome. This is simply "What" the story is about, cut and dried, to the point. However, it cannot be a boring sentence. You want nouns, qualifiers and action verbs that deliver layers of potential action, a cascade of thought-associated images. It must explode with powerful innuendo that will suck the reader/audience in and make them want to know exactly what goes on in the story, what happens to the characters, how they live the adventure.

Essentially, a Log Line delivers the outline of the story's essence. When someone asks you "What is your book (screenplay) about?" this is the succinct sentence you tell them. The majority of the people who will ask you are merely being polite, so here's a key point: If the listener is intrigued or curious, they will ask you for more information. If not, either your story holds no appeal OR they aren't really interested anyway.

Let's assume your single sentence told of a story that does not appeal to this person. Is it the story itself or the person's tastes? If it is the story itself then you need to rethink your sentence.

Always ask yourself how your story is different from others "in the same category." You can practice by writing a Log Line for five or more stories of one type such as "military romantic suspense" or "Regency marriage of convenience" or "Scottish bridal kidnapping" or "serial murderer defying police" or "rich man-poor girl rescues" or . . . You get the idea. Pick several books or movies of the same type and write a Log Line for each. Don't dwell on the words you choose. Write the Log Lines quickly. How similar are they? Why? Because they deal with similar or stereotypical characterizations or plot lines?

Now, think about your story. You have to make your story differnt, fresh, enthralling. If you don't feel that way about your story, how will you get someone else to want to read it? Your difference will begin with a powerful Log Line.

STEP ONE: IDENTIFY CHARACTER ROLE/IDENTITY

Names of characters do not create images in the reader's mind, but roles do. Think of a name as the identity of the character to the rest of the world, but the underlying power of the character is what he or she is doing in the world. Names can be changed, but that innate power demanded by various roles will not change.

All of us have many roles in our lives: Child, Sibling, Spouse, Parent, Friend, Employee, Professional Engineer, Home Owner, Church Member, Writer, Poet, Screenwriter, Dancer, Gym Member, Horse Owner, on and on with each of us obviously making different lists. Each of those roles has its own agenda or tasks, concerns, "business" that is important only to that role. In reality, each role is its own "life." Of course, some bleed over into other roles, influencing actions and choices–like becoming a parent influences spousal expectations or a boss's demands of over-time makes our bowling team mad or paying for a hospital bill means not repainting the house this year which could in turn send our neighbor into an angry out-burst--but our daily lives are moments lived in each of these roles. A story grows out of the drama of those moments.

What is the dominant role in your Main Character's life that is "in the camera's eye" for the majority of the story? What is the role central to this story with all other roles subordinate or influenced by the demands of that role? Is it a working mom, a deployed Marine, an accountant?

STEP TWO: DOMINANT PERSONALITY FACTOR

The underlying, driving force of a personality is what allows each of us to tackle the big challenges of our lives. And sometimes only our internalized self is aware of that power lurking within. Only when we are forced will that deep characteristic evolve to its fullest. That is what You-the-Writer need to yank out of a character and put to work to meet the life-changing challenge in your story. That is the characteristic you will plug into your Log Line.

Like multiple life-roles, each of us has an array of personality traits, sometimes relevant only to particular roles, some hidden deep in the essence of our mental lives and others shown every day by our actions, choices, words. All of those traits are essential to who we are as individuals. They categorize our "personality type" to psychologists. Storytellers evolve into amateur psychologists as we analyze and depict make-believe characters. You-the-Writer must carefully consider your Character Profile and select the dominant characteristic that will energize the Main Character throughout your story.

Pick that one personality factor that will be vital to the character enduring and succeeding, even if it is something to be overcome. Create a Log Line using that characterization of qualifying trait and life role to evoke images.

"A callous Southern playboy….."
"A haunted, introverted librarian…."
"A brilliant but ignored daughter..."
"A frigid female heart surgeon..."
"A ridiculously happy family man..."

Still not sure of how to describe your Main Character? Make a list of five positive and five negative personality characteristics you have. Now, pick one that your family will agree on and another that your close friends will agree on. How many of your mere acquaintances are aware of both of these? Which "face" do you show the real world? What "secret" personality trait do you harbor, waiting for the right moment, the right opportunity to use? Consider the power within your Main Character that will be called up throughout the story.

Avoid using more than one trait in your Log Line. One is enough. Choose the one that will visually communicate the power that will drive the story.

STEP THREE: IDENTIFY MOTIVATING CIRCUMSTANCE / ADVENTURE

What is the situation or "New Life" the character is thrown into? In the Hero's Journey construct this is something not normally sought. It is a change that demands more effort, a challenge to who this person is.

In category or genre fiction a writer is tempted to insert the situation common to the genre or sub genre. Resist the urge. Instead, identify what makes your story circumstance unique from every other romance or fantasy or mystery. This implies that you have read a lot in your genre and know common storylines.

Yes, it is essential to create a Log Line in the spirit of your genre. But, in the same vein, be absolutely 100% certain yours is unique to your story and not a "cookie cutter" that could be applied to any other Regency, any other paranormal, any other Navy SEAL romantic suspense . . . You get the idea.

STEP FOUR: OPPOSITION TO OVERCOME/CHALLENGE/ IRONIC COMPLICATION

Here is the point you introduce the truly unexpected twist or irony contrasting with personality trait and role. Of course, it must be logical to the circumstance and genre. Primarily it has to be wildly evocative. You-the-Writer must propose a story with any number of possibilities that can be guessed or not. They must so enthrall or intrigue the reader that more detail is demanded! You want the reader/listener to ask for the synopsis or entire manuscript.

Look over these examples of one character's story possibilities in many genres:

Romance
"A callous Southern playboy cannot inherit until he convinces the new female pastor that he's worthy."

Mystery
"A callous Southern playboy uses his prison time to network favors and find who ruined his family."

Fantasy
"A callous Southern playboy defies a curse and is whisked into a swampland world where he is the servant."

Western
"A callous Southern playboy wins a whorehouse filled with underage orphans and an outraged madam."

Log Lines are not meant to be simple; they are meant to be powerful. Think of the imagery of poetry: Every word should be evocative of a cascade of images. Remember, this must be an intriguing, defining sentence about both character and story. It is the hook that will demand your story be read. A Log Line is your introductory sales pitch. It is the line you use in your query or cover letters.

LOG LINE POINTERS

Read your sentence aloud in one breath. If you have to take a breath or hesitate, it's too long. That's why the 25 words. Again, remember that agents/editors/producers have the attention span of a gnat. So keep the sentence tight and pertinent.. Do not try to cram it with an overwhelming amount of information. You want their imagination set on fire with a cascade of images and possibilities, not flooded with so much they feel like they are drowning. Focus on primary traits, primary trials, primary goals. Not ALL traits, trials, goals. Primary means the most important to the entire story.

Watch out for passives. Any "is" verbs or use vague, genre-specific wording like "gets saddled" which is 1) passive, 2) cliché and 3) a "western" connotation. It's not "meant" to be any of those but when writing a log line for a unique genre, do not "mix your metaphors."

* * * * *

GENRE FILM Chapter 2 Exercises

Exercise 2a. List the internal and external/role characteristics of your main character. Carefully choose your qualifiers for edginess, qualities that can either be positive or negative.

Exercise 2b. What is the character's main goal that makes him or her continue to strive?

Exercise 2c. List all the possible obstacles to achieving that goal.

Exercise 2d. Now formulate your "Log Line"....in 25 words or less.
Key Points:

1) Pick your "role" noun, identify your most tantalizing and pertinent qualifiers, then put that noun in action with the most vivid verb you can come up with. Power words with lots of levels that demand to be explained. Can you make a list of more action-packed verbs that imply the action of the story?

2) Look at your qualifying clauses and your verbs. Does the agent/producer get lost between the subject (the main character noun) and the verb?

CHAPTER 3

Concepts of Suspense and Webbing/Mystery Genre

IN THE BEGINNING . . .

. . . there is a **TITLE**. You need a title for your story, even if it will change by time you begin marketing this sucker (and will most likely be changed by the producers, just as book titles are dictated by publishing houses). Titling your work gives it an "identify" in the file folders of your mind. The more you learn of your characters and their experiences, the more likely you are to change the title. Again, that doesn't matter. What does matter is you have a handle on the script's force and identity from the very beginning.

You have a Statement of Purpose and a Log Line to start you on this quest. Next you brainstorm a list of possibilities. Go for short, memorable, appropriate. If something really hits you as perfect, the next thing you do is go to the Internet Movie Database (www.IMDb.com) and do a search for movies with that title. Titles cannot be copyrighted, though they can be trade-marked. George Lucas trade-marked STAR WARS. Go figure.

Lew Hunter, Chair Emeritus of the UCLA Film Department, will demand his students re-title a script if he feels it will not act as a lure. This "Master of the Memorable" believes titling was one of his most important jobs in the seven years he was Program Director at NBC. He had his finger on the pulse of every network series and their episodes, every movie, every documentary. To this day his mantra is "Make the title memorable."

> "MAKE THE TITLE MEMORABLE."

SUSPENSE = WORRY OVER CONSEQUENCES + DOUBT OF OUTCOME

You will encounter various aspects of character anxiety throughout this book simply because it is fundamental to avoiding a story of "the happy people of the happy village." As human beings we are forced to deal with change day in-day-out. When you are storytelling, that change needs exaggerated consequences forcing the character to strive harder with more costly choices. The opposition must create such intense conflict that the characters cannot ignore the circumstance. Like all animals, humans are innately lazy. We naturally seek ease and comfort, "down time" when we can recharge and refocus. Some can ignore whatever and live separated from social order, whereas others are motivated to do something so their mind and body can be put at ease. Your job as a storyteller is to identify what will create the greatest discomfort or worry for that character (thus for the audience).

Building on the concept of "laziness," if we have a choice we would rather life proceeded without complication or interruption. "Ain't gonna happen," especially for a storyteller. Writers thrive on complication and roadblocks. The challenge for us is to identify those logical complications that will push our characters the hardest. The characters will lose or gain something of value by the choices made. That sense of importance of that loss or gain will create worry in the audience. The greater the value, the greater the sense of suspense about what will be the consequence of the choice.

Some Classic "Suspense" Tools

1) Ticking clock or a deadline
2) Misunderstandings
3) Foreshadowing of pending danger
4) Worsening conditions
5) Shift of suffering consequences to innocent
6) Tweaking of character's greatest fear/weakness
7) Confrontation with obviously more powerful opposition
8) Moral dilemma
9) Reinforcement of unworthiness/judgment
10) Audience Awareness vs. Character Ignorance

Worry tightens the screws and creates greater suspense. Writers need to learn how to hold off resolutions as long as possible. A rather clichéd tool in mysteries is to throw out "Red Herrings" that make the audience consider various possibilities and not focus on one. Our well-read, sometimes rather cynical move-going public work very hard to sift the clues and insights thrown out "in passing." The writer has to invest over-time effort to be subtle yet logical. That requires a careful consideration of the "tools" listed above as well as the variations of common suspenseful events and some techniques. Think of your own examples as you work through these lists.

TEN COMMON SUSPENSE EVENTS

1. Obstacles in Protag's life creating worsening problems
--THE MIRACLE WORKER: Parents' sympathy and guilt

2. Delays of news, event postponement, accident/illness, natural disaster
--GLADIATOR: Caesar's murder

3. Imminent danger of life, love, happiness threatened with or without Protag's knowledge
--THE COWBOYS: the rustler's trailing the herd.

4. Struggle of physical or mental conflict to achieve an outcome
--G.I. JANE: Woman enduring physical abuse of SEAL training

5. Waiting through events with characters (and audience) not knowing outcome.
-- STEEL MAGNOLIAS: Daughter's marriage and pregnancy

6. Interruptions of revelation of significant information by other character or surprise elements
-- GODZILLA: Mutated dinosaur had found a place to lay its eggs.

7. Distractions of occurrences, mishaps or a character who confuses the main issue
--THE ELECTRIC HORSEMAN: Sonny's concern for his confused old friend

8. Conflict and indecision in Protag
--SCHINDLER'S LIST: Main characters value change and principles

9. Discussion, introspection, description, exposition or philosophy which slows story progression or creates atmosphere (building a sense of urgency of "Get on with it!" in the audience)
--A BEAUTIFUL MIND: the hallucinations
--DANCES WITH WOLVES: Voice Over readings from the diary entries

10. Innocence or helplessness of character
--WILLOW: The baby being protected by Willow
--THE NET: The Alzheimer mother of the Sandra Bullock character.

EIGHT TENSION-BUILDING TECHNIQUES

1. Surprise vs. Suspense: Surprise is sudden, unexpected (JAWS: head popping from boat hole) whereas Suspense is knowing what but not when or how (JAWS : shark coming back and eventually being killed)

2. Life and Death: Threat is very real to valued ideal, image, way of life or life itself (A STRANGER AMONG US: Cynical NY detective becoming more aware of her shallowness among sincere Hassidic Jews)

3. Uncertainty of Connecting with someone to love as Protag makes an unrequited emotional investment (A DIARY OF ANNE FRANK's blossoming puberty in strained and confined circumstances).

4. Pressure of someone to hate where an Antagonist blatantly threatens the Protag (STARMAN's Federal Agent determined to capture him at all costs).

5. Worsening Complications perpetually piling up to the breaking point (ARMAGEDDON's series of crew problems proving the theory that if something can go wrong it will.)

6. Repeated Clock References where the threat is dependent on time that continues to march on toward the deadline. (HIGH NOON)

7. Genuine Doubt despite hints and foreshadowing, but nothing definitive (SIXTH SENSE's appearance of dead people not acknowledged by the doctor.)

8. The Big Scene Vacillation of the Climax where everything has led to the determination of success or failure (THE PATRIOT'S battle where Benjamin Martin is not only instrumental in leading the fighters but gets to confront and defeat his nemesis.)

CONCEPT OF WEBBING

Several screenwriting gurus including Truby, Seger and Bonnet discuss the interrelationship of the parts of the whole story. It is kind of like that game "Six Degrees of Separation." If you think of the inter-dependence of modern society and how we can trace consequences and inventions backward to related origins, a complex concept of the interrelationship of plot and subplots, characters and motivations, multi-layered consequences becomes relatively simple.

There are many visual analogies for this concept like a hub with the spokes of the wheel supporting the surrounding outer structure of the wheel's rim. Or the ripple or domino effect of a logical cause-effect cascade. Or a spider's an intricate web with the fine fibers interdependent to maintain the integrity of the whole.

Therein you have the concept of "Unity" in any story. Every word, every character, every scene must be vital for the logic of the whole to make sense. If your Statement of Purpose can be proven without a scene or character or speech, then guess what you need to do? Yup. Highlight that extraneous element and hit the delete key. The corollary in the planning stage is to identify your pivotal events, those lynchpin points that are absolutely necessary for your story to move forward, then consider the cause-effect chain of events necessary to get from one point to the next. Identify what threads you need to make the story webbing whole.

This is where you begin to eliminate artsy scenes that help to explain character motivation or set mood or prove you did you research. You hone in on the vital story threads. You only have 100 pages and a lot of territory to cover, a lot of logical life to depict that you want your audience to experience with the characters.

You have to be absolutely logical and definitively selective. Include just what events and character your story needs to enthrall your audience and keep them worried to the very end. No more, no less.

MYSTERY GENRE

Every story has to have elements of a mystery of the unknown in it. This does not mean a "crime" as is required by the genre itself, but unknown elements the script reader seeks to discover. Two fundamental audience questions not immediately answered will always be: 1) Why are these characters the way they are? 2) What will be the consequences of these actions? You-the-Writer have to create enough interest in the characters for the audience to want answers. From that first page/first minute. No puzzle to solve or care about? Any viewer will be saying "So what?" and will mentally challenge everything from that point on.

EVERY STORY HAS TO HAVE ELEMENTS OF A MYSTERY OF THE UNKNOWN IN IT.

FUNDAMENTAL CONCEPTS OF MYSTERY

1. **Open with a crime and character the audience can care about.**

- This could be a crime against social order of any kind, including family values (which isn't unlawful, of course). It could be a crime that is personal or moral, such as a breach of ethics that has dire consequences. Murder is naturally a common heinous crime because one person (or group) ends the life of another human being. Consider social institutions or factions who do not value human life and the reactions of those people that do, such as political groups who practice "The end justifies the mean" thus they use children to deliver bombs. Or the conflict that arises between cultures over the practice of human or animal sacrifice. One profoundly believes the human or animal carries messages to God while the other is abhorred at what they consider to be ignorance. Who is right? You-the-Writer have to set up both sides and decide who is the criminal and who is the detective/prosecutor.

- And the crime does have to immediately apparent, as well as the person involved, be it detective or perpetrator. The audience has to be seeking with the detective immediately. The writer who first builds interest in a character before executing the crime is writing a dissatisfying, slow story. Remember, tension has to be immediate and high-stakes for the people involved.

2. Detective must exert effort; Criminal must fool or avert attention
- In other words, the person investigating the crime must prioritize that investigation. It has to be a driving motivator in that investigator's life. Yes, that character can and should have other agenda's playing out, but everything in the story needs to draw this person back to thoughts and actions focused on trying to figure out "who done it."

- Likewise the perpetrator has to be astute and devious trying to avoid discovery. Obviously, if your criminal is caught too soon or is identified too soon that is "game over." And pay attention to evolving a multi-dimensional character who thinks the action is justified. They are not evil in their own minds. They think they are right or justified to act in such sociopathic manner, be it "I am owed" or the arrogance of superiority or whatever. The criminal has to be driven to perform the crime then to hide.

3. Foreshadow everything, but with subtlety; Coincidence is taboo
- Foreshadowing means dropping hints or insinuations. Yes, you can drop erroneous or misleading information, frequently called a "red herring." The point is to drop significant information without it seeming to be important. Anything you dwell on your audience will think "Aha, I've got this figured out. Why should I care anymore?" A slight variation on the foreshadowing consideration is not to inundate your audience with so much they can't recall the data. Hints are like spices added to a soup, a little goes a long way and you don't want the entire experience to be overcome by one.

- Coincidence is flat out cheating your audience. Yes, it happens in real life, but you are telling an exaggerated story. You want logic and carefully woven proof to reign supreme. You want to intrigue and manipulate your viewer's mind, not suddenly deliver the evidence. Respect your audience member's intellect by never, ever having evidence or explanation abruptly, conveniently delivered to your detective.

4. Outline cause-effect story events . . . then identify character reactions - The primary focus of a mystery is the events of crime-evasion-detection. Without that triad you do not have a mystery. Therefore you figure out first how the crime happens, what the criminal does to evade capture and what the detective has to do to thwart and capture the criminal. These are actions, events you need to command before you begin to describe the characters involved, their motivations, their agendas. Yes, reactions are the result of a character's psyche. However, to create a tense, credible series of events you need to formulate a devious pattern of events then fit in your characters' motivations and internalizations. Certainly as you write some things will change as you learn more about your characters, but establish and resolve the mystery in your own mind so you can make it as complex as possible for your characters.

5. Focus cause-effect on mounting suspense where options have higher stakes - Every event sets up character choices for how to react. Awareness of options will come from Character Profile, such as education, life experience, coping mechanisms, etc. Ignorance can lead to fatal errors in judgment. Awareness can lead to impossibly difficult decisions as in the "lesser of two evils" or sacrifice of the one to save the many. Truly difficult dilemmas create the most enthralling story events, but don't overdo use of this tool or you will emotionally/intellectually wear out your audience with a "Oh, not again!" And you need to make subsequent effects lead to even more difficult dilemmas and decisions with the result being "Rising Tension" of mounting suspense or more intense concern for the character's well-being.

6. Avoid gimmicks, blundering, super studs, prolonged psychoanalysis - All of the above become trite clichés that patronize the intelligent viewer. You certainly don't want to speak down to him or her. You want them caring about the story events and the character reactions. You want the audience vicariously living the story with your characters, not rolling their eyes over how ridiculous anything sounds. You want to show not on-the-nose tell character perceptions.

7. Beware use of real names/personae - Names and circumstances that have been in public records like news media or accessible court proceedings are "fair game." However, be prepared for the repercussions of maligning or distorting situations or motivations. If you are brave enough to use actual people as characters in your story, consult an attorney and get a signed release of permission. Otherwise, skew the description and names so any one person cannot pounce on you for defamation.

8. Verify law enforcement practices and criminal statutes
- The policies and procedures of each city, county, state, federal, international and even institution are all different. Only amateurs assume identical requirements. Research thoroughly training, minimum behavior requirements (right down to type of weapon allowed to carry), paperwork and accessible data (who can tap into U.S. federal records, for example). Inform yourself about how a city law enforcement department interacts with county and federal or even how a religious organization investigates and prosecutes its own law breakers (Quakers vs. Hasidic Jews vs. Vatican). When dealing with real entities, have the integrity and fortitude to portray them accurately.

MYSTERY CHARACTER REQUIREMENTS

Consider the concept of right-brain creative and left-brain pragmatist. Yes, there is evidence that scientists and Alpha males tap into right-brain creativity to problem solve. They imagine possibilities. However, the left-brain logic ultimately dictates decision-making. They identify cause and effect. They reason out conclusions, sift through dilemmas and choose actions. Suffering the consequences of any decision, the left-brain pragmatic person reassesses results, formulates subsequent possible actions and consequences. Quite obviously, both Protagonist detective and Antagonist criminal will both be constantly **left-brain** people.

So the primary personality requirement of both a mystery Protagonist and Antagonist is **highly intelligent**. I am not saying dysfunctional, ignorant idiots do not commit crimes. They do, mostly in moments when exercising very poor judgment. But these people are not fodder for Antagonists who can last for an entire or screenplay. They are not a challenge for any detective. On the Protagonist side of the equation, you want a detective who is investigating whatever who can think "outside the box." You want a unique detective, not a stereotypical Private Investigator, F.B.I. agent or police detective. You want a Protagonist who is skilled, capable, and challenged by a Antagonist who is equal or maybe even superior.

Secondly, you want both Protagonist and Antagonist to be **highly motivated** from Page 1. Of course, you do not tell all right up front, but you do show how intense both of these characters are from the moment they appear in your story. Even if the Protagonist is a slow-to-act Southern Good Ol' Boy, he must be observant and calculating, capable of attacking when necessary. He must care. The opponent or perpetrator has to be just as caring about his or her own survival. That intensity translates to calculated desperation. The suspense between the two highly motivated people weaves in and out of the entire story right up to the climax.

MYSTERY PLOT TYPES

Here we go on genre "predictability" or genre conventions, or not. You must understand the convention can open creative possibilities.

1. **Puzzle**, the game of wits where a threat is posed & salvation depends on a solution

2. **Hard-boiled/hard-core**, focused on toughness, brutal reality of physical exploits

3. **Straight Mystery**, crime committed with focus on criminal analysis

4. **Pursuit**, technology of era used in tracking the fleeing criminal
   a. **Spy:** Professional agent who infiltrated setting to obtain information
   b. **Man-on-the-run:** Spectrum from innocent accused to international arena
   c. **Metaphysical:** "Gothic" evil soul-possession alluding capture
   d. **Doomsday:** Geopolitical importance of Protagonist vs. Destroyers
   e. **Whodunit:** Emotional detective driven to solve

5. **Social Order Shattered**, entire group is threatened, laws undermined
   a. **Psychological:** Inner malice of Antagonist threatens lives
   b. **Mechanistic:** Details of all-powerful plan to subjugate social unit
   c. **Vigilante:** Laws-be damned by self-righteous individual
   d. **Caper:** Focus on criminal plan deliberately meant to break the law

6. **Camp**, any of the above reversed for comedic effect (Leslie Nielsen's many)

7. **Period**, any of the above set in the past (THE NAME OF THE ROSE, 1986, Sean Connery)

MYSTERY CONCLUSION

Can you see in the above criteria how You-the-writer can combine "Mystery Plot Types" to create a story focus? Can you also see how you can make the Mystery either the Main Plot or a Subplot to the main focus of a story? Understanding the kind of mystery you are going to weave is the starting point for identifying the elements you have to include and exactly how you weave those into your story.

MYSTERY FILM ANALYSIS

Your **goal** in analysis of each and every film is to look for the genre elements just discussed as well as to get in the habit of automatically assessing key points of characterization, story structure, and cinematic techniques. At the conclusion of each is a discussion of the Concepts presented at the beginning of this chapter that are reflected in each film.

* * * * *

WITNESS

By Pamela Wallace, Earl Wallace, Edward Feldman
1985, starring Harrison Ford, Kelly McGillis

Length: 107 minutes (not including time given to credits)

Log Line: A wounded detective learns Amish rural ways as he protects a young boy from the corrupt cops intent on silencing him.

Statement of Purpose: To prove a strong value system will not be corrupted by modern violence

Intro Image: Open field of wheat blowing in the wind = serenity of the rural life.

First 10 minutes
Who:
RACHAEL, Lovely, emotional widow
DANIEL, Tender, manly Amish male
SAMUEL, Innocent, curious Amish boy
JOHN, Attentive, hard-nosed cop
When: Contemporary (1980's)
Where: From simple rural life (Pennsylvania) to dangerous & corrupt modern city (Philadelphia)
What: Recently widowed Amish woman takes her son on trip through a city where he witnesses a murder
Why: Exposing her son to the dangers of the corrupt society, she must comply with laws of that world

Four subplots impacting the Main Plot:
Amish way of life
Corrupt police officers

Principled John Book
Attraction between John & Rachael

Time Line: A month in the summertime

Image repeats:
Fields of grain
Amish contrast
Birdhouse
Guns
Carpentry
Modern conveniences as threat

Act I = Set-up of Ordinary World
10 min Intro: Amish widowhood, train trip with Samuel witnessing murder, meeting John Book
20 min Inciting Incident: John sequesters Rachel & Samuel with his sister = Personal responsibility
27 min PP I: Samuel ID's McPhee (which sets up balance of hunt-and-hide story)

Act II = Life 180 degrees, John's life among the Amish
45 min Pinch I: Samuel finds & learns about gun (John's awareness of fears' impact on these people)
63 min Mid-Point: John & Rachael dance in the barn (Epiphany of changing relationship to possibilities of physical contact)
78 min Pinch II: Rachael bathing, John watching & her silent offer (relationship = home)
89 min PPII: Arrival of the three assassins on the farm

Act III = Resolution of story's problems: Book uses Amish farm to defeat the corrupt officers
91-103 min Climax: Kill or be killed battle with bell-ringing bringing the surrounding Amish neighbors & Paul's surrender
106 min Commitment: "You be careful out among them English."
After-story Conclusion: John leaves & Daniel arrives to claim Rachael's life. Two men are seen greeting/acknowledging one another.

Dialogue Notes:
Amish cadence
Bar scene's street & police lingo
Change in Rachael's "tone"
Change in John's "tone"

Alpha Character posturing differences:
Daniel vs John Book
Eli vs. Paul
Rachael vs. Eli

Supporting cast Unique Character Gems:
Samuel, innocent & curious
Daniel, masculine, capable
Eli, staunch, judgmental
McPhee, cold, focused
John's sister, impatient but supportive
Carter (John's partner), capable, vulnerable
Modern Storekeeper in Amish town, quick to complain

Background effects, the nuances of aura:
Horse-drawn buggies in midst of traffic
Community caring & support vs. city isolation
Fearful respect vs. conscience
Dependability of demanding farm routine
Service to community through physical labor
Stringent rules to maintain protective social cloak

Elements from Other Genres: Romance, Spiritual, Juvenile, Action-Adventure

Question: Did you perceive Daniel as a lurking threat of domination or as a legitimate suitor concerned for Rachael's well-being?

Appearance or reference to recurrence of Tension Theme in Min. **BOLD = visual of actual EVIL**. Secondary tension theme woven in of John & Rachael relationship noted, as well. Tension is always the point . . . and every page,,every scene counts!

Act I = Set-up of Ordinary World
7 "Careful among them English"
10 Samuel eyes "Angel of Death" statue
11-13 Samuel witnesses the murder
16-18 Man killed was police officer, ID, bar incident
20 = Inciting Incident John takes them to his sister
22 Pictures, out for hot dogs, sister says
26-27 = Plot Point I Samuel sees McPhee's pic in trophy case

Act II = Life 180 degrees, John's life among the Amish
28-29 John talks to Paul about boy's ID

29-30 McPhee shoots John in garage
32 John calls Carter to make paper disappear
33 Threesome to sister's house
34-38 John takes back to farm, collapses
39 Eli involves elders
40 John awakens to see Rachael sleeping in chair
41-42 Paul trying to trace Lapps
44-45 = Pinch I John's gun danger to innocent Samuel & Amish ways
46-48 Eli's lessons to Samuel on dangers of English
49 Rachael to John: more personal lessons on Amish ways
50-51 John in Amish clothes "Need my gun"
52-53 John to town to call Carter "Watch your back"
54 Rachael takes back gun & bullets
55-59 John learning Amish farm ways
60 = Secondary threat of Daniel vs. John for Rachael
63-65 = Epiphany Mid-Point John working on car, music & dance with Rachael
66-67 Eli confront Rachael about talk of shunning
68 Paul questioning & threatening Carter
69-76 Barn raising scenes of Amish life & Rachael's watching
77-78 = Pinch II Rachael's bathing & blatant offering self to John
79 John's explanation of "if" meant either he stays or she leaves
80 Tourist bus scene, John's verbal threat
81-82 John discovers Carter dead & phones Paul with threats
83-85 John's anger boils over to beating of townsman
86-88 Rachael realizes John leaving, passionate kiss
89-90 = Plot Point II Threesome arrive at farm at daybreak, guns out

Act III = Resolution of story's problems: Book uses Amish farm to defeat the corrupt officers
91-103 = Climactic Battle Threesome holding Rachel & Eli, John killing Fergie & McPhee, Samuel running then returning to ring bell for neighbors who stand in face of Paul's "evil"
104-106 = After-story Police cars in farm yard then John sits beside Samuel at pond, John & Rachael long farewell eye contact, Eli to John "You be careful among them English."
107 John leaves as Daniel arrives to take over Rachael's life

CONCEPTS DISCUSSION

You were not told exactly what to look for regarding specific mystery components in the minute-by-minute analysis of this film. Neither were you reminded to look for elements of the specific fundamentals discussed in Chapter 1. It is assumed you were paying attention to both areas. But, now let's look at the in-depth concepts demonstrated.

TITLE

The succinct title is memorable and focuses on the thrust of this movie, the child as the singular witness to a murder by corrupted cops.

SUSPENSE TOOLS

1) Ticking clock: Frequent references to timeliness related to solving the original murder then the delays created by the corrupted cops inability to circumvent the Amish antiquated communication network and knowledge that Book WILL come after them if they don't find him first.

2) Misunderstandings: Between Book & boss Paul, Book & his sister, Rachael & Eli

3) Foreshadowing: Engel of Death in the train station, Rachael's terror at seeing how violent John can get at the bar arrest, "No one else knows," John's dripping blood in the garage, Samuel shouting his echoing voice up the grain tower, the assassins backing their car from the crest of the hill.

4) Worsening conditions: John is shot, the Elders seeing John, John delirious, John hears Carter is dead, Daniel observes Rachael's discomfort around John, the Amish lady asks about John while quilting, Eli confronts Rachael about the Amish gossip & possibility of ostracism, Samuel takes the risk to return to the farm being assaulted by the assassins.

5) Shift of suffering to innocent: Innocent child witness, sister being questioned, demeaning modern tourists and townspeople insulting Amish then ultimate assassins willing to terrorize and hurt all of Lapp family.

6) Tweaking of greatest fear: John periodically reminded of threat to Amish "innocent" and simple life

7) More powerful opposition: Paul and minions involving other law enforcement & willing to threaten innocent

8) Moral dilemma: Take knowledge of cop corruption to authorities outside Philadelphia and leave Samuel vulnerable to immediate retaliation, Rachel & Eli defy Amish isolationism to heal their wounded warrior, John lays low or spends his healing time occupied with useful pursuits, Rachael & John choices of Amish world or modern world inhibiting culmination of their attraction.

9) Reinforce unworthiness: Amish way of life simple and moralistic vs. violence and hurtful allowances of modern way of life.

10) Audience Awareness vs. Character Innocence: Audience well-informed of law enforcement vs bad guy consequences vs. Amish innocence or choice to remain separate, simple, innocent.

* * * * *

LETHAL WEAPON

By Shane Black
1987, starring Mel Gibson, Danny Glover

Length: 112 minutes (not counting credits)

Log Line: A family-man-type, seasoned detective is paired with a suicidal, over-the top younger man to take down a ring of ruthless drug smugglers.

Statement of Purpose: To prove a caring human can give purpose to a damaged soul.

Intro Image: Aerial view of nighttime Los Angeles sprawl

First 10 minutes
Who:
Roger Murtaugh, aging, respected police detective
Martin Riggs, risk-taking, lonely detective
When: December 1985
Where: Los Angeles
What: Murtaugh's birthday = insecurity with aging, Riggs lonely existence = lives for the job
Why: Investigation of girl's death will throw two together

Three related subplots:
Ruthless drug smuggling
Murtaugh's family life
Riggs' recovery from wife's death

Time Line: Two weeks before Christmas

Image repeats:
"I'm too old for this shit."
Christmas décor
Family & friend banter
Suicidal
Murtaugh's neck exercise before shoot
One bullet
"You owe me."

Act I = Set-up of Ordinary World, Murtaugh as family man, Riggs lonely existence
10 min Intro: Girl's suicide/murder, Murtaugh family contrast, Riggs no home-life & violence
13 min Inciting Incident: Riggs called psycho as steps into line of fire & kills sniper
24 min PP I: "I'll see you later" Riggs' deliberate choice not to commit suicide

Act II = Life 180 degrees, Increasing risks of investigation of murderous drug ring
40 min Pinch I: Murtaugh confronts Riggs about suicidal thoughts
50 min Mid-Point: Riggs dinner with Murtaugh family & partner bonding (reaction insinuating "My life could be different and that's worth living for.")
75 min Pinch II: Murtaugh relieved that the vest prevented Riggs death (celebrates Riggs being in his life)
83 min PPII: Murtaugh and Riggs fail to rescue Rianna & all captured

Act III = Take down of drug ring proves Riggs' value to Murtaugh
94 min Climax: Murtaugh & Riggs take down the "mercs," McAllister & Joshua
109 min Commitment: After Joshua, Murtaugh's "I've got you, partner."
After-story Conclusion: Riggs at cemetery then at house with bullet, Murtaugh invites in for Xmas

Dialogue Notes:
Murtaugh: smooth, always back to logical
Riggs: intensity & emotional shifts
Murtaugh family: age/role appropriate
Joshua's tone: cold, bitter

Alpha Character posturing differences:
Murtaugh control vs. Riggs on-the-edge risk-taking
Joshua cold, macho
Captain professionalism vs. McAllister comander-in-control owed respect

Supporting cast Unique Character Gems:
Rianne, young womanhood
Trish, tolerant wife & caring mother
Joshua, no conscience, violence-focused
Psychiatrist, professional succumbing to personal buttons being pushed

Background effects, the nuances of aura:
Murtaugh home
Riggs' trailer
Police Station
Luxury compounds
Dance club

Elements from Other Genres: Action-Adventure, Western

Question: Did the bantering relieve the tension of dangers? Was it credible given the short time these two knew one another or believed because nature of police work?

Appearance or reference to recurrence of Tension or Evil Theme in Min (**BOLD = main, visual**). Important point is constant tension, gradual tightening of audience concern for character well-being. "Make them care then make them worry." Two tension themes in this movie: Riggs' tenuous mental state and the drug smugglers.

Act I = Set-up of Ordinary World, Murtaugh as family man, Riggs lonely existence
3
8
9
13-14
15
17-19
21-24 = Plot Point I

Act II = Life 180 degrees, Increasing risks of investigation of murderous drug ring
25
26-29
30-31
32-34
35-39
40-41 = Pinch I

42
45-48
50-57 = Mid-Point Epiphany
58
59-60
62-64
65
66-68
70-74
75 = Pinch II
76
77
78-79
80
81-82
83-87 = Plot Point II

Act III = Take down of drug ring proves Riggs' value to Murtaugh
88-90
91
92
93
94-102 = Climactic Battle
103-108 = Riggs' Battle
109 = Commitment
110-112 = After-story

CONCEPTS DISCUSSION

The emphasis in the above analysis was on the timing of the threat and not the scene by scene explanations. You should be able to identify this film's fundamentals as discussed in Chapter 2. But, now let's look at the in-depth concepts demonstrated.

WEBBING RELATIONSHIPS/STORY LINES

-Attractive daughters at risk, as well as remaining family members

-Wife/Family needed to keep a cop grounded

-Murtaugh and Riggs both willing to do violence for their job & for those they care about

-The Vietnam War connections, especially Riggs' dangerous Special Forces skills comparable to the mercs

-Murtaugh competent marksman, Riggs more deadly marksman

-Comparing-Contrast of homes: Murtaugh, Riggs, corrupted wealthy

-Stressors pushing people to extremes: Murtaugh & Riggs, psychiatrist, jumper, McAllister, Joshua

-Who do you rely on? : Murtaugh's family, Riggs' dog, police partners, McAllister & Joshua relationship (burning arm to prove)

* * * * *

GENRE FILM Chapter 3 Exercises

Exercise 3a. Identify the 3-4 subplots needed to enrich and give logic to the Main Plot of your story. Identify the cast of characters involved in each of these subplots. Remember that subplots are happening simultaneously with the Main Plot and you will merely be pulling out events that relate to the Main Plot of your story.

Exercise 3b. What is the time frame of your story? A week? A month? A year? When do your major story events happen along this Time Line? Jot down some notes of how you plan to indicate the passage of time.

Exercise 3c. Write your Statement of Purpose for your script. What is the Point of your story? What will the experiences of your characters prove?

1) Does your Main Character represent Principle or Society and Good or Evil? Make a list of situations that could depict what you want to prove.

2) Does your Antagonist represent the opposing Society or Principle? Make a list of situations that could depict that opposing concept.

3) Where could you drop these into your Paradigm?

Exercise 3d. A well-paced story "weaves" threat and suspense into the fabric of the everyday or extraordinary life of the characters. Sometimes it is just referenced or mentioned and other times it is visual and intense jeopardy. That threat should be one of the important subplots that you will document in each section of your Beginning-Middle-Ending.

1) What is your Main Threat that will be visually exciting and edgy for the audience?

2) Look at your Paradigm and make a dot (.) where these intense moments need to appear. Are they clustered? Is there a long time between any these intense moments (when your audience is not being reminded of the threat? Do you see a logical progression of worsening action-reaction up to the climax?

CHAPTER 4

Set-up Credibility, Character Sequencing/ Science Fiction Genre

OVERVIEW OF THE FIRST 10 PAGES/MINUTES

The first ten pages of the screenplay/minutes of the movie are the most important of the entire story. This is where you introduce fundamentals and make the audience care. In other words, you introduce the audience to the characters' "World of Woe," the problems of their "Ordinary World" being experienced now. You pique curiosity that demands the rest of the story be seen to see what happens. You establish your storytelling ability that will allow them to suspend their disbelief and suck them into the adventure of the cinematic character's life. You demonstrate the fundamental personality of the Main Character that will be instrumental to all the following events. The story so enthralls the imagination, the audience wants to go questing with the characters.

OPENING IMAGE

Right after FADE IN comes your first Slug Line and first narrative paragraph. You want it to be a "doozey," something iconic that represents all that is to follow. Unless you have the money and professional influence to direct this story, you do not dictate music or credits at this point. Your main concern is how you will visually impact the audience, creating questions while establishing the "feel" of your film.

Whatever that first image is, it must represent everything that is to follow. Here are some examples:

--A tattered flag ripples in the smoke-filled wind above a battlefield strewn with dying and wounded men in blue and gray uniforms = Civil War era and the implication of a story of aftermath consequences.

--A rifle being pulled from a saddle sheath as wild mustangs race by into a man-made enclosure = a story of man destroying nature and what can be done to stop it.

--Midwife catching the birthing baby as the chamber doors burst open on a medieval knight shouting "The king is dead!" = consequences to this newborn.

--A campfire's sparks, bright against the dark sky, drift up to settle on the needles of a nearby pine tree and burst into flame with an audible "whoosh" = consequences of careless disregard for nature

--Frantic young man behind the wheel of a car speeding through the pouring rain = story of trying to overcome consequences even at the risk of life.

--Opening and closing ring box that is then flung into a river = a man who has lost at love and is forcefully moving on.

--Rocky Mountain vista through the lens of a camera when a shot rings out and the camera's view topples to the side = a murder to be solved.

These are just examples and could go on indefinitely, but you get the idea. First image = questions of consequences. How many videos do you have in your private collection? Play just the first image and state the anticipated consequence or question that is created at the outset then answered in the movie.

FIRST IMAGE = QUESTIONS OF CONSEQUENCES.

USE OF PROLOGUE OR BACK-STORY

Some novelists will use their entire first chapter to establish back-story of relationships and circumstances. That works in select instances when that "set-up" experience has direct relevance to the consequences of the main plot. It does not work in film making because it is **exposition** or factual explanation of "why" the story is going to happen. It is preferable to just get to the story unfolding now. It is highly likely that such a "set-up" will get cut in pre-production or during film editing.

The temptation of a prologue is to imply outcome, a form of on-the-nose storytelling. Why would you want to tell the audience if the adventure will be successful or not? Why should they sit in those theater seats for the next two hours? It is more satisfying to weave in the back-story in droplet-type flavoring instead of spoon-feeding. Modern movie-goers are much more sophisticated than those of a couple of generations back. Play to their intellect and not just their emotions.

OBJECTIVES OF THE FIRST 10 PAGES

So, you open with a scene the characters are experiencing now, a scene of jeopardy and character action that demonstrates fundamental characterization. Utilize vivid imagery that will impact both character and audience. Tweak vulnerability and how the character handles that. Rely on crisp, confrontational dialogue to establish strength of character.

Your emphasis at this point is two-fold: Make the audience believe and make them care with the least amount of exposition. Explode on the screen with the five W's . . .

1) WHO the story is about. Show that Main Character in action, making things happen in his or her world. Depict a scene that demands a reaction. Showing how your Main Character/Protagonist responds or copes will set-up fundamental expectations in your audience's imagination.

2) WHERE the story is happening. Because of the nature of collaborative storytelling in cinema, the writer need not give more than a line or two about setting beyond the Slug Line. It is the job of Set Design to research and fill in the details. Consider the difference between the rugged and perpetually snow-covered Himalayas vs. the lushness revealed by the spring melt in the Rocky Mountains or the details that would reveal the differences between a modern Scottish castle-turned-bed & breakfast and a 13th century Great Hall in that same castle. Just droplets of description that establish.

3) WHEN the story is happening. Of course your Slug Line will have DAY or NIGHT, but then your narrative will define the season or the year . . . How? In my "mega-script" CROSSROADS OF LIFE AND DEATH I used a lot of SUPERIMPOSE stating place, year and month to help move the story along simply because it covered 1944-1950 and utilized so many locations of a real life journalist adventurer. It was based on a true story of historical significance. Sometimes such subtle things as swimsuit-clad kids, a carved pumpkin or a Christmas tree can be enough to set the "When." The movie STEEL MAGNOLIAS utilized the seasons and the changes in the characters to depict the passage of time.

4) WHAT is happening to the Main Character. Consider a series of consequential events in your opening 10 pages that force your character onward and not looking back. This is all part of his or her "Ordinary World" and not the "New World" that he or she will be forced into in Act II. What are the trials and tribulations of the Main Character's world building toward the pivotal event that will change the person's life?

5) WHY are these events significant to the Main Character. Whatever is happening in this character's life at the opening of the story, those events have to be important to the person. Annoyance, triumph, anger, challenge. Consider events that dig at the emotions of the Main Character and force some kind of reaction that will demonstrate the underlying personality to the audience. You want this "why" to matter enough to make the audience identify with and care about this person.

Covering these five elements in the first 10 pages/minutes will sell this story and convince the audience they want to see the rest of the movie.

MOVING INTO ACT I'S ORDINARY WORLD

Act I's focus is on cause & effect giving glimpses of back-story that created the present situation. This set-up depicts the Main Character(s) living their "normal" life with specific goals and motivations visually evidenced. The audience becomes aware of problematic habits and inhibitions while accepting the character's knowledge, basic skills and interaction with his or her imperfect "Ordinary World." The "feel" of this time period is one of anticipation.

The writer has only 25-30 pages/minutes to acquaint the audience with all the fundamental information needed for them to understand the environment, the driving forces of the characters, and the possibilities beckoning. Besides considering what subplots must be introduced, the writer must be conscious of the question "How much of the story's Time Line will this ¼ of the total story take from Introductory Image to the end of the pivotal Plot Point I?"

INCORPORATING "HERO'S JOURNEY" & ARCHETYPAL CHARACTERS

Where a novel has the luxury of length, a movie needs to move. Where a novel can be complex and explore many facets of character and complexity in-depth, a movie has to have a linear Main Plot. Two tools that can help a writer to weave a tight story are 1) The Hero's Journey and 2) Archetypal characters. Just as poetry forms can discipline a poet's efforts while stimulating the challenge of how to be unique, these two storytelling tools can help the writer defy predictability. The writer has to work to be both clever and subtle.

CALL TO ADVENTURE VIA MESSENGER = INCITING INCIDENT

Remember humans strive for comfort and security, resisting change? Between pages 15 and 20 (frequently right at Page 17) of a cinematic story the Main Character is motivated to make a change. Sometimes that comes in the form of an opportunity, evidence of a new desire or an actual person dinging the Character with a challenge. This "Inciting Incident" will be a direct cause of the pivotal event that will change the Main Character's life. Any challenge or hint of change is an uncomfortable experience. The "Inciting Incident" discomfort can 1) emphasize the Main Character's reluctance, 2) make him/her question ability to cope, 3) force questions of worthiness and 4) emphasize that ignoring the "Call" will worsen the danger to self concept or raise the stakes if accepted.

MENTOR FORCES THE MOVE TOWARD CHANGE

Some form of a good or evil intentioned "Mentor" will enter following the Call. This character's purpose is to prompt the Main Character to make a decision to take action. If a positive influence, the Protagonist focuses on humanity's higher calling (thus the Mentor is seen as a constructive influence like Obi Juan in STAR WARS). If negative, the Protag's attention turns inward to the baser, more self-serving or survivor instincts (thus the audience identifies the Mentor as the Antagonist).

RELUCTANT CHOICE TO CROSS THE THRESHOLD INTO NEW WORLD = PLOT POINT I

Again, the story emphasizes the unwillingness of the Main Character to accept the challenge. He/She does not want to change and venture into the unknown. The "Ordinary World" is a known factor with tried and comfortable coping mechanisms. Beyond the familiar lurks uncertainty. The event at Plot Point I forces the Main Character to make that choice and begin a "New Life." The positive Mentor is solemn with encouragement, while the negative Mentor is rubbing hands in glee over the angst the Main Character faces. Plot Point I's event changes the Main Character's life forever thus causing the balance of the story.

RELATIONSHIP SEQUENCING & WEBBING

> EVERY SUBPLOT AGENDA IS SIMILAR TO THE MANY ROLES EACH HUMAN FULFILLS IN THEIR OWN DAILY LIFE.

Every subplot agenda is similar to the many roles each human fulfills in their own daily life. Sometimes they influence one another, but for the most part one agenda doesn't give a hoot what is happening in the other arenas of our life. Examples: Your bank and bank account, pet or animal responsibilities, health and fitness, spiritual community, charitable organizations, money-earning job, extended family, love life. The point is each role has its own needs and expectations. Sometimes one will have some critical demand that will disrupt the other agendas. And that's where the subplots of your life spin a thread that weaves the whole together. We are the sum total of our various agendas and multi-tasking or focus as needed.

Sequencing an agenda in a screenplay means you figure out what will be going on simultaneously in each subplot. Then you pull out those events that will tie into or "web" into the Main Plot. Those are the events you depict in brief scenes. Brief. The more words or pages you give a subplot or character, the more important they will seem to be to your audience. Just as the threat is important, you need to pay attention to the length of time that goes by without mentioning a particular subplot's agenda. Too long and your audience will have to recall their importance. Too often and the audience will be asking "Whose story is this, anyway?"

Use subplot events that shove the Main Character to grow by acceptance or fail by ignoring. Do not use the mundane to establish aura. Only depict those things that will have an effect or consequences on the character. Pay attention to the logic of how you move into and out of an agenda so the transitions are smooth and will not jar the audience to the point that the illusion of continuous story is shattered. Pick what is logical and what is important that will move the story forward.

SCIENCE FICTION GENRE

Science Fiction, Fantasy and Horror writing are grouped together under the umbrella classification "Speculative Fiction," in case you encounter that terminology and are unfamiliar. However, every genre is distinctive with their own needs, character expectations and types of plots.

Science Fiction aficionados tend to cringe when their beloved genre is "type-cast" by the pigeonhole description of "technology vs. humankind." Sorry. But it is true. The "science factor" is to blame. Storytellers got on board the Science Fiction rocket way back when Jules Verne started imagining stories evolving from fantastic machinery. Actually, before that back in the

Renaissance, Leonardo da Vinci started designing very plausible machines, proposing technology that has since proven just how right he was. Ah, imagination! It was inevitable that storytellers would latch onto these tantalizing ideas and run with them.

If you have not seen the very first Buck Rogers' Sci Fi movies of the early 20th century you missed a true appreciation for just how far cinema has come. Those movies had robots made of cardboard boxes with piping for arms and the "space ships" traversed the painted star-speckled "sky" via a string. There was no such thing as "Special Effects" in those days. Through the '50's into the '60's the technology of cinema and Special Effects actually evolved. Many attribute the public demand for Sci Fi material to the TV series STAR TREK and such movies as Kubrick's iconic 1968 film 2001: A SPACE ODYSSEY. Actually before that the genre had such great novelists as Arthur Clarke, Asimov, and H.G. Wells. Is it clear that the genre has evolved from simplistic imaginings to present day techno-babble? Undoubtedly it will continue to do so as new gadgets are invented and new science uncover more and more about our own world and the universe beyond our little sphere. Sci Fi writing is the "What if" Factor gone wild. That's why it is so much fun to work with!

FUNDAMENTAL CONCEPTS OF SCIENCE FICTION

1. Read current Science Fiction and Science publications.

- One has to understand how far the imagination of others is reaching to understand how far one can write his or her own story. Remember "There are no new stories"???? If you are not constantly feeding your imagination with what is currently published in both fiction and nonfiction, you can easily fall victim to simplistic storytelling (death to a Sci Fi writer, especially a new one).

2. Humanity faces constant change both in social institutions and investigative methods, theories and discoveries, thus imagining the fantastic or hypothesizing the fantastic is essential.

- The only rule to hypothesizing the fantastic is that you must maintain absolute **logic** in Cause-Effect scientific speculation and social evolution. Science will be primary over socialization, but logic can never take a back seat to drama. Logic must drive the drama.

3. Use sound, logical, universal scientific principles, but if skew be ready to explain why and how your logic arrived at that conclusion.

- Remember you are a liar, but especially in Sci Fi, you must be a credible liar. Sci Fi folks are mostly well-educated and well-versed in many fields of science. They read the books and go to those movies to see how someone else manipulated their science in the storytelling process. They are looking or a screw-up.

4. Write a complete profile (bible) of any alien culture, peoples and their science.
- If you are hypothesizing, you have to understand what principles these other worlds live by and what is "normal" so you know where to tweak their abnormal. If you do not know and can't explain, who can?

5. Carefully chart where technology impacts characters in your story.
- Attention to this detail will allow you to research and document your technology. That prevents any vague or inaccurate references and allows you to provide consistency. Technology is a major factor in any Sci Fi story, so do your homework!

6. IMPLICIT: Not by formula but through human conflict.
- Yes, you have to have technology, but it means nothing if you do not have humans responding to it, using it, suffering because of it. SPACE ODYSSEY would have been a boring film if not for the computer "Hal" confronting the Astronaut "Dave." The technology must create some consequence by its very existence.

SCIENCE FICTION CHARACTER REQUIREMENTS

Ignorance does not win a battle against anything in Science Fiction. Nothing happens by coincidence. Therefore, the main characters must be **highly motivated, intelligent, skilled and adaptable**. Portray survival of the fittest through the smartest. Both Protagonists and Antagonists must be **credibly questing** to obtain their definitive goals and must be **willing to manipulate their environment** to survive. There's a saying in law enforcement that anyone can be taught to shoot a gun, but ultimately it will come down to who is **willing** to fire it. Flip that concept in Sci Fi to the character willing to think outside the box to create a new, survivable environment.

SCIENCE FICTION PLOT TYPES

1. Far-traveling Story
2. Wonders of Science (and changing Science)
3. Man vs. Machine
4. Progress, Sciences & Social Impact
5. Progressive Man vs. Resistant Society
6. Man vs. Future (Time Travel)
7. Effects of Cataclysm
8. Progressive Man vs. Fragile Environment
9. Superpowers
10. Superman
11. Human vs. Alien

12. Progressive Man vs. Organized Religion (even Alien)
13. Imbalanced Past & Future

SCIENCE FICTION FILM ANALYSIS

Your **goal** in analysis of each and every film is to look for the genre elements just discussed as well as to get in the habit of automatically assessing key points of characterization, story structure, and cinematic techniques. At the conclusion of each is a discussion of the Concepts presented at the beginning of this chapter that are reflected in each film.

* * * * *

STAR WARS IV: The New Hope

By George Lucas
1977, starring Mark Hamill, Harrison Ford, Carrie Fisher

Length: 119 minutes (not counting credits)

Log Line: A budding Jedi knight joins rebels fighting the inter-galactic dark force bent on domination.

Statement of Purpose: To prove there are unseen forces in the world that can be utilized by focused humans both for good benefits and for self-serving, destructive intentions.

Intro Image: After the scrolling prologue, a ship in the black of space being chased by a much larger vessel.

First 10 minutes
Who: R2D2, C3PO, Princess Leia, Darth Vadar
When: Future
Where: Outer Space
What: A menacing ship is attacking a smaller, more vulnerable ship
Why: A dark military force is intent on capturing a rebel ship to intercept harmful military secrets

Four related subplots:
Luke & his Jedi destiny
Leia & the Rebel Alliance
Hans Solo's questionable businesses
Obi Juan vs the Dark Side

Time Line: Perhaps two weeks

Image repeats:
Space ships
Robots
Storm Troopers
Rebel Uniforms (cross between WWII fighter-pilot & NASA astronaut gear)
Light Saber
Acceptable aliens
Weak military minds
Useful youth-like skills
Explosions

Act I = Set-up of Ordinary World: Luke's youthful isolation challenged
10 min **Intro:** Leia's robots escape Darth Vader with her message
20 min **Inciting Incident**: Luke pries intriguing message from R2D2's workings
25 min **PP I:** R2D2 leaves safety to find Obi Juan and Luke must follow

Act II = Life 180 degrees of confrontations: Luke bonds with Obi Juan to save Leia
35 min **Pinch I:** Obi Juan call-to-adventure, Luke denies that he can take the risk
58 min **Mid-Point:** Obi Juan convinces Luke of sensitivity to "The Force"
75 min **Pinch II**: Determined Luke opens Leia's cell to rescue her
91 min **PPII:** Darth Vader strikes down Obi Juan leaving Luke on his own

Act III = Resolution: Luke instrumental in destroying the Death Star
105 min **Climax:** Rebel Alliance pilots taking on Imperial fighters until Luke hits vulnerable spot
116 min **Commitment**: Han joins the battle to assure victory
117 **After-story Conclusion**: Luke, Han & Chewy honored by Princess Leia & the Alliance army

Dialogue Notes:
Luke maturing from insecure to assured tone
C3PO's formal, literate talkativeness
R2D2's electronic sounds relaying emotion
Leia's aristocratic tones of command, judgement & impatience
Deep-throated menace of Darth Vader vs. confidence of Obi Juan
Han's manipulative business tone in contrast to his immature tones

Alpha Character posturing differences:
Obi Juan calm, confident vs. Darth Vader edgy, passionate
Rebel command style vs. Imperial officers
Han's masculinity vs. Luke's maturation
C3PO quick, precise vs. R2D2 verbose, tentative

Supporting cast Unique Character Gems:
R2D2 & C3PO personified robots
Uncle Owen & Aunt Varue, succinct yet vivid
Alien characters in the bar, each as a unique living being
Chewnacca, technologically capable, loyal, forceful yet vulnerable
Obi Juan as revitalized Jedi

Background effects, the nuances of aura:
Luke's home planet: barren, dangerous desert . . . yet survive
Pristine interiors of complex space ships big & small
Complexity of computerized innards of ships
Alien bar full of edgy, dangerous, "private" beings
"Yucky Factor" of garbage chute
Ease of familiarity with weaponry & vehicles

Elements from Other Genres: Western, Fantasy, Inspirational, Romance

Question: Do you see the good vs. evil (right down to Darth Vader in black) correlation of the struggle in the frontier to secure a safe home that is attributed to fundamental Westerns? What of Hans Solo's arrogant "gunfighter" persona? **Appearance or reference to recurrence of Evil Theme in Min:** Vader or Imperial appearances in **BOLD.** Others have notes on elements contributing to growing tension or problems.

Act I = Set-up of Ordinary World: Luke's youthful isolation challenged
2-7 Imperial attack on Leia's ship
8-10 Robots to desert
11 R2D2 neutralized
12-13 Robots "scrap" on Jawa sand crawler
14 Storm Trooper identifies craft & droid tracks
15-18 Robots bought by Uncle Owen
19 C3PO bonds with Luke
20 **Inciting Incident** = Luke triggers Leia's hologram seeking "Obi Juan"
21-23 Wonder if "Old Ben" disturbs uncle who wants memory erased
24 Luke talks of applying to academy like his friends, discouraged
25 **Plot Point II =** discovers R2D2 has disappeared into desert

Act II = Life 180 degrees of confrontations: Luke bonds with Obi Juan to save Leia

26 Discussion of dangerous Sand People then Uncle finds Luke gone next morning

27 Luke's land cruiser seen by Sand People

28-29 Luke attacked & dragged, frightened by noise & aggressive "creature" of Obi Juan

30-34 Obi Juan identifies himself, takes Luke to his home & explains Force, father's history

35 **Pinch I** = "You must learn the ways of the Force and accompany me to Alderon." Luke refuses

36-37 Vader & commanders discuss tactics & significance of Death Star, Vader demos power

38 Obi Juan & Luke find Jawa vehicle destroyed, Jawa dead, Luke realizes after his robots

39 Luke finds home destroyed, Uncle & Aunt burned corpses

40 Vader enters Leia's cell to threaten her with robot needle

41 Luke returns to join Obi Juan & go to colony

42-43 In colony Obi Juan demos his mind-bending powers "on the weak-minded."

44-45 Bar scene with Luke confronted, Obi Juan demos use of light saber

47-48 Intro Han & Chewbaca, negotiate transport

49-50 Han orders Chewy, confronts bounty hunter about Jaba, shoots

51 Luke & Obi Juan followed

52-53 Intro Jaba & Han's debt, followed

54 Intro Mellenium Falcon "piece of junk"

55 Storm Troopers shooting, lift off then ships shooting so jump to light speed

56-57 Leia taken to commander to demo power of Death Star as destroys Alderon

58-61 **Mid-Point:** Luke performs fighting exercises, Obi Juan "feels" Alderon, Chewy & robots play holographic chess "Let the wookie win" – contrast to Luke's "I feel the Force." Then Han's "hokie religion no proof to control my destiny"

62 Leia's intel only deserted base, Falcon arrives but no Alderon

63-65 Imperial fighter toward "moon" that is actually Death Star, Falcon pulled into bay, no one aboard

66 Vader identifies "presence I haven't felt in some time,." Crew emerges from hidden compartments

67 Troops with scanner board, noise

68-69 Obi Juan going after tractor beam, warns others stay, Han sarcastic, droids find Leia

70-71 Going to terminate, must rescue, Han will do it for money

72-74 Go to detention level as Storm Troopers, shoot men & equipment, Han awkward come-back

75 **Pinch II** = Luke opens Leia's cell "I'm here to rescue you." (he's her hero!)

76 Vader sense Obi Juan "My old Master"

77-78 Fire fight with Storm Troopers, blast wall, dive into garbage chute

79-81 Trapped in garbage chute with creature, Luke grabbed/released, walls closing in

82-83 Comm link to C3PO then R2D2 shuts down all garbage chutes.

84 Obi Juan to power column to close off beam

85 Out of chute, Leia takes charge

86-87 Encounter troops & Han leads away, Luke swings Leia across to open platform

88-90 Obi Juan confronts Vader & they fight

91 Plot Point II = As crew runs to Falcon, Luke sees Vader cut down Obi Juan (leaving Luke alone)

Act III = Resolution: Luke instrumental in destroying the Death Star

92 In Falcon, Luke devastated at loss as take off

93 Han directs him into fighter seat

94-95 Han & Luke shoot down all attacking Imperial fighers, celebrate, jump to hyperspace with beacon

96 Leia tells Han he'll get his money but worries about ease of escape

97 Luke asks about Han's interest, "Good" and arrive at Rebel outpost

98 Leia directs download of R2D2's memory bank with Death Star plans, Death Star has followed

99 Rebel pilots listen to explanation of one vulnerable spot requiring precision bomb drop

100-103 "May the Force be with you." As pilots to ships, encourage, Han prepping to leave

104 Luke "hears" Obi Juan's voice. 15 minute until Death Star clears & can fire.

105-115 Climax = Imperial to Rebel fighters battling, Luke "Trsut your feelings." Vader takes to a fighter, several failed tries due to fighting & Rebel losses, Vader hits R2D2, Death Star clears

116 Commitment = Falcon/Han return to blast at Vader (who escapes) allowing Luke to drop the bomb into the "chimney" and Battle Star explodes. "Luke the Force will with you always."

117- 119 **After-story =** Crews joyfully greet one another, Luke, Han, Chewy spiffed up to receive commendation from Princess Leia before assembled Rebel army & accept roaring applause.

Progressive CONCEPTS DISCUSSION

You were not told exactly what to look for regarding specific science fiction components in the minute-by-minute analysis of this film. Neither were you reminded to look for elements of the specific fundamentals discussed in Chapter 1. It is assumed you were paying attention to both areas. But, now let's look at the in-depth concepts demonstrated.

Opening and Act I

Hands down this is Luke Skywalker's "Hero's Journey." In this story the dramatic problem filled the first ten minutes rather than focusing on the Hero. So the audience was immediately set to wondering, asking questions they wanted answered and is armed with knowledge of the value of the droids. In essence, these 10 minutes were a Prologue.

However, the 5 W's were definitive for the imagination, the exposition clear.

Moving into the "Ordinary World" the audience meets the hard-working Luke who just wants to get on with life. Like many a young man he years to test himself against the world or, rather, the vague forces out there threatening his concept of civilization. He has already learned many survival skills and is willing to fight if necessary. His willingness is a primary factor in fulfilling his destiny. We see him respecting his aunt and uncle. We see him discovering a mystery and a "Call to Adventure." He wants to learn more. Then along comes his mentor Obi Juan who actually gives him the "tool of the Jedi trade" as the light saber. It all sounds good until Luke is actually asked to leave the familiar and dive into the adventure. That he isn't quite willing to do . . . until the only home he has known, the only family he has known are killed. At that point he is free and wants to take part in ending such atrocities.

One by one he is joined by the Adventurer and his side-kick and eventually the romantic interest, the damsel in distress. However, not one of these characters is flat, stereotypical and predictable. They have their own paths to follow and will allow only so much nudging to "play well with others." Their personalities are distinct and only enhanced by their experiences.

As an exercise, highlight how often one single character (other than Luke) appears and reappears in the outline. Consider their essential role and how that role shifts and morphs into something else when needed . . . yet their fundamental personality remains unchanged.

Also, look at how many times the visuals explained without a word being voiced.

Now, consider how you can weave in your jeopardy in your story while paying attention to the needs of the archetypal story telling.

Concepts to Consider:

1) Appropriate Title
2) Types of Suspense utilized
3) Webbing of related elements
4) First 10 minutes prepared audience for the balance of the story
5) Character consistency after Introduction

* * * * *

STAR TREK

By Robert Orci, Alec Kurtzman based on Gene Roddenberry TV series 2009, starring Chris Pine, Zachary Quinto, Leonard Nimoy

Length: 121 MINUTES

Log Line: An arrogantly brilliant Star Fleet cadet motivates unique fellow academy graduates to stop the destructive actions of a vengeful alien ship commander.

Statement of Purpose: To prove that the challenge in life is not mere survival with self-fulfillment but to find compatibility and relationships in one's true calling.

Intro Image: Exterior of Star Ship Kelvin moving through space (under attack).

First 10 minutes
Who: Parents at time of birth of James T. Kirk
When: "Star Date 2317.04" Kirk's birthdate
Where: Space
What: Kelvin being attacked by Nero demanding someone identify Spock
Why: George Kirk saves lives of 800+ Kelvin crewmen and wife as she gives birth then sacrifices himself as crashes Kelvin into Nero's massive ship.

Four related subplots:
Spock's Star Fleet career
Kirk's Star Fleet Career
Friendship between McCoy & Kirk
Relationship between Ohura & Spock

Time Line: Glimpses of Kirk's birth & childhood to Star Fleet senior year & days of Nero journey

Image repeats:
Star Ship exteriors
Nero's ominous ship
Womanizing down-time
Red Matter
Competition

Act I = Set-up of Ordinary World: Kirk's birth to rebellious kid to defiant Youth
10 min **Intro:** Nero destroyed Kelvin at Kirk's birth on escaping shuttle
24 min **Inciting Incident**: Pike challenges Kirk to attend Star Fleet Academy
35 min **PP I**: Distress call from Vulcan demands all cadets to active duty = Call to Adventure

Act II = Life 180 degrees of Complications: Enterprise to foil threat of rogue Romulan ship
44 min **Pinch I:** Kirk awakens to hear similarity to Kelvin anomaly
54 min **Mid-Point:** Kirk the hero of destroying Vulcan drill & accepted as crew member
79 min **Pinch II**: Old Spock tells of life-long friendship
94 min **PPII:** Kirk emotionally assaults Spock until the Vulcan retaliates almost killing Kirk

Act III = Resolution: Enterprise engages and defeats Nero
105 min **Climax:** Kirk fights Nero while Spock destroys earth drill
113 min **Commitment**: Kirk with Spock offers sanctuary to Nero but refuted
After-story Conclusion: Kirk's commendation & given captaincy of Enterprise with Spock aboard

Dialogue Notes:
McCoy's dry wit
Kirk always witty or confrontational
McCoy's speech cadence
Chekov's thick Russian
Vulcan cadence
Scott's crusty Scots burr

Alpha Character posturing differences:
Kirk always arrogantly Alpha to Everyone
Spock-the-son vs. Sarek-the Vulcan-father & Spock as competent Star Fleet officer
Ohura's bearing as woman vs. persona as Star Fleet Officer
Pike mature commander vs. Nero stressed to point of violent commander

Old Spock mellow vs. young Spock still questing
McCoy sarcasm vs. everyone else

Supporting cast Unique Character Gems:
Nero on the edge
McCoy, Ohura, Sulu, Scotty . . . Compare to TV series personas
Pike the competent, focused commander, George Kirk courageous, decisive
Sarek logical & accepting, Old Spock mellowed & accepting
Boy Spock angry & defiant, Boy Kirk just as angry & defiant
Scotty's alien protégé cute helper (pet-like)

Background effects, the nuances of aura:
Well-lit & pristine Star Ships vs. dark, messy Romulan ship
Open Iowa countryside with Star Ship construction site in middle of field
Rugged Vulcan exterior with educational chambers
Star Fleet Academy like any college campus
Frozen planet with Scotty's "empty" outpost

Elements from Other Genres: Action-Adventure, Western, Romance

Question: Were you distracted by trying to reason out the "the disruption in the time continuum" (especially when young Spock met Old Spock) or did you merely suspend your disbelief and go with the flow? And, secondly, if a drop of the Red Matter caused such horrific implosion, why wasn't its entire release more horrific, its Black Hole more powerful?

Appearance or reference to recurrence of Evil Theme in Min: Rogue Romulan Nero in **BOLD** but perpetual cascade of dangers to life

Act I = Set-up of Ordinary World: Kirk's birth to rebellious kid to defiant Youth

2	Nero's threat
7	No Spock so kills Kelvin Captain
8	Evac Kelvin, PG wife to Medical shuttle, Loss of auto-pilot
9	George stays, Wife's delivery
10	Collision Course, James T. Kirk born
11	Impact & George dies
13	Juvenile Kirk driving car on Iowa flatlands
14	Chased by cop, jumps free = Kirk is risk-taker
15	Contrast Vulcan children, tenacious & defant Spock
17	"Control your fears so they don't control you."
20	Spock decline the Science Academy for Star Fleet
21-23	Youthful, womanizing Kirk fights in bar

24-26 **Inciting Incident**: Pike researched father & ID's Kirk's genius
27 Kirk do Star Fleet Academy in 3 yr, meets McCoy
29-30 3 yrs later: Nero's 25 yr wait to capture a ship
31 Ohura's documentation of Klingon transmission about destroyed ships
33 Kirk's 3rd Kobiashi-Maru exercise, nonchalant, malfunction, defeats test
34 Call for council investigation, Spock confronts with "Cannot cheat death"
35 Plot Point I: Vulcan distress call with all cadets called to duty

Act II = Life 180 degrees of Complications: Enterprise to foil threat of rogue Romulan ship
37 Kirk not listed, McCoy decides to help him
38 Ohura confronts Spock for Enterprise assignment
40 Dock with Enterprise with Kirk ill
42 Launch of Enterprise, intro Sulu as pilot
43 Intro Chekov with description of "lightning storm" anomaly near Vulcan
44 **Pinch I:** Kirk awakens hearing about storm = Greatest fear ship loss like Kelvin
45 Nero's drill into Vulcan
46 Kirk explain anomaly compared to Kelvin as "Attack"
48 Arrive amid debris of destroyed ships
49 Nero attacks then hails Enterprise
51 Red Matter, Pike to Romulan ship
52 Pike selects 3 for shuttle & makes Spock Captain & Kirk First Officer
54-60 Mid-Point: Kirk & Sulu "fly" to drill platform, battle, Nero launches Red matter
63 Beam aboard then Spock to disintegrating planet, loses mother
65 Vulcan implodes into Black Hole
68 Nero explains plans & threatens Pike with slug
72 Spock & crew discuss time continuum, Kirk & Spock argue
75 Kirk shuttled to frozen planet
78 Kirk's crab-like creature chased away by Old Spock
79 **Pinch II:** "Have been and always shall be your friend" = recognition of life-long friendship
80 Mind-meld story of "129 years from now Super-Nova"
83 "Did I know my father?"
84 McCoy vs. Spock on Enterprise
85 Old Spock & Kirk to outpost, Intro stranded-as-punishment Scotty
87 Old Spock explains Trans-warp theory that Scotty "invented"
90 Spock cites #619 emotional compromise
91-96 **Plot Point II:** Kirk & Scott aboard, water turbine, Confrontation, No Captain

Act III = Resolution: Enterprise engages and defeats Nero
98 Chekov's theory, Spock concurs & volunteers, Kirk joins
100 Nero arrives at Earth to drill
101 Enterprise fires, Spock & Kirk transport to Romulan ship
104 Find Old Spock's ship with Red matter, it recognizes Spock, less than 4.3% chance
106-111 Climax: Kirk fights Romulan's & Nero as Spock destroys drill
109 Nero orders fire on Spock despite Red Matter
110 Kirk fights Romulans, finds Pike as Spock aims ship at Nero's ship
112 Spock and Kirk with Pike transported back to Enterprise by crowing Scotty
113 Commitment: Kirk offers logical compassion to Nero, Nero declines
114 Red Matter implosion in to Black Hole
115 Warp doesn't work to pull away until Scotty releases dilithium for explosion
117-120 **After-story:** Spock meets Old, Kirk commendation & Captaincy, Spock on board

CONCEPTS DISCUSSION

You were not told exactly what to look for regarding specific mystery components in the minute-by-minute analysis of this film. Neither were you reminded to look for elements of the specific fundamentals discussed in Chapter 1. It is assumed you were paying attention to both areas. But, now let's look at the in-depth concepts demonstrated.

RELATIONSHIP SEQUENCING & WEBBING

Obviously this was a film written "after-the-fact" of Gene Rodenberry's TV series and subsequent movies. The crew relationships had long been established so the screenwriters, director and cast had to work to comply with the audience expectations of basic personalities and relationships. That demanded a lot of attention to exposition and set-up of the histories of people already known to the audience. The purpose of the film was to establish how they all came together in the beginning. To be satisfying, yet logical in the time frame allowed, only glimpses of exposition and moments of high tension could be depicted. "Showing Moments" crammed with innuendo delivered, in my opinion, without boring.

The physical similarities as well as the speech and facial habits the actors mimicked their predecessors bringing credibility to the characters. The only "surprise" was Ohura and Spock's budding romance. The other thing was that these young people were given their rank relatively early in their careers. "Logically" one can then question lack of advancement until as late as in 100 years later (?) . . . However, the tasks they had to perform on the Enterprise at their young ages did demand the ranks, thus it seemed appropriate to accept this convoluted point "for this story."

Look at how the crew members were woven in and out of the unfolding story. The screenwriters did a commendable job of using their skills and knowledge at appropriate times and not leaving them for long. There was a definitive webbing of the crew's relationships to one another, such as Spock talking with McCoy who classically asked him "Are you out of your Vulcan mind?"

The problems with Nero and his ship were referenced but actual "seeing" him and his threat was shoved aside to set the stage for the crew members until, of course, the Climactic battle. Did we need to see more of Nero? Referencing him and second-guessing his plans provided adequate tension relevance. The whole concept is meant to remind the audience of that subplot on a regular basis to heighten their concern.

Progressive Concepts to Consider:

1) Appropriate Title
2) Types of Suspense utilized
3) Webbing of related elements
4) First 10 minutes prepared audience for the balance of the story
5) Character consistency after Introduction

Here are the first five of 24 concepts you must pay attention to in your writing and in your analysis of each and every cinematic story.

* * * * *

GENRE FILM Chapter 4 Exercises

Exercise 4a. Time to actually write your first five pages (and anticipate the five pages to follow).

POINTS TO PONDER for Opening's 10 Pages
Here are questions to ask yourself as you plan and write these pages:

About the start of story:
1. How will the opening image/event/scene ultimately impact the story?
2. What vivid, dramatic opening event would reveal maximum information with Show vs. Tell?
3. What event would involve/challenge/impact vital characters, even if pre or post actual story time?

About Character Revelations:

1. Which characters must the audience immediately meet?
2. When does the Major Antagonist enter the story? As a subtle or a blatant threat?
3. What elements from Character Profiles must audience have to empathize/understand/establish motivation?

Exercise 4b. Examine your depiction of setting with a critical eye. Succinct yet evocative? Are your narrative paragraphs brief enough or do you need to break them up more? It is acceptable to have a new paragraph for each change of camera view. You are not saying what is seen through the lens, merely implying. Note: The more you do this the more your mind's eye will begin to "see" those camera views and that's how you will write.

Exercise 4c. Examine each character's first appearance. Would your brief character description set an actor on fire and create a desire to play that role? Is the dialogue crisp, progressive and characterizing with attitude and innuendo?

Exercise 4d. Write pages 6-10 with attention to cause-effect events and dialogue.

Exercise 4e. What subplots and supporting cast members did you introduce?

Exercise 4f. Make a list of questions you think the audience would be asking at this point . . . questions they really want answered in the rest of the story. (If possible, ask someone else to read your 10 pages then your list of questions and see if they agree.)

CHAPTER 5

Signpost Events, Opposition, Point-of-View/ Fantasy Genre

SIGNIFICANCE OF PLOT POINT I

Probably every person reading this can think of an incident that changed the direction of his or her life, a moment that in fact caused the rest of your life to unfold as it did. Loss, triumph and recognition, an educational or circumstantial challenge that demanded a change in the status quo, a new responsibility, meeting a special person are just a few examples. If you were to write the fictionalized screenplay of your life that incident would be Plot Point I. It put a cap on your "Ordinary World" and launched you (by choice or forcefully) into a totally "New Life."

Movies are fictional accounts, not documentaries. So, even if you are writing about a true story based on diary or historical accounts, you must remember that you are fictionalizing the retelling. You might add "Thank God it is not a documentary!" Fiction exaggerates both event importance and characters. That's what makes films about historical figures so fascinating. We are imagining what went on in their lives, even in their bedrooms. It doesn't have to be flattering . . . but it absolutely must be cinematic high drama. Plot Point I is the epitome of such drama for the film character's life is going to change because of that event.

Yes, Act I events depict the character in action, alluding to untried skills or demonstrating character flaws and propensities. When the audience arrives at that moment of the Plot Point I event, anxiety's tension must be high. Jeopardy resides in awareness of options and the choices made. How will you visually describe that?

If you are not certain what event you want to throw at your character, then brainstorm an intense "What if" list of logically caused circumstances the character could arrive at. Do not go for the most logical, but work to create the most dramatic, angst-filled situation you can. Grab the audience by the throat and have them on the edge of their seat hurting, agonizing, as fearful or stunned as the Main Character who is forced to act in a manner that will mean leaving the predictable "Ordinary World" and slamming headfirst into a totally "New World" because life whirled 180-degrees from what was expected by the character.

Finally, think about how Plot Point I consequences will work to prove your Statement of Purpose.

DEFY PREDICTABILITY

This is the moment when a lot of new storytellers and screenwriters in particular will begin to worry about formula writing. Formula only results when the prescribed steps are blatantly apparent. Your job as a writer is to keep the audience so involved in what happens next, they don't stop to analyze. Only when you hesitate to provide undue emphasis in amount of time, character rumination or dialogue references will the audience be made aware of the progression of a story's signposts, the "prescribed" events of "The Hero's Journey." Defy predictability through the intensity of cause-effect story progression.

YOUR JOB AS A WRITER IS TO KEEP THE AUDIENCE SO INVOLVED IN WHAT HAPPENS NEXT, THEY DON'T STOP TO ANALYZE.

CHANGING MAIN CHARACTER'S GOAL

Remember in Act I how you were asked to depict the Character's passion for a Tangible Objective? Sometimes that goal changes in the "New World" and sometimes it doesn't. The "New World" may just make it more difficult to go after that Goal. The lessons the character learns and confidence-shift with new skills and new knowledge may just result in redefining what is necessary to live a satisfying life and what becomes insignificant. That's okay. Why? Because life is messy and not as linear as some movie makers have portrayed. Your job as a storyteller is to "mix it up." Making the character want something new may be one of the changes.

A transient goal is quickly realized with no long-term impact. A more significant goal is the elusive one that the character must work hard for, sacrifice for. Don't make your main characters shallow and predictable with those short term (and predictable) goals. Give them the deep, hard-won kind that will impact their inner character (thus attitude) and result in outer action or visual evidence of the worthiness of the character.

Complex characters take the audience along on their experiences and growth. If the audience doesn't care because of predictability or shallowness, they will grow disgruntled and critical of character choices. Over-simplification of obvious choices and consequences will have the same effect on the audience.

The writer walks a tightrope. What will make that "walk" easier? Growing confident in pushing the envelope and not always playing it safe. Going for the most outrageous, riskiest, most exaggerated choices with an eye to "making sense of it all" in the end. Look at writers like Quentin Tarantino.

The one iron clad rule is that the subsequent events after Plot Point I are at least plausible and not pure, illogical idiocy. The goal and the rock-and-a-hard-place choices create tension (worry about consequences) but maintain audience interest. Write the pivotal Plot Point I, consequences and maybe even a change in goal concept that makes You-the-Write feel edgy and excited. That indicates you are exploring new territory as well and that is fun!

INTENSIFYING OPPOSITION

The opposition of antagonists comes in two guises: 1) minor short-term irritants and 2) major long term problems. Minor irritants make the characters trip . . . and swear. The major problems force choices that have consequences. Every single scene needs to have some sort of opposition to what the characters are trying to make happen. That opposition creates the tension of conflict the characters cannot ignore. The minor oppositions annoy and irritate to the point of temper flare-ups. The major problems force action of some sort. Remember, that means for the Antagonist (Character), as well as for the Protagonist (Main Character). Don't forget to tweak and annoy your Antagonist to give the audience glimpses of chinks in his /her armor that can be useful in the future.

And here you need to rid yourself of some of your own "baggage" by depicting those irritants that drive YOU up the wall. People who cut you off in traffic, "pen clickers" or whiners, even the catty, insincere "smiler" in the office who is actually the most vicious back-stabbing gossip. This is one area where writers have the opportunity to play amateur psychologist . . . for themselves. Writing about these petty things and actually depicting a viable response is a liberating experience for a writer.

SCENE POINT-OF-VIEW

The conventions in novel writing make it comparatively easy to depict who is viewing a given scene. The camera is more omniscient, but the POV is still an issue the screenwriter needs to be conscious of in every single scene.

Three movies are recommended to concentrate on Point-of-View: To fully understand character focus in a script as a whole watch AMADEUS, 1984, as told by Soleari. Intentionally conflicting stories were depicted in COURAGE

UNDER FIRE, 1996. And shifting focus with an ensemble cast was skillfully portrayed in THE FAMILY STONE, 2005.

The focus of each of these different kinds of stories will give you clear examples of "how to guide the camera" to tell the scene's story from a single character's point-of-view. You won't actually be telling the director and cinematographer. Your narrative and dialogue will simply have that kind of focus.

Points to consider:

1) WHO is the scene about?
2) WHO is impacted the most significantly by the scene's events and dialogue?
3) WHO is causing drama vs. who is reacting to the drama?

One of the most common revisions in later drafts of a screenplay is a change in a scene's focus to the leads or to what impacts the leads.

FANTASY GENRE

The second type of popular "Speculative Fiction" is Fantasy which plays into imaginary worlds and societies and connects with an audience because the character problems are recognizable, credible, comparable to common human problems in our real world. Quite obviously, Science Fiction shares story-style with Fantasy when the imaginary place and characters come from a society/societies beyond our human experience. Just as all Science Fiction is not necessarily Fantasy, not all Fantasy is Science Fiction. Tolkien, *THE WIZARD OF OZ*, ancient mythology and fairy tales are prime examples. Those push the envelope of the imagination without the manipulation of science and technology.

Some Fantasy stories are light with laughter, easily resolved problems and simple triumph of good over evil as seen in many innocent childhood favorites on the Cartoon Network or in hundreds of cute and much-adored children's books. Other Fantasy stories are dark and angst-ridden such as the Tolkien's LORD OF THE RINGS trilogy and the movie GODZILLA (1998). And were the King Arthur and Robin Hood legends based on historical fact or pure fantasy?

Speculative Fiction as a whole, whether Fantasy, Science Fiction or Horror, is based on one premise: creating plausibly fantastic situations that are the **extremes** of the storyteller's imagination. Think how that explains the myths of ancient cultures. Fantastic make-believe entities were created to tell stories in the Inca, Aztec, North American Plains Indian, Maori, Australian Aborigine, Swahili, Celtic, and Nordic peoples. Every race, every culture fantasized, mostly to explain their natural world or to teach the young life lessons.

Thankfully, the tradition continues even more fervently in our modern culture. Why? Because our fertile human imaginations continue to hypothesize life lessons experienced in strange places by entities different yet similar to us. The one common factor is logic. The reader/audience has to be able to logically follow the plot and connect with the characters.

FUNDAMENTAL CONCEPTS OF FANTASY

1. Read both the past and the current prominent Fantasies.
- Especially pay attention to the sub-genre you intend to write to understand how the genre has evolved and not infringe or copy another's imaginings. This is not an area where copying or building on another's world and characters is a form of flattery. It is plagiarism. Be original or don't do it.

2. Write a complete profile of the culture or cultures and histories of the peoples.
- Remember, you must believe they exist, that they have existed prior to the point of your story. Create the cause-effect logic for the evolution of the politics, monetary system, clothing, adornment, Activities of Daily Living, food preferences and preparation, family structures, for everything, so you feel the societies and the lives of the people.

3. IMPLICIT: Anchor your society and characters with analogies to our human reality, no matter how bizarre your rendition.
- The point is to connect your reader/audience to the bizarre through their own awareness as in "That's just like people in our town."

4. Play close attention to the Diction (style of speaking-formal/informal) and Syntax (grammatical arrangement of words) of your characters' speech patterns.
- Even different fantasy genres use specific diction and syntax in the narrative as well as the character dialogue, such as the soft, simple, almost musical quality of "Arthurian" stories vs. the harsh, abrupt wording in Germanic, Anglo-Saxon, Nordic stories. Consider even the naming of objects and animals. Example: How did Yoda speak vs. the Zeus in Greek mythology?

5. Carefully mix and contrast fantasy creatures/people to create subtle casting impressions or points.
- Consider the roles, behaviors, personalities of fantastic creatures/peoples that function as "repeat images" quickly painting emotional impressions on your reader/audience. This is one less-than-obvious Fantasy tool to carry your story and avoids blatant telling.

FANTASY CHARACTER REQUIREMENTS

The creatures/peoples in Fantasy are **humanoid personifications of motivation and thought.** The Protagonists and Antagonists are **risk takers capable of change** for it is the risks they take and the changes they make that guide the story.

FANTASY PLOT TYPES

1. Sword & Sorcery with Mythic Hero Protagonist
2. New Worlds encountered
3. Ancient Mythology or Legends retold
4. Personified Animals
5. Allegory

- ALL elements of plot, place and characters reflect and represent circumstance in our world.

TYPES OF FICTION

At this point in discussing speculative Fiction, it is particularly appropriate to point out the three general types of fiction, designated by the storyteller's approach to the overall story. Remember, these are literary considerations, but they may help you in deciding how YOU want to focus your story.

1. **Mimetic** Fiction . . . imitates actual life . . Sit-coms . . . . Contemporary Romance
2. **Premise** Fiction . . .. .revised reality . . . . . Anecdotal, Hamlet . Arthurian Legend
3. **Dream** Fiction . . .. creates own logic . . . DUNE, myths . . . . AVATAR

FANTASY FILM ANALYSIS

IMPORTANT: Identify 1) the type of Fantasy story told, 2) the Fantasy characters and archetypal characters used in the story, and 3) the evolution of the Fantasy elements that made you "believe" in and become involved in the story. How does the story work to make you "suspend disbelief?"

* * * * *

LADYHAWKE

By Edward Khmora, Michael Thomas, Tom MacKenzie, David Peopls
1985, Starring Matthew Broderick, Rutger Hauer, Michelle Pfeiffer

Length: 114 minutes

Log Line: A manipulative young thief helps a vengeful warrior-by-day-wolf-by-night and his agonized lady-by-night-hawk-by-day in their quest to end their cursed existence.

Statement of Purpose: To prove that true love's righteousness can overcome adversity and evil.

Intro Image: To V.O. "Nothing is impossible, Lord." a hole is dug through a mud-encrusted wall.

First 10 minutes
Who: Phillipe-the-Mouse, a thief confined to Aquila's inescapable prison
When: Middle Ages (by clothing, customs & use of crossbow)
Where: France (by French names)
What: He is escaping the atrocities of the Bishop's prison through the sewers
Why: The Bishop has ordered his hanging

Three related subplots:
Navarre & Isabeau's love story & journey
Imperius vs. the Bishop's spirituality
Phillipe's reluctant journey of redemption

Time Line: One week (from Phillipe's escape to the sun's eclipse when Bishop hearing annual clerical confessions in Aquila)

Image repeats:
Hawk flying
Vicious wolf
Navarre's sword
Crossbow
Phillipe's groveling vs. curiosity
Cathedral
Lowly/mean priest attire vs. Bishop's finery

Act I = Set-up of Ordinary World: Phillipe seeing Navarre & Isabeau's shape-shifting
10 min **Intro:** Phillipe escapes Aquila into the countryside with Bishop's men pursuing
16 min **Inciting Incident**: Navarre pulls him onto his horse claiming him as cohort against Bishop
22 min **PP I**: Phillipe witnesses the wolf attack then magical gentling by the strange lady

Act II = Life 180 degrees Confrontations: Selfish Phillipe joining in the quest to end the nightmare
33 min **Pinch I:** Navarre asks for help getting into Aquila but Phillipe fears return
57 min **Mid-Point:** As Imperius diverts soldiers, Phillipe bravely assists Isabeau, sees her transform
75 min **Pinch II**: Hawk glides to Phillipe bypassing Navarre
82 min **PPII:** Wolf falls into frozen water to be saved by Phillipe, Isabeau desperate for resolution

Act III = Resolution: Battling the Bishop and recovering to humanity
99 min **Climax:** Navarre battles his nemesis, can't stop bell ringing, ultimately has to kill Bishop
112min **Commitment**: Navarre & Isabeau embrace as humans, enjoyed by Phillippe & Imperius
After-story Conclusion: Imperius praises Phillipe with expectation he will make it to heaven

Dialogue Notes:
Phillipe's tonal shifts from arrogance to manipulation to caring
Navarre's commanding warrior tone vs. lover
Bishop's authoritarian voice
Isabeau's gentle femininity
Imperious's sloppy diction = loss of pride

Alpha Character posturing differences:
Phillipe, a survivor always on the edge of arrogance
Navarre, the Alpha male warrior and lover
Imperius, guilt-ridden bent on redemption
The Bishop, self-righteous superior owed whatever he wants
Cezar, vicious hunter l

Supporting cast Unique Character Gems:
Imperius, guilt-ridden but caring
Bishop, masterful, willing to manipulate, yet innately fearful
Cezar, willing agent who savors the kill

Background effects, the nuances of aura:
Bishop's opulent residence
Forrests, fields & castles of Aquila
Imperius's disintegrating castle
Cathedral

Elements from Other Genres: Romance, Action-Adventure, Comedy, Inspirational

Question: Did having the story POV from Phillipe's instead of Navarre or Isabeau enhance the audience suspension of disbelief and allow "participation" in the journey or was it "strained comedy"?

Appearance or reference to recurrence of Evil Theme in Min: Darkly powerful Bishop and his forces in **BOLD**. By now you have concluded that CHARACTERS cause the consistently more difficult complications that are on the plain numbered pages in the cause-effect storyline series of events. The actions have consequences that increase the tension.

Act I = Set-up of Ordinary World: Phillipe seeing Navarre & Isabeau's shape-shifting

1 Soldiers, Cathedral with priests
2 Bishop's envoy & soldier seeking Phillipe who has escaped prison
3 Soldiers searching
5 Phillipe climbs to grate in Cathedral floor as Bishop's entourage enters
6 Bishop informed of Phillipe's escape, widespread search ordered
8-10 Phillipe steals from soldiers, into countryside & forest, steals clothes
11-15 Village scene Phillipe bragging, soldiers reveal, Ex-Capt of Guard Navarre intro & fight
16 = **Inciting Incident** when Phillpe running & Navarre pulls him onto horse to escape, Hawk's help
17-21 Navarre to peasants hovel, bed in barn, talk of "one day," Navarre's helm, Phillipe talking to self, hears woods, runs back to barn
22-24 = **Plot Point II** Phillipe sees peasant axman taken down by black wolf, trying arm crossbow, intro Lady Isabeu, calming him then out to calm wolf, terrified Phillipe climbs to loft rambling about "magic"

Act I = Life 180 degrees Confrontations: Selfish Phillipe joining in the quest to end the nightmare

25 Bishop's Capt racing back to Cathedral as Navarre, Phillipe, hawk in woods for the night

26 Phillipe tells Navarre of enchanted woman he saw

27 Navarre implies quest, sleep, Captain at Castle

28-30 Captain confers with Bishop about Navarre's return & asked about hawk, sends for Cezar

31 Phillipe manhandling sword, Navarre warns & explains family significance & plan to kill Bishop

32 Navarre needs Phillipe guide into city

33 = **Pinch I**: Saved my life, can't repay. I have no honor but better than return to Aquila, sword threat convinces him otherwise.

34 Isabeau chasing rabbit finds Phillipe tied to tree & he talks her into freeing him, wolf howl.

35 Hawk to mounted Navarre wrist, search for Phillipe, Soldiers capture Phillipe

36-38 Solders-Navarre fight, crossbow arrow hits & downs Hawk

39 Navarre wraps Hawk, hands to Phillipe, orders to ride Goliath to Imperius at ruined monastery

40-41 Phillipe riding, bird bites, Phillipe arrives & calls out, intro Imperius, no ordinary hawk

42-43 Imperius hurried & worried, sends Philippe out

44-45 Imeprius searches for herbs, Phillipe sneaks in to find Isabeau with arrow protruding & makes connection, Imperius forces him away.

46-47 As Imperius pulls arrow, Bishop having restless dreams, Isabeau screams, wolf howls

48-51 Imperius tells Phillipe of Isabeau & Navarre's love and Bishop's jealous bargain curse

52-53 Bishop examines Cezar's useless pelts, find the hawk & will find the one who loves her

54 Phillipe watches as Isabeau awakens, talks of Navarre wanting her cared for

55-56 Near dawn, troops arrive at monastery, Imperius announces found way to break curse in 3 days

57-60 = Mid-Point Epiphany: As Imperius distracts soldiers, Phillippe leads Isabeau to tower roof, door breached, Isabeau falls in first rays of sun to shape-shift to hawk, Phillipe cowering on outside wall, threatening solider hit by Navarre's crossbow, "Pays to tell the truth, Lord."

61-63 Navarre grateful but distrusts Imperius when says can reverse the curse, Phillipe calls Isabeau "Ladyhawke" to Navarre & pushes that she has fiath, he vows to kill the Bishop as he swore.

64 As Navarre rides, Philippe chatters, Imperius in mule cart

65-69 Inn scene as shelter in barn, Phillippe steals clothes for Isabeau, music, dance, laugh

70-71 As Phillipe cradles sword, the two run into Cezar's wolf-pelt-laden horse. Philippe wields sword, but as he rides away, Isabeau jumps on Goliath and follows into rainy forest

72-73 Isabeau creeps forward, Cezar sets another trap, one wolf caught & yelping, Cezar stands over him as Isbeau attacks, snarling Navarre/ wolf approaches, Isabeau kicks Cezar into own trap killing him

74 Imperius hurrying mule "Going to snow."- Navarre awakens Phillipe in morning camp

75 = **Pinch II:** Hawk glides to Phillipe bypassing Navarre , emabarrassed, passes her back

76-78 Fumbling explanation of night, Jealous of every moment "Tell me every word." Sad but remembered how happy, Hawks & wolves mate for life so not even that

79 Imperius arrives to tell of eclipse, Navarre scoffs, rides off with hawk.

80-81 At snowy night camp find Isabeau and convince of plan

82-85 = **Plot Point II:** Imperious & Phillipe dig hole, Isabeau watches & hears wolf, as crosses ice it breaks, three humans hurry to save floundering wolf. Isabeau holds. Phillipe into water & wolf claws across him to get to ice. Isabeau crying in desperation "We cannot live like this."

Act III = Resolution: Battling the Bishop and recovering their humanity

86-88 At sunrise, Isabeau rubbing wolf, Barest moment wolf to Navarre, hawk's eyes change & flies out of shelter to Navarre's roar of agony.

89-90 Navarre told sword fell through ice as saved him from drowning, sees Phillipe's clawed chest & told happened in rescue, "show you hwo to cage a wolf."

91-92 Return to Aquila at night, Soldier stops cart, finds snarling wolf in cage

93 Morning bells as Bishop prepares and Phillippe swims into sewers

94-97 Imperius "Soon " Phillipe inside with dagger, Cathedral processional, sees skylight, Navarre gives over hawk, if hear the bells I have failed so give her a quick death, Phillipe creeps to door

98 Navarre on Goliath "As your former Captian" Solders allow pass, Phillipe struggles to unlock & lift bar.

99-111 = Climax: Navarre rides into Cathedral, priests cower as Bishop watches, Captain rides his charger in for battle, both fall for sword combat, Phillpe slides sword to Navarre, overhead skylight broken as eclipse begins, soldier rings bells (Navarre thinks Isbeau dead so more enraged) Bishop "Kill me curse forever." Then looks to doorway horrified. Navarre glimpses her, forces Bishop look at the two of them. Navarre & Isabeau embrace, she carries hawk hood & josses to Bishop. Upon return to Navarre, Bishop tries attack & Navarre throws sword, impaling him.

112 -113 = **Commitment**: The couple savor seeing one another in the sunlight pouring through the skylight then recognize & thank "You two" Imperius & Phillipe

114 = .**After-story**: As walk to doors, Imperius "expect to see you at the pearly gates" & Phillpe replies "Even if I have to pick the lock" While Navarre lifts his lady who joyfully spreads her arms.

CONCEPTS DISCUSSION

You were not told exactly what to look for regarding specific fantasy components in the minute-by-minute analysis of this film. Neither were you reminded to look for elements of the specific fundamentals discussed in Chapter 1. It is assumed you were paying attention to both areas, as well as noting the lengthening list of concepts previously discussed. But, now let's look at the just-discussed in-depth concepts demonstrated in this film.

CHANGING CHARACTER GOAL

Initially, Phillipe's only goal was to be free of Aquila, a simple and reasonable goal. Navarre's intervention saves him from capture thus the young thief is indebted but he refuses to help the knight on his quest because to return is a greater risk than to defy Navarre. Then he encounters Isabeau and is drawn into their story through his own insatiable curiosity. His once pointless existence now has purpose and a definitive higher purpose at that.

The story events that bring the characters together likewise changes each one's goal: Imperius finds salvation from his unforgiveable sin of breaking the sanctity of the confessional that set all in motion, Isabeau's endurance gives way to desperate hope of a solution and Navarre is finally convinced that revenge is not his purpose but redemption.

Each character entered the story with one goal but each changed because of the events of the story.

POINT OF VIEW

An intriguing factor in this film was the story used the point-of-view of a supporting character observing and caring about the shape-shifting main characters. That allowed the audience to take his role, ask his questions, begin to emotionally invest in their quest. Navarre and Isabeau's dilemma gave Phillipe a purpose higher than his own survival. Also, his essential ignorance and superstitions allowed the audience to believe in the shape-shifting and the Bishop's black arts in that time period.

Pulling the catalyst Imperius into the story gave Phillipe the reasonable explanation for Navarre and Isabeau's dilemma, as well as amped up the tension by dangling the carrot of a solution that the warrior Navarre won't believe because he is so focused on revenge. Phillipe's innate curiosity also allows the audience to hang on Imperius's every word with Phillipe as the story is told. We are as fascinated as Phillipe in the circumstances that created the problem.

Believing what is happening actually motivates Phillipe to become braver, try harder, resolve to help where before he was reluctant. Step-by-step his part in their story strengthens him into becoming a better, more selfless person. The audience experience of his transformation would not have been possible if the story had been told from, say, Navarre's revenge focus or Isabeau's POV of feminine desperation.

Interestingly, the audience is drawn into Phillipe's quest for freedom before exposed to the shape-shifting. That emotional involvement allows us to share Phillipe's doubt of what he is seeing and we can empathize with his trepidation . . . and eventual capitulation to personal involvement in their quest.

Progressive Concepts to Consider:

1) Appropriate Title
2) Types of Suspense utilized
3) Webbing of related elements
4) First 10 minutes prepared audience for the balance of the story
5) Character consistency after Introduction
6) Unique defiance of predictability
7) Opposition intensity increased

* * * * *

HARRY POTTER & the Sorcerer's Stone

By Steve Kloves from novel by J.K. Rowling
2001, starring Daniel Radcliffe, Richard Harris, Maggie Smith

Length: 144 minutes

Log Line: When a bright, tolerant boy turns 11, he is whisked off to a wizardry academy to learn his calling and confront the evil being who killed his parents.

Statement of Purpose: To prove that intelligence and fortitude can create the courage to confront fears and evil.

Intro Image: Owl flying at night

First 10 minutes
Who: Harry Potter, neglected but tolerant 11 year old boy with mischievous sense of humor
When: Contemporary times
Where: English suburb
What: Couple & spoiled son harass and subjugate boy living with them
Why: Harry endures by trying mischief like removing glass between cousin & big snake at zoo

Four related subplots:
Voldemort's manipulations
Gryffindor vs. Slytherin rivalry
Hermione's contrasts
Harry's heritage

Time Line: One school year

Image repeats: Owls, cloaks, stair cases & corridors, brooms & wands, mythic creatures & beings

Act I = Set-up of Ordinary World . . . From England to Hogwarts
10 min **Intro:** From Harry's Muggles to Hogwarts destiny
17 min **Inciting Incident**: Hagrid tells Harry he is a wizard
30 min **PP I**: Threat of Voldemort and the meaning of Harry's scar

Act II = Life 180 degrees . . . Complications of Life at Hogwart's
53 min **Pinch I:** Professor Snape tells Harry fame isn't everything = he must prove himself
70 min **Mid-Point:** Harry & Ron take on the escaped troll for Hermione.
93 min **Pinch II**: Harry sees his parents in the Magic Mirror
107 min **PPII:** Harry is confronted by the dark, cloaked form sucking the blood of the dead unicorn

Act III = Resolution in the "Restricted Areas" of Hogwart's to uncover Voldemort's cohorts & plot
130 min **Climax:** Harry defies devious Quirrell & stands up to the spirit of Voldemort
136 min **Commitment**: In the hospital Dumbledor explains Harry's threat to Voldemort
After-story Conclusion: Gryffindor wins the annual House Cup because of Harry, Ron & Hermione.

Dialogue Notes: Compare & contrast speech diction & syntax (tho all British accents)
Dumbledor's dignity vs. "tone" of the other professors
Quirrell's deliberate stuttering wimpiness
Hermione's superior prissiness
Hagrid's gruffness

Alpha Character posturing differences:
Harry's confidence even in his muggle home and subtle assertiveness blossoming after Quidditch game
Dumbledor's leadership persona vs. Hagrid's lumbering "care-giver"

Supporting cast Unique Character Gems:
McGonagill, "Wise Woman" instructor
Hagrid, lumbering essence of a "protector" who can relate to children
Malfoy, snide, spoiled, self-serving
Snape, sniveling, creepy, suspicious
Quirrell, always expecting the worse behavior
Goblin bankers, small but powerful

Background effects, the nuances of aura:
Harry's isolated closet "bedroom" at Muggles vs. open, cozy dorm at Hogwart's
Medieval grandeur of Hogwart's
Floating candles
"Living" paintings
Giant Chess pieces
The isolation of Hogwarts (in the Scottish Highlands)

Elements from Other Genres: Science Fiction (defiance of scientific principles), Juvenile, Action-Adventure

Question(s): 1. Did this first movie in the series adequately present the varying levels (ages) of Hogwart's students or did it seem to have an over-abundance of entry-level students Harry's age? Or did you see this as merely a matter of Harry's POV? **2.** What did you think of Harry's quick "catch up" to Ron and Hermione's level of wizardry awareness?

Appearance or reference to recurrence of Evil Theme in Min:

Act I = Set-up of Ordinary World . . . From England to Hogwarts

2	Scar on baby's forehead & demeanor of three bringing Harry to the stoop
8	Snake

12 Continuing delivery of letters & increasing number of owls
16-18 = **Inciting Incident:** Hagrid's appearance at the house on the rocky island
20 Everyone in the Marketplace in awe of Harry's name
22 Goblin escorts into the vaults
26 Trying power of the various wands
30 = **Plot Point I:** Hagrid's story of Voldemort & his scar's curse

Act II = Life 180 degrees . . . Complications of Life at Hogwart's
34 Through the wall to get to the Hogwart's train
39 Arrival at Hogwart's via boats at night
42 Entering the dining hall to be "judged" and restrictions stated
47 Harry chanting "Not Slytherin."
53 = **Pinch I** Snape's potion class where professor snarls "Fame isn't everything." (Harry's fear of helplessness)
56 Mention of Vault 713 was broken into, the one Hagrid took something from.
57 Malfoy challenges Harry to broom-riding contest
62 Three-some venture into restricted area & encounter 3-headed dog
70-74 = **Mid-Point:** Halloween treats, announcement troll escaped, Harry & Ron rescue Hermione
75 Harry guesses what dogs guarding (Nimbus 200)
76-84 Quidditch with Harry capturing the gold
85 Hagrid's abode
86 Anticipation of Christmas, but Harry not going "home"
88 Gift exchange where Harry receives "invisibility cloak"
89 Harry into restricted area via cloak
93 = **Pinch II:** Harry sees his parents in the magic mirror
95 Ron at the mirror
96 Dumbledor explains "Desperate desires of the heart"
98 Harry's owl flying (only flies for a reason)
99 Hermione's book reveals "the Sorcerer's Stone"
100 Harry, Ron & Hermione to Hagrid's shack
101 Norbert-the-dragon hatches
102 Malfoy reports their unauthorized venture
104 Three punished with detention in the forrest
106 Follow figure among the trees
107 = **Plot Point II:** Harry sees evil (Voldemort) drinking blood of the dead unicorn

Act III = Resolution in the "Restricted Areas" of Hogwarts to uncover Voldemort's cohorts & plot
108 Centaur comes to their rescue
111 Courtyard discussion, Hagrid, The Sorcerer's Stone

113 Solution of how to get by the 3-headed dog
114 Accusation of them being "up to something"
115-116 Herminone uses her wand, cloak to get by dog & enter cavern with vines
119 Barely escape attack by flying keys
120 Harry mounts his broom to catch THE key
121 They enter the chess room
124-127 They play "Wizard Chess" with pieces exploding, Harry "Checkmates"
128-129 Snape discovers & releases Troll
130-135=Climax: Mirror shows Harry with stone, Quirrell unwraps turban to show Voldemort's face, Voldemort attempts escape & tempts harry to give him the stone, Harry firm tho hands in pain as Voldemort touches the stone
136-138 = **Commitment**: Harry awakens in hospital where Dombledor explains Voldemort's pursuit, Mother sacrificed for love of her son, reunited with Hermione & Ron
139-143 = **Afterstory:** End-of-year banquet, Gryffindor wins House Cup because of threesome's extra deeds, Leaving on train, Hagrid gifts the photo album

CONCEPTS DISCUSSION

You were not told exactly what to look for regarding specific fantasy components in the minute-by-minute analysis of this film. Neither were you reminded to look for elements of the specific fundamentals discussed in Chapter 1. It is assumed you were paying attention to both areas and the progressive list of concepts you are learning. But, now let's look at the just discussed in-depth concepts demonstrated in this film.

PLOT POINT I SIGNIFICANCE

Plot Point I has to be the eventful disruption of the Main Character's Life, the pivotal moment when that character is faced with circumstances that will change his or her life. For Harry it is the discovery of the evil entity Voldemort and the story behind the birthmark on his forehead. Up to that point his escape from his demeaning muggle existence and introduction into the magical world has been one of wonder and amazement. At that point it turns serious. He must choose to engage in the whole experience of Hogwarts to discover his own meaning and why everyone knows him. He is launched on his quest.

With some stories the Hero is literally forced to make the choice of the "New Life." They prefer the known to the unknown or feel incapable. But their life is still whirled 180 degrees because of this one decision to "engage" in the adventure.

DEFYING PREDICTABILITY

The British author J. K. Rowling had access to many legends which she then elaborated on, using a mix of everyday details from villages, cozy cottages and parlors to dorm-style living and educational systems. She utilized exaggeration that the set designers, costumers and special effects people could elaborate on to create the curiosities and minute details of Hogwarts. The unpredictable was based on the familiar thus it was easier for the audience to "live vicariously" in the story and accept when the unpredictable appeared.

Make a list of every item in this film already present in mythology and legend in one column then beside each item note how it was changed in Harry's world. Here is the essence of Fantasy. The audience has to be absorbed in "How is this going to be different?" rather than saying in disgust "How stupid is that?" Consider the classic THE PRINCESS BRIDE that was rife with exaggeration based on the familiar. Yes, some of it was blatant comedy's juxtaposition, but we became involved in the characters and their world. Disbelief was suspended. That too, was the fantasy power of the entire Harry Potter series. We looked for the familiar and how it became more in the stories.

INTENSIFYING OPPOSTION

The essence of creating characters who grow is to perpetually throw them up against one opposition after another, each obstacle more threatening than the last. To avoid melodrama that opposition has to be logical to the story circumstance.

If you walk through this film with Harry you see him confronting the obstacles of the unique circumstance in his uncle & aunt's home, with his cousin, then challenged by the discomfiting idea that others recognize his name and by the challenge to make choices he doesn't understand because he has no frame of reference. Like any student starting in a new school, he faces positioning himself among his fellow students, identifying relationships good and bad, and fitting in with his new teachers (the people who control his environment) . . . and so on. Each scene, each situation becomes more important than the last. The suspense and tension grows. By the time you reach the end of Act II, Harry is knowledgeable and responsible for his choices and the consequences of his actions are life-and-death important.

This should impress upon you the importance of cranking up the power of each challenge, each obstacle, each antagonist as your story progresses to make your audience "worry" about the outcome. The more worried they are about unpredictable outcomes, the greater the intensity your story innately projects.

Progressive Concepts to Consider:

1) Appropriate Title
2) Types of Suspense utilized
3) Webbing of related elements
4) First 10 minutes prepared audience for the balance of the story
5) Character consistency after Introduction
6) Unique defiance of predictability
7) Opposition intensity increased

You now have been exposed to seven of 24 or about one-fourth of the storytelling concepts that make up a cinematic story. Learn these and identify them regularly to become a skilled and knowledgeable craftsman.

* * * * *

GENRE FILM Chapter 5 Exercises

Exercise 5a. Write Pg 11-15, leading up to your Inciting Incident.

Exercise 5b. Identify your "Messenger" who will motivate your Protag to think. Now, examine each scene so far for the presence of Opposition, minor and major.

Exercise 5c. Write Pg 16-20 through your Inciting Incident.

Exercise 5d. How did you Protag respond to the Challenge the Messenger presented? Who was the POV character in the Inciting Incident scene?

Exercise 5e. What was the logical consequence in the scene following the Inciting Incident? Did you introduce or refer to the Major antagonist or threat that will build throughout the story? Or did you throw the character into a subplot agenda that will complicate his/her "Ordinary World" at this point?

CHAPTER 6

Concepts of Character Profiling, Back-story on Dialogue/Comedy Genre

Rarely will you encounter a "seat-of-the-pants" screenwriter simply because they understand how carefully structured a film needs to be, and that requires meticulous planning. The film's foundation is the screenplay as its blue print. A sloppy blue print will not motivate and guide all those artists who will turn the outline into a real film. So, screenwriters have to be the epitome of planners.

Chapter 1 reviewed the fundamentals of both story and character. In this chapter we are going to more carefully examine how you work-up a Character Profile then build on it to discover the vital elements you are going to utilize in your story. We will also discuss how you utilize back-story for character and complications and what a driving force that Profile is in creating unique dialogue.

A WRITER'S CHARACTER PROFILE IS NOT AN ACTOR'S

Your job as a writer is to give birth to the character then to allow the character to mature and evolve with all the nuances of life lessons already learned. An actor's job is to crawl into the skin of the character and interpret those lessons in order to breathe life into the cinematic being. The writer and the actor share the empathy for the character, but the actor's experience is much deeper than the writer's. The writer is concerned with the total presentation, whereas the actor works at a visceral level. After all, the actor has to sublimate self and become the character. The writer "merely" has to orchestrate the movement and speeches of the character.

Truly good actors do not just "read" a role. They spend time developing an understanding for what drives every movement, every spoken word, every habit, every prejudice before stepping on a set. Example: Dustin Hoffman spent a lot of time at an institution for autistic adults before actually studying the script for RAIN MAN. You did not see Dustin Hoffman in the autistic savant Raymond Babbitt. You merely saw Raymond. John Wayne won an Oscar for his role as Rooster Cogburn in the original TRUE GRIT. Whether a war movie or a western, John Wayne was John Wayne (demeanor, swagger, dialect) . . . until Rooster Cogburn. Think of Johnny Depp's many characterizations vs. Tom Cruise, Tom Hanks vs. Harrison Ford, Daniel Day-Lewis vs. Jim Carrey. The point is an actor's job is to abandon self and portray the character, not to a stereotype but to become that unique human being in that particular circumstance. The characters lived for the writer in the original script, but the actor gives them visible life.

REFLECTING THE PROFILE

When you complete the General information on a Profile, you are establishing an identity much like authorities do in the Witness Protection program. You are creating fundamental memories for that character of birth, childhood, family, education, work experiences. Moving into the Personal information you are grounding the evolving human in relationships and preferences, giving credence to habits and expectations. Ultimately, you are rounding out a human being who will have the potential to grab hold of story events and make things happen because of both General and Personal background.

You-the-Writer must believe both General identifying information and the Personal data to understand what motivates your character, what triggers emotions and actions as you move him or her through the story. You have to respect the vital need for the Profile before you start writing. You must understand where your character is in life before you start the story that will change the character because of the experiences about to happen to him or her.

Your profile will provide all the information you need to identify exactly where to annoy, where to stress, where to anger, where to hurt that character.

AUDIENCE EXPECTATIONS

There is a generality in creative writing that characters need to be 65% universal so the audience can identify and empathize with their experiences . . . and only 35% unique so they can soar with them in their adventures. Just because you can predict from a Profile how a character will react, doesn't mean the audience will. They are not privy to all you know. Yes, you want them guessing the option choices the character is considering, but you know where you are headed and the audience doesn't. Your job is to keep them caring about the consequences and hoping the character will make the "right" choices or not suffer unduly if wrong. You are the puppeteer who cuts the puppet's string and lets the character flounder and fail or struggle and succeed . . .

according to where you are headed in the story. Just take the audience along for a memorable ride!

LIFE STAGES

Just about every decade in life has its own "stage" of development and tasks, just as psychologists and sociologists have identified relationship, marriage, career, educational, body image "stages." If you have never thought about these concepts or taken a course that addressed them, I strongly suggest you invest in one book that brings it all into focus very succinctly for the working writer: *The Writer's Guide to Character Traits* by Linda N. Edelstein, PhD. She is a practicing clinical psychologist who truly gives some eye-opening information that you can utilize immediately in giving depth to your characters, no matter their age or "Life Stage." Edelstein identifies 21 personalities. I strong recommend her insights into both personality and life stages. You will find concise concepts and many spring boards for creating unique life circumstances.

You can also explore the Internet for "Life Stages" and "Human Growth and Development." The vast array of charts and concepts can help you advance your skills as an amateur psychologist. The point is not to qualify you to go on the lecture circuit talking about these charts and statistics.

The idea is for you to discover where your character is at in his or her life and depict that person moving forward in a dramatic "take control" fashion. Your job is not to explain, but to demonstrate through visual action and succinct "in your face" dialogue. The better you understand your character's history and expectations wherever he or she is in life, the better you will be able to challenge and nudge their reactions. Understanding puts you in control . . . of every single character be they leads, supporting or extras.

HISTORY'S INFLUENCE ON DIALOGUE

The study of dialogue is worthy of its own intense course. In Chapter 1 you were given eleven points to ponder when writing dialogue. The one point pulled from the Character Profile is #10, diction and syntax. The sound and cadence of a character is ingrained from early childhood when that person was first learning sounds equal meaning. Consider English-speaking actors who "sound" like their native Ireland, London, Australia when being interviewed as themselves, yet can assume a credible Southern drawl, Boston "twang" or Midwestern smoothness in a character role.

A common criticism of Kevin Costner in ROBIN HOOD, PRINCE OF THIEVES was that he didn't sound like the native Brit Robin Locksley was supposed to be. He sounded . . . American, whereas Morgan Freeman's Moor sounded like a Moor. Another friend and fellow writer criticized the lack of a "true Irish" accent by Val Kilmer playing John Patterson in THE GHOST & THE DARKNESS. That friend had no exposure to the more highly educated Irish. She did not know that the thick brogue most think of as Irish is comparable to street slang. Kilmer had a dialect coach and sounded like the regimental colonel and college-educated civil engineer he was portraying.

Of course, your job as a writer is not to write dialect in dialogue. You merely state character origins and influence in the narrative's succinct characterizing sentences. The one thing you can do in dialogue is insert here and there an idiom appropriate to the Scot, German, South African, Ozarks, Hispanic or whatever. Let the Actor and the Dialect Coach handle it from there. Of course, when you have unique sentence structure such as Yoda's, you will be consistent with that character's speeches.

Diction and syntax can also be influenced by education and training. Consider how hard the U.S. military and intelligence people work to attain a natural flow to the foreign languages they learn, especially those who will be covert operatives. Watch the movie GOOD WILL HUNTING and pay attention to how and when Will loses the frequent use of the "f-word" in the university atmosphere . . . but reclaims it when back around his friends and when under stress with the doctor's psychological pushing.

Note on cursing/obscenities: Not only is cursing a mental habit, it also indicates two things, 1) lack of a vocabulary thus a form of mental laziness out of ignorance and 2) as an emotional release valve. Beware overuse no matter how often your young people or military types would "normally" use it. In those instances, a sprinkling is enough to make your point and give authenticity. Too much and it becomes ineffectual and vulgar over-emphasis to the audience.

And don't forget the influence of personality types and gender. A generality is that unless con artist, lawyer or salesman, most men are relatively brief communicators. For women the generality is they like to have the last word or emphasis on their point. Yet, personality types also influence speech patterns. The Stoic vs. the Extrovert, the self-deprecating Whiner vs. the sunshiny Pollyanna, the fearful and withdrawn Abused vs. the mouthy Braggart.

Bottom line: Not only do you want to keep your dialogue short-short-short, but you also want to develop an ear for how well it portrays who your character is and how he or she communicates in this particular scene.

BACKSTORY'S INFLUENCE ON PLOT

In the beginning of your story, characters and your social order are coming from somewhere with a long chain of preceding experiences. When your audience suspends their disbelief, they also give up "the need to know" all that happened before. Their focus and yours is on the now of the story they are going to live over the next two hours. Everything that happened before essentially means nothing . . . until it becomes relevant to the now of the story. When the character needs or refers to something in the past is when the audience will want to know what happened.

Many storytellers (like Garrison Keillor, the laconic, mellow-voiced Lake Woebegone creator) utilize the style of set-up and aura to talk around the sweeping circle to get to the point of the story. Screenwriters do not have that luxury. If said writer was a novelist first, that "build" is a hard habit to break. But, consider the high cost of being long-winded in a screenplay. How many movies are longer than two hours? More importantly why do they run longer than two hours? Is it usually because of lots of dialogue or essential action? Repeat this mantra: A movie is more a short story than a novel. A movie is more a short story than a novel.

All that background and insider information movie-goers want after seeing the film can be found on the DVD or the documentaries of "The making of. . . ." The DVD's extras also provide the scenes that were cut to create the shortest film possible to allow for theaters to show it so many times on the same screen in one day. A shorter film means more revenue potential. That's nothing to sneeze at. Watch those "Extras Scenes" on the DVD. They will educate you in the how's and why's of film editing, as well as imprint on you what exposition was not needed to tell the story.

Foe example, note the scenes cut from Ron Howard's A BEAUTIFUL MIND and the entire subplot cut from Ridley Scott's KINGDOM OF HEAVEN. Sometimes you will find answers to transient questions you may have had when you first saw the film . . . yet you will realize that the essence of the story was intact as shown in the "Release Version" vs. the "Director's Cut." The extras merely enhance your awareness and enjoyment after the fact.

BEWARE FLASHBACKS

At the opening the spec script for PAYING THE PIPER, a bagpiper is seen putting on his uniform regalia with brief (only paragraph-long) flashback glimpses of the death of his police officer wife. One flashback is of the man in his dark suit holding the hands of his two small children beside a piper playing at the funeral. You subsequently find out that the gig he plays that day is his first in the six months since his wife's funeral. Her passing, his mourning and the piping for that particular event are pivotal to the balance of the story. They are all back story exposition yet relevant to the piper's experience at the very opening. They are visuals establishing his state of mind and motivation.

Lengthy flashbacks in film are as digressive as full-scene flashbacks are in novels. They have to be confined to glimpses of the past relevant to the present. They should be a transient, rarely used tool only. That brief reference to a past event that sheds light on the present should be enough. Screenplays do not have time for a list of long-winded explanations or elaborate depictions of the past. Too much information, too much delving into the past drags the pacing of the present time of the story. It becomes like a repeat "Breaking News" interruption to your favorite TV show. Audience is interested in the "now."

COMEDY GENRE

Humor cannot be an isolated moment of levity in either a book or a film. To truly be successful it has to permeate the entire work.

Example: Playwrights are rarely invited to rehearsals. A neophyte received an invitation to the rehearsal of her serious one-act drama. The playwright sat immersed in the actors putting "life" into the words. They got to one humorous line given to one character the playwright had intended for the character to lighten an awkward moment. The actress delivered the line then froze with actors and director turning to look at the playwright. The director asked "That is the only funny line in the whole play and it jars the dramatic tone. Is that what you really want?" Of course, the playwright changed it.

If you are asking why they had to point it out and ask the playwright's intent, it is because a rule of live theater is no one changes lines except the playwright. Not so in screenplays. Cinematic dialogue can even get changed by the actor as the scene is being shot, but plays are sacrosanct. Always? Get real. Theaters out in the boondocks will alter whatever to fit their venue and their audience.

The point of the above story is obviously that rare bits of humor dropped into serious situations or by normally serious characters shatter the window of illusion. The writer may think the moment of levity is needed but the ultimate reader/audience will disagree. One moment of levity disrupts the unity of the whole in a dramatic story. If you want to use it, give the line to a character who is consistently a smart-mouth klutz needing rescue. Create the expectation for light moments amidst the dark.

A resource I can suggest for those who want more is *What are You Laughing At?* by Brad Schreiber. He speaks to the writer who is not a naturally humorous person, the kind of writer who has to think hard, plan harder. These are commonly the people who can make dead-serious comments in e-mails that are interpreted as sarcastic hyperbole (exaggeration), but whose intentional puns are groaners. Some writers accidentally fall into making a humorous comment. They envy their peers and people like Robin Williams who are Natural comedians or punsters. These are the people who need to study this genre a lot and carefully plot and meticulously craft humor.

WHAT IS HUMOR?

Essentially, humor is a three part structure of **setup-expectation-reversal.** The longer the set-up the tighter the rubber band of tension at expectation and the faster the bounce of reversal will assail the reader/audience.

Look at the panels throughout one page of the comics in the newspaper to reinforce these concepts. Carefully assess each for Panel One = Set-up, Panel Two = Expectation, Panel Three = Reversal. If it is one long panel, remember your eyes move left to right and you will discover the same pattern.

Now, examine a paragraph or an entire humorous scene from a particularly funny book you really enjoyed or film that seemed to have laugh after laugh. Mel Brooks or Monty Python films are good studies. Look for the unfolding of that structure.

But there are two more very important elements overlooked by that neophyte playwright: Timing and Relevance.

Timing is something comedians, especially stand-up comedians work very hard at. It is the build and the illusion created in the set-up, the spinoff of the expectation and the bah-bump-bum delivery of the reversal. Go too long and the reader/audience won't care. Too illogical or abrupt and they won't get it.

Relevance means 1) placement in the structure of the whole, 2) the meaning to the whole AND 3) the characters playing to the audience. In the 1998 film PATCH ADAMS, Robin Williams played a true life young physician who based his medical practice on lightening the serious with humor and successfully founded a hospital to that end. Laughter releases pain-relieving, mood-elevating endorphins that Patch Adams scientifically documented improved the tolerance of painful procedures and the longevity of cancer patients of all ages. The delivery of the mood-elevating humor was all in the timing at the relevant point the patient (or family) would be ready to acknowledge the perspective and laugh.

Ever heard the phrase "That's about as funny as a screen door on a submarine." That's the commentary when the reader/audience did not "get it" because it was inappropriate humor or the audience lacked the experience to relate to and create expectation. Hospital, police and military humor is frequently not appreciated by "civilians."

For the comedy writer, the meaning to the whole is how consistently the humor is woven into the entire story with this character or this circumstance. And, finally, the audience has to believe and laugh with this character, not the demeaning laughter at this character.

THE AUDIENCE HAS TO BELIEVE AND LAUGH WITH THIS CHARACTER, NOT THE DEMEANING LAUGHTER AT THIS CHARACTER.

FUNDAMENTAL CONCEPTS OF COMEDY/HUMOR

1. Fumbling through ordinary life/circumstance gone awry in a domino effect.

- Who hasn't had one of those days, weeks or months when nothing works for you and the complications keep piling up as a result? Maintaining a sense of humor is key to survival of the frustrations. And how close can laughter be to tears? Which is the better emotional release at this point in your story?

2. Never rely on simplistic "vaudeville" slapstick silliness.
- Contrived, obviously orchestrated events will fall flat. Silliness can create reader/audience smiles, but rarely will belly-laughs result. Think of an accidental squeeze of a chocolate syrup bottle that results in a smearing, squirting food fight . . . that leads to a sensual love scene. And bonking someone on the head can create a very real concussion of the brain rattling in the enclosed skull with swelling and severe pain resulting. Now, tweaking someone's nose on the other hand . . .

3. Play real people in uncontrollable, exaggerated circumstances
- But here you have to pay close attention to your timing and the length of your humorous build. The best impact is quick in, quick out to get the laugh. And focus on laughing with, not at the characters. If the characters don't get it and only the audience laughs, half the impact is lost.

4. Pay closest attention to your twist or reversal because that should have some kind of consequence.
- Stand up comedians frequently "relate" their spousal or family humor to one or more people in the audience because that person will be thought-associating consequences. In a story/novel/film if the comment or event does not have consequences, then it should be deleted.

5. It is acceptable to stretch Cause-Effect almost to the irrational limit but do it quickly!
- In trying to create humor in a situation you play the "What if . . ." Game to its wildest extreme then consider the rational or logical. Whatever comes up as the **opposite** of what the character/audience expected will most likely be humorous. Get to that point quickly so your character/audience arrives there not expecting that effect! Too much time establishing expectation and the intelligent character (and audience) will anticipate the possibility of the reversal, thus your humor falls flat.

6. For humor to have depth there must also be an element of pathos.
- That concept goes back to the Greek plays and still rings true today. The ridiculousness of MRS. DOUBTFIRE played off the reality of a man legally separated from his precious children and willing to try anything to maintain that connection. Examine your favorite humor and identify the underlying serious situation the humor lightens. Pathos will force you to avoid slapstick.

COMEDY/ HUMOR CHARACTER REQUIREMENTS

Of course your character has to be **capable of recognizing and appreciating humor.** The best comedic character is one who is **well-meaning but unfocused/preoccupied.**

COMEDY/HUMOR PLOT TYPES

1. Family changes
2. Business
3. Government/Military life
4. Environmental contrasts
5. Relationships of any sort
6. Coming-of-Age bumbling and trials
7. Life stage gone awry
8. Routine gone awry
9. Animal antics

Let's tack on a couple more concepts that work in film and fiction as well: romantic comedy and AIRPLANE creator David Zucker's discussion of comedic points you need to carefully consider when doing exaggerated humor.

HOLLYWOOD'S FAVORITE: THE ROMANTIC COMEDY

There can be humor sprinkled throughout a drama, but in the end it is focused on tension and jeopardy to life and limb. Comedy, on the other hand, relies solely on 1) set-up, 2) expectation, and 3) reversal. The chain of events makes you smile and feel light-hearted. The circumstances can be serious, but the events flow with the anticipation of warm fuzzies, non-life-threatening confrontations and upbeat resolutions.

Billy Mernit's *Writing a Romantic Comedy* is an in-depth look at that type of cinematic story. His approach to the Romantic Comedy in the "The 7 Beats for Romantic Comedy" aligns perfectly with the Plot Paradigm (and Romance's Relationship Plane, Appendix N). Here is my interpretation/explanation of his approach:

The 7 Beats for Romantic Comedy by Billy Mernit

(Note: This concept builds around the Three-Act structure, simply shifting the main points to fit a romantic comedy and Mernit's terminology/semantics.)

1. Set-up (the chemical equation)
2. Catalyst (the cute meet)

3. First Turning Point (a sexy complication)
4. Mid-Point (the hook)
5. Second Turning Point (the swivel)
6. Climax (the relationships' dark moment)
7. Resolution (joyful defeat)

1. Set-up's chemical equation: Scene sequence of events identifying both the exterior Identity and interior Essence conflicts. After the opening scene it tells the audience about the lead character and what is lacking in that character's life.

2. Catalyst's cute meet: Event that brings the man-and-woman together and into conflict, irrevocably changing both their lives. A "good" romantic comedy makes the meeting genially meaningful. It resonates and sets the hook in the audience's imagination.

3. Turning Point's sexy complication: The ending of Act One event that has male and female "thinking" of the other, thus the balance of the story is their new life together. This event is a startling development that defines the character goal, making the internal conflict of the two people drive their external actions. Think of this Plot Point II as a kind of explosion forcing awareness and changing the two people.

4. Mid-Point's hook: An intense heightening of sexual tension and emotional involvement, implicating the relationship's outcome and creating higher stakes awareness of what is to be lost or gained. Blatant depiction of story theme.

5. Second Turning Point's swivel: At the end of Act II, this is the event that jeopardizes the protagonist's chance to succeed at his/her goal and is the main character's "point of no return" in the internal conflict, the character arc. The only option is for the character to take action to either a) choose love over his/her original goal or b) sacrifice love to get the goal. There's the dilemma, but, of course, since this is a romance, the choice will be to choose love).

6. Climax's dark moment: The consequences of the "swivel" decision create an intense confrontation where private motivations are revealed and relationship as well as worthy goals are on the verge of being lost.

7. Resolution's joyful defeat: The Relationship wins with the reconciliation and re-affirmation of the primal importance of the two-as-one, sometimes with the personal sacrifice of the main character's external goal.

Walk this 7-Beat Structure through any of your favorite romantic comedies. By about the fifth film you will begin "seeing" the concepts without list in hand. Your mind will look for them.

David Zucker claimed in his 20 years of writing, producing, and directing comedy he "never read a book about it." Times have changed and there are a lot out there now. Regardless, Zucker's list of what not to do has some very good points you should think about:

15 Simple Rules of What NOT to Do:

1. Joke-on-joke: stacking two jokes at one time.
2. Unrelated humorous background: what's going on behind the action. See #1.
3. Acknowledgement: characters "explaining" to someone what's going on with the joke.
4. "Breaking the frame" : author intrusion to make sure the reader/audience "gets it."
5. That didn't happen: a glimpse of something illogical that was suppose to be funny.
6. Can You Live With it?: Will your consequences not be logical or funny?
7. Ax Grinding: repetitive jokes making the same point
8. Self-conscious: on-the-nose dialogue that is blatant reminder of whatever
9. Trivia: clichéd humor that only the perpetrator "gets" thus falls flat
10. Straw dummy: contrivance you create to "stage" the humorous event/ dialogue
11. Play off known Comedian or staging a joke or event to mimic well-known style
12. Technical Pizazz: mindless action orchestrated without immediate comedic pay-off
13. Piling It On: re-using overused current affairs jokes known to general public
14. Hanging On: playing out the reversal for too long.
15. There Are No Rules: ignoring what makes you laugh.

COMEDY FILM ANALYSIS

Your goal in analysis of each and every film is to look for the genre elements just discussed, as well as to get in the habit of automatically assessing key points of characterization, story structure, and cinematic techniques. At the conclusion of each is a discussion of the concepts just explained that the film utilized.

Also pay attention to the lengthening list of previous film concepts you should be watching for. A useful habit is to watch a film looking for specific concepts then watch it again looking for others. Unless you have a photographic memory, repetition will be your best instructor.

* * * * *

MRS. DOUBTFIRE

By Randi Mayem Singer and Leslie Dixon
1993, Starring Robin Williams, Sally Field, Pierce Brosnan

Length: 120 minutes

Log Line: When he loses custody of his beloved three children, a resourceful actor returns to their lives as a witty British granny.

Statement of Purpose: To prove the power of parental love can transform personal values and self concept to preserve relationships.

Intro Image: Cartoon "Voice Over" (demo separation of make-believe and reality)

First 10 minutes
Who:
Daniel Hillard, an impulsive, irresponsible father of three
Miranda Hillard, interior designer, over-worked, stressed-out mother
Lydia, lovely, studious 13-yr old daughter
Chris, athletic, fun-oriented 12-yr-old son
Natty, bright, cute 5-yr-old daughter
When: contemporary times
Where: San Francisco, California
What: He goes to the extreme to entertain his children by hosting a wild, messy party that infuriates his wife.
Why: Unsuccessful as an adult, he wallows in childish joys that push his grounded wife to demanding a divorce

Three related subplots:
Daniel & Miranda
Miranda & Stuart
Daniel & court-ordered employment

Time Line: Approximate four – six months, Summer into Fall

Image repeats:
Characterizing by voice
Contrasting energetic granny movement with male athleticism
TV
Food
Financial Success = Control, Labor = Resourceful
Time Management = Responsibility

Act I = Set-up of Ordinary World: Daniel's loss of place in his children's lives
10 min **Intro:** Establish Daniel's childish irresponsibility, driving Miranda to demand divorce
18 min **Inciting Incident**: "I will do anything to be with my kids."
26 min **PP I:** Miranda refuses Daniel's after-school care & advertises for a nanny

Act II = Life 180 degrees: Mrs. Doubtfire's impact on family & Daniel's life
40 min **Pinch I:** Miranda confesses to Mrs. DF how difficult life was with Daniel
50 min **Mid-Point:** Mrs. DF firmly takes control of defiant children & thanked
67 min **Pinch II**: When Daniel's disguise exposed to Lydia & Chris, they support him
87 min **PPII:** Daniel confronted with conflict of Lundy meeting as himself & Miranda's birthday party with family as Mrs. DF at the same restaurant

Act III = Resolution: Exposure to both Lundy & Miranda with consequences
102 min **Climax:** Restaurant confrontation & court consequences
116 min **Commitment**: Miranda allows Daniel after-school supervision
After-story: Mrs. DF show commentary on the many different kinds of families that love one another.

Dialogue Notes:
Daniel's acting ability to change his voice per personality
Distinct tonal differences between parent-child & adult communication
Uncle Frank & Aunt Jack
Differences as children change from whiney to worried to observant

Alpha Character posturing differences:
Irresponsible Daniel vs. subservient Daniel vs. confident Daniel
Miranda vs. Mrs. Doubtfire
Daniel vs. Stuart (consider each reflecting a concept of manliness and self-concept)
Daniel vs. Lundy (consider the life role and life stage of the two men)

Supporting cast Unique Character Gems:
Lydia, Chris & Natty, children representative of their age
Stuart, suave, focused, arrogant
Uncle Frank & Aunt Jack, free-spirited, caring & accomplished
Lundy, aging business man who wants to be proud of his accomplishments
Mrs. Sellnan (Social Worker), focused, detail-oriented, by-the-book
Bus Driver, responsible, safe yet on-the-prowl
Mr. Sprinkles, aging, clueless

Background effects, the nuances of aura:
Hillard cozy home (safe environment)
TV station/studio
Daniel's cramped apartment
Country club pool
Crowded up-scale restaurant
Austere Courtroom

Elements from Other Genres: Juvenile, Romance (where it goes wrong)

Question: Was Stuart's role as attentive male credible or a touch forced/stilted as a "foil" to Mrs. Doubtfire? Either way, do you believe it was dictated by the script, director or actor?

Appearance or reference to recurrence of Evil Theme in Min: Society's Sense of Responsibility through Miranda's role in **BOLD.** Daniel's mistakes contribute to his own cascade of other problems.

Act I = Set-up of Ordinary World: Daniel's loss of place in his children's lives

2	Daniel fired over argument with director so picks up kids for at-home birthday party
5	Miranda at work, intro Stuart interest, "Emergency" at home
6-8	Miranda arrives to chaos of petting zoo & police ticket, music & rapping
9-10	Miranda & Daniel argument over who's responsible, 14 years & it's over. I want a divorce
11-12	Daniel at Frank's who talks with mother about marriage on hiatus, stay with make-up artists
13-14	Court: joint custody but Daniel live separately, Daniel leaves
15-16	Daniel talking to kids about not their fault
17	Meeting with Mrs. Sellnan, Crt Liasion about home & job
18 = **Inciting Incident:**	When confronted with unbending expectations, "I'll do anything to be with"
19	Wise-cracks at studio job, "Lots of luck smart ass."
20-22	Miranda meets Stu, long time, go over drawings (nervous)
23-25	Kids dinner at messy apartment, miss you, sarcasm about Miranda, MY time
26 = Plot Point I:	Turns down Daniel care after school, placing ad for nanny

Act II = Life 180 degrees: Mrs. Doubtfire's impact on family & Daniel's life

27-30	No choice, Daniel changes phone number, calls with diff. voices then as Mrs. Doubtfire
30-34	"Make me a woman" so Frank & Jack do make-up, nails, wigs, mold mask, dress, cheer

35-37 Euthagenina Doubtfire arrives to meet, charms Natty with Stuart Little, Chriss strapping lad who likes soccer but studies before athletics, lovely Lydia not argue in front of children

38-39 Lovely home, tea in kitchen, wonderful resume

40 = Pinch I: Daniel hears how difficult it REALLY has been for Miranda

41 Hired, must ride bus & oogled by driver

42 At appt encounters Mrs. Sellnan making at-home visit, ID's as his older sister

44-48 Alternating between Daniel & Mrs. DF, seen by neighbor boys, mask into street & destroyed

49 Picks up ne mask from Frank "Why wasn't I born an only child?", TV job, change to DF

50-57 = **Midpoint Epiphany:** Kids watching TV, controller into fish tank, labor at chores or homework, on fire making dinner, picks up and table set as Miranda arrives to spotless house & quiet, "I miss Dad." Lydia thanks DF "Long time since Mom's smiled."

58 Bus driver REALLY hits on DF this bus ride

59-61 Soccer with Chris, biking with kids, dance with broom, prepping dinners (lobster per Julia Child) reading to Natty, defeats purse snatcher

62-64 Stu intro to children, Miranda shares feelings with Mrs. DF who warns & suggests celibacy

65-67 Studying with Lydia, bathroom break, seen by Chris, exposed

68 = **Pinch II** Lydia & Chris accept & support his disguise

69-70 Watches old man taping bad dinosaur kids' show & criticize to Lundy, OK

71-75 Miranda converses with Mrs. DF about bad marriage to Daniel & crying self to sleep

76-80 Trolley to Stu's country club to swim, drinks as watches, jealousy, "run-by fruiting."

81-82 Daniel acting out dinosaur rap, Lundy invites to dinner to discuss proposal

83 Kids at Daniel's neat apartment for dinner, Daniel offers again but can't fire Mrs. DF

85-86 Miranda picking dress for birthday dinner date, mrs. DF caution again, You join us

87 = Plot Point II: Daniel can't get another appt with Lundy so trapped in alternate personas

Act III = Resolution: Exposure to both Lundy & Miranda with consequences

88-92 Arrives at restaurant, sees restless Lundy, wants smoking area across room, phone call about being late, to Bathroom to change, Stu gives expensive bracelet, Dan lots Scotch to catch up with Lundy & drunk

97 As Mrs. DF, drops dentures in wine glass, back to Lundy who notes perfume, order, then powders red pepper (allergic) on Stu's plate in kitchen

101 Accidentally back to Lundy as Mrs. DF so intros new children's show host

102-104 = Climax A: Stu gasps on spiced shrimp then inhales & chokes, Mrs. DF to the rescue but vigorous action dislodges mask & Daniel is exposed to startled Natty & enraged Miranda.

105-108 = Climax B (Consequences): In courtroom Daniel loses all rights for one year with only supervised visitations. He speaks on being addicted to children which moves Miranda.

109 Interviewing nannies going badly.

110-115 Miranda hears Mrs. DF voice on TV show, goes to studio, talks with Daniel about children being happier.

116-17 = **Commitment:** Daniel arrives to pick up children after school

After-story: Mrs. Doubtfire speaking on her show about all kinds of families but if there is love binding the members together, they will be all right.

CONCEPTS DISCUSSION

Maintain your analytical mindset and consistently look for the story and character principles of Chapter 1, as well as the Progressive Points learned previously. As those become habit then pay attention to the genre expectations of techniques, character and plots. Let's look at the just discussed concepts demonstrated in this film.

REFLECTING THE PROFILE

Obviously, the Character Profile of Daniel Hillard would have reflected his acting ability and devotion to "having fun in life." That **talent** was essential to his "lot in life," his chosen profession of being an actor who could switch voices on cue. The audience also sees his lack of self-discipline and self-control at the beginning of the film that gradually changes. In the beginning, he charms those who join in his escapades and simple interests, but creates chaos for the more responsible adults (right down to his own mother and gay brother) and even creates questions and caution in his own maturing children. His fundamental role of "Father" in life is also his greatest challenge.

Out of that part of his Profile the storyteller can identify and use both the **tools** of his trade (his voice, quick wit and sarcasm) and the bungling of his **opportunities** (the voice-over work and inability to keep his mouth shut to more serious supervisors). His talent lacks the discipline to guide it to fulfillment with the tools and opportunities he encounters. So, his Profile provides the storyteller the means to create a cascade of consequences he must deal with.

The audience doesn't need an in-depth view of his home life as a child when we see his gay brother and hear his mother sympathizing over the phone. The innuendo is that the siblings were encouraged to "be themselves" with little structure, but the **family resources** are at least dependable. Daniel's older brother appears to have more stability and security in his creative and home life than Daniel, thus Daniel can rely on him "in a pinch." He is a sympathetic ear, yet you still get the implication that even he expects Daniel to "settle down." He is ecstatic when Daniel seriously carries through with the Mrs. Doubtfire role.

The one consistent factor in Daniel's life is his devotion to his children, from the beginning of the story to the end. They provide his **motivation** to attempt the outrageous, as well as his **goal** to be a positive factor in their lives. His action and his dialogue repeatedly turned back to those issues like the compass needle seeking true north, whether he was in his Daniel persona or as Mrs. Doubtfire.

The melding of the Profile into the cause of the plot is essential to good storytelling.

LIFE STAGES

We will not walk through children's "Growth & Development Guidelines" (Appendix F) until Chapter 7's discussion of Juvenile film needs, but be aware that the writers of this script paid close attention to the maturation needs of the 12-yr-old son and the 14-yr-old daughter, as well as the innocence and expectations of the 5-yr-old daughter in orchestrating the events in the Hillard home. The characters were consistent and credible. There were no attempts to make any of them "more mature than their years" or more insightful. Particularly telling was the scene when Daniel is "discovered" by Chris so that young man remains cautious and his dad respects that.

The maturation stage of the couple places them in their late 30's, smack-dab in the midst of focus on career and creation of family routines and memories. They are at the height of life's responsibilities, obligations, pressures. They have been married for 14 years so the "new" has worn off, the children have their school schedules and activities and any deviations cause stress. Without supreme effort on the part of both adults to divide the burdens and work to alleviate the major stresses, misunderstandings and resentments are inevitable. So the circumstances that caused the initial problems are easily identifiable to the audience. The whole point of the conflict wasn't about caring but about realistically managing responsibilities. Since the partners were not on the same page in awareness and priorities, the rift was reasonable.

Taking the adults to deeper level, let's look at their self-concepts. Neither Daniel or Miranda are at "optimal" places in their lives. Yes, Miranda has a secure, well-respected position as an interior designer, but her self-concept is not being reinforced in her personal life. She is at a late child-bearing age and beginning to feel the dissatisfaction of insecurity about her self-image as a woman. She demonstrates her insecurity when told of Stu's interest and even when trying to decide what dress to wear to the restaurant. Her eventual recognition of Daniel's capabilities result in her accepting a reasonable solution of the family problems.

Due to the "busy-ness" of life, Daniel had not been yanked down from his "teen playboy" mindset though he periodically tried to argue his "adult" point-of view. He is perpetually put in the position of supplicant rather than decision-maker. It isn't until he faces devastating loss that he decides to change. He does not truly "wake up" to his own ineptitude until Miranda shares how much she cried, how overburdened her husband made her feel. Faced with loss of that which he lives for (his children), he uses the resources he has and begins to mature and evolve into a responsible adult. He does not change his essential ability to have fun, only how he controls his behavior and manages his responsibilities.

HISTORY'S INFLUENCE ON DIALOGUE

Obviously, the late Robin Williams' brilliant vocals contributed to this story, but it provided an interesting undertone of conflict to have his Doubtfire persona as a "muddled" British accent and Stu's sophisticated execution and awareness as a foil. Daniel's consistency of attitude in Mrs. Doubtfire's diction and syntax contributed to the credibility of his dual role. That also enhanced the poignancy of his confidences shared with Miranda. The humor and contrast were ramped up when he had to bounce back and forth with the social worker's visit then when his speech slipped at the pool with the attractive girl and as he became increasingly intoxicated at the restaurant.

The children's dialogue also had an evolution to it as they grew from whining about their lots in life to accepting the circumstance, even capable of bantering. Children are resilient. On the whole they tend to sublimate anxieties and live in the moment.

The dialogue of "male bonding" was particularly interesting. Compare and contrast Daniel with his director at the beginning to his interactions with his impatient supervisor at the studio to his ultimate exchanges with Lundy. As his confidence grows so does his masculine persona. Consider how he spoke to Chris when he was "exposed," as well as when he shook hands with Stu after saving his life at the restaurant.

The point is You-the-Writer need to have such control over the nuances of your character dialogue, not ultimate control, mind you, for that is the realm of the actor and director. However, you can orchestrate diction and syntax to "aim" your audience where you want them to go.

Progressive Concepts to Consider:

1) Appropriate Title
2) Types of Suspense utilized
3) Webbing of related elements
4) First 10 minutes prepared audience for the balance of the story
5) Character consistency after Introduction
6) Unique defiance of predictability
7) Opposition intensity increased
8) Character demonstration of profile history
9) Consequences of back-story

* * * * *

National Lampoon's **CHRISTMAS VACATION**

By John Hughes
1989, Starring Chevy Chase, Beverly D'Angelo, Randy Quaid

Length: 92 minutes (with credits at beginning, runs 97 minutes)

Log Line: When Clark tries too hard to make a memorable holiday season, the Griswold family's December turns into one disaster after another.

Statement of Purpose: To prove that the best of intentions cannot overcome ignorance, inevitable logic or common sense.

Intro Image: Family car driving along snowy highway with Christmas music playing.

First 10 minutes
Who:
Clark Griswold, idealistic, well-meaning but accident prone family man (thinks he's Alpha)
Ellen Griswold, supportive, tolerant wife who always compensates
Audrey, 16-yr-old daughter who barely endures, tad spoiled
Rusty, 14-yr-old son who resists cooperating, but helps when no choice
When: Contemporary December (1989)
Where: Northeastern U.S. (steep roads, pine trees)
What: Family driving to cut down their own ideal Christmas tree

Why: Clark is obsessed with creating a memorable "old-fashioned, fun-filled family Christmas."

Three related subplots:
Clark's company
Family dynamics among in-laws
Intolerant sophisticated neighbors

Time Line: Three weeks before Christmas

Image repeats:
Advent Calendar
Christmas decorations
House covered in white lights
Gifts
Memorabilia
Company bonus
Sacrificing for family happiness
"Have's & Have-Not's" vs. Pride
"Griswold Family Christmas"
"When have I ever . . ."

Act I = Set-up of Ordinary World: Clark forcing family into Christmas celebration
9 min **Intro:** Country excursion to obtain tree punctuated by typical disasters
10 min **Inciting Incident**: "All my life I have wanted a memorable Christmas"
17 min **PP I:** Clark & Russ set out multiple boxes of lights, overdoing "right to be proud."

Act II = Life 180 degrees: Clark sets up one disaster after another in quest for "Great Christmas"
40 min **Pinch I:** Repulsive Cousin Eddie & family arrive
53 min **Mid-Point:** Ruby Sue asks if Clark is Santa & he realizes he must come through
62 min **Pinch II**: Clark looks at family gathered at dinner table in "moment" of classic joy
73 min **PPII:** Clark crying over "Jelly of the Month" instead of expected financial bonus

Act III = Clark regains composure at loss of bonus & confronts kidnapped boss
78 min **Climax-A:** Clark leads family reaction to squirrel

83 min **Commitment-A**: His dad convinces Clark to read "Twas Night Before Christmas"
87 min **Climax-B:** Police cars & SWAT converge on house
90 min **Commitment B:** Boss changed his mind.
After-story: Uncle Lewis's cigar ignites sewer gas sending lawn reindeer & sled across the moon & Clark's concluding statement about creating a memorable Christmas "I did it."

Dialogue Notes:
"Comfortable" exchanges between Clark & Ellen
Undertones of criticism of the in-laws
Uncomfortable formality of Frank, Clark's boss
Teen whining
Cynical snippiness of Neighbors
Clark's habitual "Freudian slips"
Eddie's braggadocio speeches

Alpha Character posturing differences:
Clark when serious/focused vs. Clark the buffoon
Extreme contrast of Todd and Eddie in Clark's life
Clark vs. Eddie
Clark vs. his father & father-in-law
Clark vs. Rusty

Supporting cast Unique Character Gems:
Cousin Eddie, well-meaning but pathetic, ignorant, crude
Audrey & Rusty, put-upon teenages
Clark Sr. & Nora, Art & Frances, judgmental, narrow-minded in-laws
Cousin Catherine, Rocky & Ruby, unsophisticated, ignorant, "trying"
Uncle Lewis & Aunt Bethany, crotchety, forgetful seniors
Todd & Margo, selfish, intolerant yuppies

Background effects, the nuances of aura:
Out-of-doors cold
Relative luxury & décor of Griswold home
Busy coldness of Clark's company offices
Grossness of rusted RV
Neighbor's ultra-modern house
Suburbia

Elements from Other Genres: Juvenile

Question: Since Clark Griswold had the where-with-all to attain a company position (of 17 years) in a highly competitive company, did you ever question how he could be so "oblivious" and idealistic in his personal life? OR did the character suck you in and make you WANT to believe in his lack of common sense and his perpetual desire to want the most from life?

Appearance or reference to recurrence of Evil Theme in Min: Reminders of importance of legitimate problem (bonus) in **BOLD.** Remaining disasters Clark set-up or had to deal with. Note pacing of 1-2 page cycles of set-up, expectation, reversal.

Act I = Set-up of Ordinary World: Clark forcing family into Christmas celebration

1-2 Driving on country road singing Christmas music, kids withdrawn

3-4 Clark responding macho to red-neck harassment

5-7 Escaping crash to tromp through snow for tree though forgot the saw

8 Neighbor sarcasm, huge tree in living room

9 Sap on fingers while talk of bickering in-laws coming, "Holidays about resolving differences."

10 = **Inciting Incident**: Ellen reminds him of unrealistic standards. "When have I ever . . ."

11-12 Dec 16. Clark mention bonus to co-worker, shows pool model, deposit, "Last true family man" boss with minions, use idea at trade show. "Merry Christmas" sarcasm.

13-14 City images to Clark in lingerie dept & busty clerk, Freudian "hooters, nipply" Russ catches

16 Family doing Christmas things when doorbell with both sets parents & chaos of quick criticisms

17 = **Plot Point I:** Clark with Rusty setting out multiple boxes of lights, determined to "be proud."

Act II = Life 180 degrees: Clark sets up one disaster after another in quest for "Great Christmas"

18 Rusty "Might be overdoing it." When was the last time," Neighbors want him to break neck

19-20 Ladder collapse, nailing lights & sleeve to eaves

21 Audrey coercing mother to rearrange sleeping & control grandparents

22 As nighttime, Russ drops reindeer, Clark nailing lights on room, slide off causing ice to break Neighbor window, Ellen calls to Clark in bushes

23-24 Neighbors find damage as family in nightwear to yard, 25,000 bulbs, Griswold Family Christmas, nothing, disgust.

25-27 Clark figuring, "imagine it" family sleeping while Clark checking bulbs

28-29 Clark sneaking presents into attic (pull-down ladder) , dusty Mother's Day from '83

30-31 Frances closes ladder, Clark can't open, family leaving to shop & don't hear him

32-33 Sees drive off, finds discard clothing then Griswold Family Christmas 1955 home movie, teary as watches past until returned Ellen pulls open trap door.

34 Neighbors observe Clark's persistence, Clark with Santa "avoiding family"

35-37 Clark's frustration over lights not working, "Plugged in?' Mother flips switch, brilliance causes accidents at Neighbors & power station drain, off again, Clark kicks Santa

38-39 Ellen flips switch as Clark mans plug, All see lights, Halleluiah Chorus. "It's a beaut!"

40-41 = **Pinch I:** Cousin Eddie's arrival with rusted RV, Rocky's sore, Ruby Sue's eyes uncrossed, Rottweiler "Snots",

42-45 Couple alone time in RV, Eddie admiring tree as dog drinks dry, clueless Eddie breaks Christmas décor, relates daughter in clinic & son with Carney, staying for month, Clark spews nog.

46 Dec 18. Clark takes gift to boss in conf. room (identical shape to others on credenza) Awkward exchange.

47-48 Night on sledding hill, applying lubricant to saucer for land speed record, Eddie 's metal to plastic plate in head, Clark rockets down hill, through trees, across highway.

49-50 Dec 19. Toying with pool model, co-worker no bonus yet but envelope to house

51-52 Clark at kitchen window "sees" pool with family, Eddie transforms into lingerie model who strips suit & throws at window.

53-54 = **Mid-Point:** Ruby Sue "Uncle Clark, are you Santa?" Refocuses Clark. Denies, asks if excited, chastises crudeness, she tells of getting nothing year before so Santa all crap, Clark promises this year

55-56 No man with letter, morning chaos at table, looking out at gross Eddie emptying chem.. toilet into sewer already filled with gas.

57-59 Out of work 7 yr, holing out for management, Clark & Eddie at store loading cart with huge bags dog food, Eddie admits impoverished status, Clark wants to give Christmas, Eddie gives him a list

60-61 Dec 24. Clark assists Bethany & Lewis into house. Clark lifted & replaced wig. Rusty in the Navy? Did I break wind? Rusty with mewing box=wrapped her damn cat, "gets confused" Eddie with box leaking lime Jello.

62 = **Pinch II:** Clark looks around full table at family awaiting festive dinner.

63 Aunt Bethany recites "Pledge of Allegiance" instead of "The Blessing." Eddie stands & salutes

64-65 Catherine's turkey REALLY dried out, family eats anyway, Eddie gross, Ellen flicking food to side, cat playing with tree's wires

66-67 Clarke reports pilots saw Santa, Eddie "You serious?" dog yakking under table, probably into garbage, Clark & Ellen cleaning spilled garbage in kitchen, Lewis calls for Clark to get his stogies

68 Clark to living room finds lights out, plugs in electrocuting the cat under chair, Carry smoldering to curbside, like to fumigate, smell something?

69 Return to dessert, Lewis with cigar at tree, puff of fire, Clark checks Lewis back to charred tree, turns & old man on fire. Art tells him ugly tree anyway.

70-72 Clark angrily to door for delivery boy with envelope, "My bonus" All react to his ecstasy, he announces putting in pool and plans to fly all down to celebrate. Apologizes fro being short but money

73-74 = **Plot Point II:** Clark opens, numb midst family clamor then crying & angry, certificate for "Jelly of the Month Club." Shreds, gulps eggnog, rants about wanting to drag his boss from Melody Lane mansion, Eddie thinks then RV pulling from driveway.

Act III = Clark regains composure at loss of bonus & confronts kidnapped boss

75 Wild Clark with chain saw looking around yard. Neighbors at table as tree crashes thru window.

76-77 Clark in Santa suit cleaning hands, Elle chastises, Clark even saws off loose newel post (echo of IT'S A WONDERFUL LIFE), family again settled in living room. Bethany "What's that sound?" Then Clark looks into tree

78-80 = **Climax A** (Clark defending his home): Squirrel from tree, Mom faints, "Where's Eddie he eats these things?" Plan to trap, smack with hammer, Frances faints, Father "Going in with you." Sees squirrel on Clark's back, dog loose from porch & chases squirrel through house . . . Margo demands Todd punch Clark so goes to do herself . . . as Clark opens door so squirrel + dog land on her.

81 Family with bags stopped by Clark who insanely demands they WILL stay to finish up the "fun, old-fashioned Christmas." "Don't make ti worse." "How could it get worse? We're on the threshold of hell."

82-83 = **Commitment A:** Clark Sr. consoles his son about being good intentioned and a good man who just wanted a perfect Christmas. "How'd you get through?" "Jack Daniels . . . you should read "Twas the Night . . ." Clark smoothly reading to relaxed family & wide-eyed children.

84 "Eddie with a man in pajamas wearing a big bow" Ho-Ho-Ho, Wife calling police, "You're fired and you to jail." Clark accepts responsibility

85-86 Clark apologizes for losing temper but 17 years counting on bonus, "Sometimes good on paper, don't see the people it hurts. Last year plus 12%" Cheering.

87-89 = Climax B (Action end to crisis): Police cars & SWAT attack the house, break down neighbor's door, FREEZE as into living room,

90 = **Commitment B:** "All a misunderstanding. Not pressing charges since this man called me on something.." Frank's wife & police chief also criticize cutting bonus. Children outside to see Christmas sky

91 Lewis drops cigar into sewer, explosion sends yard sleigh across moon as Bethany sings "National Anthem with family & police saluting. Ellen kisses Clark with "Merry Christmas, Sparky."

92 = **After-story:** Clark looks up at sky with "I did it!"

CONCEPTS DISCUSSION

The first viewing of a film should enthrall you in the story and characters, but every film has positive and negative lessons to teach. Identify the storytelling basics. If you don't "get them all, watch it again. Next, watch for the elements from the Progressive Concepts list. Finally, watch fort the genre expectations, character and plot type. Here's a discussion of the just-discussed concepts present in this film.

AUDIENCE EXPECTATIONS

The entire concept of "genre branding" is aimed at marketing to build audience expectation, to attract the targeted audience. That is also the concept behind playing off of successful films in their sequels. This film built on the 1983 VACATION and 1985 EUROPEAN VACATION. Audiences already knew Clark Griswold and his family, though ages of the children were juggled a bit. It didn't matter. The concept of well-intentioned plans going awry had already been established successfully in the first two films. This film had a built-in audience.

Clark Griswold is perpetually trying to create "special memories." He never anticipates objects and people failing to cooperate, thus he must blithely deal with the reversal's consequences. Yes, the antics are frequently vaudeville slapstick, but the audience is suspended in a state of anticipation for that very thing. So, like any successful humor, we are set-up then the exaggerated opposite delivered. Though Clark consistently states a smattering of insightful lines of dialogue (like at the office to his boss's minions as they pass him and his ignored comebacks to the pathetic Cousin Eddie), he shuts down his common sense and tries "one more time" to focus on fun. Even when at his angriest, he vents with every vulgar name he can think of then works to move on in the poignant moment with his dad asking "How did you make it work?"

What did the writers deliver but humor: "With a bottle of Jack Daniels."

> ULTIMATELY, YOU-THE-WRITER HAVE TO FOCUS ON CONSISTENCY OF SET-UP, ANTICIPATION AND REVERSAL TO WRITE SUCCESSFUL COMEDY.

Ultimately, You-the-Writer have to focus on consistency of set-up, anticipation and reversal to write successful comedy. And it has to be done on all levels from scene-by-scene dialogue to pay-off of sequences to the structuring of each act.

BACK-STORY'S INFLUENCE ON PLOT

Eddie's ignorant and crude intrusion into the Griswold Family Christmas is a perfect foil to Clark's attempts to go all out. We are given bits and pieces of his essentially pathetic, under-achieving history. His life is one failure after another. He lacks education and social graces. His persona is one of barely surviving and needing the help of others. Clark has material security and a degree of sophistication he has worked for . . . along with a desire to create warm, fuzzy memories. He knows his generosity is enabling the dependent behavior but the innuendo is he will not insult this relative or ignore need. His generosity extends to that pathetic, clueless family . . . with the predictable results that the he will suffer exaggerated consequences.

Now, one step up the social evolutionary ladder is the Yuppie neighbors, Margo and Todd. Everything in their world is modern, pristine and above the vulgarity and chaos of the Griswolds. Of course, that provides an ideal subplot for enhancing outrageous negative consequences to everything Clark is trying to enjoy. Their outsider experiences emphasized the insanity. They were the "straight man" to Clark's punctuating actions.

Clark Sr. and Nora along with Art and Frances grounded the holiday story in universals of extended family "come to judge." These are the people who knew the adults as children. Each couple has their own life-style and yet they are still the parents Clark and Ellen are trying to please. Nora pats her son's cheek when the lights don't work, but Clark addresses her "safety" when she faints at the "attack of the squirrel." Frances cringes at Clark's hugs and chides her daughter for smoking. Art sees Clark as a perpetual buffoon who should be ignored while his dad sympathizes with Clark's efforts. These glimpses deliver a cascade of thought-associations to how these people perceived the past and arrived at how they intend to react to the present.

Uncle Lewis and Aunt Bethany were the epitome of every very elderly relative anyone has invited over for a holiday get-together. And like all the other characters, they were exaggerations of the worst. Of course, we saw Uncle Lewis in his younger days in the 1955 family movie Clark watched in the attic. He was consistently crusty with cigar-in-hand in old age. Though

Alzheimer's is definitely not funny, the humor around Aunt Bethany's forgetfulness punctuated the Christmas Eve gathering right up to and including her singing the National Anthem to the sleigh's air-born trip across the moon and her ending "Play Ball!" There was no drama over inappropriate behavior or sadness over "what had been." In the moment Bethany was hysterically funny. We weren't laughing at her but with her exuberance of the moment.

Ultimately, the extended family figures provided the "every man" grounding yet opportunity to exaggerate for a humorous pay-off. We ask ourselves, "How many times did I want to laugh instead of cry?"

BEWARE FLASHBACKS

Remember that flashbacks are digressive and the movie audience is interested in the here and now. Logically that means you can have brief excursions, glimpses and references to the past, but you only do that for vital information and NOT to establish aura.

Back-story was provided in this movie through interactions more than explanations. From the kids' impatience with their parents, especially Clark, to the grandparents' innuendos, to transient references of work history, to even the neighbors' reinforced disgust with Clark. No long explanations had to be given that would have pulled the story to a halt for that explanation. We wanted to see what happened next, not rehash the past

Three times we were given longer bits about the past: when Clark watched the family of 1955 and the two times Eddie gave Clark more information than he wanted, first about their true financial status and secondly about the metal plate in his head being replaced by plastic. All three instances provided set-up information for subsequent events and a play off of images.

The most poignant scene was when Clark Sr. talked with his son about the evening's catastrophe and his awareness of the fine man and father Clark had become. He builds Clark's self-confidence by stating he knows he is a better man and deserves to be the one to continue the family tradition of reading "Twas the Night Before Christmas." The reference to the Jack Daniels recalled that 1955 family movie and put all in perspective.

Bottom Line: Comedy or not, you have to consider how you are going to optimize and condense every scene and make each significant to the whole.

Progressive Concepts to Consider:

1) Appropriate Title
2) Types of Suspense utilized
3) Webbing of related elements
4) First 10 minutes prepared audience for the balance of the story
5) Character consistency after Introduction

6) Unique defiance of predictability
7) Opposition intensity increased
8) Character demonstration of profile history
9) Consequences of back-story

Repetition is reinforcement of knowledge so the concepts become habit. That's the reason for the cumulative list. You now should have these nine of 24 total committed to memory.

* * * * *

GENRE FILM Chapter 6 Exercises

Exercise 6a. Write Pg 21-25 right thru Plot Point I's life changing crisis event that forces the Protag/Main Character out of the "Ordinary World" and across the threshold into a new way of life.

Exercise 6b. Time to consider the Protag's immediate reaction to facing a life spun 180 degrees and headed in a new direction. What are the possibilities? What has to be dealt with immediately? Remember, though the character is inherently a catalyst, this way of life is still new and must be learned.

Exercise 6c. Consider what elements from the subplots that will logically create need for new skills & knowledge, tests, meeting of new friends and glimpses of the growing threat. Now is another opportunity to create more "What If" lists of possibilities that will assault the Protag.

Exercise 6d. Write Pg 26-30 of first encounters with this "New World."

Exercise 6e. What are the challenges to the Protag and subplot events afoot in the Antagonist's world?

Exercise 6f. Are there any new Allies in the New World's people? Who contrasts with the Protag? Who enhances the Protag? Who annoys the Protag? How does the Protag respond to these new personalities? Any reminders of the back-story's past that discomfits the Protag?

CHAPTER 7

Character Arc, Inherent Sex & Violence/Juvenile Genre

All human beings are constantly changing, whether they are 8 or 80. Our experiences invade our consciousness and trigger thoughts and questions. Sometimes we have light-bulb moments of awareness and other times we are frustrated and motivated to learn more or try another coping mechanism. Life demands we change or perish, mentally, emotionally, socially or even physically. Not learning, not maturing puts our inner and outer being at risk. All of that is documented psychological fact.

So, how can a writer (playing the amateur psychologist) take advantage of this evolving humanity?

FROM ORDINARY WORLD TO NEW WORLD OF ACT II

At the outset of your story and throughout Act I you established a baseline of personality factors your audience can recognize. You gave them a character goal and demonstrated how this character routinely copes with situations and people encountered in the "Ordinary World." The outer appearance of your character's actions, facial expressions, mannerisms and dialogue depicted visual evidence of this person's inner values and self-concept. Quite obviously, this was your set-up.

THE OUTER APPEARANCE OF YOUR CHARACTER'S ACTIONS, FACIAL EXPRESSIONS, MANNERISMS AND DIALOGUE DEPICTED VISUAL EVIDENCE OF THIS PERSON'S INNER VALUES AND SELF-CONCEPT.

Then along comes that Plot Point I and forced the character in a "New World" where he or she learns to live in a new manner or perish on all or one level. The more levels at risk, the higher the stakes, the greater the tension.

THE CHARACTER ARC

Seat-of-the-pants writers hate the need to contemplate this, but, as stated before, planning is a necessity for screenwriters to create the tightest script possible. So, it is time to drag out that Paradigm again.

IMPORTANT QUESTIONS AT THIS POINT OF THE FIRST HALF OF ACT II:

1. How is your boy or girl doing? How is this person reacting to the new experiences?
2. Has the Main Character learned any new coping mechanisms or have these been resisted?
3. What disturbs the character and what soothes the character in the New World?
4. Remembering that a cinematic character is an inherently dramatic character, how has your Protag demonstrated externally what is happening internally?

The Character Arc is the internal change caused by external events and demonstrated by a change of attitude. Yes, it can evolve and explode into awareness in the second half of Act II. However, it is more satisfying for the character to continue questioning his or her capabilities to truly succeed until the Climax of Act III proves the change and the ability. Act II is the testing ground of trial and error. This goes along with the concept of never portraying "the happy people of the happy village."

So, look at your Main Plot progression and what is going on in the subplots then consider how you want to test your Main Character's **Inner Essence**, that self-concept and resolve that creates motivation. Don't forget your Statement of Purpose, either. As you plan the evolution of the Main Character's Arc, consider those events or experiences that will provide more evidence to prove your Statement of Purpose.

QUESTION OF GROWTH vs. DETERIORATION

It is a fact of life that humans like to cheer for heroes who represent the best of us. We are profoundly disappointed in those heroes who later prove to be flawed to the point of ineffectual. The more serious or heinous the flaw, the deeper our disappointment. Sometimes the stories of such down-falls work to call attention to their existence. Shining a light on weaknesses and their consequences creates an entirely different sense of story in the audience. They see what not to do. And that's okay, as long as you are aware that you cannot have it both ways in the short span of a film. Either the deterioration results in consequences (STAR WARS Episode III) or redemption is the reward to a spirit that defies "The Dark Side" (Luke and his father Anikan in STAR WARS Episode VI).

If you choose to do a deterioration story, you need to start Act I with a likeable but flawed character where the life-changing Plot Point I is the "last straw." The subsequent Act II is a cycle of the Protag's Opposition growing stronger. In this story the Protag will be the "Evil" side of the story equation. The struggle or vacillation creates the meaning of the story, even though the Protag will lose in the end. A prime movie example of this is the masterfully re-arranged scenes of MEMENTO.

ANOTHER USE OF STATEMENT OF PURPOSE

Your two fundamental (and succinct) tools are your Log Line and Statement of Purpose. The Log Line explains the thrust of your Main Plot. The Statement of Purpose guides your consideration of what needs to impact the inner essence of your Main Character. Both allow you to identify what you can exclude and what you need to include in your story. Do not take them for granted. Think of them as you do your Character Profiles, Paradigm and actual writing. They will keep you focused and progressing, as well as preventing your digression into unnecessary side trips.

HOLLYWOOD'S NEED FOR SEX & VIOLENCE

Hollywood is fickle and there is no such thing as a "trend." Why? Every power figure in the industry has his or her own preferences and absolutely no one can predict what will click with the ticket-buying public. There will be a lot of "copy cat" projects, however, after a successful film. But, think about it. How long does it take for a script to go from concept to financing to development to production to the screen? The public could move on to some other "flavor-of-the-month" by the time your rendition of a similar story makes it into the theaters.

The only constant in film making is no one wants to read/see the story of "the happy people in the happy village" thus dramatic conflict is essential in every genre. The most basic essence of conflict is "want is blocked by a powerful obstacle" and the two basic human wants are the continuation of life and perpetuation of the species . . . thus violence and sex are common elements in every kind of genre. Doesn't get any simpler than that.

THE TWO BASIC HUMAN WANTS ARE THE CONTINUATION OF LIFE AND PERPETUATION OF THE SPECIES . . . THUS VIOLENCE AND SEX ARE COMMON ELEMENTS IN EVERY KIND OF GENRE.

DEFINITIONS FOR THIS DISCUSSION:

Sex: Chemistry of physical attraction vital to establishing a loving, trusting relationship that will lead to sexual intercourse, whether visualized or inferred.

Violence: The threat or actual physical jeopardizing of human life, be it disruption of status quo or actual death.

SEXUAL CONTEXT OF THE VARIOUS GENRES

To begin with, we are not talking about sexual intercourse on screen here. Consider multi-published romance author Linda Howard's Twelve Steps of Intimacy, the titillation of inference, the unspoken assumptions shown on screen of this physical progression.

Linda Howard's "Twelve Steps of Intimacy"

1. Eye to Body
2. Eye to Eye
3. Voice to Voice
4. Hand to Hand

* * *

5. Arm to Shoulder
6. Arm to Waist
7. Mouth to Mouth
8. Hand to Head
9. Hand to Body

* * *

10. Mouth to Breast
11. Hand to Genitals
12. Genitals to Genitals

The logic of this physical progression lies in **trust, acceptance and permission**. The more one trusts, the more access to the body will be wanted and allowed. On a primal level, each step makes the person more vulnerable to a lethal attack. Think about that as you again look down the list. Each move actually invades another's space more. Each exposes the body to attack or allows total control of a body part that could have been protected or defended previously. Hand holding keeps one from running and each subsequent movement pulls the body closer. Mouth and head are where breath moves in and out and where one exposes the fragile spine and vital blood vessels. Each allowed step gives freer access to vulnerable body parts and surrenders control by responding, becoming more stimulated and willing.

Let's put these concepts into a cinematic context.

ON SCREEN CHEMISTRY & SEXUAL INNUENDO

What does someone mean when they say "That couple has great chemistry" or "I don't believe the attraction because the on-screen chemistry is just not there"??? Yes, actors who possess that sexual charisma and great acting ability can turn a simple conversation into a raging seduction scene. But, I think screenwriters have to create the characters, the fundamental choreography, the subtle dialogue that gives the actors the tools to work with. Visuals, visuals, visuals at all three levels of characterization, movement, speeches.

> VISUALS, VISUALS, VISUALS AT ALL THREE LEVELS OF CHARACTERIZATION, MOVEMENT, SPEECHES.

Time and again you will hear some industry people say "The barest hint of what is going on or closing the door will create greater titillation for the audience than if you film an R or X-rated sex scene." Some call these scenes "tasteful illusion" and others roll their eyes and say "That's a director cheating to get by the censors." I believe both are right. However, an artful screenwriter can heat up the screen with the characterization, movement, and speeches to the point the audience members are squirming in their seats because their vivid imaginations are racing.

Probably the singular most common tool of playing off sexual assumption is the touching or partnering of spouses, parenting referrals, pregnancy or the presence of children, even the image of a double bed. Small children will not even think about the underlying assumption that sexual congress is implied in all of that. Cartoon guys getting "bug-eyed" when a curvaceous cartoon gal walks by swinging her hips is humorous, but for different reasons to different levels of maturity. So the teen films that show skin and hormonal boys are alluding to the assumption of thoughts of sex. An elderly couple holding hands are at what stage in Howard's Twelve Steps of Intimacy? Is the contrast between those two examples in the assumption of vigorous activity for the purpose of procreation or pleasuring a partner? What exactly is the implied difference? And, yes, it does matter that you understand it.

Here is where the romantic script writer has to very deliberately plan the sexual visuals you will use in your story by specific orchestration of Howard's Twelve Steps, the titillation of inference or the unspoken assumptions.

.Keep a list of the visuals that will depict thoughts and emotions, such as his hand sliding around her bare, sweaty midriff and her gasp and shiver then verbal denial as "What? No, nothing's wrong. You just startled me." He frowns then pinches his eyes to concentrate harder.

Movie-making is about the visuals you give the actor and director to tell the story. The physical "signaling" is how the audience connects with the character's thoughts.

Here's an interesting exercise to get you in that visual mode: Put in your favorite movie that you watch over and over . . . sans the volume. Watch how the body language and facial expression show the story.

Of course, as a writer you will not depict every nuance, just insinuate what a good actor can latch onto. To describe every expression, every physical move is called "micro-choreography" and will get your script promptly sent back to you or thrown in the recycle bin. Imagine yourself as an artistic actor who wants to recreate a memorable character on camera. As an actor do you want somebody who wrote the thing three years ago dictating to you how to do your job? Instead, O Screenwriter, you must think of macro-managing.

VIOLENCE DOES NOT MEAN BLOOD & EXPLOSIONS

Think of violence as "increments of jeopardy." Crewella Deville in 101 DALMATIANS was a violent woman who wanted those puppies to die. The horrors visualized at Omaha Beach on D-Day in SAVING PRIVATE RYAN were as visually accurate as it could get. At the other end of the spectrum you have the mother warning her misbehaving son with "The Look." No violence is committed, just the threat of something the boy would not like. The same thing could be said about gunfighter opponents and the stare-down scene where one relaxes and looks away, unwilling to act. No violence was enacted, merely a threat resulting in the response of allowing the Alpha Male to reign supreme.

So here's the formula:
M + G + O = Dramatic Conflict
(Main character) + (Goal) + (Opposition) = Dramatic Conflict

And here's the VIOLENCE formula:
W. M. + W.G. + THREAT = Jeopardy
(Willing Main Character) + (Worthy-of-Risk Goal) + THREAT = Jeopardy

Examine each of those components and you will discover the LEVEL of violence you must have in your story.

WILLINGNESS TO TAKE RISKS

Highly motivated people are logically more willing to take risks. The more confident and skilled the person, the greater the risk they will be willing to take. At the other end of the spectrum is the innocent, ignorant character who makes assumptions and takes risks without awareness of the consequences. So, you must examine Character in each scene for these two extremes.

Cinematic stories are about exaggerated circumstances, so goals have to be big, very big. The more important the goal, the greater risks the motivated character will be willing to take to achieve that goal . . . within the parameters of their personality. Think back to the innate personality traits talked about previously. What would motivate a devoutly religious character to respond violently and take a human life? The most decorated soldier of WW I, Sgt. York was a registered conscientious objector with Quaker roots, yet when he committed himself to defending the rights of people to live freely rather than under tyranny, he killed and captured more German soldiers than any other one man in the history of that war. He committed to both his willingness and a worthy-of-risk goal that motivated him to the ultimate of violent acts, taking other human life. By instinct, animals are willing to do whatever it takes to survive. Consider that in your formula. A devoted gentle mother who initially appears wimpy can become a violent lioness when her children's lives are threatened.

The greater the threat, the greater the level of jeopardy, as well. Think about how stalking can escalate, yet every level is frightening to the victim. Every level is an invasion of territory, a disruption in the continuum of a safe, secure life. Practical jokes are a threat. Holding a door closed, forcing someone to eat something, putting a bug or snake into someone's backpack or bed . . . all of these disrupt and threaten the security of the moment. Restraining someone, whether body-to-body or with some sort of tie-down, is a threat to physical freedom for the person being restrained. In hospitals, law enforcement or military actions this act may be necessary for the safety of the majority, but it is still a threat to the one restrained.

Up to this point I have refrained from using specifically personal references, but I am doing so now because of a strongly held principle. I have great personal difficulty identifying the entertainment value of the violence of multiple car wrecks like in THE BLUES BROTHERS or in the gore and terror of "slasher" movies. Having worked in an Emergency Room for years I saw the reality of human suffering. And, yes, I had a tough time sitting through the battle scenes of SAVING PRIVATE RYAN and my beloved BRAVEHEART. The cinematic drama of the violence ripped right to my soul, which was appropriate for the story and the theme of those movies. The battle scenes were there for MORE than entertainment value . . . which cannot be said of the gratuitous scenes in THE BLUES BROTHERS and the various "slasher" movies.

When you choose to depict violent scene or incorporate violence it had better be relevant to the core of the story. Never ever write it in simply because you think it would appeal to a certain demographic of viewers.

LEVELS OF JEOPARDY from VALUE OF GOALS

All of that said, let's go back to the concept of "jeopardy" in the more sedate romantic movies. The Main Character or Hero and Heroine must be willing to risk their personal well-being for the ultimate sake of the relationship. That is what makes O. Henry's Christmas story " The Gift of the Magi" so intensely meaningful: the husband and the wife loved one another so much they were willing to give up the one thing they treasured most to make the other happy.

How to consider "jeopardy" is simply a matter of identifying what the character values most then listing the many different ways that "thing" could be diminished, tarnished, or destroyed completely. Some assaults merely undermine the value whereas other actions can malign and destroy the essence of character values.

Every single character should have their own set of "golden idols," those things that are sacred to them. Of course, as human beings we will share some common values . . . but most of us hide and protect those "things" that are the most sacred to each of us alone. Those sacred things are what make each of us vulnerable because nothing--not one thing, not one institution, belief, or physical possession, not one relationship, one human ability--is above attack or beyond destruction.

Stephen Hawkins is the most brilliant man of our world but he is trapped in a deteriorating body and must rely on machines to communicate his brilliance. Our human shells are fragile. Our belief systems are certainly even more fragile. Who is right and who is wrong? When will the truth be known for certain? One man's truth is another man's abhorrent way of life.

So, each writer must create each character with his or her own set of values and personal idols then create a story experience that will assault those values. You-the-Writer have to suck the audience in to care about that character's values in Act I then depict all the trials and stressors that strain and jeopardize those valued ways of life in Act II and finally force the character to defend the well-being of that character's values in Act III.

Here's an important point when trying to identify what is jeopardized: Intense drama results when the person has two choices and both are horrific, both will hurt or destroy something of value to the character. That is called a "**dramatic dilemma**." Story is predictable when the choices are merely between right and wrong or between two rights. But when the choice is between two wrongs, the tension becomes glaring anxiety. Dilemma creates even a greater sense of jeopardy for the character who must act!

JUVENILE GENRE

The idea of Cross-Genre Appeal takes a different slant when one is considering the Juvenile market. In all the other genres you can mix-and-match, but in

Juvenile you must shave the other genre contrivances to fit the requirements of this genre. In other words, the needs and expectations of the children viewing juvenile material come first. Yes, a juvenile story can have elements drawn from mystery, inspirational (Christian), historical, western, action-adventure, science fiction, fantasy, horror, humor and romance . . . but only at the age-appropriate level of the target audience. That is a sacred responsibility the writer needs to understand.

THE NEEDS AND EXPECTATIONS OF THE CHILDREN VIEWING JUVENILE MATERIAL COME FIRST.

The lower or simpler the language and maturity level of the viewers, the less conceptual wiggle room the writer has. Granted, modern technology-savvy children are becoming increasingly sophisticated in their awareness of story conventions and human problems. However, you cannot push adult awareness of story-telling devices and mature subject matter onto the evolving mind of a child. The censors and juvenile film watchdogs who oversee juvenile material absolutely will not tolerate it. Don't hold up the Harry Potter and Twilight series as examples of exceptions, either. They weren't. They were written to a particular age group and simply taken up by younger kids as tolerated by the adults (and advertisers) in the juvenile world.

So, your job as a writer of juvenile stories is to know your audience, the age group you are writing to. The Society of Children's Book Writers & Illustrators has a plethora of resource materials to help authors. Interview teachers and children's librarians who work in the age group you want to appeal to. Evaluate your story and character.

Being a parent or simply having lived through childhood yourself is not adequate training to understand audience expectations. Your perceptions are skewed by your anecdotal experience. For example, a man in the bag-piping community pitched a late elementary boy's story, a fantasy about an empowered boy. Then he submitted the first three chapters. The editor was stunned with the college-level (and beyond) vocabulary he used. The author was asked to revise to make it age appropriate. He refused saying "When I was that age I hated being talked down to. I want my book to challenge kids." The editor explained how most of his words could not even be understood by context. The targeted reader would have to drag out a dictionary which would shatter the window of illusion. The book was not contracted and the author still has not found a publisher so anticipates self-publishing. His problem of using himself as a reference point is that he has a remarkably high genius I.Q.. He was not an ordinary 6th Grade boy and could not speak to an ordinary 6th grade boy!

Look at the "Growth & Development Guidelines" of Appendix G. You will find an explanation of the general type of material each stage of childhood demands. Quite obviously, Young Adults can handle the concepts closest to mature adult material, but even there you need to research your market. Watch

YA movies and TV shows specifically looking for differences from adult and elementary-age entertainment. Talk with the young people who watch those and ask their opinions. Immerse yourself in the expectations of the age-level you are targeting. Do not think you can push the envelope beyond those and expect a producer of juvenile films to give you a chance. Just like in any of the other specialized markets, those producers know their audience (and the censors) much better than you think you do.

And, always remember the industry pays attention to the censor rating. For example, a feature film may be rated PG-17 for theater distribution, but the cursing may have a voice artist over-ride to change the words or scenes may actually be edited out for the TV rating. If you are not familiar with the censoring process, do an Internet search on "Censor Ratings" to get the most up-to-date information and categories.

FUNDAMENTAL CONCEPTS OF JUVENILE FILM

1. TRIAD: Protagonist POV, Demonstrate character growth, Clear problem resolution.

- Children of all ages need to identify with the main character experiencing the story. One, not a cast of a dozen.

- Every event is consistently filtered through this one character's perspective. That focus allows the child to vicariously live with that character, to identify with that character.

- The main character or protagonist must evidence some change in awareness or appreciation of whatever the situation is. Yes, children like to be entertained but they are watching how other children learn to cope with their world.

- Each story must have a clear goal or desire identified by the protagonist.

- The opposition can be many kinds but appropriate to the circumstance and age-awareness of the child.

- The main character must exert effort to overcome the opposition and the problem must be clearly resolved.

- In general, children lack the life experience and education to decipher complex motivations in others and to envision complex consequences.

- Simple problem, manageable complications and problem resolution. Beginning-Middle-Ending.

2. Understand the Juvenile Film Market needs of:

a. Pre-School: vivid visuals with simple dialogue tell the stories related to child's current experience

b. Early Elementary School: Simple problems (humor preferred), smart solutions, strong characters

c. 'Tween Stories/Middle Grade: Ages 10-14 with similar or older characters & more worldly/adventurous problems

d. Young Adult: more adult-like, independence-oriented stories, role-models ages 15-20

3. Evaluate story's Main Type of Problem (to control detail & complexity)

a. Difficult or unrealistic protagonist ***goal***

b. Level of threat of ***situation***

c. Demonstrate ***options*** available to protagonist

4. Understand essential internalizations of evolving childhood:

a. To love & be loved

b. To belong

c. To achieve

d. To gain security

e. To know

5. Clean, distinct, successful endings for Protagonist

- Though we all know life is messy and rare clear cut, successful stories for children delivery a satisfying ending that clearly defines the success of the Protagonist. Children lack the life experience to rationalize or contemplate vague endings. If they identified with the Protagonist and vicariously lived the story with that character, they want to feel successful, positive, empowered at the end. They want o walk away thinking "I could do that."

6. NEVER talk down to, sermonize to or overload a young viewer

- Talk to juveniles as if they are reasonable, attentive people, whether they are 5, 15 or an illiterate 25-year-old. Write vivid, short, action-oriented dialogue that triggers sensations and emotions. Forget delivering numerous facts you think the kid needs to remember. Facts are not interesting, but the characters living life are!

7. Watch movies of the market and read Human growth-and-Development texts

- Respect your juvenile audience enough to know what they are watching and where they are at in life. Spend a few hours every month browsing new releases in your favorite video store or children's section of the library. You cannot write what you do not know. You have a responsibility to understand current market and your market.

JUVENILE CHARACTER REQUIREMENTS

The majority of juvenile viewers will chose stories about characters who are one to four years older than they are simply because they are seeking role models or problem solvers they can emulate or imagine as a "best friend." So, the character you use must be a **positive role model** capable of coping and smart enough to learn and grow from the story.

It must be emphasized that the children populating your story must be **"iconic children"** as in representative of their age group. So fill out a detailed Character Profile that depicts all aspects of this kid's life to make him or her resonate as a living, breathing kid.

JUVENILE PLOT TYPES

The conventions of the juvenile market are restrictive because You-the-Writer are being given an almost sacred responsibility to touch the fragile and easily influenced mind of a child. Think about that.

1. **Coming-of-Age**, the Protagonist matures from one stage into a more responsible stage
2. **Young Romance**, the first stirrings of extraneous (beyond family) need to love & be loved
3. **Changing Family**, through death, divorce, loss or gain of family with dynamics change
4. **Animal Story**, an animal changes the child's awareness of life
5. **Nature Story**, climate or geography impacts, challenges, teaches the child
6. **Innocence vs. the World**, simple immediate focus is threatened & changed into negative awareness of vulnerability.
7. **Physical / Emotional Challenge**, undeveloped or weak body or mind confronted by physical or reasoning demands that seem beyond the child's ability.
8. **Heritage / Ancestor Awareness**, learning of unknown or new awareness of discomfiting social relevance.
9. **Role Model Story**, child becomes fascinated by someone worthy of being an idol
10. **Education / School Story**, the challenges of intellectual and/or social aspects of school life
11. **Moral / Values Challenge**, child is made aware of accountability and consequences

JUVENILE CONCLUSION

Most likely You-the-Writer can remember stories as examples of several of the above plots and possibly even films or books that combined several circumstances into one story. The main consideration is always that child's POV. Adult perspective is forever skewed by their broader awareness, their lessons learned. One book and its film adaptation come to mind: TO KILL A MOCKINGBIRD. The father Atticus had an entirely different awareness of what was happening than did his young daughter Scout. I would not say this was a juvenile story but it was told from a juvenile POV.

JUVENILE FILM ANALYSIS

Before you have been reminded to identify storytelling fundamentals and the previous Progressive points then think about the genre expectations depicted in these films. This time you need to be able to discuss why this story appeals to each particular age group. You should not be surprised to have a list for each of the various ages as well as adults.

* * * * *

THE LION KING

By Irene Mecchi, Jonathan Roberts, Linda Woolverton, plus 25 more
1994, Starring Voices of Matthew Broderick, Jonathan Taylor Thomas, James Earl Jones, Jeremy Irons, Moira Kelly

Length: 81 minutes (not counting credits)

Log Line: A guilt-ridden young lion abandons his kingdom but must eventually reclaim his heritage from his evil uncle.

Statement of Purpose: To prove the mistakes of youth can be overcome with courage and focus beyond self.

Intro Image: Sunrise on the African plain as animals gather.

First 10 minutes
Who:
Mufasa, Reigning Lion King
Shenzi, Prince's Mother
Rafiki, Baboon wise sooth-sayer
Simba, Lion Cub learning of his legacy

Scar, the darker, watchful & calculating male lion
When: Summertime
Where: African plain/savannah
What: Lion cub son needs to learn the "Circle of Life" balance
Why: For one day he will take his father's place maintaining order

Four related subplots:
Mufasa/Simba vs. Scar
Simba & Nala childhood friendship into Love Story
Scar & his manipulations of the Hyenas
Timon & Pumba's "Akuna Matada" philosophy (contrast to Mufasa's responsibility lessons)

Time Line: 1-3 years (From Simba's birth to adulthood)

Image repeats:
Dominance & Cooperative Respect vs. Intimidation
Rafiki's Tree
Stars
Forbidden areas
Pride Rock vs. harsh rock vs. lush grasslands & jungle
Chase & Capture
Visions & Perceptions
Responsibility vs. Blame

Act I = Set-up of Ordinary World: Simba discovers his World
8 min **Intro:** Simba introduced to the animals & the "Circle of Life"
11 min **Inciting Incident**: Scar insinuates only bravest can go to forbidden zone
17 min **PP I**: Cub Simba recognizes danger & his responsibility of leading Nala to Graveyard

Act II = Life 180 degrees: Simba tests his place in the world as a naïve cub then as a young lion
22 min **Pinch I:** Mufasa chastises Simba emphasizing mature responsibilties vs. Simba's impulsiveness
35 min **Mid-Point:** Simba finds Mufasa dead after stampede & accepts Scar's accusation
53 min **Pinch II**: Mature Nala is thrilled to find Simba alive
60 min **PPII:** Nala confronts Simba with world destroyed under Scar

Act III = Resolution: Simba fights to win his rightful place in the world
72 min **Climax: Simba battles Scar**
80 min **Commitment**: Atop Pride Rock Simba roars

After-story : Animals return to greet Simba's son to complete the Circle of Life

Dialogue Notes:
Scar's seductive voice
Young Simba vs. Mature Simba
Caricature of Hyenas
Chattering Zazu
Silliness of Timon & Pumba

Alpha Character posturing differences:
Mufasa vs. Scar (attitudes, demeanor, dialogue tone)
Manipulative Scar vs. intimidated Simba (innocent vulnerability vs. manipulation & bullying)
Empowered Simba (change in awareness reflected in tone & demeanor)
Nala vs. Simba (as immature cubs then as mature adults with responsibilities)

Supporting cast Unique Character Gems:
Zazu, the herald
Rafiki, the Mentor
Scar, the Shadow
Timon & Pumba, Comic relief
Nala (Playmate to Mate)
Hyenna, the henchmen

Background effects, the nuances of aura:
African plain from lush grass to drought-ridden dead zone
Safety of grassland to jungle vs. stark & rugged terrain
Treacherous graveyard
Thorn thicket when small animal can hide but barricade to larger predators
Throne-like Pride Rock

Elements from Other Genres: Comedy, Action-Adventure, Romance

Question: 1) Was the illusion of variety of animals respecting lions credible? Did this play up childhood idea of all creatures "getting along?" 2) Was the subservient role of female lions sufficiently countered when mature Nala found Simba, as well as the females of the pride barely tolerating Scar? How could that whole dynamic been handled differently while maintaining the concept of the male lion as "King?"

Appearance or reference to recurrence of Evil Theme in Min: Devious Uncle's jealousy and his henchmen hyenas acting out in **BOLD**.

Act I = Set-up of Ordinary World: Simba discovers his World

1 At sunrise, animals migrating to a common destination
2 Mufasao surveys his plains kingdom, greets Rafiki, who presents cub Simba to animals.
3 After animals bow, sullen Scar captures mouse
4 Mufasa vs Scar confrontation
5 Simba vs. Mufasa strong & could beat him
6 Rain on tree with Rafiki painting Simba picture
7 Simba waking parents "You promised" youthful exuberance
8 Surveys kingdom & Mufasa warns against "forbidden area" then teaches "Circle of Life"
9 Zazu (messenger) to be "victim" as Mufasa teaches Simba to pounce
10 Mufasa to the hyenna problem leaving Scar to manipulate Simba with sarcasm
11 Inciting Incident = Scar tweaks curiosity about lure of Elephant Graveyard only for bravest
12 "Our little secret" but Simba conspiring with cub Nola before mothers' bathe
13 To waterhole with Zazu, "betrothed"
14-15 "Mighty King" song with animals
16 Simba & Nala tumbling into the forbidden zone of Elephant's Graveyard
17 Plot Point I = Simba recognizes danger & his responsibility of leading Nala to the Graveyard

Act II = Life 180 degrees: Simba tests his place in the world as a naïve cub then as a young lion

18 - 20 Hyennas stalk as trespassers, cubs run, Zazu caught, Simba tries fight but weak
21 Mufasa attacks then confronts Simba with "You disobeyed"
22 - 24 **Pinch I =** Mufasa teaches "big prints to fill," brave when you have to be, stars are kings of past
25 – 28 Hyenna vs. lions, brought zebra offering, Scar "I will be king, so be prepared."
29 – 30 Scar leads Simba to gorge, everybody learns. "To Die for"
31 – 32 Wildebeast chased by hyenna, stampede, Scar tells Mufasa Sima there
33 Mufasa gets Simba to tree in midst of stampede
34 Mufasa climbing rocks, Scar prevents & he falls to death
35 -37 Midpoint = Simba searches, finds Mufasa dead, Scar convinces his fault & he must run away
38 Scar directs hyenas to chase & kill, Simba escapes in the brambles
39 Scar announces to the pride deaths of Mufasa & Simba & new world with hyennas

40 - 41 Rafiki watching, Simba collapses on parched plain, found & saved by Timon & Pumba
42 – 45 Simba recovers with "Akuna Matada" and bugs
46 Evolves into carefree GROWN Simba still living carefree
47 – 48 Imprisoned Zazu, Scar told by hyenas no food, lionesses must go far to find
49 – 50 Simba thoughtful at stars remembering lessons, walks away from Timon & Pumba
51 Rafiki seens vision of Simba alive
52 Pumba chasing bugs as lioness out of grass chasing him "She's gonna east me!"
53 -54 **Pinch II =** Simba attacks Nala, recognition, introductions, Everbody finds somebody
55 Nala tells him he's the king, refuted
56 – 59 talking playing, rubbing, "Love is in the air" Trio now 2,
60 Plot Point II = Nala tells of devastation at Pride Rock & his responsibility, can't change past

Act III = Resolution: Simba fights to win his rightful place in the world
61-64 Rafiki follows Simba who looks in water & sees Mufasa, He lives in YOU
65 - 67 Simba looks to stars, Remember who you are., run from it or learn from it, heads back.
68 Nala startles Timon "Carnivores!" won't find here since he's gone back to challenge his uncle
69 Nala running "Wait up" then "If I don't do it who will?" followed by Timon & Pumba
70 Area parched "fixer-upper" Timon & Pumba distract hyenas with "live bait**" hula**
71 Scar strike Shenzi when told herd has moved on
72 Simba appears, nuzzles stricken mother, Scar simpering, "One reasin shouldn't rip you apart"
73 Climax (Begin) = Scar points out hyenas & threatens secret of Mufasa's death
74 Simba admits, Scar stalks to edge, lightning strikes, "Just the way your father looked"
75 Hyennas attack Simba but lionesses attack them in turn
76 As Zazu, Timon & Pumba join, Simba chases Scar to edge
77 Cowering Scar blames hyenas, Simba tells him to run.
78 Climax (End) = Simba attacks, knocks Scar into rocks where hyenas close in on the turncoat
79-80 **Commitment =** Flames consume area then rain ends drought, Simba greeted by lionesses. Rafiki points to Pride Rock "It is time." Simba takes his place with Mufasa's voice, Simba roars

81 **AfterStory =** Lush area, animals again gathered, Simba & Nala on Pride Rock as Rafiki holds up cub.

CONCEPTS DISCUSSION

The Juvenile genre, like children's medical care, demands attention to detail for you are speaking to a sensitive and vulnerable imagination. That is an enormous responsibility. Pay attention to every detail, as well as every framework necessity.

CHARACTER ARC

It does not always have to be the Main Character or Protagonist who is the character changed by the events of the story. However, there is a heightened sense of "rightness" when this is the case, especially with juvenile stories, such as in THE LION KING. When the Main Character is moved from youth into a more mature realm of life, the "coming of age" sequences are logical to push and pull the character through the stages of growth and development in order to reach the understanding and acceptance of awareness and responsibilities of that more mature stage of life.

When the character who changes is a supporting character witnessing the events, a person who learns by observation and subsequently changes (such as the POV character of Phillipe in LADYHAWKE) it works only when that character is integral to the evolution of the events of the story. The supporting character has to be in the audience's face in most of the scenes with the main characters. Their subplot has to be evolving with a beginning-middle-ending to it, right along with the Main Plot.

With a firm grasp of the Statement of Purpose or what you are trying to prove with the events of the story and considering where your character is in the beginning, it is relatively simple to imagine those experiences the character needs to encounter to prove your point. You can hypothesize the change or arc you want your character to show because of the story. Remember, you do have to show by the deliberate choice of actions how this character has evolved to be braver, more astute, more willing to demonstrate faith, whatever the journey's culmination will require to demonstrate that arc in a satisfying manner without explanations. Show, don't tell and "Actions speak louder than words" in cinematic story-telling.

And, yes, every successful film has some kind of "Aha Moment" when the character makes a significant change of behavior and the audience is taken along for the ride. All that had gone before Nala's confronting Simba about his responsibilities closes in on the young lion and he is forced to remember and accept his duty-bound role in life. It is part of the "Circle of Life" and the audience is right there with him, especially the kids in the audience. Here is the visual example of taking responsibility for one's actions no matter how hard it is, no matter how scared you may be of consequences. It is the right thing to do.

GROWTH vs. DETERIORATION

Since cinematic stores are meant to mirror life, we know that not everyone on that screen will "live happily ever after." In THE LION KING the manipulative and selfish Scar was not meant to be rewarded or to grow because of his devious actions and lies. His world deteriorates because he lacked the positive energy to motivate the continuing growth of the "Circle of Life" around Pride Rock. He is a user and his subservient creatures do not care about their effectiveness. His lack of growth and learning led to the consequences of his downfall, his just desserts. Where Mufasa had the broader vision of how all the creatures "fed" one another, Scar is only concerned about himself.

Now, consider any darken principled story or characters who have truly nefarious or negative life energy intents. Storytellers can twist story events initially to show them off as being rewarded such as Commidus in GLADIATOR, Magua in THE LAST OF THE MOHICANS, or Colonel Quaritch in AVATAR. Ultimately, however, these negative characters eventually receive their "come-uppance." Their reward in life was transient and the eventual consequence is that the character loses as a result of their own actions, obsessions, and choices caused by their character flaws.

> THE CHARACTER LOSES AS A RESULT OF THEIR OWN ACTIONS, OBSESSIONS, AND CHOICES CAUSED BY THEIR CHARACTER FLAWS.

So, Writer, when you are planning your story events, remember you need to create the beginning's set-up, middle's confrontational problems then ending's resolutions for the negative character's subplot in order to satisfy your audience when it comes time for consequential pay-off of his deterioration. You can nudge your audience to want that to happen, but withhold the manner of the consequence.

LEVELS OF JEOPARDY FROM VALUE OF GOALS

Quite obviously, life and death issues are the highest stakes for most of us humans. There are some humans, however, who perceive of things that could be worse than death. When you are creating your character profiles you are establishing your character's priorities in life, those principles, people or things that character would do anything to protect and preserve. From priorities you move to goals and the levels of projected situations or things the character is willing to sacrifice to achieve.

In simple juvenile stories it is relatively easy to identify **Maslow's Hierarchy of Needs** and what the juvenile understands at their level of maturation. A pre-school child does not comprehend how a flame from a grill lighter can consume curtains, furniture and lives, nor that brackish water in the backyard could be thick with death-causing bacteria the child drinks it. That same child will understand that if cold it needs covers and if thirsty it needs water.

In THE LION KING Simba the cub did not perceive any threat around his uncle but he did know he wanted his father's good opinion of him. He did understand the encroaching danger of the stampede and the snapping snarling hyenas, but not the dangers of the parched land he escaped into. So his poor choices created dangerous situations he was not prepared to figure out. He lacked the experience to compare, contrast, consider consequence and choose differently. However, by the time he had matured into a full-gown lion aware of his own power (in size and his mighty roar), he was capable of doing that higher level of thinking. He perceived the jeopardy and chose to confront it because of his higher goal beyond his own selfish needs. That created a satisfaction in the audience vicariously experiencing this story with him.

So, Writer, you need to consider with every one of your characters what they are willing to do, what they absolutely refuse to do and what they need to learn to become aware of different choices. Never make anything coincidental. Make the character have to work for it. Remember Joseph in FAR AND AWAY who had bought a horse for the Oklahoma land race then came out of the drinking tent to find the aged animal dead? The only other horse for sale was a wild, barely-broke young horse that he had to fight to ride in the race.

Make your Character have to fight every inch of the way! If they become too comfortable or complacent like Simba did living with Timon and Pumba, that's when you throw another confrontation in his path like Nala who piqued his conscience and his love interest.

Progressive Concepts to Consider:

1) Appropriate Title
2) Types of Suspense utilized
3) Webbing of related elements
4) First 10 minutes prepared audience for the balance of the story
5) Character consistency after Introduction
6) Unique defiance of predictability
7) Opposition intensity increased
8) Character demonstration of profile history
9) Consequences of back-story
10) Identification of Character Arc
11) Use of Sex and Violence blatant or subtle

* * * * *

SHREK

By Ted Elliott, Terry Rosslo, Joe Stillman, Roger S.H. Schulman
2001 Mike Myers, Eddie Murphy, Cameron Diaz

Length: 86 Minutes

Log Line: A self-deprecating Ogre goes on quest to reclaim his home but finds live instead.

Statement of Purpose: To prove character strength, courage and lovability are not dictated by appearance.

Intro Image: Fairy Tale book with V.O. about "Love's First Kiss"

First 10 minutes
Who:
Crude, loner Ogre Shrek
Wise-cracking, irrepressible Donkey
Many familiar Fairy Tale personas being ensalved
When: Once-upon-a-time
Where: Make-believe land surrounding Shrek's swamp
What: Fairy Tale personas being enslaved so escaping to swamp
Why: They will not be hunted in the Ogre's swamp because villagers & soldiers afraid

Four related subplots:
Reluctant friendship of Shrek & Donkey
Farquaad's pursuit of Fiona for her kingdom
Fiona's secret & love story
Persecution of the Fairy Tale personas

Time Line: About a week

Image repeats:
Castle
Soldiers
Villagers
Crude humor
Day-to-Night cycles
Safety-yet-threat of illusions

Act I = Set-up of Ordinary World Shrek's simple swamp life invaded/ disrupted
10 min **Intro:** Shrek's gross swamp invaded by donkey & other Fairy Tale personas
14 min **Inciting Incident**: Donkey tells of Farquaad's eviction & need for sanctuary
19 min **PP I:** Farquaad is going to have a tournament to determine Princess Fiona's rescuer

Act II = Life 180 degrees: Shrek goes questing to regain his swamp
36 min **Pinch I:** Shrek finds the beautiful Princess but merely awakens & drags along
50 min **Mid-Point:** Fiona overhears Shrek's self-deprecating & decides to be nonjudgemental
58 min **Pinch II**: Fiona entices Shrek with flirting
66 min **PPII:** Shrek overhears only portion of Fiona's Ogre comments & thinks applies to him

Act III = Shrek confronts Farquaad to claim Fiona
74 min **Climax:** Donkey convinces Shrek to forcefully interrupt wedding to proclaim his love
81 min **Commitment**: Love's First Kiss changes Fiona permanently to an Ogre like Shrek
82 **After-story Conclusion**: Shrek & Fiona wedding with Fairy Tale persona celebration

Dialogue Notes:
Shrek's Scottish accent
Donkey's rapid-fire wit
Farquaad's demanding & manipulative tone
Tonal exaggeration of Fairy Tale personas

Alpha Character posturing differences:
Shrek cranky, sarcastic vs. Donkey, energetic,
Shrek vs. Farquaad
Shrek vs. Fiona
Changes in Fiona between Princess & Ogre personas

Supporting cast Unique Character Gems:
Fairy Tale personas
Farquaad's laughable "evil"
Female Dragon's attraction to Donkey

Background effects, the nuances of aura:
Shrek's hut
Crumbling Castle & lava moat
Shrek's swamp
Non-threatening aura of the forest
Atmosphere of the castle

Elements from Other Genres: Romance, Fantasy, Action-Adventure

Question: Could Farquaad have been portrayed as more evil-intentioned and meaner than the wimpy character we saw? Remember Prince Humperdink in THE PRINCESS BRIDE and how gruesome his tortures were, yet that is a children's favorite.

Appearance or reference to recurrence of Evil Theme in Min: Farquaad's selfish/sinister persona in **BOLD** and most of rest evolved consequences from choices.

Act I = Set-up of Ordinary World Shrek's simple swamp life invaded/disrupted

1-2 Fairy Tale book with V.O., Shrek tears out paper for outhouse use.
3 Villagers hunt the Ogre but are terrified
4-5-6 Fairy Tale personas are enslaved, talking donkey, flying runs to Shrek where wants to stay
8 – 9 Continues to follow Shrek, I'm an Ogre, This is my home
10 "I like my privacy" "Can I stay, please?" No! Sleep outside
11 – 12 Mealtime, watched by Donkey, shadows of Blind Mice
13 Wolf in bed, throwa out finding characters in yard, "Why are you in my swamp?"
14 Inciting Incident = Didn't invite you, Lord Farquaad evicted us
15 Donkey with Shrek to confront Farquaad, no singing.
16 Farquaad in castle, torture Gingerbread Man, Do you know the Muffin Man?,
17-19 Plot Point I= Magic Mirror choice of Cinderella, Sleeping Beauty, Fiona, chooses Fiona who needs rescuing so plans a tournament to select someone to rescue her FOR him.

Act II = Life 180 degrees: Shrek goes questing to regain his swamp

20-21 Shrek & Donkey arrive, frighten gatekeeper, Shrek in armor, imperfect world
22-24 Trmpet & far. Announces tournament, Shrek enters
25 Shrek wins & announces wants his swamp back if frees Fiona, Far. agrees.

26-28 Donkey joins, Shrek like onion = sticks, layers, Not everybody likes onions
29-30 Find bridge to castle over molten lava, cross, don't look down, Shrek backs Donkey across
32-35 Donkey to handle dragon as Shrek to highest room, Girl Dragon fancies Donkey
36 **Pinch I** = Shrek finds beautiful Fiona, shakes awake, rescuing you, drags with
37-39 Fiona rebels "What kind of knight are you? One kind. Donkey handles Dragon
40-41 Fiona Praises Shrek & wants remove helm & kiss, "Not your type"
42-44 You're an Ogre! Sent by Farquaad. Need true love, Shrek carries, woods cave
45-47 Night sky, Shrek telling Ogre stories, Ogre against the world
48 **Mid-Point** = Fiona behind cave door listens & watches
49-53 Beautiful Princess, sing/bird explodes, burps, I won't judge you
54-57 Confront & battle Robin Hood's men, Donkey arrow, embarrassment
58-60 Pinch II = Shrek & Fiona playing & flirting
61-62 Dark, Fiona in building, Shrek denies like
64-65 Donkey goes in finds Oger "Ate the Princess" No AM Fiona
66 **Plot Point II** = Fiona talks of spell and how everyone hating ugly Ogre as "horrible, ugly beast" Shrek hears, drops flowers, leaves campsite.

Act III = Shrek confronts Farquaad to claim Fiona
67 Back to beautiful Princess, Shrek standoffish
68-69 "Who could love a hideous beast" Farquaad arrives, wants married today
70-71 Shrek offends Fiona and Donkey, Living useless life, Fiona ready for wedding
72 Farquaad in crown, Shrek alone, Donkey alone, Dragon crying, Fiona alone
73-75 Donkey build wall for half of swamp, Friends forgive, Ask Fionna, whistles for Dragon
76-78 Climax (Begin) = Dragon fly them to castle, wedding "Get to I do" Wait for love, can't marry unless for love, romantic crap, "I object" Ogre can fall in love with a Princess
79 Preposterous, (sun setting) Fiona transforms, Far. "Disgusting"
80 Climax (End) = Far pulls sword, Dragon through window, Shrek & Fiona fight together
81 **Commitment** = "You are beautiful" Fiona kisses and she stays Ogre with enchantment done
82-86 **After-story** = Shrek & Fiona wedding followed by lots of Fairy Tale personas celebrating

CONCEPTS DISCUSSION

Like most Disney movies, this one followed the Hero's Journey so the storytelling elements should have been easy to note. Perhaps you were also able to identify the Fantasy elements as you marched through the Progressive points you've learned so far. But, here again is a G-rated movie that has mature elements that appeal to different ages. The total package makes for memorable cross-genre appeal.

USE OF STATEMENT OF PURPOSE

If a writer does not know the POINT of the story, then the chances are high that the story will wander and even prove to be vague and disjointed at times. With a definitive objective in mind the story, characters, plot and details remain focused and purposeful. That is especially important in juvenile stories where many innuendos and literary or artistic cinematic illusions are lost on the child seeking a straightforward story and not something they have to contemplate and figure out.

The "message" of SHREK is simple and definitive. Every character, every scene, every event, every speech served to prove the point of the story. The charm rested with the familiar made to be unique and humorous. That contributed to the overall point that we can be comfortable with those we like and love, no matter what their appearance!

Both when planning and when in the throes of writing fast, if a writer has a solid statement of purpose it is simple to identify what kinds of characters and events one needs in that story. In SHREK it was logical to have a Main Character who was ugly and ostracized, a loner who like being alone . . . then prove to him that he shouldn't be alone, that he could be appreciated and like for who he was, not what he looked like. Logically then you had to create characters who needed him. In proving his ultimate integrity and willingness to sacrifice, he proved himself worthy of their caring. And to the audience as well. His ultimate journey prove the statement of purpose of the overall story. The simplicity of that statement of purpose made it appeal to juvenile audience members.

HOLLYWOOD'S USE OF SEX & VIOLENCE

Interestingly, the attraction or sexuality of SHREK is treated "as a matter of course" without any titillating innuendo. But it is still there. What is it about the beautiful Princess Fiona that makes her so much more appealing in the general context of "a pretty girl?" Then why is it so "right" that Shrek marry a female Ogre and that they share "Love's First Kiss?" Why do people marry? Why do they kiss? The flirting and hand holding is natural but children do not think of it beyond that "natural state." Yet the implication is there: ultimate procreation (which they did have the triplets in a sequel). Family, home, sharing life with others. That is the essence of Shrek. And the flirtatious dragon with Donkey creates such an incongruity that one's funny bone is tickled, but the concept is still attraction for the sake of mating.

And jeopardy and Violence was rampant in Shrek's life. The villagers came to attack him. They didn't mean to tie him up and swat him for being naughty. They meant to kill him. Look at the assault on the Gingerbread Man. Here was an entity who could talk and feel and his legs have been ripped off. And what about that martial arts display by the Princess Fiona with Robin Hood's men? Children's stories are rampant with threats of violence and heroes coming out triumphant. Of course there isn't as much graphic violence as in the battle scenes of GLADIATOR and BRAVEHEART.

> A FACT OF LIFE IN HOLLYWOOD IS THE CENSORS ARE PARTICULARLY VIGILANT OF JUVENILE FILMS.

A fact of life in Hollywood is the censors are particularly vigilant of juvenile films. If you think of it as a lack of blood and demonstration of pain, a lack of titillating details that children would not relate to, you can easily see where juvenile stories need to skim or allude to in order to meet reasonable standards for the sensibilities of children.

Does every adult story need explicit sex or graphic violence to be deemed truthful and authentic? Of course not. Those elements are enhancements of the events of the story, they are not the most important facets of the character's journey. If you think so then you do not as yet understand the meaning of storytelling and character development. The words "WHEN APPROPRIATE" need to be carved into your brain. If you are faithful to that concept, you will know when to skim and when to use detail in your screenplay.

WILLINGNESS TO TAKE RISKS

What makes SHREK a great hero is that he valued one thing all children can identify, his home. He was willing to leave the safety and security of his swamp to confront a power greater than himself. He was willing to risk his safety to regain control of his swamp and his concept of home. We had been shown how he confronted and scared off the villagers, but now he is going to castle that has men in armor and archers who could take his life. What does he do there but accepts the challenge of rescuing a princess just so he can have the privacy of his swamp back. And what does he end up fighting for? A love that he wants to last his lifetime.

Your Character Profiles will identify those things people care about, what they hold dear, as well as their willingness to take risks to protect or regain what they value. That willingness to take risks must be as unique as the goals of each human being. A farmer who has had a multitude of dogs through the years sees them as helpful animals but not as valued companions. Most farmers will not spend hundreds of dollars on a dog's health care if they develop a disease like cancer. But for a young boy who cherishes his dog, he will stand up to his parents and may even risk humiliation to beg the veterinarian to give his dog the medications he needs to live as long as possible. Do you see the difference in values and willingness to take risks?

Great Protagonists are not only vulnerable in some way, but they are also willing to step beyond their own safety zone to take risks of the known and unknown kinds. Think about that, known and unknown.

Progressive Concepts to Consider:

1) Appropriate Title
2) Types of Suspense utilized
3) Webbing of related elements
4) First 10 minutes prepared audience for the balance of the story
5) Character consistency after Introduction
6) Unique defiance of predictability
7) Opposition intensity increased
8) Character demonstration of profile history
9) Consequences of back-story
10) Identification of Character Arc
11) Use of Sex and Violence blatant or subtle

At this point, you should be comfortable and familiar with 11 of 24 film concepts utilized to analyze films you watch and in your own script. Anything is possible when tackled a little at a time. Recite them, identify them, practice them.

* * * * *

GENRE FILM Chapter 7 Exercises

Exercise 7a. Write Pg. 31-35 playing up subplots, insecure character reactions to risk.

Exercise 7b. Where have you paced your "Jeopardy" so far in Act II? Have you depicted your Protag reluctant to react physically or the opposite: too much the instinctual hothead? (Remember that even verbal sparring implies risk/jeopardy to the calm routine.

Exercise 7c. Write Pg 37-41 thru Pinch I, the startling awareness of greatest fear Protag would prefer to avoid at all costs then reactions of avoidance/over-compensation/change of subject. Focus on expanding field of influence, learning, achievement of new skills or reinforcement of latent skills.

Exercise 7d. Track your Protag's dialogue so far for false bravado rather than arrogance, subtle vulnerability and self-doubt created by the worsening challenges of the New World. How many new characters have appeared so far in Act II? Has there been any face-to-face interaction between Antag and Protag yet?

Exercise 7e. Have you categorized your story according to your Main Plot? Have you identified any of the other genres' elements and/or their plots that could be reflected in your subplots?

CHAPTER 8

Pinches, Anxiety Curve, Antagonist/Horror Genre

If it seems to you that you are being asked to periodically back-track in this book to recall previous concepts, you are absolutely correct. The reason is that you must constantly be thinking of cause-effect consequences. Everything that has gone before should be reflected in what follows.

Chapter 7 discussed the Character Arc, the impact of the events on the Main Character's **Inner Essence** that changes his or her attitude and actions, his or her **External Identity** as seen in the role played out in the movie. Two sign-posts aimed directly at depicting that Inner Essence are 1) in the middle of the first half of Act II, Pinch I that depicts how the Character reacts to the spotlight shining on his or her greatest fear . . . and 2) in the middle of the second half of Act II that Pinch II which is the prideful moment for the Main Character when the Mentor or the public acknowledges the character's abilities or "greatness." Both are nudges at the Main Character's self-concept.

PURPOSE OF PINCH I

Somewhere close to Pg 37 of your script you should have a situation that truly rattles the Main Character. It doesn't have to be related directly to the Antagonist. It does have to shine a spotlight on the Main Character's awareness and acknowledgement of that which is most feared, the one thing hidden in the deepest part of the Character's psyche because it is too painful, too disturbing to tell anyone else. If you just thought that the Antagonist should have such a flaw, too, you are absolutely correct . . . but your story is about the Main Character.

This Pinch I signpost allows the audience to empathize with the inner humanity of the Main Character. We all have fears we prefer not to share in "touchy-feely" moments. They hint of vulnerability being judged, inadequacy being pointed out. Acknowledging this fear should make the character feel less worthy of what he or she is trying to accomplish. It is the chink in the psyche's armor. And guess, what You-the-Writer are going to do with it, once you have introduced it? Yup, you will refer to or call it up it at some key point latter then use it by forcing your Main Character to confront that fear and over-come it with "Herculean" emotional effort.

Example: Indiana Jones in RAIDERS OF THE LOST ARK. His greatest fear was snakes. What happened at Plot Point II of the movie? He was thrown into a deep vault literally crawling with thousands of snakes. <Shiver> Did he become a screaming, insane maniac? Nope. He was set up as a problem-solving, physically resourceful man so he defied his fear and escaped. His inner most fear had been introduced early on in the movie then used. The power of his character dictated he overcome that fear when it became a life and death issue.

THE POWER OF HIS CHARACTER DICTATED HE OVERCOME THAT FEAR WHEN IT BECAME A LIFE AND DEATH ISSUE.

PURPOSE OF PINCH II

Close to Page 67 (approximately half way between Mid-point's Epiphany and Plot Point II's Dark Moment) the Main Character (and the audience) need a "feel good moment" when accomplishment is acknowledged in the story. The Mentor says something along the lines "You have exceeded my expectations" or the agent calls to say that one of the top talk show hosts wants an interview or the adopted daughter throws her arms around the soldier dad proclaiming "Having you home is the best!" The event has to be equal to what the character has achieved in the story on a visceral level that will make the character feel proud and confident. It is a visually emotional moment.

Pinch II is an important signpost because just beyond the horizon lurks assault, defeat, failure. This moment is important in the ebb-and-flow of a story that is not all action-adventure, but about how the events make the character feel. If you have done your storytelling job well, the audience will feel and appreciate the same positive "warm fuzziness" the character experiences. Self-concept is at an all-time high and the character forges ahead, confidently determined to attain the ultimate goal.

Do not think the Protag has completed his or her Character Arc. That will not come until the true test in the Climax.

CONCEPT OF THE ANXIETY CURVE

Any writer who carefully manipulates anxiety in a story knows how to control both character and plot.

Anxiety is commonly recognized as "feeling troubled." In reality it is more than that. A normal amount of anxiety is

ANXIETY IS COMMONLY RECOGNIZED AS "FEELING TROUBLED." IN REALITY IT IS MORE THAN THAT.

necessary for human beings to survive. Hunger stimulates concern enough to seek food. Feeling cold leads to the creation of shelter, clothing, and artificial warmth. The threat to life or life style prompts offense, defense, or flight. These are all actions growing out of anxiety over well being. The responses are called coping mechanisms.

Normal coping mechanisms and the perceptions of options are learned from life experiences, such as trial and error deductions or focused education. A dependent child cries to be fed, later learns to complain, and ultimately is trained to seek and prepare its own food. A physically or mentally weaker person may not perceive any option but to endure or surrender to tyranny, whereas a conditioned soldier will choose deliberate actions to ensure survival.

A concept known to health care providers is called "The Anxiety Curve." What a simple model that writers can use in storytelling! Refer to the diagram of the U-shaped horseshoe figure in Appendix H.

At one end is total **panic** wherein the person's thoughts are too scattered to direct purposeful action. The adrenaline-fed "fight or flight" response is the side of the curve climbing toward panic. The person trembles, sweats profusely but the mouth is dry, heart pounds, eyes dilate with darting gaze registering nothing. The mind cannot focus. If thoughts fire so fast the person cannot grasp one the result is Panic.

At the other end or pole of the U-shaped spectrum is **apathy**, total surrender of the "will-to-live." This person is limp, unresponsive to any stimulation, staring with a blank, almost marble-like gaze, a state psychology calls "Catatonic." The emptiness in the blank expression makes the observer shiver. Depression is an early manifestation of the slide up this side of the curve. The skin is cold and pale, heart rate slow, pupils pin-point. This person is withdrawing inward. Apathy.

Most humans exist at the apex of the Anxiety Curve, one day excited in response to new challenges to survival, the next day exhausted and wanting only to be left alone to relax and vegetate or giving in to spurts of self-pity and depression.

When you think of it logically you realize this ebb-and-flow or advance-and-retreat manner of coping with life maintains a balance of physical and mental health. Remaining too long on either limb of the Anxiety Curve results in overload on the struggles to cope.

So, what happens when the world's stressors push the person further and further either toward panic or toward apathy? What happens when intense or traumatic events push that person beyond their ability to cope? And how can the writer maximize the drama of the Anxiety Curve concept in the storytelling process?

An incredibly well-crafted example exists in a Diana Gabaldon novel, *OUTLANDER.* In the climax the hero ransoms his lady's release from prison with his own body. The antagonist had been lusting for the warrior from early in the book. Jamie Fraser agrees not to fight the rape if his Claire is set free.

The released woman finds help to raid the stronghold. They find Jamie near death. As she nurses him she realizes his body is recovering, but his self-concept had been so shattered that Jamie is sliding toward apathy. Desperate to pull him back from surrendering his will to live, she anoints herself with the perfumed oil favored by the rapist and goes into Jamie's darkened room. Rather than surrender again, the terrified man calls up his warrior mode of coping, swings around that Anxiety Curve, and fights, nearly killing the woman he loves . . . but once again challenged to live.

Think about intensely dramatic moments in movies like FOREST GUMP, GONE WITH THE WIND, and even Disney's POLLYANNA. The characters exist by habit more toward one end of the Anxiety Curve but are forced toward the other end. Is it always from apathy to the "fight-or-flight?" Think about all the characters, not just the main players. Sometimes the slide of a supporting character is what prompts the response of main character.

CHARACTER ANXIETY FOR STORYTELLERS

Classically, writers start with characters seeking some goal but encountering opposition. Conflict thus story results. To heighten the drama, how far can story characters be pushed from their "normal" coping mechanisms?

Human beings truly do learn what coping mechanisms work best for them as individuals. A child identifies something wanted and considers how to get that thing, be it an extra portion of dessert or to accompany a reluctant sibling on an excursion. Whining works with Mom but only makes Dad more likely to say "No." Perhaps manipulation of the sibling, even bribery achieves the goal. Frequently children and sometimes even adults move through a series of trial and error to identify what works and what doesn't.

When the goal is denied how do different humans respond? Some react with dark, ugly physical anger to release the inner frustration and regain a sense of control over something. The eternal optimist, on the other hand, shrugs and looks elsewhere for satisfaction. Experience of results and an inner awareness of consequences and options all contribute to these diverse and unique **coping mechanisms**. Sometimes even delay tactics can be a manner of coping since delay can provide time to research, to gather more data, to consider more options.

FASCINATING CHARACTERS ARE THOSE WHO ARE NOT SIMPLE REACTORS TO STRESS, BUT THOSE WHO THINK, OBSERVE, CONSIDER OPTIONS AND ARE INTELLIGENT.

Fascinating characters are those who are not simple reactors to stress, but those who think, observe, consider options and are intelligent. These are the characters who act and cause the subsequent events to happen. They "cope and cause." Yes, the audience may catch on and attempt to predict how a character will cope with whatever challenge is thrown at them, but the careful writer will weave in that unpredictable factor of character enlightenment of sudden understanding. Thus the audience encounters (with the character) the choice of an unpredictable option.

How does a thinking writer achieve this without being obvious? Every major player in any story requires a Character Profile describing each character's unique life history of experiences and deliberate education. Remember coping mechanisms are learned from these incidents. When a new character is "born" in a writer's imagination with a detailed history, the writer can naturally predict and describe how that character copes, how that character acts in each and every situation.

Basically, once in-depth Character Profiles have been developed, the writer should be able to elaborate three simple factors and use them to tell the story:

1) How does this character demonstrate anxiety?
2) What coping mechanisms does the character perceive as options and habitually use?
3) Where is the character's "breaking point" that will dramatically send him/her sliding toward either end of the Anxiety Curve?

Here's a simple formula to rely on:
Profile + Personality Type + Stress = Coping Style

ANXIETY MADE APPARENT

Think of how you or anyone you know demonstrates anxiety. That baseline will provide you a relative "normal". . . or make you aware of unique habits, stress-relieving habits. Examples could be as simple as nail-biting, fingers through the hair, or rambling conversation. More subtle habits could be bursts of criticism, gossiping, or selective attention.

Now, consider your character's background from childhood right up to the moment of your story's opening scene. Do not choreograph every nuance, but understand and write in how your character habitually responds to typical stress, both physically and mentally.

Give the character depth with unique qualities and habits the audience can look for as indicators of mounting tension. The simple result is no more stereotyping!

FOR THE PLOT: POSSIBILITIES OUT OF ANXIETY

A writer who knows the characters well can plan events that will push each character's buttons and produce logically yet vividly dramatic events. So, yes, you can apply the Anxiety Curve concepts to all characters.

Do you know people who ignore the disorganization of clutter in home and office yet become agitated when schedules are not kept? If sarcastic anger or manipulative coaxing is how this person copes with an unacceptable stressor, wouldn't the writer want to use this in the story plot?

Taking it one step further, the writer can select pivotal events that truly push the character to the limits of their ability to cope. The result is logically rising tension. Identify each character's emotional breaking point then put that person on the dramatic path that will demand the supreme emotional effort . . . in their effort to return to the "normal" apex of their Anxiety Curve . . . and take the satisfied audience along for the high-power ride.

DRAMA REQUIRES AN ANTAGONIST

"Opposition" was addressed in Chapter 5 with a discussion of major and minor antagonistic elements. And by this time you should have concluded that each genre has its own conventions of the "kinds" of antagonists needed to meet audience expectations. Now, it is time to enhance your concepts of subtleties of both major and minor antagonistic elements.

Protagonists are only as powerful as the Antagonists they have to overcome. Every primary Antagonist absolutely must be as motivated, powerful and interesting as the Protagonist. From your Log Line and Statement of Purpose you were able to identify the essential opposition the Protagonist must face. Did you profile that person or persons?

What motivates the Antagonist should evolve as the main threat to the Protagonist throughout the entire story. Obviously, that motivation had better be pretty important to keep the Antagonist actively determined. An Antagonist need not be a dark and savage Villain with evil, abhorrent thoughts and behaviors. An Antagonist is simply opposed to allowing the Protagonist to succeed. They do not see themselves are evil, merely as right and the Protagonist as wrong. The days of "black hat vs. white hat" people and values died with the 1930's westerns. Your job is to depict an opposing character the audience can understand and even empathize with. As the story evolves, the values and motivations must make the audience identify more with the "Good" side of the equation.

An Antagonist complicates the Protag's way of life and makes him or her work harder to achieve the desired goal. On the other hand, a dark, repulsive Villain has zero redeeming qualities and is out to destroy life, principles, the social order simply to further his or her own agenda. This kind of negative or evil force lacks conscience or appreciation for the value of life and answers to no one. Their motivations and rationalizations are focused on self actualization. Look at each genre's antagonist qualities then consider you Log Line and your Statement of Purpose. Does your story require only an Antagonist or is your drama better served by a Villain?

Do not overlook the antagonistic elements that can be found in Nature's uncontrollable impact or the expectations of Social-Cultural-Moral or Professional agendas. These can be merely antagonistic or villainess. The tornadoes in TWISTER even had "monster" type growls. Many a story has grown out of a restrictive, demanding, punitive social-cultural-moral society. What happened between Tevya and his youngest daughter Chava in FIDDLER ON THE ROOF?

Ultimately you must choreograph how the Protagonist responds to worsening confrontations. What makes your Protagonist shift from reaction to action, from recipient of dictates and consequences to the force that changes or causes events? That "taking control" to overcome the Antagonist(s) is the last half of the story. Credible success or failure is up to your storytelling ability.

Pay attention to what experience will make your Antagonist/Villain feel triumphant. The last half of Act II is where you build your story to create that event when the Antagonist shoves the Main Character into a no-win situation, a corner where he or she has only two choices of give up or come out fighting. Every situation, reaction, dialogue exchange, subplot contributions, the emotional tweaks of your Pinches, has built to this moment when you Antagonist has won and your Protagonist is defeated. The Antagonist is celebrating as the Protagonist weeps. The Antagonist is swinging up his or her Anxiety Curve on the euphoric, pulse-pounding side while the Protagonist is crawling toward his or her Apathetic cave to lick wounds.

HORROR GENRE

The final third of the Speculative Fiction genre is Horror wherein a human's worse nightmares are made realistic and credible. The end result is the audience experiences the emotion of fear--deep, visceral fear--that is termed horror. The stories depict and the characters experience vulnerability, loss of security and the threat of pain and death, elements that human beings fight to avoid and overcome. So, what is the allure of such stories? Isn't it exactly that hope of the capacity to battle, overcome and survive?

From the Horror Writers Association website: "In his 1982 anthology *Prime Evil,* author Douglas Winter stated, 'Horror is not a genre, like the mystery or science fiction or the western. It is not a kind of fiction, meant to be confined to the ghetto of a special shelf in libraries or bookstores. Horror is an emotion.' He was correct and his words have become a rallying cry for the modern horror writer."

Think of the eerie and chilling atmosphere created by such masters as Poe, Shelley's *Frankenstein* or Stevenson's *Dr. Jekyll and Mr. Hyde,* Stephen King and Dean Koontz, right down to the simplistic "slasher" and "hauntings" stories of pop culture.

One uncomfortable discussion related how vividly terrifying images came from disturbed or "enhanced" mental images as when Stephen King's *Kujo* was written when he was high on cocaine. This explained a lot of the story to fans. If you're curious how mind-altering drugs can impact the mind (but appropriately unwilling to give it a try), read any of Carlos Castenadas' books describing the frightening monsters that appear to those using hallucinogens as part of their Native American religion. Many a cancer patient receiving chemo therapy will tell you of similar such visions the couple of nights after each chemo-therapy treatment. Chemo therapy drugs are almost caustic thus can cause changes in the neurological pathways in the brain with vivid, horrifying nightmares resulting. All who have experienced this are thankful the side effect is very transient.

Your most powerful horror stories will evolve from your own greatest fears. You may even be able to better cope with and understand those fears if you depict and control them in a Horror story! For example people with snake phobias had their greatest fear played out in RAIDERS OF THE LOST ARK between Indie and those snakes. Avid swimmers with vivid imaginations vicariously experienced the persistent attack of that damn shark in JAWS!

INCORPORATING HORROR INTO ANOTHER STORY

Dig into your own mind for a specific, almost therapeutic reason. When writers truly examine what hurts them the most, they depict an intensity that more generalized writing treats in a shallow, ho-hum manner.

It's like a 12-year old 6th grader writing a story with a cast of adults. The kid simply does not get it right. But when the story is re-casted to the 12-yr-old's POV, the perception of the events and reactions makes the story credible. The adult audience member can see beyond the child character's perception to evaluate what they think was really going on with the adults. But the child character attains credibility for his/her own level of understanding and a very poignant story can result.

WHEN WRITERS TRULY EXAMINE WHAT HURTS THEM THE MOST, THEY DEPICT AN INTENSITY THAT MORE GENERALIZED WRITING TREATS IN A SHALLOW, HO-HUM MANNER.

So, some psychology practice theories encourage repetitive problem issues or phobias be fictionally depicted with a positive resolution the person controls as a way to rid the mind of reliving and thinking about the negative possibilities. People who have written like this experience rare subsequent nightmares.

One of the Horror films analyzed here is LAST BREATH, (written, directed, starred by Ty Jones), an incredibly moving story with an ultimate moral that will leave you profoundly changed. That is not exaggeration or hyperbole, but a phenomena reported at every theater the film was shown in around the U.S. and overseas. Ty used his own "worst nightmare" scenarios, paired them with an available location for the climax of the film and played out lessons to be learned from preventable human errors. Even for those who are not fans of Horror film, this one will be a unique and moving experience. It is solid, laudable storytelling by an independent film-maker.

FUNDAMENTAL CONCEPTS OF HORROR

1. Make the audience care about the characters then focus on the frightening, not the logical.
- According to the sophistication of the targeted audience, it generally takes a lot of the unpredictable and unexpected to truly engage the fear factor of a Horror enthusiast.

2. Play to the wildest extreme of fears in the Protagonist and force that person to face the power of the Antagonist.
- Perpetual hiding and escape does not make for a tense, enthralling reading experience. The Protagonist must confront and sacrifice to the Antagonist until the ultimate Climactic Battle.

3. Play the ebb-and-flow game of threat-injury-recovery until the supreme test.
- Slowing of down time through exposition and description must ease the audience's tension/concern to provide a truly engrossing story that involves the audience's intellect and all the senses. The audience has to experience the story with the characters!

4. Draw from the Protagonist's Character Profile to attack both strengths and vulnerability and keep attacking until Protag either fails or grows!
- The sequencing of the Protagonist's journey to avoid pain and survive demands a masterful melding of Alpha and Beta characteristics. Too much Alpha, the Protagonist can become melodramatic and humorous, but too much Beta will create a character the audience sees as too weak to root for. Carefully identify each character's contribution and role in the Survival Game.

5. Avoid stereotypes and predictability by multi-layering character motivations, threat and skills.
- Do not model but break the mold. Always. One method is to play off your very own worst fears, your very own nightmares. That will personalize your story and shine through your writing.

6. SURPRISE is not suspense.
- Suspense builds gradually with more risks, more at stake, tightening the tension of the fear toward the panic state, toward the state of unable to think what to do next with fewer options available. Abrupt flashes of a threat will surprise the audience but not necessarily frighten. Avoid the gimmicks and clichés at all costs because they too will not create suspense.

HORROR CHARACTER REQUIREMENTS

Since Horror stories can evolve in any of the other genres, the representative Protagonists must be susceptible to one factor all human beings share: **fear of the loss of control.** Antagonists in Horror stories are focused on **over-powering and controlling**, be it delivering pain or actually taking life.

HORROR PLOT TYPES

1. End-of-Time/Apocalyptic
2. Catastrophe/Natural Disaster unleashing the unknown
3. Alien Invasion
4. Animal/Nature gone awry
5. Shape-shifting/Vampire/Werewolves
6. Ghostly haunting/Dark Afterlife
7. Insanity/Psychopath
8. Oppression/Persecution/Revenge
9. Torture/Entrapment/Isolation
10. Nightmare-to-Reality
11. Monster evolution and attack
12. Satanic/Cult coming to power
13. Witches and Warlocks

HORROR FILM ANALYSIS

These repetitive forms of analysis are intended to train your mind and imagination to look for key elements of character, story and genre. The Progressive Concepts should become a checklist for you to note and, hopefully, pay attention to in your own screenplays.

* * * * *

LAST BREATH

By Ty Jones
2010, Starring Ty Jones, Mandy Bannon

Length: 83 minutes (running time after credits)

Log Line: Struggling with a disintegrating marriage, a couple is imprisoned by a sadistic stalker and forced to make choices that will ultimately determine their family's survival. .

Statement of Purpose: To prove that parental behaviors can have dire consequences on the innocent.

Intro Image: Disheveled masculine figure approaching building at night

First 10 minutes
Who:
Michael, workaholic, distracted husband & father
Caleb, idealistic elementary school-age son trying to "get it right" with father & mother
Tina, impatient, insecure wife and mother, with a drinking problem
When: Contemporary
Where: Suburban area with tidy houses & business potential
What: Tenuous family members on edge with one another
Why: Son's fears of seeing stalker ignored, frustrated mother's careless habits create short-temper, hyper-critical husband admired at work for his ambition

Four related subplots:
Husband's infidelity
Wife's alcoholism
Family relationship errors
Stalker's efforts

Time Line: Two weeks of marriage disintegration with ultimate flashbacks of lifetime of bad choices

Image repeats:
Family portraits
Female seductress
Rats
Knife
Polaroid photos

Eavesdropping
Phone conversations

Act I = Set-up of Ordinary World: Establish fractured, superficial, selfish family members
10 min **Intro:** Family of insincere promises, superficial caring efforts, loss of values
9 min **Inciting Incident**: Michael leaving his job to be on his own
19 min **PP I:** Michael has bought the dilapidated building for his dream factory

Act II = Life 180 degrees Stalker captures & ritualistically tortures couple separately
25 min **Pinch I:** Michael & Tina discover they are locked in the building
42 min **Mid-Point:** Michael awakens tied to tilt-table
49 min **Pinch II**: Tina concerned about Michael's status
55 min **PPII:** Loss of any control, "You've got 30 minutes

Act III = Resolution: Couple escapes tormentor but drawn back by conscience for redemption
59 min **Climax:** Michael knifes tormentor, Tina escapes but returns for Michael
89 min **Commitment**: Tina with Michael returns to comfort fallen tormentor
After-story Conclusion: "When I was little I felt safe because that was love."

Dialogue Notes:
Tina's whiney, demanding tone
Michael's manly "in control" attitude
Gradual shorter communications of Caleb
Stalker's growling anger

Alpha Character posturing differences:
Michael vs. Tina, focus & strength vs. insecurity & loss of control
Michael vs. Caleb, undermined father figure vs. needy child
Michael vs. Stalker, problem-solving man losing control to vicious torturer
Tina vs. Stalker, terrified woman bent on escape but emotional open

Supporting cast Unique Character Gems:
Caleb as "silent observer" in flashbacks
Stalker's persistence and deliberation

Background effects, the nuances of aura:
Dilapidated warehouse
Comfort of the middle class homes

Elements from Other Genres: Romance, Juvenile, Inspirational

Question: 1) Were the intro image of the Dark Figure and Caleb's complaining of seeing "somebody" at his window appropriate or misleading "Red Herrings?" 2) At what point did you "get" the Stalker/Tormentor?

Appearance or reference to recurrence of Evil Theme in Min: The vengeful Stalker/Tormentor appearance will be in **BOLD.**

Act I = Set-up of Ordinary World: Establish fractured, superficial, selfish family members

1 Glimpses of dirty, bloodied, violent-tempered man approaching building at night
2 Michael's "When I was little", promises
3-**4** Caleb with camera, fear of rats, **Polaroid of figure**
5-6 Caleb bumps mom dumping cake, her anger
7-8 "Excited for family" arguing, son listening & crying
9 **Inciting Incident:** Michael's construction crew "Miss us"
10 Your dad, Flashback of dad chastising him = Parenting example
11 Tina with photo album, apologizes
12 Letter from dead mother about love, **bloodied hand on window**
13-14 Michael's secretary Sara "Tonight?" "No, busy." Tina's suspicion,
15-16 "I believe in you." Back & forth shots, "Meant to be" empty OJ & Vodka bottle
17 VO of temptation as flashback affair & pained expression
18 Drive to warehouse, Tina waiting, doll floating in water
19-**20 Plot Point I:** Michael bought the building, enter, talk of factory, **bloodied hand of stalker**

Act II = Life 180 degrees: Stalker captures & ritualistically tortures couple separately

21-22 Consulting, cell call from Sara "I love you."
23-**24** Loved when with you, Please?, No!, separate, It's over, **bloodied door handle**
25 **Pinch I:** Locked/jammed, trying other doors, loud noise in warehouse
26 No cell signal, 2 more exits locked, noise, startled, hovering
27 Boy's recorded voice over sound system
28-29 Tina confronts Michael, shoves & runs off, collapses crying
30 Blood drips from pipes, stalker appears, running, Michael beating on door
31 Tina running, falls, hitting head, unconscious picked up by stalker, Michael reads message written in blood
32 Tina awakens in small, locked room, scurrying sounds

34 Rats emerge from pipe into room, Michael calling, tries overhead door, finds Polaroid

34 Footsteps then baseballs flying, stalker swings bat

35-36 Rat are on Tine, escapes thru duct work, rats follow, falls to floor

37-38 Stalker drags Michael, in chair, "When you hunt someone," "What you've done."

39-40 Tina trying doors, watch thru glass, Intercom voice, "Stop it!"

41 Pole with wires whirling toward her, beating, Injection

42 Blood dripping, Michael awakens on tilt table, noting electrical connections

43-45 Mid-Point: Tormentor forces to drink dissolved Viagra & takes photos, Explains stimulation will cause complete circuit & electricity, Sick, Michael: Whatever you want. Why buy this building? Not for family, Michael admits.

46 Can't go back: Flashbacks of childhood

47 Plastic over face "How does it feel?" = Everything about how Michael FEELS

48 Tina awakens, "Why doing this?" "I was listening . . ."

49-51 Pinch II: (Tina thinks connects with Stalker) Stalker folds message, "Where's Michael?" "Why care?" Photos, "You gave up so easily." "Tell me what I've done?"

52 Michael struggling until contact, electricity & screams

53.-**54** Tina: Mother kick then get in bed , gritting her teeth, Stopped feeling & listening, "What hear with heart?"

55-56 Plot Point II: Tubing, Stalker injects Tina, "You've got 30 minutes" Goes to Michael, sharpens knife

Act III = Resolution: Couple escapes tormentor but drawn back by conscience for redemption

57-58 **Stalker:** "Ever been cut? Must feel pain to feel pleasure or anything else. Same as sex drugs. Some just euphoria of pain. Dreamt of this place, this moment." Michael: "I don't even know you!"

59 Climax: Michael loosens one bolt, rams knife into Stalker, Gets out.

60 "Who are you?" Kicks, Opens door, iron pipe, Fight.

61 Tina strains against rope, frantically frees herself

62-63` Wedding ring, Michael staring at Stalker

64-65 Tina again running fleeing staggering Stalker, in bathroom stalls "Tina, have to hurt you." She escapes out hole in wall & finds Michael.

66 Tina watches Stalker kneeling with note, yelling at Michael.

67 Tina tries to awaken Michael

68 Vent to outside, sees man, can't leave Michael

69 Cell phone "Mom?" lost connection, Stalker

70 Tina finds room with Caleb's pics surrounded by torture photos, Wall bleeds onto photos.
71 Toys bloodied, hand grasps, Outside door opens, V. O. freedom & no more pain
72 Flashbacks of pristine moments of love & joyful life.
73 Door starts to close, Tina turns racing back to find Michael in chair, Man's hand
74-76 Tina awakens chained to chair beside Michael "I'm sorry, Trying to impress my dad. If I had you, I had everything." "I love you." Fingertips touching, Stalker watching through hole & staggers away.
77-78 Get out of bonds, hugging, Stalker collapses as they run to door where Tina hesitates with V.O "When your child is hurt"
79 **Commitment:** Tina returns to Stalker, clutches his bloody head: Flashbacks of Caleb listening to arguments, seeing moments of betrayal in teen years, baseball, knife for self-mutilation, her alcoholism, finding Tina's suicide note, what happened to me?, shootings, "Mommy!" Playing in the park, "lovng" Tina and Michael witness his "Last Breath."
82-83 **After-story:** Tina and Michael find themselves clean and unscathed, Stand to hug one another, car arrives at house where Caleb runs to greet them. "When I was little I felt safe because that was love."

CONCEPTS DISCUSSION

Identifying what works and why gives you the mental logic to apply the same storytelling elements in your own process. Look for them, think about them then apply them yourself. The procedure is: Fundamentals, Progressive Concepts, this genre's expectations.

FOR THE PLOT: POSSIBLITIES OUT OF ANXIETY

The plot events of LAST BREATH all grew out of what the boy Caleb perceived his parents had caused. Those factors that made the boy feel insecure, unsafe, unloved were reflected directly in the punishment dealt out by the "Stalker" (or grown and corrupted Caleb). In every scene, every page of this story the anxiety was only briefly allowed to drift toward Manageable middle of the Anxiety Curve when another threat was delivered. That sort of ratcheting of the stress level keeps the audience concerned about the safety of the characters and questing for the "Why" driving the tormentor.

When you look at the flaws of Tina and Michael, you see a natural evolution of consequences that the innocent child eventually brought down on them hoping there is a chance they will learn from their suffering to identify what he suffered with them throughout the years of his childhood.

Ultimately, every storyteller can pay attention to those motivations, conflicts, rising tension and resolutions that are natural to the point you want your story to prove.

DRAMA REQUIRES AN ANTAGONIST

What makes LAST BREATH so brilliant is that the Main Characters "created" their own Antagonist, the corruption of the innocent son based on their actions, not his. Yes, the Stalker/Tormentor made deliberate choices of how to torture Michael and Tina, but the adults were the originators in creating their own demented Antagonist. Their learning about themselves and the consequences of their behaviors allowed them to rise above the nightmare. Their acknowledgement allowed them to reverse their behavior thus prevent what "could have happened."

Ultimately the Antagonist proved to be the salvation for the couple, their road to redemption for a lifetime of selfish, hedonistic choices.

Evaluate the power of each Major Antagonist and create visual situations that will showcase the worst this character can be, the most challenge to take the Protagonist where you want him or her to prove they are worthy of triumphing.

Progressive Concepts to Consider:

1) Appropriate Title
2) Types of Suspense utilized
3) Webbing of related elements
4) First 10 minutes prepared audience for the balance of the story
5) Character consistency after Introduction
6) Unique defiance of predictability
7) Opposition intensity increased
8) Character demonstration of profile history
9) Consequences of back-story
10) Identification of Character Arc
11) Use of Sex and Violence blatant or subtle
12) Demonstration of Anxiety Curve
13) Contrasting qualities of Antagonist to Protagonist

* * * * *

THE GHOST AND THE DARKNESS

By William Goldman
1996 Paramount movie staring Michael Douglas & Val Kilmer

Length: 105 minutes

Log Line: An Irish engineer building a bridge in 1898 Africa must hunt two man-eating lions.

Statement of Purpose: To prove humans can control their fear and overcome Nature.

Intro Image: Tall grasses of Tsavo

First 10 minutes
Who:.
V.O. Samuel: The African Storyteller
Protagonist: Patterson: Confident, focused, competent engineer who will not be intimidated
**Minor Antagonist: Beaumont: Tyrannical, powerful man-in-control
Love Interest: Helena, Patterson's adoring, proper, well-spoken Victorian wife
When: 1898 (Superimposed on-screen)
Where: From luxurious England to chaotic, exotic Africa
What: Assignment of building a bridge over the River Tsavo in a designated period of time
Why: Competition is on their heels & project will make or break Patterson's reputation

**Note: The MAJOR Antagonist in the story is obviously Nature in the form of the man-eating lions but Beaumont's demands shove Patterson into their path.

Four related subplots:
Lions/Evil/Fear
Railroad/Job
Clash of Culture/Religion/Superstitions
Family References (all characters)

Time Line: Ten Months
Spring: Intro with Helena three months pregnant
24 hours: In Africa
3 months later: Pinch I, Starling's death & "behind schedule"

December: Mid Act III when Remington wishes "Merry Christmas. 'Tis the season.")
Ending: Helena arrives with two month old son.

Image repeats:
Grasses of Tsavo (that hide the threat)
Birth of child
Thorns
Helpless hospital patients
"Sort it out"
Control your fear
Owl (Symbol of Death in African Culture)
Claw necklace (Reminder of courage)
"Lions don't do this"
Flames consuming

Act I = Set-up of Ordinary World: Life from England to Tsavo
10 min **Intro:** From England to spectacle of Tsavo & Patterson's anticipation
17 min **Inciting Incident**: Patterson's One Shot
25 min PP I: Maheena's death by lion

Act II = Life 180 degrees: Hunting the lions
37 min **Pinch I:** Starling's death by 2 of them (Patterson's greatest fear = Helplessness)
60 min **Mid-Point:** Remington & his Masai hunt with Patterson's misfire
68 min **Pinch II**: Remington acknowledges Pattern's trap
71 min **PPII:** Hospital Slaughter by 2 Lions = Lions are Superior

Act III = Taking fight to the Lions
99 min **Climax:** Patterson's battle to kill the last lion
102min **Commitment**: Workers return, Helena & baby Son arrive
After-story: Samuel's V.O. Chicago's Field Museum "Still be afraid."

Dialogue Notes:
British speech patterns
Irish cadence (Kilmer had a speech coach, though I have heard some unfamiliar with the Irish culture criticize that he wasn't "Irish" enough . . . he is spot on with the educated Irish in contrast with the "common man" Irish.)
Samuel's "learned English" speech cadence
Abdullah's "learned English" speech cadence
Remington's Southern drawl

Alpha Character posturing differences:
Beaumont . . . flaws? (Contrast the arrogance with his demeanor)
Patterson . . . . flaws? (Contrast his waffling insecurities with his courage)
Remington . . flaws? (Contrast his "wounded warrior" essences with his pride in skill)

Supporting cast Unique Character Gems:
Samuel, intelligent, communicator, loyal, dependable
Maheena, confident, inner & outer strength as role model & motivator
Abdullah, leader by intellectual manipulation and mouthy, judgmental
Starling, hard-working, devout, determined to overcome wimpy affect
Dr. Hawthorne, alcoholic, sarcastic, competent & caring of patients
Masai, clique-ish, courageous warriors
Lions (actually used three, two from U.S. one from Europe)

Background effects, the nuances of aura:
Sophisticated English setting
Freedom & openness of the African vistas
Organized chaos of multi-cultural railroad camp
Crude hospital
Eeriness of Tsavo at night, both when clear or in ground fog
Vulnerability in the tents, on the grassy plains, in the cave lair
Difference of close quarters in tents vs. in the rail-car trap & hospital tent
Threat of mob vs. working together demonstrating effect of "Proxemics"

Elements from Other Genres: Historical, Inspirational

Question: Did you feel the panic of the hired guns in the railroad car trap was credibly choreographed? How would YOU have set-up and written that scene?

Appearance or reference to the Lions (recurrence of Evil Theme) in Min:
The unnatural Lions
Note: **BOLD** = Actually "see" the Lions . . . On the Paradigm along that line of the Lion subplot, a DOT would be placed every time the lions are brought up or depicted. Note greatest intensity the lions are present on-screen longer, but frequently mentioned or used when not on screen.

Act I = Set-up of Ordinary World: Life from England to Tsavo
15 Intro problem of lion attacks
16-18 Inciting Incident: Tree stand & "One Shot"
20 Maheena's story & looks to grasses
22 Lion POV, claw necklace
24-26 Plot Point I: Lion attack on Maheena

Act II = Life 180 degrees: Hunting the lions
27 Description of abnormal Lion feasting
29 Lion POV, Report of another kill
32 Lion in the grasses
33 Lion POV, watching
34-38 Pinch I: Lion attack, ID two, Starling's death
39 Image of lions trotting with V.O., Tsavo "A place of slaughter"
40 Fear & discussion with Abdullah
41-43 Report to Beaumont, about 30 dead, trap plan
44 Discussion & thorn wall, Lion's POV
45-47 Trap, panic, Lion escapes
48 Tracks beside trap
50 Remington's Masai out of grasses (like Lions)
51 Remington's hunt role
52 Remington tells doc of prints outside Hospital
57-62 Mid-Point: Thicket glimpses, Patterson faces, misfire
64 Masai call them the Ghost & the Darkness, leave
66 Lion roars
68 **Pinch II:** Blood & gore plants at Hospital, Remington admires trap
69 Lion pacing, shadows, sounds
71-74 Plot Point II: Lions attack slaughter in new hospital

Act III = Taking fight to the Lions
75 Claw necklace for bravery
77 Discussion "Only lions" & paw prints into hills, go after them
79-80 Finding cave lair of bones, "For the pleasure"
83 Lion roars O.S. during camp scene
84-85 Macan, about 100 killed, "They're after you."
86 Nervous, tethered baboon
87 Lion's POV, Lion's eyes
88 Owl knocks Patterson off macan, Lion attacks but escapes
89 Lion's eyes as being hunted
90 Lion's leaping attack & shot dead by Remington
91 Lion roars O.S. during camp celebration
93-94 Dream of Lion out of grasses onto Helena & baby
95-96 Remington's tent shredded & bloodied, panicked Patterson tracks
97 Lion roars O.S. as cremate of remains, fire the grasses
98 Grim Patterson firing rifle to "Sort it out" at the bridge
99-101 Climax: Lion attack, into tree, jump for gun & finally kills last one
102 **Commitment:** Sees actual Helena & baby waiting, looks to grasses to be sure
104 **After-story**: V.O. about Field Museum, "You will be afraid."

A GENERAL DISCUSSION OF THIS SCRIPT

Goldman's Spec Script is posted on line at www.weeklyscript.com. Click on Movies then "G" and scroll down to "The Ghost and The Darkness. The 107-pg script can be downloaded and printed out free of charge. Note all the white space and succinct, one-line narratives.

IMPORTANT NOTE: This copy is of William Goldman's original Spec Script. It has camera shots in it because Goldman (Like James Cameron) is a movie-maker. All Spec Scripts by others will be written in "Macro Scenes" with narrative descriptions, no camera directions, no actor directions.

By the time this got to the actual Shooting Script and had been casted, "Red Beard" became "Remington." And the Scenes were revised with numbers of each scene in both the left and right hand margins because scenes are shot out-of-sequence according to the availability of cast and locations. The Script Supervisor and Continuity Supervisor are charged with making certain the details of costuming, hair, props, background, etc. look the same.

For the full appreciation of this film, read the original Spec Script after seeing the film then go back and watch the film again with the original script, marking where changes were made (especially dialogue) and scenes inserted or deleted. This will give You-the-Writer an awareness for how a Spec Script evolves into the film,

Goldman had a major degree of control of his script, whereas most original writers do NOT. Their script is bought outright and sometimes they are contracted for the first re-write, but more frequently not. Other experienced writers or writers favored by producers and directors will get the assignment for the rewrites. Being contracted to be on-set to do the "Shooting Re-Writes" is only for the very brave and thick-skinned who thrive under intense pressure when demands are made like "The Director/Star doesn't like this scene. You have 20 minutes to re-write these five pages before the angle of the sun changes and we lose the entire day's shoot."

Weather and locations play havoc with film-makers. I call to your attention the hospital scene right after Maheena's death by the lions, as Dr. Hawthorne is discussing his "findings." The rain is pouring down outside. That was the only scene that could be shot for a three-week rainy period, yet idle crew and cast still received their pay and had to be fed and housed out of the production budget. The torrential downpours were so bad that the fake partial bridge built for the opening scenes was washed away and had to be rebuilt.

PINCHES

Remembering that Pinches demonstrate what strikes a cord within the Main Character, this film's Pinch I or Greatest Fear was the fact that there were two lions and one so "easily" eluded Patterson's gun and killed the most purely motivated of the characters. Patterson has to face that he was helpless and lost any sense of control. His reputation and engineering career had been based on his ability to control, to evaluate and create this man-made bridge where there had not been one before. His confidence and even arrogance was that he extended his abilities into a realm where he had no control and someone close to him paid the ultimate price. He then applied his skills and reasoning to building the "Contraption" so when he's feeling vulnerable and insecure, a man's man acknowledges and praises the principle of his idea. It is quick, but it is still a "warm fuzzy" that Remington tossed to the hurting Patterson.

Both greatest fear and "Silver Chalice" moments tweaked emotions from Patterson's Character Profile. His most vulnerable and a small reward when he most needed it to rebuild his confidence. So, the showing was not just events, but a revelation of emotions tweaked by the events.

ANXIETY CURVE

Throughout this entire film, Patterson is on a journey that ebbs and flows. One moment he is being praised, the next he is being attacked and forced to behave differently His success does not come easily. He only progresses in small steps with logical conflicts setting him back the instant he feels in control.

The Anxiety Curve is where you can most easily create "What if" events that torture and test your Main Character. Always consider what emotions will "pop" from a given event. And remember that you need the definitive "ebb and flow" cycle to sustain the audience's emotional investment, as well.

THE ANXIETY CURVE IS WHERE YOU CAN MOST EASILY CREATE "WHAT IF" EVENTS THAT TORTURE AND TEST YOUR MAIN CHARACTER.

Progressive Concepts to Consider:

1) Appropriate Title
2) Types of Suspense utilized
3) Webbing of related elements
4) First 10 minutes prepared audience for the balance of the story
5) Character consistency after Introduction
6) Unique defiance of predictability
7) Opposition intensity increased
8) Character demonstration of profile history
9) Consequences of back-story
10) Identification of Character Arc
11) Use of Sex and Violence blatant or subtle
12) Demonstration of Anxiety Curve
13) Contrasting qualities of Antagonist to Protagonist

Can you close your eyes and recite these 13? You have 11 more to go. Memorize them a little at a time. These are the tools of your creative arsenal that will make you an accomplished, knowledgeable screenwriter. Take them on, a little at a time.

* * * * *

GENRE FILM Chapter 8 Exercises

Exercise 8a. Write Pg 42-46 paying attention to Protag's learning stressors and build to Mid-Point's Epiphany coming next.

Exercise 8b. Have you demonstrated consistent coping mechanisms or the worsening antagonistic elements stressing both your Protag and your Antag in the first half of your script? In other words, have you "foreshadowed" possibilities of the final straw of your main players?

Exercise 8c. Write Pg 47-52 through Mid-Point's Epiphany, that emotion-riddled experience where the Protag finally realizes the value and meaning of his or her potential in the "New World." (By now you should be catching on that you are challenged to write before considering more in-depth concepts about each section of the screenplay. The purpose of that is for you to spew it out" then learn how to analyze it. The important writing always comes in the revision stage.)

Exercise 8d. Pay attention to where you are at in the agendas of your subplots and supporting cast. The tension of stress from the Main Plot should be having an impact on them, as well.

CHAPTER 9

Mid-Point, Change of Focus to Active Role, Scene-Sequel/Romance Genre

What important event happened at your Mid-Point? That is a vital question to maintaining the momentum of your story. Lots of people think the Beginning and the Ending are the most important parts of a story . . . and they would be wrong. How can you understand the meaning of those two without the struggles and climb in the middle? And how can you achieve the progress without and understanding of the building blocks of story, the elements of each scene?

MIDPOINT'S EPIPHANY

So far you have had your character responding to the new world, gradually attaining insights and skills. Now it is time to swing the hammer that hits him or her right between the eyes with the meaning of the journey. The drama of this half-way point is equal to the power of the ending's Climactic "battle." The Mid-point event depicts the explosion of the Main Character's mental, spiritual, emotional, and physical power on the screen and forces him to recognize his value. The Main character now takes charge of his or her role in the New World.

> THE MID-POINT EVENT DEPICTS THE EXPLOSION OF THE MAIN CHARACTER'S MENTAL, SPIRITUAL, EMOTIONAL, AND PHYSICAL POWER ON THE SCREEN AND FORCES HIM TO RECOGNIZE HIS VALUE.

You've lived with your character for going on eight weeks (if not longer). By now you should be familiar with how this person thinks and reacts. Mid-Point is the payoff for that knowledge. You must create a stunning moment of revelation for the character. Start with a list of "What-if's" to be sure you are choosing the most dramatic and not the "easiest." How will the character show the audience that internal intensity and motivation has changed?

Related to the above question is how vividly dramatic a scene can you create that will be a pivotal experience for both the actor and the director? That is no small thing. This excitement of this scene will be proportionately as invigorating for the audience as will be for the cast and crew. The camera's eye picks up on flagging energies. If the cast and crew believe this to be a pinnacle moment in their careers, the audience will be aware of the power of the scene they create. You-the-Writer have to give them that scene.

Example: One of the best Mid-Points that stays with me is in the original KARATE KID. Daniel leaves a party and goes to Mr. Miyagi's house. His mentor is very drunk. On the low table is an almost empty bottle of booze, a box displaying the Medal of Honor, a newspaper with headlines of the Japanese-American Internment Camps of WWII, a photograph of a very pregnant young Japanese woman and a telegram stating "We are sorry to inform you of the death of your wife and son in childbirth." Daniel helps Miyagi to bed then returns to the table to look over the material. There is no Voice Over. He frowns as he reads the telegram then reverently sets it back down. Daniel then walks to the bedside of the sleeping Miyagi, puts his palms together and bows to him. He gets his significance to his teacher just as the audience gets it . . . without one word of dialogue. From that point on Daniel is motivated to do his very best without Miyagi nagging him. He has taken responsibility for his own actions.

IMMEDIATE AFTERMATH INTO ACT II

The challenge does not stop with the Mid-Point but leads directly into the consequences of that scene. The Main Character is now motivated to act, to make things happen, to live up to the potential of his or her inherently dramatic personality. The second half of Act II has to be a series of more intense scenes than played out before. The writer needs to tighten the tension of the screws. Make each scene riskier than the one before. Create more desperation in your Antag, more heroic effort (and confidence) in your Protag. Take the internal struggles and manifest them in actions.

ONE SCENE AT A TIME

Dwight Swain thoroughly explains Scene (and Sequel) in his *Techniques of the Selling Writer*. Though Swain speaks to the novelist, the logic of the concepts translate perfectly into screenwriting. By breaking down the parts of the scene into these units, you can identify where you need what to happen in the most succinct form possible and where you can "break away" to a contributing subplot and maintain optimal tension and forward progression without confusing your audience. Understanding Scene and Sequel will change the way you write.

First, you must understand that we are not talking about the theatrical "French Scene" concept of a stage play's live theater where a scene begins with the entry of any character and ends with any exit. Obviously, that convention is for the convenience of rehearsals. X-Actor is needed for these so-many scenes. In screenwriting it refers to an Action Scene, a unit of time.

SCENE

"Scene is a unit of conflict lived thru by character and audience/reader." The Scene's purpose is to depict interesting character action where the character is confronted by opposition. This unit of time moves the story forward making your audience care about the outcome.

The Scene formula is G + C + D

From moment one, the character appears with a short-term, immediate **Goal** in mind. It can either be one of Achievement "I AM going!" or one of Resistance "I refuse to go!" The **Conflict** is created by whoever or whatever opposes the character. That opposition can be vastly over-powering and important or it can simply be a common daily routine annoyance. Obviously the Character anticipated some kind of problem in confronting the situation with a specific goal in mind. However, the next element comes as a surprise. **Disaster** is delivered in the form of **new information** the Character had not anticipated but is forced to deal with. End of Scene.

A scene can be one paragraph or one page/minute of screen time. The whole grouping of Scene and Sequel related to one major event is a screenplay **Beat**. Those Scenes related to the agenda of one character or one subplot is **Sequencing**.

The next movie you watch, studiously look for these microcosms. As you identify them, you will also come to understand how a cast and crew film a movie scene by scene and can film out of sequence. (Usually that is done because of limited actor or location availability.)

SEQUEL

"Sequel is a unit of transition that links two scenes." Where the Scene left off, the Sequel takes up. Its purpose is to transition the events of one scene through what happens because of that scene, moving through those events, conversations, whatever to the **consequence** that is the Goal of the next full Scene. Sequel presents information (exposition) the character needs in order to figure out what to do next. It can telescope reality by jumping over the mundane and getting to the important stuff. The depiction of what transpires in the sequel—ruminating, emotional outbursts, suffering, etc—and the passage of time provide an element of pacing. The Scene lives the moment, but the Sequel creates leaps of logic to the next important Scene. The audience is carried along this bridge of logic from one Scene to the next.

First in the Sequel is the **Reaction** to the Scene's Disastrous information. That Reaction will be consistent with the Character Profiles and the Character's normal coping mechanisms. Audience interest is high here. That is followed by the presentation of Choices, whether depicted, stated or implied. The more unsatisfactory those choices, the greater is the **Dilemma** the Character faces. Ultimately the Character must make a Decision of what choice to or option is best. That **Decision** provides the motivation for the Goal of the next Scene.

The formula for the Sequel is R + Di = De

An entire sequel can be accomplished in one paragraph or it can take a couple of pages. A valuable tool in Sequel is "**implication**." The astute audience (and you will always assume your audience is intelligent) can connect the dots of what happened bridging two major scenes. Example: The couple is in the back seat of the car, sweaty and passionate. War Zone Slug Line. An explosion and a helmet rolls. Smoke drifts over the body glimpsing the male's face as he dies. Hospital Slug Line. A middle age woman hurries down the hall and slams open the door of the room where the young woman labors to deliver a child. Not one word of dialogue, but the visuals skipped from Scene to Scene to Scene taking the audience on that fast roller coaster ride of action-consequences. Reactions, dilemmas, decisions of what happened in between the Scenes were all implied.

WRITING THE SCENE-SEQUEL UNITS

At the outset of a Scene you establish time, place circumstance then demonstrate the Character's Goal through actions. Don't write small. Choose power words. Live in the moment, not in an irritating flashback. Don't accidentally summarize. Your Character deserves his or her time to "shine" in the throes of drama, intent on something, denied whatever and delivered a blow that will lead to Sequel's reaction.

In Sequel is the time to compress the trivial and mundane. Focus on dominant emotions the character experiences (and the actor will interpret). This is where you will prove your credibility as a writer because you must weave in backdrop, important choreography, relevant subplots as they play on the Character's responses and external emoting. Choreographing external evidence of thought is a tough thing in screenwriting, but a necessary one, as well. You can't talk the thoughts to death but must *show* them in action.

Think of the Scene as a big square. Inside that square you write an uppercase G followed by a big C in the middle and that D at the other side of the square. Draw a line from that box to another box. That line is Sequel.

Atop the Sequel line an uppercase R then "Di" in the middle and "De" at the end. Next Box G-C-D. Line with R-Di-De. There you have a schematic of cause-effect storytelling that you can use to create viable scenes, tight sequels, and ultimately identify when and where to plug in your subplots. You will also be able to identify when you insert something that doesn't contribute to that scene or where you skipped a piece of logic the audience (and characters) needed.

HOW TO BREAK AWAY TO ANOTHER SUBPLOT

Trust your audience. Give them credit for the ability to "get the logic" of what is most likely going to continue on when you cut away to another series of events in another subplot. After hitting Goal and Conflict in a Scene if you cut away to another subplot, you may confuse your audience. A better moment is right after Disaster. Better yet is in Sequel's Reaction that leaves the audience hanging (wanting answers). That's the most common place episodic network TV cuts away to commercials. It is also how an ensemble cast living their own stories is juggled. Cut to another character's Scene with Goal-Conflict-Disaster then return to the first storyline at the point of Decision into Scene with Goal-Conflict-Disaster . . . and so on. The audience is led back and forth for the hour episode of the TV series and the character's own storyline is advanced.

THE AUDIENCE ASSUMES THE ABANDONED STORY IS GOING ON SIMULTANEOUSLY SO WHEN THEY ARE RETURNED, THEY MAKE REASONABLE ASSUMPTIONS ABOUT WHAT TRANSPIRED.

This ability for the audience to figure out what happened while away "living" another series of events is exactly how those episodic TV shows carrying 2-3 character stories can jump back and forth between them. The audience assumes the abandoned story is going on simultaneously so when they are returned, they make reasonable assumptions about what transpired. The more intense the scene, the greater the tension created in the audience. That means the "pay-off" eventually has to be pretty darn good or your disappointed audience will be frustrated. On TV that means they switch channels. In a screenplay being read by an agent or producer, it can mean the difference between a "Pass" or "Consider" or Recommend."

Can you see how you can "pace" a story by how much you dwell on any one part of either Scene or Sequel? Can you see how it is preferable in a screenplay to hit the action high points of an important scene then tighten the exposition of character depiction and story information in the Sequel? Consider how many times visuals immediately supply information the audience needs to "get it."

An example of the analysis of Scene-Sequel-and- Break away can be found in Appendix I where the opening to the spec script EYES OF THAT CAT is broken down.

CREATION OF A BEAT SHEET

In this context a "beat" could be seen as those scenes and their sequels related to one event in the plot. A Beat Sheet provides the outline for those scenes that need to carry the story from Act I throughout Act II and culminating in Act III. A beat sheet consists of approximately 36 to 48 "groupings" broken into Act I, Act II, and Act III. These provide the "spine" of the story for your screenplay. Note: Many Movie DVDs come with a scene list that is similar to a beat sheet, if you need coaching. An example of the Beat Sheet for Act I of the spec script EYES OF THE CAT can be found in Appendix J.

ROMANCE GENRE

Since this textbook' s PART TWO: ROMANTIC SCREENPLAYS 101 explains this genre in-depth, the following information will only touch on essence and highlights for those who want to understand how it works to add a relationship to their "other genre" story. Yes, romantic relationships are definitely one element that can be woven into any genre story.

Romance addresses the human need for someone to share life with. Once-upon-a-time romance meant only the male-female pairing, but here at the beginning of the 21st century we are seeing stories of nontraditional, same sex relationships. They all depict people in search of a partner. At one time it was the female making the male aware of his need for her. Now, it can be stated **"A romance is the story of a couple struggling through life's changing saga until one transforms the other's awareness of the need and value of the other."** They start out as separate human beings and end up committed to being a couple, facing the world and its problems together.

A love story is not necessarily a romance. People can experience the gamut of emotions attraction ignites from curiosity to obsession, from want to lust. A romance is different in that the two end up as one. Examples of love stories are the movies SOMERSBY, LOVE STORY, and BRIDGES OF MADISON COUNTY. In each the people were alone at the end. In SOMERSBY the male sacrificed the relationship for the laudable cause of principle. She died in LOVE STORY. BRIDGES was a story of attraction and succumbing to adulterous lust then separating for the sake of social morality.

Most definitely each of these stories depicts the evolution of a loving relationship, but the relationship did not culminate in a commitment that completed the cycle. Yes, they all ended logically for who and what the characters were, but the relationship did not win. In a true romance, the relationship moves forth into the after-story as the unit of the committed couple.

An aficionado of romance knows the couple will be together in the end, so to find out the ending is not the purpose of a romance. Devotees of this genre seek how the couple comes to that commitment point. Period.

NOTE to the groaning males: Here's the generalization. Women are inherently nest builders seeking a mate to create family, whereas males may desire the security of a relationship but are more concerned about the world, not the nest. They seek the challenge of "spreading it around," attracting as many females as possible . . . as a side-line hobby, not as a vocation. The human male is about survival (jeopardy), whereas the female is about assuring the continuation of the species (consequences of sex). That's the lowest common denominator in our biology.

FUNDAMENTAL CONCEPTS OF ROMANCE

1. Plot moves through meeting, misunderstanding, separation, commitment
- So, yes that is a formula, but the twists and turns can be orchestrated as uniquely as each human life! Examine the Relationship Plane that is woven into the three-act structure to help meld this concept into you script. (Note the elements of this diagram will be pointed out in the Romance Film Analysis.) You already have Linda Howard's 12-steps of Intimacy to help you choreograph the growing relationship.

2. Motivated character driven, not complex plot driven.
- Character driven stories focus on the evolution of the internal awareness of people experiencing whatever. Plot driven stories depict people responding to the events making the plot more important than the people. It's as if the plot events would happen no matter who was casted to experience them. In character-driven stories the audience is more interested in the characters than the plot events.

3. Heavy on emotional emoting because devotees demand character awareness of emotional response.
- In general, female writers "get" this and male writers struggle. Women "nest builders" hone in on the details and emotions that go into carving their place in the world, whereas men tackle the "big picture" and the effort it takes to achieve a role, a place in that world. Thus women tend to analyze whys, motivations and emotional triggers, whereas men consider the tasks to accomplish the goals necessary for survival. Those mindsets can certainly vacillate, but since the majority of the romance audience is female, the romance writer needs to rely on the feminine need for emotional situations, not just the physical acts performed.

4. LOVE scenes, not sex scenes.

ROMANCE FOCUSES ON THE SINGULAR RELATIONSHIP CULMINATING IN THIS GIVE-AND-TAKE SCENE, THE NEED FOR THIS ONE PERSON TO BE MADE WHOLE BY THE PARTNER, TO BE MADE TO FEEL SPECIAL TO THIS ONE PERSON.

- Whether the sexuality in a book or film is sweet (hand-holding and kissing, references to nothing below the shoulders) as required by Young Adult and Christian or detailed as in erotic romance, the writer must pay attention to portraying the arousal of characters' awareness of love for one another, not just the physical sensations demonstrated. Porn or pure erotica (for the sake of base proclivities) depicts the foreplay and sexual act for the sole purpose of titillating and arousing the audience's sexual fantasies. Romance focuses on the singular relationship culminating in this give-and-take scene, the need for this one person to be made whole by the partner, to be made to feel special to this one person.

5. Must keep Point-of-View consistent but alternate female-male.
- Even as recently as the 1990's the romance stories were told from only the female perspective. Now, more sophisticated, more demanding audiences want to know stresses on both partners and see their reactions, the consequences of how they cope. This adds depth and credibility to the relationship.

6. Subplots/minor characters/ environment must affect the relationship
- When the relationship is the Main Plot driving the story, anything that does not impact the relationship is not necessary and can be deleted. The reason the audience wants this story is for the relationship. However, if the relationship is a complication to the main plot of, say, a mystery, then of course, the attraction will play off the unfolding plot events and not the other way around.

7. The romantic partners are introduced within the first ten minutes of the romance film.
- The singular people destined to be a couple must enthrall the audience's concern early in the film. The romance aficionado will be frustrated if the romantic interest is not introduced until after the Protagonist steps into the "New Life" of Act II or middle of the story. Withholding introduction until then implies this relationship is not as important as the events . . . thus the story is not a true romance. This is a tenant or convention of the genre. Good writers satisfy, not frustrate their audience.

ROMANCE CHARACTER REQUIREMENTS

Heroic factors play heavily in romances, but there are some other nuances to note. One of the two partners, the **stronger "male-type," is Alpha-Beta, highly motivated yet vulnerable in some way**. The **softer "female type" is Beta-Alpha, relying more on thought and emotion but capable of motivation toward empowerment**. The masculine partner is called to help empower the feminine one, while the feminine one triggers the masculine person's emotions. The complexity of how this interfaces does not have to be by formula, but can be as uniquely interesting as the characters.

It is vital to well-crafted romance that the main characters be flawed, complex, and empowered to make things happen. The two people are always risk takers within their own realm, willing to do whatever it takes to survive. They are not weakened by the emotions they discover. Rather, they are stronger, more determined because of them. Where life was tenuous before, the relationship intensifies the sensations and meaning of being alive. That is all related in visual evidence of reactions, body language, attention focus You-the-Writer put on paper.

ROMANCE PLOT TYPES

Time-Place Plots

1. Contemporary: Occurs within past 20 years to present
2. Historical: Within documented past played against historical events
3. Western: Plays in a Frontier or Old West setting
4. Medieval: European Middle Ages setting of castles, knights, serfs.
5. Regencies: Early 1800's England (pre-Victorian era)
6. Scottish**:** Scotland and/or Scots, from ancient to contemporary
7. Paranormal: Ghosts/Vampires/Werewolves/Time-Travel

Themes Plots

1. Innocent being initiated
2. Cynical, hardened becoming vulnerable
3. Marriage of Convenience
4. Forced Marriage
5. May-December Story
6. Social/Professional Barriers
7. Shared Adventure
8. Medical
9. Law Enforcement
10. Military/Government profession

INTERNAL ESSENCE vs. EXTERNAL IDENTITY

Knowledgeable gurus have shared their insights, wisdom and opinions about romance over the years. Screenwriting lecturer and book author Michael Hauge proposes a solution to many a romance relationship problem. And this may help the males to understand. The true lovers are attracted to the inner essence of each other, totally apart from appearance, external role or **identity**, the world's perception of persona. That's where the "Getting to know one another" comes in. Yes, pheromones need to be activated in the sexual attraction part of the relationship, but that has nothing to do with abiding love that looks deep into the other partner's very being, beyond what the world sees.

NOTE: To work, a cinematic romantic story requires a lot more nuances than this brief overview can provide. A well-crafted romance requires use of detailed pacing and a tone of pull-and-push, attraction and reluctance, recognition of intense need and willingness to act on it. There are over 10,000 members of Romance Writers of America who are avid students of romantic relationship stories. If you are seriously considering writing a romance into your script, study beyond this over-view.

ROMANCE FILM ANALYSIS

Of course, once you believe the attraction, you will be looking for obstacles and the couple's gradual recognition and acceptance with the ultimate pairing becoming one unit despite all the obstacles. The turning points of the relationship are the turning points of circumstances of the background plot. All subplots impact the relationship.

* * * * *

AVATAR

By James Cameron
2009, Starring Sam Worthington, Zoe Saldana, Sigourney Weaver

Length: 155 Minutes (Theatrical release)

Log Line: A paraplegic marine inhabits an alien body on an exotic planet and becomes torn between the alien culture and its destructive exploitation by his fellow humans.

Statement of Purpose: To prove a man of conscience and integrity can bond with and defend a race with laudable values.

Intro Image: Aerial flight over lush trees.

First 13 minutes
Who:
JAKE SULLY, wheelchair-bound former Recon Marine willing to take risks for a warrior's life
GRACE, biology/sociology expert who loves an alien race enough to fight for them
COL. QUARITCH, hard-core Marine commander on alien Pandora willing to violently exterminate the natives
PARKER, narrow-mined corporate head of Pandora's mining colony focused on corporate profits
When: Future (2154 per dates on Jake's recordings)
Where: Earth to Space to Pandora's mining colony
What: Handicapped vet given chance for new life
Why: Unable to afford quality life on earth, he takes advantage of having identical g-nome of dead twin brother and volunteers for duty on exotic Pandora to help humans communicate with indigenous people.

Four related subplots:
Mining colony goals
Grace's science
Na-vipolitics & culture
Jake regains manhood as Na-vi

Time Line: Main story on Pandora is 4 months

Image repeats:
Eyes
Trees & Home Tree
Floating "Seeds" (Pure spirits from Tree of Souls)
Arrows
Helo Gunships
Manned robotic soldiers
"I see you"
"Re-breather" masks
Links (mechanical, nervous system, Na-vi fibers with creatures, ground, trees)

Act I = Set-up of Ordinary World: Jake's intro to Pandora, mining politics & his avatar
13 min **Intro:** Jake takes assignment to Pandora in his twin's place to use his marine skills

18 min **Inciting Incident**: Jake emotionally bonds with his healthy & whole avatar .
30 min **PP I:** Jake's avatar is forced to escape into the jungle of Pandora

Act II = Life 180 degrees: Jake learns the Na-vi way of life and falls in love
46 min **Pinch I:** As Moat judges, Jake fears rejection by the Na-vi (thus would be a failure)
81 min **Mid-Point:** Jake passes his test and accepted into the Na-vi clan then mates with Neytiri
97 min **Pinch II**: Jake desperately proclaims his love for Neytiri and the clan
104 min **PPII:** Colonel's forces destruction Home Tree then "pulls the plug" on the avatars

Act III = Resolution: Jake leading the Na-vi in battle with humans and winning
135 min **Climax:** Jake as the Toruk-Macto leads all the Na-vi on attack of Colonel's forces
155 min **Commitment**: Jake's last report
After-story Conclusion: Jake aabandons his human body for permanent life as a Na-vi

Dialogue Notes:
Jake's self-deprecating tone & marine jargon
Col. Quaritch tough military narrow-minded tone
Parker's whiny yet corporate arrogance
Grace's intellectual arrogance
Na-vicadence

Alpha Character posturing differences:
Jake vs. Quaritch, vs.Tsu-tey vs. Norm (note his confidence evolution from subordinate to leader)
Neytiri vs Tsu-tey vs. Jake (note her softening as she accepts Jake and falls in love)
Grace vs. Parker & Quaritch (note tone & demeanor as jocking for superiority control)

Supporting cast Unique Character Gems:
Grace, Norm, Parker, Trudy, Max
Tsu-tey, E'tukan, Mo-at

Background effects, the nuances of aura:
Pandora (especially at night) with variety, lushness & threatening environment
Colony & strip mining operation

Home tree
Tree of Souls

Elements from Other Genres: Sci-Fi/Fantasy, Inspirational, Action-Adventure, Western

Question: Since "survival" of a species was the theme of BOTH the humans mining "unobtanium" for the over-crowded "dying" Earth AND the exploited Na-viand their Pandora, did you ever empathize with the selfish humans?

Appearance or reference to recurrence of Evil Theme in Min: greedy, arrogant Culture epitomized in the narrow-minded Quaritch and his military is in **BOLD.** I've *italicized* pages with romantic elements and italicized & BOLD elements of the Relationship Plane.

Act I = Set-up of Ordinary World: **Jake's intro to Pandora, mining politics & his avatar**

1 Eyes open in capsule with V. O. about his brother (establish pattern of V.O.)
2 Jake at Tommy's funeral cremation with men making job offer
3 Ship to Pandora
4 Landing on Pandora, "One life ends, another begins."
5 Soldiers disembark, Jake in wheelchair off ship
6 Marines on earth/hired guns here, enormous earth-moving equip & huge manned robot
7 **Col. Quaritch addressing new arrivals about threatening Pandora's wild life & the Na vi**
8 "Nothing like Old School lecture," to lab with Norm
9 Jake sees his avatar "got big" :Looks like you" told about documenting science
10 Told of Grace, as she comes out of link
11 Grace greets Norm, disgusted with Jake & tromps off to confront director
12 In control room, Grace demands, Parker reminds lucky with marine
13 Parker angrily points out value of unobtanium 20mill per kilo funding her research
14 Grace escorts Norm & Jake to links, " Just go into a hostile environ with no training?"
15 Jake into link, Max sees "great brain activity" Jake closes eyes, "neuro rush"
16 Jake awakens in avatar body, responds, sits wiggling toes, off cart
17 Jake stands, grinning, unsteady then joyfully running out of lab

18 **Inciting Incident** = Encounters other avatars playing basketball, running, deep breathes
19 Avatar Grace greets, day's end to settle in beds, "Don't play with that" (filaments in braid)
20 J. wheeling in helo hangar with Trudy, "need another gun"
21 Col. Quaritch lifting weights, recites J.'s record then his own & about scars
22 Denigrates science, Recon Gyrine in avatar body, useful intel
23 Walk-quack but report to me, J. agrees, rotate home to get your real legs back, sounds good.
24 J. into link, Grace warns, on helo, flying over Pandora, landing in jungle
25 J. dismount, gun in hand, stay, J. wary, sees lemur
26 "Relax, Marine" then taking samples of tree roots as Jake wanders
27 J. collapses flowers, rhino creature roars, gun up
28 Grace "Don't shoot, hold your ground. Just territorial." J. charges & it stops.
29 Turns "Run to mama." As huge black thanataur jumps behind J. "Definitely run"
30 **PP I** = J. runs with thanataur on heels, dives among tree roots, gun grabbed away

Act II = Life 180 degrees: Jake learns the Na-vi way of life and falls in love
31 Jake chased until forced to jump into falls & river, using knife to make spear
32 Cautious thru jungle, Neytiri on limb above, notches arrow, "seed" floats to arrow, lowers
33 Trudy's helo circling, call in due to no night ops, J. in dark making torch, noises
34 Fire shows many stalking creatures, keeps at bay
35 J. swings torch, 6 legged with vicious teeth come closer, attack & fight, Neytiri arrow & knife
36 N. drives away, J. watches (***Look)*** as throws torch into water, finds whimpering, clean kill while murmurs
37 J. "sees" iridescent foliage all around, "Thank you" but N. ignores.
38-39 Impressed, N. moves off, J. follows (J. showing ***Interest***), "Don't thank. Sad. Your fault!" (**True meeting**), like a baby, Why not let kill?, Strong heart, Teach me!
40-41 Across high limb, Where learn English?, Go back! Many seeds float, settle on him, N. awe (N. showing ***Interest***)
42 "Come," awkwardly follows, "What's name?" bolo knocks off log, riders on hexapedes

43 Warriors, Tsu-tey chides Neytiri, "A sign from Eywah." Take J. to Home Tree

44-45 J. brought before Na vi, N. explains to father Eytukah

46 **Pinch I:** As Mo'at judges, Jake fears rejection by the Na-vi (thus would be a failure)

47 "Daughter will teach" despite N. negative "attitude", "See if insanity can be cured." Joins in meal

48 N. then J. into tree hammocks to sleep. Grace awakens J. in link

49 Is avatar safe? Won't believe, colony mess hall story of thanataur chasing J. , Quaritch "Jarhead clan?" Learn to be one of them, You have three months until dozers get there.

50 Parker learn what Blue Monkeys want, Home Tree sits on largest deposit

51 Grace teaching pronounce names, Don't do anything unusually stupid

52-53 Intro hexapede, & "the bond" "Forward" falls to Tsutey's ridicule, N. Again. (***Engagement***)

54 J. explaining Home Tree structure overheard by Max, w/c to lab where packing up "Getting out of Dodge." To Halleluiah Mts/floating mts of Pandora

55-56 Trudy flying helo into mist VFR with enormous earthen, vine & waterfall globs suspended in air, J. awestruck, land isolated shelf with two "boxcar-type" labs with links

57 J. sees G.'s avatar pics of school, "Use me as way back into clan."

58-59 Top of Home Tree, N calls dragon-like ikran/banchee, Bond for life. J. envies flight (***BOTH giving Permission to share & appreciate the sharing***)

60-61 J. record at link, "need rest" Days blurred, N. repetitious with bow "Skoum means moron," Norm with language "See you as *into* you," run farther every day, N. tracks & feel forest.

62 While recording, Grace tells "See forest through her eyes." N. jumps leaf to leaf descent with J. clumsy effort, "Learn fast or die."

63 G. avatar back with kids, as human finds J. sleep & puts to bed, N. correcting J. stance with bow finds correct = prolonged eye contact & back away (***BOTH acknowledge Attraction***)

64 J. V.O. about "life energy as Na-vifuneral, Jake stalk, downs "deer" then kills with knife as chants. N. admires & tells "You are ready" meaning to choose ikran. (*She is admitting **Liking***)

65-66 Hexapedes climb to thick connecting vine, "Go where the banshees are." J. with Na-vi& Tsutey scampering along "bridges, jumps to climb up dangling vine

67 -68 Arrive at rocky top, N. lands her ikran, "Jake will go first." "How knows it chooses you?" He will try to kill you." Outstanding."

69-71 Swing's bolo checking various ikrans, one screeches back at him "Let's dance." Catches, onto back, N. "Make the bond!" it knocks him off. J. comes back, captures head, bonds. "Stop" N. urges flight to seal, J. says "Fly?" They dive off rocks with J. yelling.

72 "Shut up & fly straight" levels out & Jake giving directions.

73-74 "May not be a horse guy but born to fly." With N., J. wearing apparel, Shown most sacred Tree of Souls (*J. showing **Liking**/sharing flying*)

75 G. at links "Die to get samples"

76-77 "Stone cold killer" with N. "Dive" attack by Toruk into jungle & escape, laughing. (***Connection***) At Home Tree N. shows skull of Toruk, "Final Shadow." Grandfather rode & only five since time began . J "Everything's backward now."

78 Lab record about confusion, shaves.

79-80 At colony meets with Col. 2 weeks, thought lost you, getting legs back, J. wants to finish & go through test of manhood, to be accepted & negotiate truce. "Get it done, Corporal;."

*81***Mid-Point =** N. paints & he is accepted as Omatacaya by Eytukah & all people link, N. & J to "Tree of Voices

82-83 Link fibers to hear the voices of ancestors, N. "You are Na'vi & can choose a woman." She lists he rejects "I've already chosen but she must choose me." "She already has." (***BOTH admit LOVE***)

84 Kiss, embrace, beginning to mate "for life" (commitment), J. awakens in link "What the hell are you doing, Jakie?"

85 N. awakens in J. arms to tress being dozed, cannot awaken J.

86 J. at link with G. forcing food on him & he gulps then quickly tranfers.

87-88 "Wake up, Jake!" He jumps up, waving arms, driver stops, Parker pushes control forward "See? He moved." Jake scrambles up dozer with rock to smash cameras, gunfire, & J. & N. escape. Tsutey & riders see devastation.

89 Col with Parker watching tape & recognizes Jake "Get me a pilot." Na'vi at Home Tree talk of war with G. trying calm.

90 J. & N. arrive to speak. Tsutey "You mated with this woman?" N. "Before Eywah" "Not my brother." "Not your enemy. They're out there & very powerful." Looks at N. "Words are stone in my heart."

91-92 Col at link, pushes past Norm, hits G. link & she drops. "I was sent—" His link hit & he drops. Tsutey starts to cut throat but N. knocks him away & protects (***MISUNDERSTANDING***). J. awakens "Out of your mind?" "Crossed the line. Get a little tail?" "Listen to Grace!"

93-**94** G. tells of tree link & communication system more than human brain. Parker sarcastic "Just trees." Col. plays J. recording that Na'vi won't negotiate & never leave Home Tree.

95-96. Col proposes to Parker gas first then blast the tree. He agrees. Trudy tells lab rolling gunships. G. tries to reason with Parker "Families, children, babies." He allows to link back to avatars "One hour to get them to move."

97-98 **Pinch II**: J. addresses people telling "The sky people are coming to destroy Home Tree." Mo-at "You are certain? J. explains why he came then desperately proclaims his love for Neytiri and the clan, but is rejected & tied up. N. heart-broken by betrayal. (***SEPARATION & Relationship Tension Increase***)

99-102 Helos & Col's ship appear above where J. & G. tied p, Na'vi shoot ineffective arrows, gas cannisters lobbed into Home Tree scattering the people & Hexapedes, Col sees J. "Diplomacy failed. Fire the incindiaries" Explosions, people running "Scatter the roaches." Mo-at freees J. & Grace "Help us."

103 Col. "Bring it down." Trudy backs off and flies away.

104 PPII: Switch to missles (to bring down columns & fell Home Tree) Warriors to ikrans, blast staggers E'tukan

Act III = Resolution: Jake leading the Na-viin battle with humans and winning

105 People running, staring in disbelief

106 Col. "Good work, drinks on me" Ships fly away, N. finds dying father pierced by wood

107 E'tukan gives his bow "Protect the people" dies as J. arrives "Sorry" N. screams "Get Away."

108 Parker has links cut. G. falls among escaping people then lone J. falls, pulled from links fighting.

109-110 J., G. & Norm in lock-up, Trudy brings food cart then knocks out guard & Max releases, racing along corridors to get to helo bay.

111 Controller alerts Col who recognizes w/c, grabs rifle, burst out door firing as copter takes off

112 G. "Ruin my whole day" wounded, Fly to labs, Norm avatar help attach ropes to fly one with links to near "Tree of Souls."

113-114 J. Injects into pale G. "Why would they help us?" Lab set down. J. to link without plan.

115-116 J. awakens in gray burned world "Take it to new level" His ikran lands, flying above Toruk & dives then leaps onto back.

117 At Tree of Souls, linked people singing. Shadow stops as Toruk descends & lands, people in awe.

118 Tsutey recognizes as Toruk Macto, N. "I see you" & they touch with love (***Both acknowledge NEED for one another***), asks T. to address.

119 T. "I will fly with you." Grace is dying, Carry to tree "I need to take some samples."

120-122 Mo'at instruct power from human to avatar "but very weak." People chant as fibers invade., then light darkens, G. briefly "sees Eywah" then gone. "Wounds too great."

123-124 J. addresses with T. translating. Stop the sky people who killed their own mother Earth, Cannot take out land. Call all the other clans. Tell Toruk Macto calls them.

125-126 All mount ikrans, N, with J on Toruk, to plains people then to ikran people of Eastern Seas.

127-128 Col. lecturing to packed hall at colony about gathering Na'vi soon 20,000 & over-run, think protected by their deity but we will destroy.

129 Max reporting on mobilization Trudy hoping not martyrdom, keep them from Tree of Souls, bring the fight to us, our advantage

130 J. to Tree of Souls to link & pray asking for help. N. overhears. & says "She protect balance of life" "I had to ask."

131-134 Position for attack, J. leading ikran (with Tsutey & Neytiri), Norm with hexapede warriors against footsoldiers & mechanical robots

135-144 Climax: Battle of ikran attacking copters, Trudy shooting at Col & shot down, Norm on ground with hexapede turned back, Tsutey on board bomb ship but shot & falls into jungle below, N. chased by copter with ikran hit & killed, J. telling fall back, ground troups stop then attacked by line of "rhino-like" as J. sees waves of solo ikran descending, N. screaming "Eywah has heard you!" N. finds thanataur bowing to her.

145-151 J. cripples bomb ship which crashes, then goes after Col's, He ends up falling into forest using trip through leaves as N. taught. Col into mechanical robot jumps from plane as crashes & sees link lab through foliage. As approach, N. through forest on thanataur & leap on him. Col finally viciously knifes thanataur trapping N. J. arrives & they fight. "You think you are one of them? Time to wake up." One of links smashed, J. attacks As Col holds to kill, N. shoot two arrows into him, Col dies.

152 N. can't arouse J. avatar. J. out of link, falls to floor & gasps for final breath. N. into lab & places mask over his face call "My Jake." He awakens "I see you." (***Love's COMMITMENT***)

153 Na'vi, some avatar people & some humans have colonists (including Parker) lined up loading onto transports to send back to earth.

154 **Commitment:** J. V.O. "Time of great sorrow ended so Toruk Macto not needed" See Toruk flying free. J. last recording "don't want to be late for my own birthday party."

After-story Conclusion: Na-vi chanting with Mo'at & Neytiri over J. human & avatar bodies at Tree of Souls. Jake abandons his human body for permanent life as a Na-vi

Note: Note that though this movie is 155 pages/minutes, the overall paradigm and balance of 1/4 Act I, ½ Act II, and 1/4 Act II still works. The pacing of the romance also works out and the POV is consistently Jake Sully's even though the cast is large.

CONCEPTS DISCUSSION

You should have paid attention to the relationship evolution that was impacted by the plot then caused the plot, for that is the focus of a romance. The fundamentals of story and character and the Progressive Concepts are easily apparent on analysis. James Cameron wrote this script 12 years before the industry had the technology to bring his story to life. He indicated during those waiting years he frequently took out the script and tweaked it to be certain it was the best it could be. That is the kind of attention you need to give to each of your screenplays.

ANALYZING SCENE AND SEQUEL

AVATAR is a great movie for analyzing the "blocks" of Scene events (Goal-Conflict-Disaster's new Info) and the "lines" of logical links of Sequel (Reaction-Dilemma-Decision). You can actually clip right down the pages and identify the specified elements of each. (I suggest you do this to "get a feel" for the logic of how it works).

> MOST OF WHAT IS CUT IS EXPLANATORY EXPOSITION.

Another advantage of using this movie for such an analysis is that it is so long and evolves in a steady ebb-and-flow of Jake Sully's experience and how he impacted those around him. As Jake is learning facts, so is the audience. As Jake is becoming more confident and understanding, the audience recognizes those experiences and other characters that caused that.

When you are analyzing Scene & Sequel, just as when you are plotting and writing the units, walk through the logic of what the story has to show and what the audience can figure out "happened" at different intervals. Another learning tool is to get the DVD's and not the scenes and entire sequences of a particular subplot that were cut to reduce running time. James Cameron's movies are always very, very long, but the cut scenes are just as interesting to learn deleted information that truly enhances deeper understanding of story and characters. Most of what is cut is explanatory exposition. Lack of that information does not truly change the story pattern; it merely enhances the audience experience with the characters.

ANALYZING THE ROMANCE

Of course, you noted that the romance did not begin until Jake was thrown into the exotic world of Pandora in Act II, which is reasonable, yet the Relationship Plane evolved steadily from there in the expected manner.

Progressive Concepts to Consider:

1) Appropriate Title
2) Types of Suspense utilized
3) Webbing of related elements
4) First 10 minutes prepared audience for the balance of the story
5) Character consistency after Introduction
6) Unique defiance of predictability
7) Opposition intensity increased
8) Character demonstration of profile history
9) Consequences of back-story
10) Identification of Character Arc
11) Use of Sex and Violence blatant or subtle
12) Demonstration of Anxiety Curve
13) Contrasting qualities of Antagonist to Protagonist
14) Consistently logical Scenes with smooth Transitions
15) Definitive build from Mid-Point on

*****

ROMANCING THE STONE

By Diane Thomas and Eddy Grant
1984, Starring Michael Douglas, Kathleen Turner, Danny DiVito

Length: 103 minutes

Log Line: A romance novelist leaves security and fantasy in New York when she partners with an adventurer in Colombia to rescue her hostage sister.

Statement of Purpose: To prove that a courageous woman can attract and convert a cynical male.

Intro Image: Fantasy western bad guy breaking into heroine's cabin.

First 11 minutes
Who:
JOAN WILDER, reclusive, inhibited romance author
GLORIA, pushy, worldly publisher
ZOLA, sinister murderous man on-a-mission
When: Fall
Where: New York City
What: Joan finishes latest western novel & focused on getting manuscript to publisher
Why: She has deadline and is devoted to her fantasies & readers, with no awareness of sinister threat bearing down on her.

Four related subplots:
Zola's quest
Elaine's hostage story
Ira & Ralph's quest
Joan's writing career

Time Line: Approximately two weeks (Fall in NYC, Spring in Colombia)

Image repeats:
Joan's books
Policia or Military
Sailboat picture
El Corazon & hearts
Hungry crocs
Knife/machete

Act I = Set-up of Ordinary World: Joan's quiet life disrupts by sister's request to come to Colombia
11 min **Intro:** From fantasy to mundane invaded by sinister man willing to murder
17 min **Inciting Incident**: Elaine asks if has map & can bring to Colombia
23 min **PP I**: Joan's wrong bus wrecks on mountain road putting her at mercy of Zolo & Jack

Act II = Life 180 degrees: Joan & Jack quest to follow the map and get to Cartegena
38 min **Pinch I:** Joan & Jack at gorge (threat of failure)
49 min **Mid-Point:** Joan & Jack connect in plane wreckage
72 min **Pinch II**: Couple make love & become partners on quest
83 min **PPII:** Survive trip over big falls but on opposite sides of river so Joan must trust Jack

Act III = Resolution: Rescuing Elaine & escaping vengeful Zolo:
91 min **Climax:** Zolo's attack on Joan
99 min **Commitment**: Jack tells Joan "You're going to be all right. You always were."
After-story Conclusion: Jack parks his sail boat at Joan's apt. bldg & asks her to join him.

Dialogue Notes:
Ralph & Ira's "Bronx" cadence & idioms
Gloria's educated sophistication
Jack's charm & arrogance
Joan's changing tone from wimpy to assertive

Alpha Character posturing differences:
Joan's personality evolution vs. Gloria & Elaine
Jack vs. Ralph & Juan (drug dealer)
Zola vs. Ira

Supporting cast Unique Character Gems:
Ralph, Ira, Zola as grasping, focused survivors, power-hungry
Gloria, Elaine, typical females, comparatively shallow
Juan & his henchman, violent, self-centered opportunists though gracious

Background effects, the nuances of aura:
Tropical jungle
Crude Colombian villages
Luxury compound
Crowded, dirty & chaotic airport & bus
Crumbling old fort

Elements from Other Genres: Action-Adventure, Comedy, Western

Questions: 1) Was Joan's naïveté and lack of preparation credible when she was an intelligent woman? 2) Was Ralph's perpetual appearance exactly where he intersected Joan & Zolo a bit contrived?

Appearance or reference to recurrence of Evil Theme in Min: Terrorizing, greedy elements in **BOLD.** I've *italicized* pages with romantic elements and italicized & BOLD elements of the Relationship Plane.

Act I = Set-up of Ordinary World: Joan's quiet life disrupts by sister's request to come to Colombia
1-3 Joan's V.O. as visual of her western romance where bad guy breaks down heroine's cabin door, she throws knife the rides horse, sees

brothers then hero Jesse appears & shoots the brothers, they ride toward one another, kiss then he puts her in front of him and they ride off.

4 Grungy Joan types "The End" then can't find tissue as crying over happy ending, Notes all over

5-7 Talking to cat, celebrates with candles, bottle from cabinet of collection miniature bottles, toasts then glass into fireplace, stares at book cover poster of Jesse.

8-9 Black gloved hand dials phone. Phone awakens Joan but no voice there. Notes time. Hurries to take manuscript to publisher but stops to help elderly neighbor who hands her envelope from her sister. Street venders plague Joan as she hurries. Sinister Zolo enters bldg. He's prying her door when stopped by janitor who gets knife in gut.

10-11 Publisher Gloria sits with Joan characterizing males at the bar Joan admits hopes high to meet her Jesse

12 Joan & Gloria talk of her sister whose husband was murdered, In Colombia, furtive Elaine leaves apt, drives car from garage with kids playing in the street.

13-14 Kid swings bolo knocking her out, drives car to seaside where Elaine dragged from car to boat.

15 Ralph on phone to cousin Ira observing the abduction, Ira feeding cros

16 Joan home to ransacked apt, cat screeches, phone from Elaine, Joan stunned when "I'm in trouble."

17 **Inciting Incident**: Elaine asks if has map & can bring to Colombia, Hotel Cartegena, tell no one

18 Gloria following Joan in apt as she hurries to depart, cat crate, on street warned of motion sick

19 Zolo watches Joan from car. Jt flies across moon. Joan crosses chaotic, peasant-filled airport, dragging suitcase

20 Book in hand, Ralph moves thru crowd, Zolo misdirects non-Spanish speaking Joan to wrong bus

21 Ralph sees her on wrong bus. Bus traversing mt road. Peasant-filled bus, Zolo in back.

22 Joan opens filthy window seeing jungle foliage, to front of bus, step on pig.

23 **PP I**: Joan distracts bus driver who runs in to broken-down jeep, people get off, taking crates of birds from jeep & walking up road.

Act II = Life 180 degrees: Joan & Jack quest to follow the map and get to Cartegena

24 Joan finds suitcase, Zolo observes people out-of-sight

25 Zolo pulls gun & demands map, Jack approaches on ridge above, Zolo shoots at him, fires back, Joan under bus. Zolo runs off up road.

26 Jack approaches talking to himself about ruined jeep & missing birds

27 Jack looks under bus at Joan (***MEETING***). Zolo stops little car on rutted road driven by Ralph, flashes badge, R. agitated, Zolo tries French when gets in car.

28-29 Jack finds sailboat pic, Joan needs phone & tells about to Cartagena, Who? Man with gun. I need help, Lighten up, Life & death so I'll pay,

30 Bargaining & agree on $375 in Travelers Checks, Joan walks, Jack drags suitcase & drops beside her then walks ahead. Zolo arrives at village Policia.

31 Torrential rain, Jack trudging, Joan dragging suitcase, asks what in it. Decent walking shoes?

32 Pitches case down embankment. As Joan curse, gives way, first her then him sliding down mountainside in mud, She lands in deep puddle, Jack ends up head-first between her legs

33 Jack "What a ride! Are you hurt?" Name? Joan Wilder, Welcome to Colombia.

34 Ralph on phone to Ira, Mobilizing for Iwo Jima here, Sees his wanted poster

35 On yacht Ira tells Elaine sis being tracked by butcher who killed Elaine's husband

36 Jack finds sailboat pic, rain stopped, Joan checking torn clothes, chops heels off shoes

37 Fired on, Zolo with troops, **"**After you.**"** I'm a romance novelist, sister's in trouble, run into jungle, Jack hacking with machete

38 **Pinch I=** "Wake up to ruin a man's life?" Where? Following trail, Come out edge of gorge, bridge pre-Colombian art (Trapped)

39-40 Jack heroically hunkers down as troops approach, "Stay behind me," he doesn't see Joan starting on bridge, almost falls thru, undeterred, board gives & she grabs vine swinging to other side, Jack swings on vine but hits wall.

41 Jack climbs up as Joan drinking one of miniature bottles, Zola's soldiers firing

42-43 Raining again, Jack stops hacking, Joan takes machete & leads, Jack looks at long legs (***Jack's Interest***), Joan screams at skeleton hanging out crashed plan, Jack comforts, inspect wreckage

44-46 In cargo plane of marijuana, 40 yrs in States, life here, "I've been to college." As Joan pats dry, Jack finds pilot bag & bottle of liquor, Elaine's favorite, Tell me about your sister, (***Engagement*** *invitation*), Husband killed & here to comfort, Truth & pulls map from her bag, Devils' Fork..

47-48 Burning marijuana for warmth & getting high, Joan eating olives & questions him, What you want, All you care about, Save self (***Permission*** *to share)*

49 **Mid-Point =** "Look at me!" Jack heroically hacks snake over her shoulder & pulls out poisonous "Bush Master"

50 Policia encounter Zolo's troops who deliver uniform. Joan drinking as Jack cooking snake & reading magazine. "Doobie Brothers are dead?"

51-53 Jack T. Colton, how long down here? Came to get money for boat to sail around world, By self? Sounds lonely (prolonged eye contact = ***ATTRACTION***) She passes out, so he looks over map again.

54 Ralph asleep in car on roadside as Zolo's troups pass. Joan & Jack walk into mt. village, followed by henchman as walk.

55 Hombre! Jack clicks safety off on shotgun as turn, Joan quickly asks about a car (*Joan **Liking** enough to protect Jack*). Bell maker.

56 Connect with drug running Sh-h-h! Rings bell & knocks Hang back (*Jack **Liking** enough to protect Joan*)

57-58 Juan opens peep door, You speak English, want to rent or buy a car, extends pistol, turn to face henchmen with drawn guns. "Write us out of this, Joan Wilder." Juan: THE Joan Wilder? I read all your books, henchmen smiling, waving. They enter luxurious villa, shown her books, Xerox broken.

59 Zolo & men arrive in mt. village, shows knife to old woman, boy sneaks off to villa

60 Schmoozing Joan, gives Jack one of her books. Have a car? Talk about my little mule Pepe,

61-64 Crash jeep thru garage door past Zolo, Miss fav. Pig, pointing out "sites," Zolo's jeeps pursuing & shooting, speeds past cornfields, road, no bridge, ramp elevates & launches across strem then blocks Zolo's jeeps.

65 Dried off Joan picking wild flowers on mt. side beside Pep, as relaxed Jack reads her book. Then stands & sees the map's Devil's Fork, hurries to be on their way to village below.

66-67 Ralph in village on phone to Ira, lost her, turns see dismount from Pepe "Lucky s.o.b., she's here with some guy. Jack rooms & Xerox big enough for map. Joan on phone then Elain OK & hands Jack checks

68 Jack: take to dinner, go get cleaned up & I'll buy us some clothes. Key "Lucky No. 7" Mine, too as she walks away. Joan out of shower finds beautiful clothes on bed.

69 "Beautiful" Thank you, Jack. He's definitely attracted! Read your book, impressed. My way of living in another age., Jack gives her heart necklace (***CONNECTION***)

70 Ralph sees her bag by table, "Let's dance" I don't know how. Ralph under full table between as Jack teaches Joan to dance.

71 Woman diner discovers Ralph, pulls up & beats, while Joan getting into sexy salsa dance, swings her out & back into his arms.

72-73 **Pinch II**: Kiss with fireworks behind & crowd dancing around them, Jack's boat picture as abed naked, Take you around world & back (***LOVE***), Why haven't taken map? Know close, We could get treasure.

74 Have to give up to save Elaine, Of course, Let's go for it, As kiss his hand pulls map from mattress & replaces in her bag. (***MISUNDERSTANDING***)

75 Zolo arrives in mt. town**,** They sneak out second story, , throw gear into closest car (Ralph's who is under blanket in back), Hot wire, Try key.

76-*77* Drive past shrine, horseback soldier radios location, stop, Joan: "Hear that?" Folds map to show a waterfall, Couple wading into behind waterfall, in caves "La Leche de Madre?" Mother's milk.

78-79 Ceiling formation dripping into milky pool, digging, Joan: You're the best time I've ever had." "Never been anybody's best time, Jack pulls up bundle, opens on "rabbit statue, Joan tells of writing about hiding IN a statue, VIOLA = Huge Emerald "El Corazon" We're in a lot of trouble.

80-82 Ralph behind with gun: Put in the bag. Arrive back at car with Ralph: At least I'm honest and wasn't trying to romance it from under her! Zolo coming. Couple into car as Ralph running. Follow that stone. Jack tackles & grabs bag as Joan drives down hill. Horses & vehicles surround Ralph. Joan drives into swollen river & swept toward huge falls. Jump!

*83-**84*** **PPII:** Survive trip over big falls but on opposite sides of river so Joan must trust Jack (***SEPARATION***) Name hotel. You've got the map. But you've got the stone. Shooting. I'll meet you there!

Act III = Resolution: Rescuing Elaine & escaping vengeful Zolo:

85 Battered Joan arrives at Hotel Cartegena, phones Ira. See fort? Take water taxi, 2 hrs, by yourself

86 Joan checks on Jack Colton, Not checked in (*Distrust* = ***Tension Increase***), Night taxi to fort, cautiously looks around.

87-88 Sees burning fire down corridor, "Over here. Stop. Let me see the map." See Elaine who is trust into archway. Joan pulls out map, drops & backs as ira & men approach. Ira wears loupe to view map's authenticity. "Joan Wilder, you and your sister . . . can go!"

89-90 Sisters hug, gunfire**,** Jack trust into another archway **"**Missed you at the hotel." Pushed forward with gun in back. Zolo to Ira, takes & burns map, battered Ralph crawls forward threatening Ira. Zolo: "Where is stone?" Joan: Didn't find.

91 Climax Begin: Zolo drags Joan to crocs, cuts so dripping blood attracts, Jack: "I got it."

92 Jack hesitates & soldier slams crotch, barely grimaces then shakes leg until stone rests on top of his boot. "Choke on it!" He kicks launching Stone in an arc.

93 Zolo reaches out to catch stone & croc bites off the extended hand, Jack grabs gun as Joan & Elaine crouch & run into fort corridor. Crazed Zolo follows them, grabbing hunk of wood.

94 Ira's men on top of wall fire down providing cover, Zolo after the women, Jack sees big yellow tail crawling away.

95 Ira & men run off out-distancing Ralph, into boat, Send it back for you, Jack grabs tail of croc as tries to go into water.

96 Zolo corners women, Die slow or fast like a shooting star, Joan Wilder? She snaps open knife & throws but stuck in wood, Ealine faints, Zolo Closes, backing Joan sees Jack below & calls for help.

97 Holding croc, Jacks sees struggle, (*recognizes **NEED** for one another*), lets go but but can't crawl wall fast enough, Zolo & Joan fall onto lattice-work over croc pit, Zolo with knife.

98 Joan grabs cigar & rams into stump of arm, Zolo screams, she leaps away, staggering zolo falls on lamp & set on fire, staggering around falls into croc pit. Police sirens. Hugging Elaine as Jack arrives. **Climax End**

99 **Commitment**: Jack: Don't mention my name to the police. Joan: You're leaving me? Jack "You're going to be all right." Deep KISS. "You always were." Dives off into bay. Joan fingers locket "Damn."

100 Back In NYC, Gloria finishes script "Your best. Love when he dives off then meets her at the airport and they sail around the world. Now, a world class romantic." "A hopeful romantic."

101-102 Walking thru street venders to apt bldg. Huge sailboat on trailer parked at curb, Jack kicks rope ladder for her to climb, Yellow croc hide boots, Died a terrible death right in my arms. Joan steps into his arms "Nowhere else I'd rather be." I even read one of your novels. "Know how they all end. (***COMMITMENT*** *to one another*)

After-story Conclusion: Sailboat being pulled down avenue with Jack & Joan kissing on deck.

CONCEPTS DISCUSSION

This is a classic Hero's Journey for Joan, as well as "gorgeous good girl meets hunky bad boy" romance. The story structure and cast is tight with mounting tension and unique escapades that create an exciting ride for the audience. If you didn't catch the Progressive Concepts so far, watch again just for those.

MID-POINT EPIPHANY & AFTERMATH CONSEQUENCES

Remember that Mid-Point event is to be an awakening, an event that causes the POV Main Character to see life from a new perspective and act more assertively. In this movie, the plane wreckage scene was one of "freeing of inhibitions" for both Jack and Joan. Up to that point she had been taking her survival cues from Jack. Throughout the balance of Act II and into Act III Joan is definitely a more confident, assertive "Warrior Woman" to Jack's arrogance. She is more willing to tackle the adventure rather than just react to it. Yes, she had underlying courage and commitment to her beloved sister, but she had a rather wimpy life-force that Jack sets afire.

She has seen several instances her man's physical courage from chasing off Zolo at the bus to guiding her through the tropical jungle to killing that snake. Intelligent and observant, she is ready to poke and prod this real life "Jesse" to understand what makes him tick, to test if she can dare to hope. But, being intelligent she is also reluctant to trust everything about this adventurer, especially once they find out the enormity of the Stone's value. He comes through at the fort when Zolo is hurting her and tried to get to her as she fought her own physical battle. Then Jack gives her the greatest praise he could with "You're going to be all right, Joan Wilder. You always were." Where she had been reclusive and dowdy before Colombia, afterward she is fashionable and sparkling with life-energy, a true mate to the heroic Jack who goes to all that trouble to come for her.

So that is how you evaluate that approximate middle of any story. You look for what shifts the mind, emotions and spirit of the POV character to make him or her the catalyst for the rest of the movie events.

Progressive Concepts to Consider:

1) Appropriate Title
2) Types of Suspense utilized
3) Webbing of related elements
4) First 10 minutes prepared audience for the balance of the story
5) Character consistency after Introduction
6) Unique defiance of predictability
7) Opposition intensity increased
8) Character demonstration of profile history
9) Consequences of back-story
10) Identification of Character Arc
11) Use of Sex and Violence blatant or subtle
12) Demonstration of Anxiety Curve
13) Contrasting qualities of Antagonist to Protagonist

14) Consistently logical Scenes with smooth Transitions
15) Definitive build from Mid-Point on

By this point your mind should be picturing the Paradigm and slotting in the signposts and storytelling concepts the moment you think of each of these 15 of 24. Only nine more to go.

* * * * *

GENRE FILM Chapter 9 Exercises

Exercise 9a. Write Pg 53-57 depicting you Main Character in action and focused.

Exercise 9b. Does your character take charge and assume responsibility with confidence now? How do the supporting characters react to this? How does the Antagonist react?

Exercise 9c. Write pg 58-62 to Pinch II with your Protag forging ahead into the future and the Antagonist strengthening.

Exercise 9d. Pay close attention to your succinct narrative for any tendencies to "direct" both actors and director. Make sure you are "Macro-writing" not "micro-choreographing."

Exercise 9e. Compare your Act II evolution with the Hero's Journey. Are you feeling satisfied or struggling and feeling frustrated with the conventions? Mark any scenes that seem stilted to you for revision after you reach THE END.

CHAPTER 10

Plot Point II Dark Moment, Character Intensity, Ensemble Cast/Westerns

Here we are at the 75% point in the script, the Dark Moment when the Hero gets his or her "comeuppance" after the glory moment of Pinch II. Just as all that has gone before has logically led to this point, this moment also should not be predictable. It absolutely must be poignantly dramatic. Again, you should have done a "What if" list of possibilities that will come close to destroying your Hero.

IMPORTANCE OF PLOT POINT II

By now the audience has a deep emotional investment in the welfare and success of the hero. They should also feel they can figure out what the Antagonist is going to do, but in both instances you are going to manipulate and trick that audience. You are going to make this Plot Point II event worse than the audience could possibly imagine.

> YOU ARE GOING TO MAKE THIS PLOT POINT II EVENT WORSE THAN THE AUDIENCE COULD POSSIBLY IMAGINE.

In our society we tend to not anticipate the worst-case scenario from people. That's why people in power are able to cover up bad and even heinous behavior. We cannot imagine they would stoop so low when they hold such lofty positions of respect and responsibility. We want our leaders and our heroes to be exemplary human beings. Well, storytellers are in the business of bursting those idealistic bubbles. We portray human beings at their very worst, their most vicious, at a level where they no longer control their animalistic baser instincts.

Plot Point II of your story is meant to crush the "Good" side of the equation and celebrate the triumph of the "Evil." That is high drama. Why? Because it forces the Hero to either surrender, give up, die in dishonor OR . . .

fight. This is the ultimate test of the "Good" that will motivate the Hero into well-thought out but risky action with no guarantee of success. The Character Arc will be headed toward completion because you are about to demonstrate the ultimate proof of your Statement of Purpose.

At this same time when the Antagonist is feeling triumphant and proud, you do need to pay attention to how to demonstrate the possibility of ultimate victory on the side of "Evil." Remember, a powerful Antagonist motivates a Protagonist to do more than he or she thought could be achieved. Hold your audience in a grip of uncertainty with those "shades of gray" vacillation and worry over outcome. Will Good or Evil triumph?

AVOID MELODRAMA AT ALL COSTS

Melodrama ranks right up there with predictability in things to be avoided. Fiction is lies. We all know that from the start. The trick is to maintain the credibility of your lies to the point that the audience is involved and cares about the lives of the characters in the story. They want to suspend disbelief and live the characters' story. The moment you go over-the-top either making the character act illogically, "out of character" or stupidly, you will lose that audience. They will scoff, shattering the window of illusion and begin picking apart everything from that point on.

Any storyteller knows that a motivated character encountering forceful opposition will act out dramatic conflict. Drama is defined as "any series of events having vivid, emotional, conflicting or striking interest or results." Melodrama goes one step further as "a form that does not observe cause and effect and that intensifies sentiment and exaggerates emotion." A dramatic scene delivers credible insight to the audience; melodrama delivers laughs, groans, and even squirming discomfort. Drama builds illusion, whereas melodrama destroys it. Yes, you want bigger-than-life characters, empowered people who create change . . . especially at the pivotal Plot Point II. What you do not want is a story, an event, a character that is unbelievable for even one moment. Even if they sneak up on a devious or glorious action, the point is the audience must believe it.

Look for excess in dialogue and in over-reaction. Even intense comedy is reality based. Think of CLUELESS, MRS. DOUBTFIRE, THE FULL MONTY. Each film had moments of silliness and immaturity that were balanced with moments of pathos and potential. The mistakes and absurd actions of the characters had a sense of "Yeah, that could happen." Melodrama does not provide balance because it goes that one step too far. Powerful storytelling avoids melodrama by maintaining "The Three R's: Real, Relevant, Riveting."

You create an awareness that this could be **real** if the logic is aligned, the discoveries gradual, the audience eased into the evolution of worsening events with the characters. The audience has to believe these characters would act this way! You need the audience believing while asking "What does this event/ speech/character mean to the rest of the story?" As the person in control, it is the storyteller's job to make it **relevant** and important to both the character and the story. For example, if you have an emotional outburst in your story--like the crying jag in A LEAGUE OF THEIR OWN--you have to have a "pay-off" within a reasonably short time. In LEAGUE it came when the player repeated the mistake and the barely-in-control coach says "We'll have to work on that." Ultimately, in the play-offs, the significance become **riveting** and . . . she indeed gets it right. The whole sequence was not emotional patronizing the audience's sympathy. It was important to character and story.

You will find an extremely fine example in THE COWBOYS where Will Anderson is telling the boys about how the fighting works between the old bull with the experience vs. the young bull who is stronger and quicker. The riveting pay-off of this analogy comes at Plot Point II.

How riveting are these examples? They are fundamental to their stories and their characters. The emotions and drama had a reason. Intense emotions have to have an outcome and that takes planning. Live with your characters and they will tell you when they are feeling intense emotion. It is then your job to depict it as real, relevant and riveting.

Twist the knife into the emotions of your characters where they are most vulnerable and your audience will feel it too. Plot Point II must be the epitome of angst for your cast . . . thus for your audience.

JUGGLING AN ENSEMBLE CAST

Only episodic TV series toss the ball of the "lead" back and forth. When it comes to a film there will be leads, the characters who are the Point-of-View, action-causing people in the story. Does anyone doubt that James T. Kirk was the lead in any of the STAR TREK movies? And, yet we had a wonderful ensemble cast from the TV series.

Two fine examples of rich ensemble casts are THE COWBOYS and THE FAMILY STONE. John Wayne made THE COWBOYS in 1972 and his final film THE SHOOTIST in 1976. They were his "swan song" films with themes he devoutly believed in and messages he wanted to impress on the movie-going public and his fan base. The main POV character in both was the lead played by the Duke but the balance of the casts of both were memorable. In the 2005 THE FAMILY STONE, Sarah Jessica Parker was the up-tight character causing all the problems during the final Christmas gathering with the matriarchal Diane Keeton dying of cancer. The film was about all the family members as they revolved around the one outsider.

The POV character simply is, while the rest of the cast reflects their essence off that person in an ensemble story. You achieve ensemble uniqueness by carefully considering the importance of each person to the plot. Then you create Character Profiles the actors can explode on the screen in each of their scene appearances. Ignore the stereotypes by making them highly motivated with their own powerful personas. Finally, understand the Life Stage and each person's Anxiety Curve coping mechanisms. Think about the amount of screen time each character will have. When each is in a scene focused on their "story" or agenda, give them command of the scene.

Carefully assess the ensemble cast of THE COWBOYS and how they all impacted and reacted to Plot Point II.

WESTERN GENRE

Though the heyday of the Western played out in the 40's, 50'and 60's, the genre and its mystique will always have a cyclical attraction. The generally accepted reason is that the persona of the cowboy and the atmosphere of the frontier epitomize the American psyche. TV movies and mini-series and features for the movie theaters will appear in a perennial ebb-and-flow, cyclical manner. Do not discount the iconic plot and character types that make Westerns a significant part of storytelling the world over. Know where the genre is almost as popular as in the U.S.? Germany and Japan. Go figure.

DO NOT DISCOUNT THE ICONIC PLOT AND CHARACTER TYPES THAT MAKE WESTERNS A SIGNIFICANT PART OF STORYTELLING THE WORLD OVER.

Quite obviously, most of what applies to Historical stories applies to the western genre. However, there are contemporary westerns, stories being told of rural and rodeo life, and contemporary range issues, such as federal management of grazing and wildlife areas. One simply has to read any number of magazines dealing with the various horse breeds, the cattle and sheep industry, even modern communities of the far western and Inter-mountain West to realize not all westerns need be historical. The challenges of nature's frontier are still evident.

Founded in 1953, Western Writers of America was one of the first professional genre writing organizations. You can investigate more at their website www.westernwriters.org.

Most avid writers of the genre are devoted students and researchers with extensive personal libraries. One of the most valuable reference works is the Writer's Digest book *How to Write a Western Novel* by Matt Braun. The books is not only a valuable resource, but it reflects the brilliant, award-winning, late author. His work and that of other late-greats like Louis L'Amour, Elmer Kelton, Don Coldsmith, and Jory Sherman are written with authentic detail any screenwriter can find stimulating. You cannot "fake" authentic details, historical basis, and the sense of place.

So, do you get the impression that you need to **research** era, professions and daily living to write credible westerns? Ultimately, you must research until you feel comfortable in the skin of the character living the story.

FUNDAMENTAL CONCEPTS OF WESTERNS

1. RESEARCH all things western right down to food, clothing, tools, daily life.

- History buffs, especially those who are either living the contemporary western life or who harbor profound respect for place and era will catch errors such as two vs. three pronged barbed wire in the wrong year or the Nez Perce Appaloosa horse being ridden in the plains 20 years before the breed was even evolved in the Northwest.

2. Incorporate Western or Frontier Values

a. **Rugged Individualism** because the majority of people moving west were doing so to rebuild shattered lives. The culture respected a man for what he was at that moment, not what he had come from. Questions were not asked and information was offered sparingly.

b. **Frontier equality/integrity expect** so rarely was a man (or woman) judged by comparison but rather by their word or how they chose to represent themselves. Mostly the concept was "You will be judged honest and truthful until you prove yourself otherwise." Many a binding contract was forged on a hand shake.

c. **Survival and hospitality made frontier people dependent on one another.** These values were born of isolation and distance. When one stayed at a stocked cabin, one was expected to leave it better than found and to drop off something the next traveler could use. Respect and good manners were highly regarded commodities, quietly assessed, sternly expected. If one did not comply, that person's unreliable reputation spread. Survival did not tolerate fools.

d. **Visions of social order vs. anarchy** grew out of questing to build secure homes and rear families, to establish quiet, prosperous communities where hard work was rewarded with respect and improved business opportunities. Elements recognized as symbols of civilization and refinement were prized, such as music, books, churches, laws that forced the undisciplined to respect the lives and property of others.

e. **Moral justification** drove many conflicts of who was more right and who had the power to enforce that belief, be it the wealthier rancher, the biggest man, the best fighter, the sheer numbers and social machine of the white over the Indians, or even vigilante acts when laws were nonexistent or not enforceable.

3. Profile Characters first then outline the western cause-effect plot.
- Profiling allows you to understand life experience that prescribes option awareness appropriate to time and place. Awareness of actual events unfolding at that time and place should always be a consideration of how this character would fit into whatever was evolving. Western characters will give you plot, not the other way around.

4. Identify your primary conflict, thus the type of western plot.
- When you understand the cause-effect of the conflict you know where to twist and turn the results to create less predictable plot events.

5. Identify potentially "flat stereotype" and work to give depth of characterization
- Yes the fittest survive but the how's and why's can be changed so the perpetually "Big Man-Alpha Male" becomes complex, more highly motivated for more convoluted reasons. Both Zane Grey and Louis L'Amour created novel after novel with stereo-typical Protagonists. Their most memorable were memorable because they were different! Remember that. *How the West Was Won* became an iconic movie spectacle, just as actors John Wayne, Sam Elliott, and Tom Selleck enthusiastically sought roles in the film versions of L'Amour's stories.

6. Put emphasis on effects of Frontier or Nature on the humans.
- It matters not if the place is Pre-American Revolution Great Lakes or crude Sitka, Alaska Gold Rush or modern Yosemite National Park or the Australian Outback. Weather and geography are major players in the survival day-to-day. Weather and frontier are both common denominators or great equalizers that have to be dealt with, no matter the technology.

WESTERN CHARACTER REQUIREMENTS

The essential characteristics of westerners are a **deep motivation to establish home, need to achieve their own perceived status or role and drive to attain an acceptable identity**. So, the once rich Southerner who lost all in the Civil War learns to farm, is reclusive with his painful memories and finds contentment in day-to-day living, not shallow social conventions . . . but is willing to let loose his violent fighting skills if threatened. The poor son of a coal miner hungers to be a powerful cattle baron, the abandoned wife fearlessly establishes a brothel to put food on the table for her two children while hiding her charitable acts of kindness. Makes no difference if the character is Protagonist or Antagonist, these western characteristics apply across the board.

The other character area that needs development is a westerner is a **survivor capable of adapting.** If you didn't catch Hawk Ostby's COWBOYS

& ALIENS in the summer of 2011 you missed connecting with a couple of iconic character types: wealthy local cattle baron (Harrison Ford) and dangerous loner (Daniel Craig). Of course, that movie is a prime example of mixing genres that comparatively succeeded.

You may think most human beings fit into the above categories, but you would be wrong. Most people want the optimal return for the least amount of effort, be it comfort or food or wealth or public acclaim. The exceptional people are the ones who are willing to sacrifice, accept the consequences and survive them because they are capable of adapting and changing direction to achieve their end. They are not willing to merely exist. They push the envelope, no matter the circumstance. They will not be denied!

WESTERN PLOT TYPES

As you think about these remember you must consider 1) time period's acceptable conduct, 2) historical events of the era, and 3) place. All three will change the dynamics of character and of reasonable plot events. Think about one of Polti's (Appendix F) in one of these plots.

1. Railroad/Union Pacific Story
2. Ranch Story
3. Building-an-Empire Story
4. Revenge Story
5. Ethnic/Cultural Values Clash
6. Marginal Hero Challenged
7. Townspeople vs. Lawless

- Note: A dominant percentage of townspeople had either fought to establish their homes OR were former Civil War combatants who were fighting and weapon savvy. Keep that in mind!

8. Indian vs. Society
9. Environmental/Mining
10. Trail Drive
11. Cavalry vs. Indians
12. Outlaw Story
13. Marshal/Lawman Story
14. Flight-Pursuit Story
15. Escaping Past (that catches up)
16. Mountain man/Frontiersman Story
17. Ranch vs. Farm/Sheep Story
18. Defying Government Control
19. Wagon Train Story
20. Abandonment/Coming-of-Age

Consider that many of these issues or plot types can be presented in any genre. However, when placed in a rugged frontier context with unstable social order (even lawlessness), independence and personal integrity at issue, the stories present an edginess that just cannot be created when convenience and comfort are easily attainable in a predictable modern social order.

WESTERN FILM ANALYSIS

As you analyze for the signpost events, the significance of the characters, and the stress created by the obstacles, you also will find your eye considering the authenticity of the backdrop of place, props, and costuming to create credibility. Those may not be the elements in the control of the original screenwriter, but they quickly become the canvas of the painting.

* * * * *

THE COWBOYS

By Irving Ravetch, Harriet Frank, Wm. Dale Jennings
1972, Starring: John Wayne, Bruce Dern, Roscoe Lee Brown

Length: 125 minutes

Log Line: An aging Montana cowman teaches young boys how to be men as they herd cattle to market.

Statement of Purpose: To prove that integrity, courage and character can be taught by example.

Intro Image: Rounding up a lot of horses into "breaking" them

First 10 minutes
Who: Will Andersen, aging rancher with a stern work ethic and sense of responsibility
When: 1875 (gold discovery in Montana, son's death on headstone 1856 "... would be 40 now.")
Where: Montana
What: Loses adult cowhands to a gold strike
Why: Needs to get 1,500 head of cattle across Montana to market before snow flies

Four related subplots:
Aging
Boy vs. Man
Rustlers
Cimarron as fatherless boy

Time Line: Few weeks of fall

Image repeats:
(Times 3 Rule of Intro, Refer, Use)
Knife: Cimarron-Slim fight, Asa holds to Dan's throat, Dan cuts rein
Guns: Boys give up, Boys take from chuck wagon, Boys use
Brave vs. Strong Man: Andersen calls Asa Liar, Young vs. Old Bull fighting, Asa vs. Andersen fight
Nightlinger's strength: Boys'cabin tale,"feel to be afraid," "those I have killed, those I am about to."
Southerner Asa: Civil war, Carpetbaggers, insults Nightlinger
Booze: Andersen & Nightlinger drink, Boys drink, Nightlinger offers Andersen when dying
Charley: Jew tried to fit in everywhere, One of the boys, Mourned at death
Dan's Glasses: Loss causes Charley's death, Handles while mourning, Asks back then Asa breaks
Cimarron: Anderson "I'll have to think you over," "Big mouth don't make a big man," Beloved father
Widowhood: Sisters buried their husbands, "You return safely," tombstone
First sexuality: Hooch-Kooch dancer, Nightlinger's Osceola, Temptation by soiled doves

Act I = Set-up of Ordinary World: Ranch life of rounding up livestock
10 min **Intro:** Needs men, boys will be boys
17 min **Inciting Incident**: Boys show grit by riding "Crazy Alice"
35 min **PP I:** Asa caught in lies, Will prefers integrity of his boys

Act II = Life 180 degrees: Life on the trail drive
45 min **Pinch I:** Boys saying good-by to families (facing very real dangers)
69 min **Mid-Point:** Near drowning brings Cimarron in & forces confrontation of man-boy stutter
93 min **Pinch II**: Boys drinking talk appreciated by Andersen & Nightlinger
71 min **PPII:** Rustlers invade, Asa intimidates, fights then shoots Andersen

Act III = Resolution of all Issues: Boys take on the manly role of revenge & herd recovery
118 min **Climax:** Boys (with Nightlinger) kill every rustler coldly administer justice to Asa
123min **Commitment**: Boys drive cattle thru Belle Fouche
After-story Conclusion: Boys order & place the headstone

Dialogue Notes:
Andersen: Directness, Confidence
Nightlinger: Educated/experienced musical cadence
Asa: Southern drawl, manipulative & vicious tones
Kate: Seductive pleasant tone

Alpha Character posturing differences:
Andersen, tough, hard-working, stiff-necked, principled
Nightlinger, competent, insightful, loyal, caring, a romantic
Asa, manipulative, demanding, arrogant, vicious and enjoys hurting others
Charles Honeycutt (oldest boy), born leader, quiet, confident, willing
Cimarron (Hispanic bastard), belligerent, defensive, tough, hungry for respect

Supporting cast Unique Character Gems:
Annie (Will's wife), gentle, hard-working
Anse (store clerk), understanding, problem-solver, supportive
Fats (chubby boy), cautious, willing, sense of humor
Dan (glasses), tentative but willing, insecure so vulnerable to intimidation
Bob (stutterer), very insecure, defensive but willing to prove himself
Charlie (Jewish boy), gentle, hard-working, always friendly
Kate (madam), opportunist, hard, manager with loftier plans

Background effects, the nuances of aura:
Food, fatigue, routine of driving cattle, camp life

Elements from Other Genres: Juvenile, Action-Adventure

Question: Is John Wayne's Will Andersen credible or "over-the-top" demanding of the western boys?

(Appearance) or reference to recurrence of Evil Theme in Min: Hard/Dangerous Life with rustlers in **BOLD.**

Act I = Set-up of Ordinary World: Ranch life of rounding up livestock
07
11

14-20 Inciting Incident: Riding Crazy Annie" (Means boys trying a man's job)
21
25
28
29 Guns into wagon
31 Young & Old bulls fighting
33-35 Plot Point I: Asa lies then threatens when Andersen won't hire

Act II = Life 180 degrees: Life on the trail drive
37
40
41-43
45-47 Pinch I: Parting from families, starting the drive
50
52
54-57 Epiphany Mid-Point: Near-drowning, Cimarron, name-calling challenge
60
65-69 **Pinch II:** Boys take risk of drinking & voicing views on Andersen (as "men")
72-74 Dan caught by Asa
76-77
78-81 Charlie killed
82
84
90-92 Being followed
93-104 Plot Point II: Rustlers invade, Asa intimidates, fights, shoots Andersen

Act III = Resolution of all Issues: Boys take on the manly role of revenge & herd recovery
105-106 Nightlinger finds Andersen dying
108-109 Boys bind Nightlinger & take back their guns
110
112 First killing
113 Second killing
114-115
117
118-120 Climactic Battle: Remaining men chased, trapped, killed, Asa's death deliberate
121
123-124 **Commitment:** Reaching trail head & ordering headstone "Beloved Husband and Father"
125 **After-story** Placing headstone, "Burning daylight"

CONCEPTS DISCUSSION

This is one of the leanest, most complete films ever made in Hollywood. Timing of the story events is perfection. Character development is visual and gradual. When looking for all that makes a good story, you will find it here.

One element that few films have is a mirroring of the first half of the film in pay-offs in the second half. THE COWBOYS accomplished this with subtle satisfaction in everything from dialogue to actions, characterizations to scenic views, philosophies to violence. The masterful rendering of this "pay-off" element is a technique to be carefully studied.

PLOT POINT II SIGNIFICANCE

THE COWBOYS has one of the clearest, most dramatic and most logical Plot Point II sequence in cinematic storytelling. Absolutely everything prior has led to this culmination. The confidence, arrogance, and western character epitomized in Will Andersen demands his defiance of Asa and his rustlers. He is the man to his boys and the Alpha Male. At the same time the lack of conscience and bullying arrogance of Asa forces *him* to totally destroy the better man any way he can. The impotent boys have no recourse but to stand there and watch. Seeing this man they have all come to respect and, yes, love as a father figure, defying the lawless, amoral Asa and be killed for it does not destroy them or turn them into weeping babies. No, they become coldly determined to "finish the job" no matter what it costs. They change from inept, uncertain boys into focused men willing to take life and have their revenge. (And isn't it interesting that by the time they reach Belle Fouche they have reverted back to being boys, just with a different self-awareness and confidence).

Plot Point II has many names such as the "Dark Moment." The one importance of this event is that you demonstrate the strong Protagonist being defeated/brought down/shoved into a corner and has only two options: Give up or come out roaring. This event is not coincidental nor should it be predictable. It must be *logical* and it must tweak every soul-deep fiber in the Protagonist's being. It also must reflect the gloating or arrogance of the Antagonist who appears to have won the day.

USE OF ENSEMBLE CAST

Every story will have a main POV character even if others get so much screen time or story telling opportunity. In THE COWBOYS that character was obviously Will Andersen. He was the catalyst who started the story and made the story happen even in Act III when he is dead and in that After-story

Conclusion when the boys are placing his marker and all grin to his oft repeated "Burning daylight" admonition.

However, the distinctive characterizations in this script make for a good case of how to depict an ensemble cast to their very best. Every one of those boys had a distinctive history, demeanor, manner of speaking, and skill set. Their relatively close age span made for common reactions and perceptions. That could have gotten confusing, yet the circumstances given the boys put each on display to shine in his own spotlight. They were unique individuals every time they were on screen, even when working together.

YOUR JOB AS A WRITER IS FOCUS ON QUALITY OF CHARACTERIZATION, NOT THE BALANCE OF WHO HAS HOW MANY SCENES.

Analyze ***one Character at a time*** throughout an entire script or movie where a star-studded cast is presented. Look for what made each unique and memorable. Also evaluate the number of speeches and scenes each character has. When dealing with dramatic egos you have to understand the importance of quality vs. quantity. Your job as a writer is focus on quality of characterization, not the balance of who has how many scenes.

Progressive Concepts to Consider:

1) Appropriate Title
2) Types of Suspense utilized
3) Webbing of related elements
4) First 10 minutes prepared audience for the balance of the story
5) Character consistency after Introduction
6) Unique defiance of predictability
7) Opposition intensity increased
8) Character demonstration of profile history
9) Consequences of back-story
10) Identification of Character Arc
11) Use of Sex and Violence blatant or subtle
12) Demonstration of Anxiety Curve
13) Contrasting qualities of Antagonist to Protagonist
14) Consistently logical Scenes with smooth Transitions
15) Definitive build from Mid-Point on
16) Balance of Character story importance to role
17) Every Scene credible vs. melodrama

* * * * *

THE MAN FROM SNOWY RIVER

By John Dixon, Fred Culcullen
1982, Starring, Tom Burlinson, Sigrid Thorton, Kirk Douglas

Length: 100 minutes

Log Line: In 1888 Australia a young, ambitious horseman hires on at a wealthy American's cattle station finding family intrigue and a love that risks his integrity.

Statement of Purpose: To prove that character and young love can win over arrogance of all kinds.

Intro Image: Running horses

First 8 minutes
Who:
Jim Craig, hard-working young horseman of the high country
Henry Craig, hard-working small-time land owner determined to survive hard times
When: Early Fall (1988)
Where: Australia's Snowy River high country (Queensland)
What: Money-strapped son & father plan and work to capture wild horses
Why: Need horses to provide material means to maintain home and grow into future

Four related subplots:
Harrison & Jessica
Harrison & Spur history
Manly Respect
Spur's Gold Mine

Time Line: Two weeks in fall of 1888

Image repeats:
Running horses
Rearing Stallion
Mountain tops
Weather threat
Youthful risk-taking
Gold Mine
Wealth's power

Act I = Set-up of Ordinary World: Jim seeks work to support Craig homestead
8 min **Intro:** Wild horses motivate Craigs to attempt to capture but Henry killed
10 min **Inciting Incident**: Spur gives Jim the mountain horse
14 min **PP I:** Jim approaches Harrison's lawyer looking for work

Act II = Life 180 degrees: Jim's life as a hired hand falling for owner's daughter
30 min **Pinch I:** Put-down by foreman as inexperienced
56 min **Mid-Point:** Saves Jessica & admits love
72 min **Pinch II**: Clancy speaks highly
77 min **PPII:** Unworthy Jim leaves teary Jessica

Act III = Resolution: Jim earning men's respect capturing the wild horses
93 min **Climax:** Jim chasing down the mob
99 min **Commitment**: Back for brood mares & whatever else is mine, Jessica agrees
After-story Conclusion: Jim's triumphant return to his mountain homstead

Dialogue Notes:
Differences between Aussies & Americans
Both Spur & Harrison verbose
Cultured Aunt Rosemary
Crude Curly

Alpha Character posturing differences:
Jim vs. Curly, confident & caring vs. arrogant braggart
Harrison's authoritative in-control tones vs. Foreman Caine
Clancy vs. Harrison vs. Spur, man's man vs. arrogant land-own vs. happy working miner
Jessica vs. Aunt Rosemary, overly confident young woman vs. strong-willed aunt

Supporting cast Unique Character Gems:
Spur, Harrison's identical twin
Clancy, legendary horseman & frontiersman
Curly, unprincipled ranch hand
Frew, American tracker
Shortman, Bible-reader
Aunt Rosemary, sophisticated feminist
Mrs. Bailey, cook

Background effects, the nuances of aura: Rugged high country of Australia's Queensland, challenging rock cliffs, crumbling mine, Spur's cluttered cabin, Harrison's comparatively luxurious home

Elements from Other Genres: Juvenile, Romance, Action-Adventure

Questions: 1) Was Kirk Douglas's two-for-one acting a credible contrast so audience loved Spur but "hated" Harrison? 2) Did Clancy seem extraneous and just used as a point maker to bridge Jim to Harrison?

Appearance or reference to recurrence of Evil Theme in Min: Arrogant Social Power as demonstrated by Harrison in **BOLD** though have-have not social ladder also a factor throughout. Because of its strong romance, I also ***italicized*** the elements of the Relationship Plane.

Act I = Set-up of Ordinary World: Jim seeks work to support Craig homestead
1-3 Running horses (mob of brumbies), Craig mare Bess upset, Jim talks Henry into trapping
4-6 Jim using draft horse to pull logs, mob runs down trail taking Bess, Henry killed
7-8 Spur with Jim at Henry's graveside, older horsemen tell him he has to earn right to live there
9 Jim rides Spur's cart to his shack.
10 **Inciting Incident**: Spur gives Jim the mountain horse
11 Go after Bess, Forget the mare, Jim rides into town as Harrison striding beside train
12-13 Valuable colt, last of Old Regret, unload, dog makes rear, Jim helps Jessica, angers her (***Meeting***)
14 **PP I:** Jim approaches Harrison's lawyer looking for work, "Have to find you something."

Act II = Life 180 degrees: Jim's life as a hired hand falling for owner's daughter
15 Spur in mine, Horseman Clancy appears, tells of Henry's death
16 Jim to big station, Harrison "Give you a try."
17 Spur tells Clancy of Jim's share in mine, shows gold nuggets
18-**21** Foreman & cook note hard-working Jim, Curly ambles in while Jim mucking, condescending, Jessica to stable, finds halter broken, Jim helps tie (***Look***), shared laughter, Harrison rides in
22 Jim walks H.'s horse telling Curly "Tom Fools Knot," H. & Jessica bicker over unlady-like
23-24 Jim at bunk, men talk of high country muster awaiting Clancy, Jim tells his father & Cl. "mates."

25 All in yard awaiting Cl. arrival, "legend," He greets Jim "Sorry about father. He was a good mate."

26-28 Formal dinner, H. expansive**.** Cl. "You sold, I drove.," Aunt Rosemary intervenes, decanter, "Daughter has a gd mind & way with horses," No future on plains so have to go at high country, enough to ship refrigerated beef, Cl. "Tear the guts out of the country?" Lawyer "Toast to what is and what can be."

29 Jim enters with wood, Cl. Asks him about taming Snowy River, "As likely as taming the tide." H. announces has no brother

30 **Pinch I:** Curley picking on Jim, Foreman Caine announces leave at sunrise, J. told not going, "I don't make the orders; I give them."

31-32 Dawn mount up, Jim bitter as Jessica scowling at H., two watch riders depart

33-35 Jessica pounding piano to aunt's criticism, Jim with tea try & invite to share, Aunt goes for another cup, both sorry for themselves, Try make a lady, "Won't." "Sorry," Mom teach piano before died & Jess never knew hers, "She must have been beautiful because look at you." (***Interest***) Drinks & leaves. Jess playing beautifully as aunt returns. She thinks.

36 Morn Jim feeding colt as Jess enters barn, not mean bone, Curly will find one. Jess asks Jim if he could break the colt with father away for more than a week. (***Engagement***)

37-40 Scenes: Jim working colt, trust, driving reins, Jess & Jim talk, in slickers in rain & she shoves off fence with laughter (***Permission***), saddle, both petting colt, Jim listens to Jess's piano at night & see both staring as if thinking of one another (***Attraction***), brumbies running at night

41-42 Morning Jim grooming colt, sees brumbies passing with haltered Bess, leaps on colt's back "No, Jim!" Colt throws him into path of mob. Trampled then turns over to stallion rearing above him. Abed when Jess enters bunk with tray (*Jess's Concern* = ***Liking***), argue about intent, "You are a foolish boy!"

43 H. "Where is he?" "I came off a horse." "Can get back on for 20 we left on top?"

44-45 Spur looking at woman's picture as Jim arrives, Saw Bess with brumbies. Never told me had brother, Spur asks about Jessica," Quitting after find cattle," Head to bluff, eating prime Hereford, make you gd cattleman yet."

47-49 H. examines colt's saddle markings & hoof, confronts Jessica in kitchen, aunt mentions stallion back & he upset the colt, Who riding? "He-" will fire when return & you on train to boarding school, Strikes her "you're as deceitful as your mother." Jess runs out, Aunt: Broke your own daughter, "Mine?"

50-51 Jess rides off station into stormy backdrop then thru rainy forest, Jim riding through mist finds cattle bunched, making coffee in shelter, Jess leading mare at night amidst thunder & lightning, horse rears & runs, she slips over edge of cliff.

52-54 H. with Caine at dawn "She's never done anything like this." Men all drunk. "Want ready to ride in ten minutes." Caine pulling men out of bed, Jess awakens on narrow ledge of escarpment & screams, Jim with cattle notes her trail, Men "Storm brewing & my daughter's in it. Stay & rot." Jim into rocks finds mare Kit dead & rides calling "Jess!" (*Jim's Concern* = ***Liking***)

55 Jess tries to climb up but can't. Hears Jim calling

56 **Mid-Point:** Jim lowers whip handle, at his camp Jess in blanket, wet clothes on logs by fire, No more for your father-Miss seeing you. (***Connection***)

57 When trapped just thought of getting to you, Jim stands: Take back, men risking in search, Got to get cattle down. "Weren't you listening?"

58 "Finish job, take you to Spur's place, "Sorry everything so clear-stands, turns away, Jim approaches "I'm sorry." Embrace.

59 Like we're the only two people on earth, Kiss (***LOVE***), view of isolation

60-61 Dressed, riding double, "So beautiful" "But wait until that gets here, Trying to kill you, but that's the challenge, "Treat the mountains like a high spirited horse.. Never take for granted. People the same, Kiss.

62 Spur hits wall of mine, partial collapse, sees gold vein "Lovely creature."

63-66 Couple arrive at Spur, Knew him. Why should I?, Jess in & finds mother's pic, Spur in "Matihilda" "No, I'm Jessica" All grown up. Your uncle, Find gold & relatives show up, Why pic of mother? Hiding? Lot of pain rather forget, You take Jess down while I take cattle, "Like my own daughteter."

67 Jim driving cattle& leaves message with scarf on tree. Jess & Spur supper, So angry, being young, Harrison beef.

68 Spur & Jess in cart cross creek. H. men find note "Safe on way home, Cart into yard at Twilight

69-70 Aunt tucking Jess in bed, tells Jess of brothers vying for mother, one won horse race & other after gold, Spur making pass at Mrs. Bailey

71-72 Pinch II: Jim interrupts, leave, no, see Jess. As Jim opens door, H. through outer door to bed & hugs Jess, asks forgiveness. Sees Jim at doorway, "Thanks. Clancy speaks highly of you. Need to talk."

73-74 "When find her?" Yesterday. "Fond?" "I love her" Damn strange sort of love. Put in bark hut." "I'd take care of her." "If you have spark of manhood you'll walk away" (Instills doubt.) "You bastard!" Spur in the doorway. "Long lost brother." Jess & aunt into room, Jess demands to know what happened

75-76 H. leaves room, aunt tells of Spur giving colt to mother, H. let loose, Spur went to tell & H. found together & shot him. Decided to leave & so died at your birth, Jim a part because colt now the stallion. Spur wants put past, hugs Jess & aunt

77 PPII: Jim: I'm leaving, too. It wouldn't wok, Jess. (***Misunderstanding***) She's crushed. Spur in cart stopped by livid H. "Whose daughter is she?" "Yours!"

Act III = Resolution: Jim earning men's respect capturing the wild horses

78-79 In bunk, Jim covers Frew (tracker), drunk Curly insults Jess & Jim fights, Frew's rifle forces Curly drop bottle, Jim wins & invites Frew to his fire anytime.

80 Jess at window, Jim rides by averting face from her tears (***Separation***), Curly releases H. colt & knows will blame on Jim

81 Caine & Frew tracked towad mt where joined the mob. H. blames Jim, Get every man & Clancy

82-84 Night camp: Spur offering drink to Jim as partner, Clancy arrives, tells of loose colt & accusing Jim, what do when bucked off-right back on, Ask too much of a man. Man? Father raised me to be, Probably wouldn't let you ride anyway.

85-87 H. yard full of preparing riders, H. porch to back of wagon address men about colt running with mob & positioned scouts, Greets Clancy but wants Jim off, Cla. "I want him with me." H. offers money to whoever gets his colt back. Men racing off, Jim trailing. Women on porch watching.

88 Spur arrives to Mrs. Bailey's delight. Men at mid-day, Cl. With Jim. Flare. Stallion with herd.

89-90 Clancy to wheel herd, Go at the jump, chasing running mob, Clancy with whip to lead & turns as men watch, Stallion bests him & mob off again, racing through forest.

91-92 Jim rides off at angle followed by Curly who loosens bridle, at stream, Curly falls, Jim fixes bridle then racing on

93-95 **Climax:** Men pull up at edge mountainside. Jim goes right on over & down steep slope, H. "Bid the mob good-by," as men riding, Caine points at Jim chasing heard on flat, Herd runs through snow to plateau where Jim circles herd & snaps whip at old stallion.

96-97 Spur readying cart as men return, Jess asks "Where's Jim?" Frew yelling "Glory be, will you look at that!" Jim moving herd toward station, Spurs grinning, Jess hurries to watch. Horses move into corral noting Bess with broken halter. Men gather at fence, Clancy grinning & touches hat in respect, Jim with whip controls horses & stallion.

98 Unsmiling Jim leads Bess to Spur's cart as background hands lead H. colt away. Harrison dismounts to offer Jim financial reward. "Not why I rode."

99 Commitment: Jim stares at him saying "Back for brood mares & whatever else is mine," H. "She's not for you." "Jessica can make up her own mind." "I told you, lad." Spur: "Not a lad. He's a man." Clancy echoes "The Man from Snowy River." Jessica smiling as walks from father's side then young couple grin & wave at one another (***Commitment***) before Jim rides off.

After-story Conclusion: Jim's triumphant return to his mountain homestead

CONCEPTS DISCUSSION

Continuing to use previous concepts, the romance of this story was marked. Hopefully, you identified story, character and Progressive Concepts beyond the romance. In considering scene, did you compare-contrast the Australian setting with our Old West?

ANALYZING FOR MELODRAMA

Critics who discount westerns frequently refer to "melodramatic story content, predictable plot and cookie-cutter characters." And some writers will agree that the very early western cinema (and novels) reinforced those concepts, with emphasis on "early." Any of you who really want to understand the nuances that shifted this genre from melodrama to complex storytelling need to watch some of the first season episodes of GUNSMOKE then watch a few from its final season. Next, watch the early (and simplistic) Henry Fonda movie DRUMS ALONG THE MOHAWK (1939) vs. his intense performance as Frank in the 1968 ONCE UPON A TIME IN THE WEST. Or you can compare the more simplistic-almost melodramatic-1957 version of 3:10 TO YUMA to the grittier 2007 version with Russell Crowe.

Did any scene in THE MAN FROM SNOWY RIVER touch you as melodramatic . . . and, if so, do you feel it was the character or the actor? Ah, there's the rub for a writer. Is it the story itself that begs for "almost" melodramatic scenes or is it the characterization from the writer's script vs. the quality of the acting? Watch a scene and listen to the dialogue you consider melodramatic and truly rewrite it how you would resolve the melodrama.

At first viewing, some scenes came off melodramatic . . . but after repeated watching the astute critic will realize the inherent characters of Jim and Jessica were fighting for self-realization as all adolescents are. Hm, that stage of development is prone to over-the-top melodrama simply because they haven't learned to control both their emotions and their presence in the world.

Think about the deliberate melodrama of the iconic film THE PRINCESS BRIDE in contrast to some really low-budget, poorly acted (usually indie) film. What is orchestrated for intentional effect and what is squirm-in-the-chair uncomfortable that you absolutely could not believe? How emotional can a plot and the characters get before someone in the audience is rolling their eyes and groaning with disgust? Hint: Even the best actor in the world cannot save a truly melodramatic scene . . . so don't give them the painful experience in the first place.

Progressive Concepts to Consider:

1) Appropriate Title
2) Types of Suspense utilized
3) Webbing of related elements
4) First 10 minutes prepared audience for the balance of the story
5) Character consistency after Introduction
6) Unique defiance of predictability
7) Opposition intensity increased
8) Character demonstration of profile history
9) Consequences of back-story
10) Identification of Character Arc
11) Use of Sex and Violence blatant or subtle
12) Demonstration of Anxiety Curve
13) Contrasting qualities of Antagonist to Protagonist
14) Consistently logical Scenes with smooth Transitions
15) Definitive build from Mid-Point on
16) Balance of Character story importance to role
17) Every Scene credible vs. melodrama

At this point you should be comfortable and intimately familiar with these 17 of 24 film concepts. They should come to you easily because your mind sees the flow of cause-effect in the overall story. You are able to utilized them to analyze films you watch and in your own script. Anything is possible when tackled a little at a time

* * * * *

GENRE FILM Chapter 10 Exercises

Exercise 10a. Write Pg 63-67 moving from the glory of Pinch II toward the pressures of Plot Point II.

Exercise 10b. Meticulously comb through your dialogue to this point for any emotional over-the-top melodrama. Remember: Real, Relevant, Riveting.

Exercise 10c. Write Pg 68-72 / Subplot stresses, Character consequences, Antag tension up to PPII.

Exercise 10d. Evaluate the primary character traits of your Main Characters so far, looking for 1) what has been demonstrated, 2) what is apparent to other characters and 3) what character strengths and weaknesses are being challenged. Mark scenes or "What if..." possibilities you need to come back to and revise to refocus on or change those character traits. Remember: audience members do not like to be talked down to because the majority will "get it" so write scenes with a light hand trusting their intellect.

CHAPTER 11

Weaving Research Accuracy, Detail, Adaptation/Historical Genre

Anyone considering historical storytelling needs to take an historical research course. Yes, certain research techniques may be carried over to digging into history, but the kinds of materials are so different that a specialized course is suggested. Such a course was offered at the University of Nebraska at Omaha under Dr. Ruth Carrigan. A native of New Orleans, her areas of expertise just happened match one student novelist's work-in-progress. She went above and beyond her course focus to explain three important creative writing concepts.

CARRIGAN'S THREE RULES OF RESEARCH FOR WRITERS

1) Accumulate a foundation of knowledge that makes you feel conversant enough in a subject to write authentically,
2) Get on with the bloody writing and asterisk any details you want to insert for later research,
3) Make the detail as back-ground authentic as possible because your character will take most things for granted and will not dwell on them.

In other words, she grounded the novice writer on the creative writing first and taught how to rely on research as reassurance for authenticity and credibility. Now, let's examine that research realm in the context of screenwriting.

WHO IS RESPONSIBLE FOR THE DETAILS?

Remember, the narrative of a screenplay is the "black shit" that should never slow the reading. The narrative is meant to provide glimpses of background and utilize authentic jargon, as well as appropriate clothing and prop names. The narrative is not the place to demonstrate you have done your research and find it necessary to instruct the reader (agent/producer/ actor) in what is appropriate to that era. Other experts will be required to verify the details in that collaborative milieu of the film-making community. All you are doing is writing the blue print in light brush strokes, not heavy-handed details.

All three of "Carrigan's Rules" are your responsibility in the original spec script and not beyond. A screenplay does not require the descriptive detail of a novel. Your job is to create the most vivid image with the fewest words possible.

There will be a team of three who will truly authenticate the "look" of a film: the costume designer, the set designer and the prop master. It is the job of the various cinematic craftsmen to make sure the camera sees nothing out-of-place or inappropriate. Their teams of even more experts create the sceneic design, the wardrobe and accessories, the props, including maintenance, repair, and distribution to the cast members. Producers and directors are charged with finding the very best people they can to consult and organize all that is needed and who are available for pre-production preparation and the shoot itself. Nowhere in that paragraph did you see a reference to the original writer.

You absolutely have to read several historical scripts and highlight authentic details in the narrative. Once you have highlighted them, "fan" the script pages to see the detail locations or flag where these details are used. You will find very little beyond innuendo and brief nuance.

DOCUMENTING YOUR RESEARCH

Think about having a file folder for each novel and screenplay that contains all the notes utilized when writing the story. That folder should include research notes. Example: For one mega-script, CROSSROADS OF LIFE AND DEATH, the writer utilized a thick, divider organized notebook and a copy of the true life main character's memoirs published as *Slow Boat to China* containing Pegge Parker's edited letters and diary entries. The notebook and book are available to provide a foundation of descriptive detail for the movie makers. Since the story is about personal issues with the first CIA agent killed in the line of duty, the notebook is also a form of legal documentation if any official should come knocking at the writer's door.

Make it a personal disciple to have folders of data (including website URL's) with notes on event verification, occupations, procedures, anything utilized to create each story. It is not important for you to insert everything you worked hard to find. It is only important that you prove your accurate references to location, time period, skills, etc. Those notes also provide consistency if you need to refer to whatever more than once. It is just as important for a screenwriter to be accurate and consistent as it is for a novelist.

One caution, though. Do not use only one anecdotal resource or an unreliable source like Wikipedia that can be changed by anybody with a differing opinion or agenda than verified experts. Yes, a screenplay is fiction, but your reputation will still rest on intelligent authenticity.

Do not ever "footnote" anything in a screenplay. If people want to know you verified your information, they will ask. A PhD-type English professor included a bibliography at the end of one of his first scripts, just as he would any other researched document. He knows better now.

HISTORICAL ACCURACY OF DIALOGUE

Etymology is the study of the origin of words. Just as you wouldn't have certain forensic practices in the 19th century or easy access to spices and chocolate in 12th century Europe, you have to guard against using certain words in the past. I'm not talking about just slang, either. When you are writing historical fiction, you have to look up when certain reference words or conversational words came into use. Sometimes even 50 years can be a flag if your reader/agent/producer happens to be an aficionado of that time period. Regionalism can get you in just as much hot water. Avoid inaccuracies by going to an unabridged dictionary or an etymology reference. Is that nit-picky? Yes and you should be.

You may think casual conversation does not require such anal attention, but you would be wrong. The cadence of speech in 6th century Scotland was entirely different than in the 19th century. That applies to formal address in polite society right down to the crude and rude exchanges between the lower classes or indigenous peoples.

So if you are going to try your hand at historical writing, do the research homework of authenticating speech patterns and word usage.

ADPATING A NOVEL TO A SCREENPLAY

In my book *Learn Screenwriting, Part Two: Adaptation*, the entire process and details of adaptation are addressed. Here is an excerpt from that discussion:

ADAPTATION STAGE ONE: The Differences between Novels and Film

Fact One: Not all novels can be successfully adapted to the screen.

Fact Two: Novelist's voice and style are moot points in the collaborative medium of film production.

Fact Three: Novels are intended to be a private exchange between the writer and the reader, whereas films are public group orgies.

Now, if you have read the above three facts and accepted them, you are ready to read on. If you choose to argue them, read something else.

In Fact One lies the essence of adaptation. Novels are written to reach the intellect of the reader. Sensations are titillated by thought association, just as factual information or exposition is provided for reader understanding. The motivation, memories, emotional impact experienced by the characters can be explained in novels. Film relies on one concept: Visual image.

Certainly sensations can be depicted visually, whether by character reaction or audience identification. For example, seeing a steaming turkey fresh from the oven evokes that aroma, just as a pile of steaming manure at the feet of a milk cow . . . You get the "picture." What film cannot do is explain what the character feels as a novel could. Those internal thoughts and emotions are frequently the fiber, the richness, the perfection of novels that cannot smoothly or naturally translate. Some films have successfully used Voice Over to allow the character to explain, usually as a device of logic. However, over-use of this intrusive device tends to annoy the audience who is caught up in experiencing the moment with the character. The V.O. can seem to be a lecturer trying to guide the interpretations of the audience who are too stupid to draw their own conclusions. Bad reaction.

Exposition is another fiction writer's device that doesn't translate well to film. Some novels rely heavily on underlying information in a character's background or a culture's history that directly impact the character's limited options or the plot events. Scrolling information at the opening, V.O., Series Shots as glimpses, or depicting a very brief back-story scene have all been used successfully to deliver information to the audience. First, ask yourself if this back-story is vital for the audience to get it or to be sucked into the total story. Then ask yourself how the vital information can be served up succinctly, actively, visually. The joy of reading is mental immersion in a different time and place. The joy of film is the visual empathy of sharing with characters the experience of the moment. Both are illusions, one totally on a mental plane, the second on the plane of visual awareness. Novels deliver the illusion slowly, but successful film create only the immediate moment. When screen storytelling becomes documentary *teaching*, the illusion is lost and the audience grows restless. Bad reaction.

Another problem inherent to adaptation: Readers of popular work formulate their own image of what the characters look like, what their voices sound like. The casted actor and the director's interpretation will more often than not conflict with the reader's image. Perfect matches are rare. An actor turning the tide of the public image so the character is known as him is even rarer. Frequently, the novelist has to *give up* his image for the sake of collaboration, which leads us into Fact Two.

The art of prose is the unique manipulation of words that defines the voice and style of a writer. Abstract and esoteric concepts separate each writer and provide for lively comparisons in the literary world. Screenplays are not literature. Screenplays are the crisp, bare-bones blue-prints that will guide the various craftsmen and artists who will translate the written word to a visual medium. The beauty of the WORD is not primary. The beauty of the image seen through the camera's eye is everything. If the glorious description of a place cannot be matched by the location scouts or constructed by the set designers, especially within budget, then it will be changed. Workability is the key word to translating fiction to film.

"Surely a novel's dialogue will adapt well, won't it?" These are the words that reflect who the characters are and what is important for them to say. And so much of movies is dialogue. In a novel the dialogue can be subtle or direct, effusive or succinct. Then the character has the luxury of an internal response. Multi-layered dialogue for dramatic interpretation must do both. The writer must be willing to delete inane, playful, redundant conversations, then create verbal exchanges that move the story. A succinct punch ending a verbal battle in a film scene can cover an entire chapter of bitter exchanges depicted in a novel. The writer simply must remember this long-ago quip: "These are movies, not talkies."

One last comment on *collaboration*. Look up the definition of that word. Then make a list of all the roles of people involved in bringing a film to the screen. (Don't know? Scribble down their titles as the credits roll by.) Remember the screenplay is merely the blue-print. Each of these people, these artists, will uniquely interpret their contribution. Some may read the original novel for *flavor*. Others may see no point since the mediums are so different. The producer's fiscal guidance and the director's leadership are central to the *feel* of the film. Early in their careers, most novelists learn they have to give over a degree of control to editors in the publishing houses who will manufacture and distribute their books. Well, the film industry spreads that control among many more people with the producer and the director at the top of the hierarchy, or cinematic food chain, if you will. Many writers contract as associate producers to retain some of their control. Still, the writer must accept that the novel's precious words, images, characters, and events will inevitably be rearranged, deleted, corrupted, and mangled for the sake of the film story, usually as a result of collaboration. The entire production crew is responsible for the end product, not just the writer. The novel's concept of intimacy between writer and reader does not exist in a theater, which brings us nicely to Fact Three.

Reading a novel is supposed to be a very personal experience. The very nature of comprehending language is personal. A newly divorced astrophysicist from the southwestern United States will not read *Madam Bovary* with the same appreciation as a schoolgirl from a village near Paris. Logically, based on each reader's unique life experience, the thought associations, the images derived from the words will be different. The reader is alone with the writer's words. True, the story and the characters remain constant, but the experience of each reader is unique in the solitude of the words registering on the mind.

Contrast this with all these individuals coming to a theater or settling in a living room to view a film. Certainly these viewers retain their individuality and opinions, but the experience of the film is a group experience. Together the audience lives those moments with the characters. The successful film holds the audience in their seats. The outside world fades away. The experiences on the screen take over the visual awareness of the audience. Afterwards, when the credits roll and the lights come up, the illusion is shattered, the real world returns, the group disperses to digest what they experienced together.

The Group Factor of film viewing needs to be understood by the novelist, not from an economic point of view but from an artistic perspective. Of course, the novelist wants to create a best-seller. Those books, however, will still be read one at a time. To be commercially marketable, a film must relate and appeal to an audience, a group, a large number of individuals who will get it, who will lose themselves in experiencing the immediate moments of the characters on that screen.

Sometimes the characters and their stories are meant to be strictly between the writer and the reader. That storytelling deserves to be revered in its truest form as a novel. But other times, the author can see a story and its people who can come alive and transport a a movie audience.

ADAPTATION STAGE TWO: How to Adapt Novels via Outlining the Screenplay

So, how does one go about this horrendously difficult yet simplistic process of adaptation? The horrendously difficult part is identifying what to cut out and ignore. The simplistic part is outlining what to leave in according to the rules of plot points, pivotal subplots, character arcing, and movie time. And, in reality, when you do the simplistic part, the horrendously difficult part naturally falls away. Tah-Dah! Outlining. That's it.

You were introduced to the "Plot Paradigm." As explained it works for every piece of fiction, be it short story, novel, stage play, or screenplay. Each can be plotted on a Paradigm Worksheet. Title, proposed length (and final draft length) in words or pages, a *Log Line* of less than 25 words, and a succinct Statement of Purpose (what the story events are going to prove to the audience) is at the top of the Worksheet. For event-plotting purposes, the main body of the diagram is divided into Act One (1/4), Act Two (1/2), and Act Three (1/4), or the ancient storytelling scheme of Beginning, Middle, and Ending. The length of each division provides a guideline for balance and unity. The plot twist at the end of Act One, the Mid-Point emotional high, and the tightening of the screws at the end of Act Two are marked, as well as the Climax and concluding Commitment in Act Three. Below this are the lines for the various Sub-Plots (and no more than four in a screenplay since more only clutter, confuse, and lack time for conclusion). Then a space is left across the sheet to track Image Repeats, that subtle dramatic tool that saves time. Finally, across the bottom, is the Story Time Line that will aid in the logical flow of sequencing and provide a cohesive frame or unit of time for the story.

Many an author will choose to adapt one of his or her own novels to a screenplay, That writer needs to refer to that Paradigm or construct one if not done in the first place.

The novel's Log Line needs to be considered in terms of film marketability and potential audience. Is this a character-driven story that would work better as an event-driven film? Or is this a character-driven story with film potential from Mid-Point through Act Three? How would that Log Line read? In less than 25 words, of course.

Next the writer must evaluate the Statement of Purpose for the *message* that could be delivered visually. What the writer proved in the novel may not translate to film. A theater-going audience might not get it because a lot of internalization explained much. So, between my revised Log Line and Statement of Purpose, I begin a new Paradigm Worksheet for the screenplay, usually retaining the book title and, of course, writing a proposed length of 100-120 pages (easy to divide into the Act lengths of 25/50/25 or 25-50-25).

Once the focus of the story is identified as character or event, the novel's events need to be examined for the Main Plot Line that will carry the story forward. If it is character driven, revisit those book passages that impacted the character's internal change or growth. Event driven stories are blatantly easier to identify. The key here is not to let the "But's" intrude on your thinking. As in: "But this happened. But this person told her this. But he argued with himself before he decided." Simply mark down the logical flow of events directly related to the main plot line. Too many for your proposed page length? Unmercifully cut to the barest number of main events the plot will need.

Now comes the tough part, the Pivotal Subplots. Novels have the luxury of introducing minor characters that are ingenious gems of the imagination. Complex back-story and rich character flaws provide a fascinating reading, but a screenplay simply does not have the time. Four subplots, be they the love story, a friendship, the antagonist's "business," the family dynamics. Four are all the theater audience can juggle in a two-hour viewing.

For the sake of coherence and unity, these four must each have a Beginning, Middle, and Ending, and each must impact the Main Plot line in some way. They are particularly powerful if they come together to effect the Climax.

Another factor to be considered at this point in planning the screenplay is Character Arcing or Change-and-Growth of the Main Character. This is not his visible abilities, but his internal attitude that gives subtle vibes to his external actions. I think through the main plot events and the interplay of the subplots. Is the change gradual, satisfactory, logical while still suspenseful versus predictable? Are there cast members or subplots distracting audience attention from the Main Character's Arc? Or is there a hole in the logical flow of the Arc needing a different subplot? This is the time to employ the "Selective Reasoning Process." Knowing some subplots were vital elements in the novel, the screenwriter still must ruthlessly select and delete for the sake of this visual rendering of the story.

You have previously gotten a Character Profiling Worksheet that takes the 36-Point Character Profile a step further to help you delineate the differences between what is needed in a novel vs. what is needed for characterization in a screenplay. Use these to analyze what you need to pull out of your novel and what you can't. The events of a novel change the character, but the inherently dramatic character makes the changes happen in a screenplay's events. Remember that.

The final two considerations are usually fast, painless, and mere notations. Out of your Log Line and the Statement of Purpose, the Repeat Images and the Story Time Line are logical *givens*. If the story is about the Old West and a draught, what images will be used? Is it about humanity struggling in wartime? Office intrigue with criminal money laundering? Roiling clouds, muddied clothing, empty streets, holiday decorations, wild animals at play, a loaded gun, tall grass waving in the wind . . . You get the idea. Use what will visually relate an instantaneous concept every time it appears without wasting precious script page or film time. Select images your collaborators will be excited to interpret. Beware melodrama and blatant symbolism. Use what is obvious in this unique story. These images that make immediate intellectual connections with your audience must be inherent to the story's progression or you are *lecturing*, as in "Pay attention to this you stupid audience members!"

The Story Time Line will also be obvious. Consider travel time and the natural flow of business. You cannot overlook seasonal changes, national/religious holidays, or nature's life cycles. Of course, screenplay narrative generalizes such background material, so the location scouts, prop masters, costumers and gazillion others can "do their thing" to establish the unobtrusive credibility.

In summary, you identify the parts of your novel that will translate to vivid visual images, accept the fact that the final product will not be just your precious words, and understand that you must reach the masses, not just the one fan. Then you carefully plan the script, pulling only essential elements from your novel. You select the type of story and identify the necessary characters. You note the logical flow of the main plot events from the quivering Intro Image through the final concluding moment of character commitment to something. Only the most relevant subplots need to be woven into the thread of the plot line. Your Main Character's change of awareness allows your audience to share the arcing. The images you have selected are memorable and time line *bookends* the entire experience. You have a Log Line and know the point you are making with the entire story. All you have to do is write the screenplay. Simple!

HISTORICAL GENRE

Historical fiction is any fiction that deals with real events and/or real people in a time period prior to the author's birth. That designation gets a bit hazy because some purists will tack on an additional 10, 20, even 50 years so that the material must have a generational distance to it. Those producers and publishers who like historical stories will designate their own time period eras they wish to consider. Again, the wise writer is the one who believes those guidelines and does not say "Well, if they read my story, they'll be convinced I told my older brother's war experience well." No, if a producer or a publisher says they do not want stories happening after 1960, believe them. "Historical" has a relative context but seems to be any story of two generations ago. Clarify guidelines or expectations before you submit.

HISTORICAL CONVENTIONS

A variety of resources contributed to this section, including some University of Texas History Department material that is no longer on line, history magazines, several commentaries by historical writers and a couple of books about historical fiction to compile the following guidelines for history aficionados who are addicted to stories of the past:

1. ABSOLUTE RULE: Well-researched adherence to historical accuracy, close to scholarly

2. Concept of ounterfeiting (skewing) history: Fiction smudges boundaries by making assumptions where historical records are incomplete. It is acceptable because you are writing fiction!

3. Remember that hard core historians are like objective scientists and accept only provable fact rather than imaginings. They will "getcha" if you portray inaccurately and provide no disclaimer. Keep records of what you researched where.

4. When fiction assumes cause-effect, writer must not wander into "political correctness" of "Revisionist History" rewriting historical data to prove a contemporary perspective. Have a conscience or lose credibility. Revising history to make a select group comfortable with the past has the taint of dishonest storytelling. If it is done tongue-in-cheek like Mel Brooks' BLAZING SADDLES that is an entirely different matter.

REVISING HISTORY TO MAKE A SELECT GROUP COMFORTABLE WITH THE PAST HAS THE TAINT OF DISHONEST STORYTELLING.

5. Memory is flawed and often skews to the point of being anecdotal or selective based on personal perceptions and individual consequences. If you rely on one individual's memories or even one source (such as a diary), do not blithely assume that person was documenting events precisely. That person is documenting his or her own version, what that person wants to remember. It has often been said when you hear one side of the story, you have only subjective half-truths without any objective information. Many things "color" conclusions from culture to education to prejudice.

6. Because Fiction by its very nature is lies, it is not intended to be an unvarnished accounting, When critics rear their heads, fiction writers clarify accuracies researched and clearly indicate where the story deliberately moved in another direction for the **sake of drama and character.**

7. Do not "fudge" for the sake of saving time. Flimsy background is for one who lacks creative conscience and has been a flaw in many a genre story that used scant historical references and details to claim authenticity. Have the good manners to know your era and its "current events" that impact your cast and plot. Though primary sources of diaries and interviews of those who lived the true story of CROSSROADS OF LIFE AND DEATH about post-WWII China and other Far East and U.S. locations, the writer still had to verify dates, names and places. Some faulty notes and memories were identified that had to be corrected in the final script. Though the writer clarified the screenplay was not written as a documentary, the writer still relied on conscience to be as accurate and authentic as possible.

8. Claims to be "historical" can be "a kind of male-like animal begotten by the ass of fiction of the brood mare of feelings and hence a sterile monster." *AMERICAN HERITAGE*, Oct 1992. Do not do any historical research half-way.

9. Evaluate detail as convincing "background ballast" or, if you choose to be a competent, serious teller. The extra effort results in an aura of authenticity you will cherish.

10. Understand the difference between skimming details and depth of documentary flavor that makes the work come alive. For example, compare fluff of James Fenimore Cooper's novel *THE LAST OF THE MOHICANS* with the authenticity of the Michael Mann's 1992 movie. Cooper's novel was written closer to the actual events surrounding his story, but Mann's was more authentic in tone and detail portrayal. Why? Cooper was writing early in the evolution of the novel format and his time period relied on melodrama for simplistic emphasis. Mann's was more realistic and more credible.

11. Research until you feel comfortable in the skin of your fictional characters of that era. Example: Stephan Crane had never been in battle but interviewed those who had. "Crane wasn't concerned with the Civil War, the issues which hardly intrude in his novel, but with war as spectacle, with the meaning of heroism and of God's indifference to posturing, puny men." *AMERICAN HERITAGE*, Oct 1992.

12. Historical fiction writers must carefully develop very selective distortions and inaccuracies from the "What if . . ." List. They must always remember that drama wins over fact. Sometimes fact can be pretty incredible so it may be skewed to maintain the window of illusion. Fiction—like movies--is lies. Documentaries are meant to be as close to fact as possible.

FICTION—LIKE MOVIES--IS LIES. DOCUMENTARIES ARE MEANT TO BE AS CLOSE TO FACT AS POSSIBLE.

13. Do not transfer contemporary concepts and allowances to a bygone era that held markedly different values, such as social order (female liberties) or tolerances (race prejudice such as the "Infidels" of the Crusades or religious intolerances during the Inquisition).

HISTORICAL CHARACTER REQUIREMENTS

Protagonists and Antagonists alike in any historical fiction must represent the class, profession, background you have given them, no more, no less. You cannot give them contemporary attitudes or insights, such as awareness of the Freudian "ego" or skills not invented until after that era.

HISTORICAL PLOT TYPES

At the beginning of this chapter it was pointed out that this genre covers any kind of story that takes place in the past. In essence that means there are no standard "Plot Types" to this genre. However, you should review Polti's 36 Dramatic Situations (Appendix F). Some of the wording may sound archaic, but the human situations are as clear-cut throughout history into today's society and its many cultures.

HISTORICAL FILM ANALYSIS

Primarily, both writer and audience have to set aside their analytical habits and simply enjoy the ride, taking portrayal of actual time, place, and character with a grain of salt. Period production is expensive and the vast majority of actual places have vastly changed. Substitution and CGI effects have to be used. The Reader/Audience needs to compartmentalize the "politically correct" mindset that becomes easily offended to vicarious live the story as presented. Arguing or questioning authenticity indicates you are looking for a docudrama, not the enthralling experience of cinematic fiction.

* * * * *

THE LAST OF THE MOHICANS

By Michael Mann, John Balderston, Paul Perez, Chris Crowe, Hunt Lowry
1992, Starring Daniel Day-Lewis, Madeleine Stowe, Russell Means, Wes Studi

Length: 104 minutes

Log Line: A legendary frontiersman wins the love of a courageous young woman and defends her from a vengeful Indian.

Statement of Purpose: To prove strength of character will triumph to win love and maintain integrity even in a brutal frontier circumstance.

Intro Image: Aerial view of huge range of forested, misty mountains.

First 10 minutes
Who:
NATHANIAL ideal confident frontiersman
UNCAS, athletic, respectful young Indian
CHINGCHAGOOK, wise, tolerant Indian father
DUNCAN, assured, arrogant British Major
CORA, genteel, confident, courageous Colonial lady
When: Colonial Frontier during French & Indian Wars (1757)
Where: Frontier of New York province
What: Colonists along the frontier called to join the British forces at Ft. William Henry
Why: French have recruited several New England tribes to join their assault on British occupation.

Four related subplots:
Cora & Duncan
Magua's manipulations
British-French tactics
Alice's dependence

Time Line: Approximately two weeks the summer of 1757

Image repeats:
Juxtaposition of silence to sudden sound
Drums
Flags
Military protocol
Nathaniel's Mohican history belt
Flintlock rifle
Indian war ax
Threatening water

Act I = Set-up of Ordinary World Frontier life dissolving into violence.
8 min **Inciting Incident** (Note IN Intro 10-min): Magua to be guide (for ambush)
10 min **Intro:** Colonial life of frontiersmen, civilized townspeople & military
15 min **PP I:** Munroe girls & British escort ambushed by Indians

Act II = Life 180 degrees: Survival trek to then from doomed Ft. William Henry
35 min **Pinch I:** Enter hopelessly embattled fort
51 min **Mid-Point:** Nathaniel & Cora admit and act on love
73 min **Pinch II**: Nathaniel rescue Cora from column's slaughter
80 min **PPII:** Nathaniel must leave Cora to Magua for any chance at eventually saving her

Act III = Resolution: Rescue from Magua and his retribution
96 min **Climax:** Uncas then Nathaniel and Chingchagook attack the war party
101 min **Commitment**: Nathaniel returns to Cora to turn her away from the carnage
After-story Conclusion: After prayers for Uncas' afterlife, three survivors look out over mountains.

Dialogue Notes:
Clipped British accents (but not consistent) vs. American "twang"
Native American stilted cadence
Munroe's Scottish inflection
Authentic French accents (French-Canadian actors hired)

Alpha Character posturing differences:
Nathaniel vs. Duncan vs. Colonial friends
Nathaniel vs. Uncas vs. Chingchagook vs. Huron Sachem
Duncan vs. Webb vs. Munroe

Montcalm vs. Magua vs. Munroe
Magua vs. Duncan vs. Nathaniel
Cora vs. Alice.

Supporting cast Unique Character Gems:
Alice
Uncas
Chingchagook
Munroe
Montcalm
Huron Sachem

Background effects, the nuances of aura:
Lush forest, rugged mountainous terrain, isolated cabin homestead
Int & Ext of Fort William Henry, the lake-river-falls scenes

Elements from Other Genres: Romance, Western, Action-Adventure

Questions: Was there any point you did not BELIEVE the story authentic and true to the time period?

Appearance or reference to recurrence of Evil Theme in Min: Savage vengeance in time of War with Indian/Magua appearance in **BOLD.** . Because of its strong romance, I also ***italicized*** the elements of the Relationship Plane.

Act I = Set-up of Ordinary World: Frontier life dissolving into violence.

1 Men running in forest, deer is hot but death respected by NA's.
2 Cameron cabin: at night, talk of French & Indian war, call for militia
3 Nat. talks of Kentucky//Gathering of neighbors & Indians
4 Arrogant Brit. soldier asking volunteer as Brit subject, Nat. "Not subject much at all."
5 Will go to Albany & fill County levee, Nat. & Un. Play field hockey
6. Coach & escort of Maj. Duncan Heywood, arrives to militia demands & Gen. Webb promises
7 Reports for duty & sarcastic, Webb: "To Wm. Henry while I take 60th to Ft. Edward."
8 Inciting Incident: Denigrating French, calls **Magua forward as guide**, Munroe daughters waiting.
9 Dun. tells Magua 6am sharp// Dun. rides to house, finds Cora, good to see you
10 Picnic table in field: Cora awkward, friendship & respect, rely on father's judgment
11 Dun. asks to consider, Alice calls out, (silly) "What an adventure!"

12 Soldiers marching, drums & flags, sisters mounted, into forest, "Women tired." **Magua sarcastic**

13 Ching., Un. & Nat tracking separately thru forest, fire pit

14 Look more concerned, tracking// **Magua backtracking along column, tomahawk, hacks**

15-18 PP I: Firing from brush, Indians anticipate at "Fire!" Indians attack, girls off horses (Cora covering Alice's head, **vicious fighting, Duncan valiantly defends position, Indians dropping & look to brush,** (*MEETING*) **Nat sees Magua aim at Cora & brings rifle up but he's gone,** stops Duncan shoot Ching who kills escaping Indian, Un. drives off horses to Alice's "No!" Why? Ask him. Leaves tracks. Take to forest, walk fast unless wait for next raiding party, Cora picks up pistol.

Act II = Life 180 degrees: Survival trek to then from doomed Ft. William Henry

19-21 Trekking by river falls, climbing, Un. Watches Alice, Dun thanks scout but Nat. corrects him, How west to Kentucky? Head north and turn left sudden-like 'cause not your damn militia.

22-24 <u>*Sudden Silence*</u> approach cabin clearing, burned cabin, Un. touches dead Alexandra, scan charred building, Un. in midst, see leg-foot of dead child, Ching. Id print of Ottowa & 2 French, raiding party, walking when Cora challenges to bury, calls Nat. cruel, backs as turns on her. Not strangers & stay as lie. (*really LOOK*)

25-26 Night in forest, Cora to Nat position (*INTEREST*), Why? Sign of our passing YOU'RE THE ONE (out-of-the-blue comment insinuating legendary person).Apologizes, Nat: Expected, father/Ching. told breed apart & try not to understand,, Breed apart? Cocks rifle, everybody hunkers down.

27 **Ott & Fr approach but stop & refuse closer so withdraw.** Why? Burial grounds. Make allowance.

28-30 Nat tells of parents, trappers (*personal sharing/ENGAGEMENT*), Ching at age 1 or2, English school, Why defenseless place? Indentured poor homestead answering to no one, John & Alexandra Cameron. Stars & NA legend, so there'a monument to Camerons & parent. Cora: I don't understand but stirring to my blood. (*admitting PERMISSION*) When she turns on side away, Nat studies her.

31 Move thru dark forest, still cautious, Dun. encourage weak Alice, **Un. sees distant Indian tracking them.**

32-34 <u>*Sudden Distant Cannon Sounds*</u> Nighttime French cannon lines// Canoe on lake with women & Nat. in lake swim beside, explosions & smoke light up nite, workers digging trenches, lining up cannon angle, men killed, canoe at shore, disembark below cannonade, approach fort with kilted troops & torches 35-36 **Pinch I:** *Sudden Nearby Explosions*, Enter fort chaos, "Hello, boys!" See how doing & need to talk to you, weepy Alice forward with "Papa!" "What are you doing here, gels? Where my reinforcements?" Dun: Webb no idea, attack en route. Mun. thanks three. Powder supplies? Indebted. Cora & Alice with Phelps.

37-39 Situation? Bigger, more guns, digging closer, days. Webb's at Edward, not Albany. Nat: Cameron's cabin, murder by Ott. ally of Fr. So? Will attack up& down frontier. Men here have families, You are dismissed, Dun: No one spared, things done, Mun: Subordinate to interests of the Crown.

40-41 *Sudden Children singing.* Montcalm with Ott then **Magua approach, "How are things?" Report on Ft. Ed & dead couriers. Mont: Two women escorted into Ft. Wm Henry. "Will have under knife again." "Why hate Gray Hair?" "Carve out his heart, wipe seed from the earth."**

42 Nat to Infirmary as Cora bandage Un. Done holding hands? Takes piece silk cloth, hesitates, looks. What looking at? "Why you, Miss?" Smile to smile (*ATTRACTION*)

43-44 Nat & Un at fort wall with others, dispatch runner ready, Silk another 40 yards, men ready guns, runner into woods, Nat & Un. shoot attackers until longest shot to patient Nat.

45-46 Cora overhears argument to release militia, Nat word gospel & here longer than you, Agreement with Webb. What saw, Maj? Nothing to warrant releasing these men. Nat. Better with the Fr. Sedition! See you hanged. Have a real disagreement. Mun. dictates punishment of prison or shot.

47 Dun to Cora, Wimpy Al rises & leaves, Dun when back in England won't matter, Cora Persist but answer No!

48-49 Scenes of fort at night: Singing, comforting wounded, Indians smoking, as militia meet with Nat, Right to protect settlements, Brit. no longer sovereign, absolutism, each man his own. North then clear pickets by dawn, Staying? Reason have striped skirt & work in infirmary? It does & better lookin' than you. (*admit LIKING*)

50 Nat. addresses Mohawk uncle who is staying because gave word//Cora with man as he dies, exhausted & stands, looks around at waiting needy, leaves.

51-53 **Mid-Point:** Nat stops in fort grounds when sees Cora, walks by, taking her hand (*CONNECTION*)//Secluded beyond dancing, couple look, touch, Kiss to heavy petting, savoring embraces, insinuate making love, Nat. calmly holds her at dawn.

54-55 *Sudden sounds of break-in*, Nat, Un. Ching. on their feet as soldiers invade quarters with handcuffs, Ching. Asks & Nat tells of helping friends leave. Cora defend to father, guilty of sedition, but stayed, Dun, you spoke falsely. Shouldn't ask you. He didn't. Defend because infatuated, Think poorly of you now. Cora! Justice? Better with the Fr. Makes me guilty, too.

56 Cora to Nat's cell. Going to hang you. Why didn't leave, too? All interested in here. Fort will fall, stay with officers. I will find you. Promise to stay with officers. (*MISUNDERSTAND*). "All the world's on fire."

57-58 *Sudden cannons firing*, walls exploding. Fr. at gate with white flag, In Prison Nat. reminds Cora //Morn dawns with drums & Brit marching to Fr. Lines & flags. Munroe & Montcalm face one another.

59-61 Bowing formally greet, Listen to my terms of surrender, See size of Webb's forces? Intercept dispatches, junior officer reads in English, Webb can't send & suggests surrender, Dun. takes & yes, Webb's signature. Men rather die.. Mont asks listen to terms, no prison, keep guns, men leave, colonists home. Mun. disappoint another Brit officer (Webb) not support.

62-65 Maugua with Fr Indians watching// *(Sudden Night Quiet)* **Montcalm with squad, consult with Magua, "Hatchet not red, Friends with British?" Ordered to make peace. Village burned, children killed, wife married another, all because of the Gray Hair. Became blood-brother to Mohawk but always Huron. Believe him? But not Webb.**

66 *Sudden drums beating* Soldiers marching in long line from fort mixed with civilians & wounded, Cora & Alice tandem on horse, all march by Fr. Soldiers & Montcalm, Mun "The fort is yours." Nat among cuffed prisoners with Un. & Ching. alongside.

67-70 All marching on narrow road through forest-lined field, watched from trees by outlined Indians, solo braves charge line to hack at soldiers, soldiers form up, but being shot down, all nervous watching trees, Nat straining to see Cora ahead, increased rifle firing from trees as Indians charge up and down the line on both sides, brutal fighting, Nat removes cuffs & Ching gives rifle as the three charge forward toward Cora.

71 Cora & Alice off horse but protectors killed, Cora shoots Indian, Alice freaking, Nat, Un, Ching running & cutting down Indians en route, Duncan's troops decimated at lakeside.

72 Magua sees Mun & shoots his horse, bends over him announcing vengeance then cuts out & holds up heart.

73 Pinch II: Indian holds Alice as Cora attacks & he knocks her away, Nat screams as runs toward, as Indian holds to cut throat Nat clubs him then collects Cora, hugs as Un gets Alice and they run through battle.

74 **At lakeside battle, sees canoes, women into boat, paddling thru mist,** Duncan aiming "Nothing better to do on the lake today, Major?" "I'll see you hang!" All paddle intensely.

75-76 To the river, paddling into current, approach first short falls, forward hearing louder falls, to shore, climbing out & shoving canoes over falls.

77-78 Walking behind falls into cave, Hope over falls and pass by. If not? Forgo the pleasure of my hanging. Directs Un. to keep eye on begin falls trail, All powder wet, Cora asks about father, Nat holds her as in her ear, devastated, "Don't tell Alice." Continue to hold one another

79 Alice mesmerized by falls, Un. grabs back and holds, cherishes her.

80 PPII: Magua's trackers with torches approach, Un. to cave. NA language exchanges, Cora: "Yes, go!" "If stay, no chance." Dun: "Coward!" Cora: "If one something of other lives, too." Nat: "You stay alive no matter what. I WILL find you." Long stare before runs & jumps. (*SEPARATION*)

Act III = Resolution: Rescue from Magua and his retribution

82-83 Cora resigned as torches approach, Alice clutches her, Strike Dun. & kill young soldier, Magua fingers Cora's hair speaking in NA, binding wrists, lead away.

84 *Sudden roiling water*, POV struggle in rapids, Un. & Nat hold out rifle & caught by Ching. who is hauled to rocks. Up and running.

85 Indians lead prisoners, Cora falls into foliage, Nat, Un, Ching keep at run up barren rocks, **Higher up trail Indians lead tiring prisoners,** Nat finds Cora's broken foliage & running (*INCREASE*). Maintaining fast pace thru forest.

86-87 Indian women help elderly Huron Sachem to seat, addresses Magua with prisoners, Nat, Un. Ching. arrive looking down into camp seeing excited movement to center, **Magua tells bring gift of soldier & women to burn in fires, hears distant warrior whooping.**

88-90 Nat enter carrying beaded belt, shoved, slashed, bashed over head, pushed into Magua, tells Dun. to repeat in French: "Let go free to reduce anger, Magua argues in French that now French also fear Huron, Nat accuse want to become like whites infected with sickness of greed, make into what twisted him. I am son of Mohican "Long Carabine" Take me for her (*NEED*), my death an honor."

91-92 Magua: You speak poison. Sachem shuts him. "What Huron to do? You not Huron!"
Hesitates. Orders Magua take younger, return officer, burn dark haired one & Nat go free.

Dun asks them to take HIM for Cora. Magua curses Sachem as grabs Alice. Nat. "Did you tell me for her?" Indians grab Dun. "For God's sake take her & leave." Cora screaming for Duncan as Nat drags her away.

93 **Un. watches Magua with Alice, hand to Ching's shoulder and leaves to follow.**

94 **Warrior cries as Dun tied to frame & raised above fire, screaming.** Nat to waiting site, raises gun (as Cora looks away) and ends Dun. agony. They begin climb up slope away from camp.

95 Un. climbing. Far from him Ching, Nat & Cora climb. **Sweeping view of mountains to trail along ledge where war party leads Alice**

96-101 **Climax: Un. takes out front four Indians, facing Magua (older, more experienced fighter) slashing & onto rocky outcropping, Alice fearful, Magua holds, kills Un then shoves over cliff,** Ching then Nat see from afar & react, **Alice moves out to rocks as Magua approaches, she looks down at Un. body, Magua lowers knife & beckons, she jumps.** Below Cora screams, **Magua merely waves men to move on, Ching catches up with rear guard & attacks, Nat shooting others. As Ching continues, Nat picks up unsed rifles, Ching confronts Magua & uses war ax to kill him. Magua falls dead.**

101 **Commitment**: Nathaniel returns to Cora to turn her away from the carnage.

102-103 Ching & Nat. stand on mountain top saying prayers for Uncas in his afterlife.

After-story: All three stand on mountain top looking out over the once-again peaceful wilderness.

CONCEPTS DISCUSSION

Because MOHICANS is a romance, you probably noted that the signposts of the Relationship Plane were noted in the story's pacing.

CONCEPTS OF ADAPTATION

If you have read any or all of James Fenimore Cooper's "Leatherstocking Series" about the adventures of Hawkeye (Nathaniel), you will identify Michael Mann was a genius in this adaptation. Of course, there had been earlier screenplays made into films and even TV series. Several, as in 1977, 1971, 1957, 1936, 1920. Those are wonderful comparisons to Mann's version. Without a doubt this rendition is the most credible both in iconic power of story and character and in staying close to historical accuracy. Mann did what none of the others did: He defeated Cooper's melodrama.

You have to understand that Cooper wrote this book in 1826 just 69 years after the actual atrocities that were enacted by the French soldiers and their Indian allies on the British soldiers and civilians as they abandoned Fort William Henry. The circumstances of the story are historically accurate, if not the main characters. But in the early 19th century the storytelling relied on highly romanticized personas as those main characters. Cooper's Hawkeye was so countrified as to be an ignorant, bumbling fool with zero civilized social skills. His Cora was the iconic lady-on-a-pedestal who could only be admired from afar in the classic knightly manner. Yup, gag-me-with-a-spoon saccharine storytelling . . . but totally legitimate to the style of writing and readership expectation of Cooper's era.

So what if Michael Mann had lots of other cinematic material to consider before his script. His still had the tight pacing and gritty characterization that rings true. Mann's version is flat out credible, especially the acting out of the love story, as well as the brutality of the time period.

The ultimate challenge for comparison-contrast is to actually read Cooper's *The Last of the Mohicans* then watch this film again. Here you will find the demonstrated lessons of, not only how to adapt, but also how to make the story incredibly alive!

Progressive Concepts to Consider:

1) Appropriate Title
2) Types of Suspense utilized
3) Webbing of related elements
4) First 10 minutes prepared audience for the balance of the story
5) Character consistency after Introduction
6) Unique defiance of predictability
7) Opposition intensity increased
8) Character demonstration of profile history
9) Consequences of back-story
10) Identification of Character Arc
11) Use of Sex and Violence blatant or subtle
12) Demonstration of Anxiety Curve
13) Contrasting qualities of Antagonist to Protagonist
14) Consistently logical Scenes with smooth Transitions
15) Definitive build from Mid-Point on
16) Balance of Character story importance to role
17) Every Scene credible vs. melodrama
18) Smooth, unquestionable authenticity
19) Clean, credible script/adaptation

* * * * *

BRAVEHEART

By Randall Wallace
1995, Starring Mel Gibson, Patrick McGoohan, Catherine McCormack

Length: 169 minutes

Log Line: A commoner Scots patriot unifies the bickering clans to undermine 13th Century British rule in Scotland.

Statement of Purpose: To prove that passionate patriotism can motivate men to action no matter the pain or cost.

Intro Image: Aerial view of ruggedly beautiful Scottish Highlands

First 15 minutes
Who:
Young William, unkempt, curious crofter's son (anxious to grow up)
Young Hamish, his just-as-grungy friend
Malcolm Wallace, William's patriotic crofter father
Young Murron MacClannough, sweet daughter of poor, but proud couple
Argyle Wallace, educated, wealthy Scots uncle (also patriot & warrior)
When: 1280
Where: Scottish Highlands
What: English form of negotiating with Scots was to lure them to meeting then kill them
Why: William's father and older brother fall victim leaving him an orphan to be raised & educated by his uncle.

Four related subplots:
English King Edward I's politics & family
Robert the Bruce & titled Scots
Wallace's personal life
Wallace's fighting men

Time Line: Opening in 1280, most of story evolves from 1294 to 1305 with final scene dated 1314

Image repeats:
Kilts
13th century courtly dress
Chain-mail & helms
Bows & arrows

Swords
Cavalry
Rain
Castles
Crofts
Rugged Highlands

Act I = Set-up of Ordinary World: William's transition from boy to accomplished manhood
15 min **Intro:** English slaughter of male Scots leaving determined orphans
35 min **Inciting Incident**: William's marriage to Murron
44 min **PP I:** English lord cuts Murron's throat to get to William

Act II = Life 180 degrees: Wallace's popular leadership defying titled Scots & Edward I
70 min **Pinch I:** Fellow Scot actually hired assassin (thwarted by Irishman Stephen)
81 min **Mid-Point:** Battle of Stirling Bridge victory
106 min **Pinch II**: William proves intellectual equal of cultured Princess Isabelle
126 min **PPII:** At Falkirk Wallace learns of Robert the Bruce's shattering duplicity

Act III = Resolution: Robert the Bruce's conscience rebounds even when Wallace is captured & executed
99 min **Climax:** Wallace's execution as he screams "Freedom"
166 min **Commitment**: Robert the Bruce challenges Scots to join his battle at Bannockburn
After-story Conclusion: "Won their freedom like warrior poets."

Dialogue Notes:
Accurate English accents
Accurate French accents
Inconsistent Scottish accents & cadence
Titled Scots no accent (appropriate to education, but not to place & time)

Alpha Character posturing differences:
William vs. Robert the Bruce vs. Hamish
Murron vs. Princess Isabelle
Hamish vs. Stephen
Isabelle vs. Nicolette
Robert the Bruce vs. Father (the Leper)

Supporting cast Unique Character Gems:
Hamish, William's burly friend
Campbell, Hamish's tough father
Stephen, the Irishman
Nicolette, Isabelle's attendant
Prince Edward, wimpy gay heir to the throne

Background effects, the nuances of aura:
Sweeping grandeur of Scottish Highlands
Crude crofts & villages
Crude small forts
Barren, drafty castles
Misty forests
Noise, brutality, chaos of battlefields

Elements from Other Genres: Romance, Western, Action-Adventure

Question: Did you question the lack of "power" or influence of the Church in the Highlands where presence portrayed as a nicety to have when needed but not relevant to tempering the warring factions?

Analysis relying on historical references, rather than the "Evil" English subjugating, attacking and manipulating the Scots:

Act I = Set-up of Ordinary World: William's transition from boy to accomplished manhood
1280: Malcolm Wallace killed
15 min **Intro:** English slaughter of male Scots leaving determined orphan
1294: Educated adult William Wallace returns to his father's croft
35 min **Inciting Incident**: William's marriage to Murron
44 min **PP I:** English lord cuts Murron's throat to get to William

Act II = Life 180 degrees: Wallace's popular leadership defying titled Scots & Edward I
1295-97: Wallace gathers supporters & enrages Edward I
70 min **Pinch I:** Fellow Scot actually hired assassin (thwarted by Irishman Stephen)
1297: Battle of Stirling Bridge
81 min **Mid-Point:** Battle of Stirling Bridge victory
106 min **Pinch II**: William proves intellectual equal of cultured Princess Isabelle
1298: Battle of Falkirk
126 min **PPII:** At Falkirk Wallace learns of Robert the Bruce's shattering duplicity

Act III = Resolution: Robert the Bruce's conscience rebounds even when Wallace is captured & executed
1305: Wallace's capture at Robroyston
99 min **Climax:** Wallace's execution as he screams "Freedom"
1314: Battle of Bannockburn (resulting in Robert the Bruce being crown King of Scotland)
166 min **Commitment**: Robert the Bruce challenges Scots to join his battle at Bannockburn
After-story Conclusion: "Won their freedom like warrior poets."

CONCEPTS DISCUSSION

Analysis of this film and script reveal it incorporated the principles of storytelling and the Hero's journey in this rendering of William Wallace's life. Though the modern Scots laud this version, movie goers know it is corrupt with fiction's skewed facts . . . for the sake of tidy subplot closure. It is not meant to be a documentary, but a romanticized visual experience. That is the primary principle of historical movies.

RESEARCH ACCURACY

My piper husband and I travelled to Scotland in 2004 with his pipeband (to compete in the Piping World Championships in Glasgow that August). We were there eleven days. It rained seven of those days, but we were out and about nonetheless. Most of our stay was in student dorms at Stirling University, at the base of the Grampian Mountains and beginning of the Highlands, the site of William Wallace's initial victory. Of course, we spent a day at the nearby Wallace monument and another day touring Stirling castle.

Three things stand out in my memory: 1) the Scots revere BRAVEHEART even though some things were skewed for story's sake—William Wallace is their national hero much like George Washington is to us. 2) Wallace was an extraordinarily tall Highlander (over 6'4") as is apparent by the length of his broadsword on display at the monument. So native Scots joke that Mel Gibson should have played the short Rob Roy MacGregor and ROB ROY'S Liam Neeson should have played Wallace . . . but they are logically reverent of the director-actor who brought their nation's founding story to the international scene. 3) Stirling Bridge was more a narrow earthen causeway with wide, deep bogs on both sides that the real Wallace utilized to weigh down and drown heavily armored soldiers while his kilted Scots moving quickly through the battle. So the "funnel effect" (only two horsemen could ride abreast) of the bridge with the decimating effect of the bogs were not utilized in the sweeping battle orchestrated by Gibson. In reality the fighting was much messier, quicker, and truly more one-sided for the Scots.

Edward I or "Longshanks" has been documented as a wily and manipulative tactician whose kingly arrogance was recorded and provided adequate drama for the story's framework. His son was not of robust health or demeanor, but whether he was gay or not is speculation. However, that quality certainly provided contrasts for this story . . . and some "explanations" why so many incidents were bungled. In all likelihood, lack of prompt communications probably played a more important factor in Wallace's early victories.

Quite obviously, you know that the romance and sexual liaison between Isabelle and Wallace were pure fabrication. But here's the deal: Screenplays/movies are fiction. That means you utilize storylines to ratchet up the stakes and intensify the drama, whether they are true or not. Historical storytelling is not meant to be documentary with precise footnoting. The bottom line is "Tell an enthralling story." All you have to do is remain logical and consistent. Isabelle's character was set up as intelligent and disappointed while she remained a young romantic woman hungry to meet a man's man. Reared in a royal French household, her assertiveness was credible. Her disgust at being used as a pawn was a reasonable motivator for revenge.

The timeline and bickering among the titled Scots is spot on in BRAVEHEART. Ask any Scot. This story also accurately portrayed an essential characteristic of the Scottish personality: They have long memories of wrongs done to them and their people. Note: Most of the Scots we ran into in 2004 went out of their way to be friendly to Americans because, as one taxi driver put it, "Your people and our people kicked English arses, didn't we?" Another time in a corner neighborhood pub in Stirling, a man stepped into the establishment, glanced around at the locals glaring at him, and quickly left. One of the locals referred to him as a "Sassenach who is not welcome and knows it." "Sassenach" is a Scots name for an Englishman. Wallace lived at the end of the 13th century, the English defeated the Highland clans at Culloden in 1746, and we were visited in 2004. Yes, the Scots have long memories and little forgiveness.

USE OF DETAILS

Writers do indeed need to research a topic or era until they could converse about it. Therein is the "Write what you know" factor. You insert appropriate details to give the flavor or the story . . . but not in the depth that a novelist will use. When writing historically your clothing-tool-activities of daily living references need to resonate with authenticity. However, you do not need to describe any detail that is not immediately relevant to your story and characters. Remember those nuances are the responsibility of the costumers, prop masters and scenic designers. They do have to know the minute details so the visual world is accurate.

The recreation of the Wallace croft and crude life style of 13th century Scotland is particularly note-worthy. So is the scene where in the middle of the night the men gathered for the piper to play a lament for Malcolm Wallace. The English crown periodically outlawed the pipes and many other Scottish practices. The stiff-necked Scots didn't stop their customs; they merely honored them privately and under cover of darkness.

And look at the practice of "Prima Noctra" or the local lord bedding the bride on her wedding night, a truly barbaric medieval dictate so typical of the nobility vs. their lowly serfs.

Other details that stand out are the shrouding and the shallow graves, the Scots attitude toward the Irish, the disdain of the titled Scots for the commoners, the ignoring of the fact-of-life rain with life proceeding despite its inconvenience, and the hardiness of the Highland warriors in such rugged terrain.

The hand-to-hand battle scenes are gruesome. That is in direct contrast to the "sterile" cinematic battles of the past where men and animals simply fell over. When the movie originally showed, many in the audience squirmed and cowered. Some closed their eyes and let the sound effects touch their imaginations. And isn't it interesting that many of the same "kinds" of scenes are present in Mel Gibson's THE PATRIOT?

The truth is battle is not sterile; it is horrific. That is why so many of our men (and now women) come home from battle mentally and emotionally scarred by the memories of what they saw. The contrast is that in 1297 it truly was a way of life with no alternative if you wanted to survive, but today we can choose to avoid the horror . . . or duly honor those who put themselves in harm's way so that the majority of people will not have to witness what they did. Something to think about.

CONCEPT OF HISTORIC DIALOGUE

Speech is intended to be understood. That is a fundamental idea. For a film audience to comprehend what is said here has to be a certain degree of discretion given to the actors and the dialogue coaches. The Erst dialect of the Highlands mixed with the Scots Gaelic creates a garbled sound when the person attempts to speak in English. Some of the actors in BRAVEHEART were native Scots and already had the Burr. Mel Gibson is an Aussie who had to settle for cadence and inflection vs. true accent. As already stated, the native Scots had no problem with his lack of or on-again-off-again Scots accent. Stephen's Irish brogue was much the same.

Where the screenwriter indicates ethnicity, the execution then becomes the responsibility of the actors, director, and any dialogue coaches employed to tweak the "sound" of words. Again, the writer never writes the garbled phonetics. Nope, You-the-Writer simply state in the characterization and let the actor take it from there. If you want to know how trying it can get to even read an authentic Scots accent, find a book titled *The Shield of Three Lions* (Pamela Kaufman, 1983) where the hero is a Scottish knight serving with Richard the Lionheart during the Crusades. Talk about having to "translate" every speech! Well, what happens when your reader (or audience) struggles to "hear" and understand what is said? The window of illusion is shattered and the left brain logic of the reader/audience has to be employed. End of the entertaining escapism.

Progressive Concepts to Consider:

1) Appropriate Title
2) Types of Suspense utilized
3) Webbing of related elements
4) First 10 minutes prepared audience for the balance of the story
5) Character consistency after Introduction
6) Unique defiance of predictability
7) Opposition intensity increased
8) Character demonstration of profile history
9) Consequences of back-story
10) Identification of Character Arc
11) Use of Sex and Violence blatant or subtle
12) Demonstration of Anxiety Curve
13) Contrasting qualities of Antagonist to Protagonist
14) Consistently logical Scenes with smooth Transitions
15) Definitive build from Mid-Point on
16) Balance of Character story importance to role
17) Every Scene credible vs. melodrama
18) Smooth, unquestionable authenticity
19) Clean, credible script/adaptation

You are heading into the home stretch with 19 of 24 powerful concepts in your mental vaults ready to be taken out to prove you know what you are talking about when you discuss a film, let alone when you are explaining your own script.

* * * * *

GENRE FILM Chapter 11 Exercises

Exercise 11a. Write pg 74-78 focusing on the emotional action of Plot Point II. Show the antagonist's effort to defeat and aftermath reaction to victory as a counter-balance to the Protagonist's demeanor and response to being defeated. Your audience deserves to see both.

Exercise 11b. Did you make a list of many possible scenarios for Plot Point II? If you did not have any options other than one, you may have the dreaded "Predictable Event" that will make your audience groan. You want them suffering and angry (with the Protag), not sighing in disgust (over the Protag's stupidity).

Exercise 11c. Write Pg 79-83 as the "Phoenix Risen" concept of the defeated Protag choosing to come out fighting and prepare for battle. You must once again revert to "Rising Tension" mode putting life-honor-public opinion on the line. "What if" all possibilities and contemplate unexpected but logical twists.

Exercise 11d. Check the status of your subplots and identify where they need to be resolved as well.

CHAPTER 12

Climax, Visuals, Foreshadowing, Choreography/ Action-Adventure Genre

Action-Adventure relies heavily on jeopardy's tension both in plot and in risk to the Main Characters. It is a prime genre for incorporating other genres. "A-A" aficionados want the worry and the adrenaline rush of near misses. If the challenge is Nature they expect physical challenges from both the physical environment and from creatures. What they do not want is any situation to be resolved easily.

Think about that. Doesn't it apply to any genre, any drama? The characters have to walk the road less taken, choosing difficult options instead of the easiest, not saying the simplest or most inane comments. (Example: The idiot young woman who goes down the stairs into a dark basement when she hears a strange sound. Ah, can we say "melodrama" because it is simply not real???)

Action-Adventure is appropriate at this point because every single example of that genre relies heavily on the elements of this lesson. So if you have problems with them in your other genre scripts, watch about six A-A films for these specific elements. See what works . . . as well those that don't in the Steven Seagal efforts. Never over-look that once you have learned how to analyze films, you can learn as much from missing or poorly produced stories as you can from the best of the best.

CLIMAX, THE SUM OF ALL THAT CAME BEFORE

The culmination of a film comes in the "battle" whether it is a juvenile story of a child courageously confronting a mean dog catcher chasing the stray the kid has befriended, the shark ultimately getting killed, the jilted young woman finally having her say at that point in the wedding service when the clergyman asks "If there is anyone who has just reason why these two cannot be jointed in holy wedlock . . ." The Climax is the pinnacle moment when justice is served and audience expectations met.

The Climax may be the moment when "Good" triumphs as in KARATE KID and LES MISERABLES or it can be when "Evil" wins as in SEVEN and SAVING PRIVATE RYAN. The point is that one side will win. Period. The story-long struggle and questions are answered. The Climax ultimately proves your Statement of Purpose. This story has come to an end. That does not mean one cannot have elements that dangle for a sequel. What you cannot do is leave everything up in the air, without a single resolution. If it is a book, the reader usually doesn't have that long to wait for the sequel, but in the film industry it takes at least a year for the next installment in the series to make it into the theaters. If there are story elements and characters who can be franchised and kept in the public eye, that time period is a moot point. But, for most two to three film series, the initial interest may not be all that hot. The memory of a high-impact climax can imprint images that will bring the audience back for more. Example: The Bourne Series.

The climax needs to focus on giving closure to the Character Arc. It will be the evidence that the Character has indeed changed and is motivated by the altered internal forces to act differently externally. If the Arc is not the Protag's but a supporting character, this changed person must be instrumental in the Climax . . . or what purpose do they serve?

If the story's events led to a predictable, inevitable "no choice" climax (such as in THELMA & LOUISE, STARMAN, and, yes, SEVEN) be absolutely certain and confident in the climax you settle for. Analyze your "What If" list for anything just as logical that could be an alternative ending. This is not to say you have to make every ending the "happy people of the happy village," saccharine-sweet, positive kind of conclusion . . . but you must feel your Climax is "right" for this story. The three "no choice" examples are adequate evidence of the concept.

CINEMA IS VISUAL

You may consider the heading as an "obvious" statement, but nonetheless it needs repeating, especially in relation to Act III. Here is where you keep your audience emotionally involved in the conclusion. They have an investment you must honor. Emotions are more important at this moment than intellectual feeding. **Keep the visuals intense and the dialogue minimal.** Resist the urge to "explain" even in a mystery. The audience wants to live with the characters as they are making their own discoveries. Take-charge, inherently dramatic personas like your Protag do not appreciate being lectured to . . . thus neither will your audience.

Some movies like A RIVER RUNS THROUGH IT are sewn together with Voice Over's but even then the ending has to be vivid with visuals that will haunt the audience. Of course in RIVER it was the main character, now elderly, fishing on that big Montana river. Thoughts are not visual but reactions are. A screenwriter must be a meticulous architect of a vivid blue print for all those collaborators who will keep that film alive to the very last frame.

A SCREENWRITER MUST BE A METICULOUS ARCHITECT OF A VIVID BLUE PRINT FOR ALL THOSE COLLABORATORS WHO WILL KEEP THAT FILM ALIVE TO THE VERY LAST FRAME.

FORESDHADOWING: ENDINGS DO NOT STAND ALONE

Films are not "slice-of-life" pieces of the imaginary world. They are unified storytelling structures of Beginning's set-up, Middle's worsening complications, and the Ending's resolution. All contribute to the whole.

When considering the Ending, find what means 1) the characters have been logically portrayed so their behaviors and choices are not suddenly different, 2) each and every supporting character contributed a piece of the puzzle, 3) the environment (everything from actual place to props to nature and the society) had relevance to THIS ending, and 4) every speech and action had a reason that was hinted at prior to Act III.

All four of those elements are part of the concept of "foreshadowing" or "set-up and payoff." When the element is vital it involves the "Times Three Rule" wherein a concept, a prop, a visual is 1) introduced, 2) referred to later on and 3) ultimately used at a vital moment in the story. All of these variations need to be carefully considered to avoid coincidence that startles your audience with "Where did that come from?"

Each time the hint is dropped or referenced does not have to have a spotlight of attention or a big dramatic scene to emphasize its importance. Better practiced writers are more subtle and logically weave the hint into the fabric of the story events. Unless, you are talking humor, of course. Like Monty Python, the Marx Brothers, Leslie Nielsen and Jim Carey. However, even in those examples the foreshadowing prepared the audience to accept the outlandish behavior or consequences at the reversal.

TO CHOREOGRAPH OR . . . NOT?

Subtle dialogue and subtle foreshadowing are achieved through practice. You have to write . . . A lot to truly feel confident in those light brush strokes. Choreographing action-consequence is not too different. The writer writes the blue print that is needed for the basic framework of the film to be laid out. IF that requires explaining and describing specific movement, then write it.

However, if you fall into the novelistic mode of micro-choreography in lesser important scenes . . . resist the urge and revise it out. Actors and Directors, as well as Stunt Coordinators make those decisions of what the camera's eye is going to capture.

On a bigger scene scale, as in the movement of crowds or troops, the writer describes in general terms. Realistically the availability of appropriate locations and the budget will play a major role in what the director and producers decide the film needs. Consider the CGI effects that gave realism to Rome's Coliseum in GLADIATOR, the vast armies trudging in KINGDOM OF HEAVEN vs. the very real Oklahoma land rush crowd Ron Howard used in FAR AND AWAY. The original writer can write in broad strokes of "macro-scenes" but it is the producers and directors who paint in the details.

You are reminded that special effects scenes like explosions, building fires, car crashes, hand-to-hand combat and love scenes are other places where the original writer should never write with a heavy hand. Those kinds of action scenes are choreographed by the expert collaborators, not the writer. Allude to the actions, but do not choreograph them.

ACTION-ADVENTURE GENRE

The bottom line in Action-Adventure is the Alpha human. Male or female, it makes no difference. The essence of the story ebbs and flows according to amount of tension maintained. The Alpha characters are questing and at risk, but the writer cannot maintain a perpetual taut rubber-band for more than a few pages at a time. You wear out your audience right along with your characters. So, you want Alpha characters moving in and out of risk, taking the audience along for the very tense ride.

FUNDAMENTAL CONCEPTS OF ACTION-ADVENTURE

1. Protagonist is forced into physically demanding quest that will stress mind and body to ultimate limits.

- Spin your story web out from your Protagonist's Character Profile. Unpredictably challenge both strengths and weaknesses. If you have started from plotted or historical events, then you must create characters who become intricately involved and put at risk in the situation.

2. Main antagonist threatens an isolated segment or a vital portion of the world.

- Terrorists or an army on the move are human examples just as devastating natural disasters are nature examples of major antagonists that will challenge the Alpha characters.

3. Description or depiction of physical action and environmental or circumstantial barriers will comprise 25% of the story.
- Think of your favorite action movie or book and how much of the story was the "movement" in the story vs. how much as was the "strategic planning." Yes, intelligent humans explaining rationale for taking action or approaching a problem a particular way is interesting, but not as interesting as the action itself. And you can never summarize action when that is the whole point of putting your characters in this situation!

4. Must deliver accurate rendition of tools, skills, character expertise.
- A substantial portion of the people who read Action-Adventure come looking for how familiar tools and skills are put to use. The moment you come off vague or inaccurate, you have lost credibility and shattered your window of illusion. Research whatever you need to describe and use, then run it by an expert. I refer you to Suzanne Brockmann and her Navy SEAL stories (reviewed by two serving SEAL teams) and Catherine Mann and her military flyboy stories (authenticated by her flier-husband).

ALPHA MALE REQUIREMENTS

The **Alpha Male** is the dominant provider, protector, progenitor. He thinks in compartmentalized, hierarchal terms. He is action-oriented and relies heavily on habit. The "Big Man" typical of the Alpha Male is a cross-cultural phenomenon.

The **Beta Male** is the intellectually evolved survivor because he is an adaptable problem- solver. He is careful to act and relies heavily on data and the evaluation of sensation. He is highly attentive and is actually perceived cross-culturally as potentially more dangerous than the Alpha Male. The Alpha Male may be powerful, but the exercise of that power is predictable. The Beta Male's thought associations cannot be predicted.

"THE MOST DANGEROUS ANIMAL ON EARTH IS THE HUMAN MALE."

Here's a "comparison" of behaviors or how each is perceived:

Alpha Male	Beta Male
1. Gains resources	Shares willingly
2. Physically attractive	Willingly sensitive
3. Seeks sexual intimacy	Emotionally attentive
4. Child proves prowess	Sincerely wants to nurture
5. Focused on value for time	Sees relationship as exchange

A quote to remember is **"The most dangerous animal on earth is the human male."**

ALPHA FEMALE CHARACTERISTICS

When characterizing the female lead do not confuse the terminology used with the "primal origins" in the discussion of the male. Women are considered according to their dominant intellectual traits thus motivational forces symbolic of "archetypes." Yep, women truly are much simpler . . . as "types."

The Alpha Female is assertive, confident, athletic, tough. The **Warrior Woman** is willing to attack and defend. The **Whore** is sexually aggressive and adept. The **Crone** personifies the controlling matriarchal power.

The Beta Female is perceptive, emotional, maternal and soft. The **Madonna** is the attentive and vulnerable mother. The **Priestess** is the knowledgeable guide and communicator. The **Healer** is the nurturing problem-solver.

Fascinating contrasts can be created by mixing demanding traits from an unfamiliar yet logically inherent role such as the fragile Madonna girds herself as a Warrior Woman to defend her children then must become the Priestess teaching them to survive. Or think of the slut seen as the Whore who nurses the epidemic's victims in the saloon and converts the townspeople to accepting her as a Madonna figure.

Here is a more in-depth look at cinematic examples of Pinkola-Estes's concepts of female characters she explained in *Women Who Run with the Woves*, a thick tome written in PhD-eze to be read and digested in bits and pieces. Think more intensely about your heroine.

PRETTY WOMAN: Whore to Priestess to Madonna (his choice for a mate and softer in the end)
LAST OF THE MOHICANS (Cora): Madonna to Priestess to Whore to Warrior Woman
QUIGLEY DOWN UNDER: Whore to Madonna to Warrior Woman to Priestess
LITTLE WOMEN (Jo): Crone (over her sisters) to Priestess to Healer (wasn't she meeker in the end?)
DANCES WITH WOLVES: Priestess to Whore to Madonna to Healer (See that she was predominantly
Beta?)
THE BIG EASY (Ann): Crone (power position) to Whore to Priestess to Healer to, finally, Madonna

Remember these are opinions, interpretations. You might see vacillation many times in a story depending on the skills that are called upon in order to cope. "Weaker" roles are the Beta roles whether male or female and "forceful" roles call for Alpha traits. Always ask yourself who instigates or initiates whatever action in a scene to identify what roles are needed at that time and if Alpha or Beta characteristics are needed..

A person's role in a single scene will not change. The role shift comes in the subsequent scene. In the first scene Ann in THE BIG EASY is the attorney from the D.A.'s office investigating police corruption. She is in the power position. Try as he might Remy (Dennis Quaid) cannot rattle her until he manipulates her into a dependent position and fires up her hormones to respond to him sexually. However, she still has control of herself as he works his wiles and she allows herself to enjoy his seduction. BUT the evolution of the investigation throws her back into the dominant Crone role. Then she's dependent and Whore again and then she's the Crone charging Remy with taking a bribe. She shifts into Priestess mode (with Remy becoming more powerful as he gains her access to the police department). Remy makes himself vulnerable and she is briefly the Healer to his tears. But as Remy takes charge in full Warrior mode, she then is Priestess and in the final scene his bride, his Madonna.

"THE MOST UNPREDICTABLE ANIMAL ON EARTH IS THE HUMAN FEMALE."

It is impossible to have two characters dominant at the same time. Story tension will not logically allow that. From their history, you can tell who is going to be **the player in control of the scene**, each demonstrating how he or she is coping at the moment

And here is the applicable quote about women: **"The most unpredictable animal on earth is the human female."**

ACTION-ADVENTURE PLOT TYPES

1. Military/Pseudo-Military
2. Transformation of Protagonist from Beta to Alpha
3. Spy or Superhero saving Society
4. Terrorist or Espionage threatening Society
5. Martial Arts expert saving society
6. Law vs. Crime
7. Man vs. Nature
8. Escape-Pursuit (not criminal)

ACTION-ADVENTURE FILM ANALYSIS

Though a lot of A-A films turn into "blockbusters," almost without exception the appeal is to males. So, analyze these films asking what will trigger a positive reaction from a male audience. Good cinema grows out of a sound story structure, but the focus has to be on those scenes that enhance physical prowess, intense jeopardy, and high-risk environment. Look for a celebration of the fight for survival, even when the A-A leads are female or juvenile.

* * * * *

GLADIATOR

By David Frenzoni, John Logan, William Nicholson
2000, Starring, Russell Crow, Joaquin Phoenix, Connie Nielsen

Length: 149 Minutes

Log Line: A Roman general escapes assassination, finds his family slaughtered and changes his life focus from apathy to survival and revenge on Caesar who ordered all.

Statement of Purpose: To prove absolute power corrupts absolutely but can be overcome by principled people willing to sacrifice.

Intro Image: A man's hands brushing tops of golden wheat as he walks the field.

First 11 minutes
Who: Maximus, a hard-fighting man of conscience and focused purpose
When: 180 AD
Where: Germania (central Europe)
What: Fighting the barbaric tribes of NW Roman Empire
Why: Respected, favored leader of Roman army loyal to the principled but aging Caesar Marcus Aurelius

Four related subplots:
Maximus's self-concept
Commodus-Lucilla Sibling rivalry
Gladiator culture
Sublimated Maximus-Lucilla doomed love story

Time Line: Approximately one year, winter to following year's spring

Image repeats:
Wheatfield
Armor, helms, swords & other battle weapons
Brutal killing
Political intrigues
Darkness = Secrecy
"Shadows & Dust"
"Not yet"
Figurines of wife & son

Act I = Set-up of Ordinary World: Maximus the respected leader, warrior & threat
11 min **Intro:** Maximus instructing & leading his men in battle
26 min **Inciting Incident**: Marcus Aurelius tells Max. "Protector of Rome because Commodus not a moral man."
33 min **PP I:** Marcus A. tells his son he will not inherit & Com. smothers him.

Act II = Life 180 degrees: Maximus finds family slaughtered & ends up surviving as a Gladiator
44 min **Pinch I:** Maximus staggers home to find wife & son's charred remains hanging
82 min **Mid-Point:** Max. leads triumphant first battle in the Coliseum
116 min **Pinch II**: Senator Gracchus tells Max. overthrow will work with his return to army
133 min **PPII:** Escaping Max. captured & over-throw of Commodus defeated

Act III = Resolution: Wounded Maximus still fights & kills Commodus securing Rome's future
140 min **Climax:** Bleeding Max. fights unscrupulous Com. & kills him
144 min **Commitment**: Max. orders release of Gracus & men, reinstatement of Senate to honor Marcus Aurelius's dream of Rome
After-story Conclusion: Lucilla addresses soldiers about honor of Rome & Juba buries Max. figurines in the floor of the Coliseum.

Dialogue Notes:
Juba's African speech cadence
Hagen's slight Germanic speech cadence
Slightly more formal nobility & Senatorial speech patterns

Alpha Character posturing differences:
Maximus vs. Quintas vs. Juba & Hagen vs. Proximo vs. Commodus
Marcus Aurelius vs. Commodus
Commodus vs. Lucilla
Lucilla vs. 3 Senators

Supporting cast Unique Character Gems:
Quintas, Max. Second-in-command
Cicero, Max. man-servant
Proximo, retired Gladiator
Senators, self-serving manipulators
Juba & Hagen, cautious to trust, bonded by gladiator/warrior code
Lucius, Lucilla's young son, innocent & watchful

Background effects, the nuances of aura:
Winter woods of Germania
Luxury of Caesar's portable tents
Unpopulated plains Max. travelled to get to Spain
Spanish country estate with fields
Zacchabar (Middle Eastern desert country)
Various Gladiator prisons/holding cells
Coliseum & surrounding crowded marketplace
Pristine palace of Caesar
Dream sequences

Elements from Other Genres: Historical, Horror, Western

Questions: 1) Did you believe Lucilla's manipulations then forced complicity with her insane brother, as if she had no power of her own and was totally at his mercy? 2) Likewise was Quintas a bit cowed and late in supporting Maximus?

Appearance or reference to recurrence of Evil Theme in Min: Ruthless & corrupt power seen in Commodus on screen in **BOLD**.

Act I = Set-up of Ordinary World: Maximus the respected leader, warrior & threat

11 **Intro:** Respected Maximus instructing & leading his men in battle in Germania
12-13 Commodus arrives late to the battle field
14 Max honored by his men & Caesar, "Let me go home."
15-18 Com. friendly façade "brother." Evening celebration with officers, Senators.
19-20 Marcus tells Lucilla "What a Caesar you would have been. Help your brother."
21 Max. sees Com. practicing against circle of swordsmen
22-25 Max talks with Caesar about integrity of his men, Rome, & his own family
26-27 **Inciting Incident**: Marcus Aurelius tells Max. "Protector of Rome because Commodus not a moral man."
28-30 Max. speaks to Lucilla of sons, their past & serving Rome, Max prays to family figurines
31-32 Emotional talk between Marcus A. & Com about attributes & Rome's future
33-35 PP I: Marcus A. tells his son he will not inherit & Com. smothers him.

Act II = Life 180 degrees: Maximus finds family slaughtered & ends up surviving as a Gladiator

36-37 Com. announces father's death, Max. refuses acknowledge as Caeser, Lucilla slaps then kisses Com's hand with "Hail Caesar" Max taken prisoner by Quintas' guard.

38-43 Maximus kills his soldier assassins & desperately rides for home

44 **Pinch I:** Max. staggers home to find wife & son's charred remains hanging

45-57 Maximus gives into violent life as nameless Gladiator brutally fighting for survival

58-65 Commodus with Lucilla advising assumes power in Rome & provides "Games" at the Coliseum to satisfy the mob

66-74 Brutal "Spaniard" lauded by Proximo who takes in troupe to fight in Rome

75-76 Commodus demos slipping mind discussing dissolution of Senate yet need for sister's comfort

77-81 Gladiators paraded through crowds, Max. talks with young Lucius, Helm choice, "Die with honor."

82-88 Mid-Point: Com. witnesses Max. leading triumphant first battle in the Coliseum

89-95 Com with Praetorians, Max reveals himself, Com. controls rage, "Live," tells Lucilla "They don't respect me."

96-100 Lucilla visits talking of Com. insanity & risks to son, "Man of principle." Max. talks with Jube & Hagen about his great name.

101-106 64th Day of Games, Titilus vs. Max with chained tigers, Com. tells Lucilla "arranged."

107-109 Titilas pinned, Max defies Com. thumb-down & crowd calls "Maximus the Merciful." Com confronts & taunts with family's torture. Praetorians allow Max. to leave.

110-111 In crowd Cicero hands figurines to Max & he kisses them in his cell sharing Juba remembrance.

112 Com. worries about martyring him but soothed to wait.

113-115 Cicero tells Max. of ready troops, message to Lucilla, meeting with Gracchus

116-117 **Pinch II**: **Senator Gracchus tells Max. overthrow will work with his return to army, Max.**

118-119 Max. recruits Proximo's help .Praetorians arrest Gracchus

120-122 Com. finds Lucius fighting as "Max., savoir of Rome," awaits Lucilla, asks about Gracchus, touches her as falls asleep on her breast.

123-124 Lucilla warns Max. "Tired of being strong," They kiss.

126-128 Lucilla finds Com with Lucius, he tells parable of duplicity warning her

129-132 Praetorians to Gld. Compound, Proximo releases, "Strength & Honor", as men fight, Max down tunnel to see Cicero on horse with noose & is killed.

133 **PPII:** Escaping Max. captured & over-throw of Commodus defeated

Act III = Resolution: Wounded Maximus still fights & kills Commodus securing Rome's future

134-136 Com. tells cowed Lucilla she will give him heir or Lucius dies, "Am I not merciful?"

136-139 Com. listens to mob as addresses chained Max. "Death comes to us all." Kisses him as knifes into kidney. Petals float over as elevator lifts Com & wounded Max to arena surrounded by Praetorians.

140-143 Climax: Bleeding Max. fights unscrupulous Com. & kills him

144 **Commitment**: Max. orders release of Gracchus & men, reinstatement of Senate to honor Marcus Aurelius's dream of Rome

145-146 Max. collapses seeing shadowy gate & field of wheat. Lucilla "Son is safe" & she says "Go to them."

147-149 **Conclusion**: Lucilla addresses soldiers about honor of Rome, they carry Max. out. Juba buries his figurines in the floor of the Coliseum (so they are where Max. died).

CONCEPTS DISCUSSION

This is another Ridley Scott masterpiece epic with a grand scope and lots of tension and appropriate violence to the tone of the story. Marching through the elements of storytelling and the Hero's Journey is relatively simple. The Progressive Concepts are a fascinating study of visual delivery.

FORESHADOWING

To maintain the flow of subplots that are being lived simultaneously with the unfolding Main Plot, the writer has to periodically show the audience what is happening in those. If the glimpses are hints of possible outcomes, that is a form of "foreshadowing." Repeat emphasis is awkward and rather patronizing, but glimpses of consequences of a previous scene in that subplot (without resolution) contribute to the concern or rising tension in the audience. They will "get it" that the information is significant because you spend x-number of pages or scenes on the topic or the evolution of that subplot's topic.

GLADIATOR is a long movie that gave what enthralled audience members needed then moved ahead with consequences . . . but later on. It kept the audience logically moving back and forth between storylines yet always forward. The "Dramatic Repeats" of images, items, actions, even lines or references like honor, principles, mercy were consistent threads.

At 12 minutes into the film Maximus is out and about the morning after his Germanian victory celebration and sees the stripped and competent Commodus fighting off the swordsmen surrounding him in practice. Commodus does not pick up another sword until he sees young Lucius wielding a pretend sword. In his unstable state he hears Lucius say he is "Maximus, the savior of Rome." His rage is controlled but immediate and the tension increases. When Marcus Aurelius said back in Act I that his son was "not a moral man" and you see all of his vicious plotting and threats, you are NOT surprised when he stabs Maximus before facing him in the Coliseum. It didn't matter that you knew he was an able swordsman; by this time you know that Maximus is the superior fighter. Commodus's ugly act is logical, but who is the ONE supporter who witnesses his vicious ploy to guarantee his win? Second-in-command Quintas who respects his former General much more than he does this Caesar. So, when it comes time to "help" Caesar, Quintas tells his Praetorians to "Sheath your swords." He is announcing enough is enough and that, too was foreshadowed in Act I and in Act II with how he looked at Maximus.

Copy and print out the list of Image repeats, then the analysis separately. Have a set of colored pencils and put dots whenever you see one of those items appear and reappear in the film.

Also, look at each Major Character and how their subsequent behavior or reaction was "set up." Wasn't the smarmy, incestuous attitude of Commodus toward Lucilla set up at 13 minutes in that wagon headed to Germania, then sprinkled in with each time becoming more blatant and her efforts to avoid less effective until she was trapped? Cicero the devoted servant, Hagen the Germanic Gladiator. Proximo the "Gladiator-Businessman." Even each of the politically manipulative Senators. Follow each character through the story and see how their ultimately significant action was foreshadowed, not blatantly but subtly.

CULMINATION OF CLIMAX

There have been criticisms of the ending of this film, calling it bittersweet or disappointing. But, here's the deal: the ending does not ALWAYS have to be positive for the hero or heroine . . . It simply has to be logical. Each of the subplot threads played out logically as well and not "Pollyanna-saccharine."

Lucilla may not have been eligible to be Caesar but, recognizing that this brave man gave his life in removing the abhorrent Commodus from her life, beside her hero's body, she maintained her dignity and force of personality by reminding all of the "Honor of Rome" and demanding they honor the man who gave them back their Senate and principles. She had reminded Maximus of those principles and he gave his life for them; so it was the least she could do for him.

Proximo who released his gladiators was "in danger of becoming a good man" yet he was cut down in his quarters by the attacking Praetorians. Should he logically have been treated any other way for turning traitor? In reality, that actor, Oliver Reed, died suddenly during the filming. If you noticed the Figure of Proximo going to his balcony to see the Praetorians at the compound gate then walking across the yard with the keys, the camera's eye did not show his face or profile. The clips inserted were edited in from other scenes.

Quintas, in reality, was a soldier of Rome. Yes, he fought under Maximus at Germania, but he answered to Caesar. With Marcus Aurelius dead, by his creed, he answered to Commodus. It was not important how he came to command the Praetorians in Rome, but the assumption is he pleased Commodus with how he ordered the execution of Maximus in Germania. To see his former commander, a man he had well-respected, alive and bravely fighting in the arena, gave him pause, a flicker of a smile. Facing Maximus on the floor of the arena, he stoically accepts that judgmental glance from Maximus. When he witnesses the depraved and dishonorable actions of Commodus, his military code of "Strength and Honor" are insulted so he refuses to allow his Praetorians to help Commodus. Still with a guilty conscience, he at least regains a sense of honor.

Lucius, the innocent young heir, adored the "Spaniard" then admired the heroic Maximus despite his uncle's threatening manner. He bravely walked to the arena and proudly walked behind the men carrying Maximus.

Cicero, quietly and confidently served Maximus in Germania, respecting his shrine to his family and was tempted to pull that sward when his master was arrested. He watches the Coliseum fighting with admiration and speaks as a friendly messenger willing to notify the Roman army that Maximus needs them. When he is sacrificed, he apologizes for failing, a mark of true courage and integrity.

Hagen died giving Maixmus, the man he grew to respect, his chance at freedom.

Juba, the African kidnapped from his village and family, showed the insinuation in the final scene that he would find his way home because he was not slated to die, "not yet."

Commodus had to die. His escalating insanity and dishonorable actions totally built audience anticipation of his life coming to end by way of Maximus. He deserved what he got. If Maximus had merely severely wounded him and had him imprisoned, he would have still been Caesar. Nope, justice was served.

Maximus had to die as well, not because history dictated, but because from the first image you know he wishes to be in his fields greeting his family. Repeatedly throughout the movie, his devotion to their memories, his apathy without them, even his pure pleasure of holding and kissing those figurines emphasize where his heart and soul truly wanted to be. Though he and Lucilla had reconciled their past, she still understood and said "Yes, go to them."

Being with them again was his reward for all he had done, all he had suffered. Though a touch melodramatic, it was logical.

As you are planning your Climax, you need to cover all those subplots and all those characters who have been major players . . . but the one thing you have to do is be dramatic. Be courageous enough not to be predictable, but be smart enough to be logical.

Progressive Concepts to Consider:

1) Appropriate Title
2) Types of Suspense utilized
3) Webbing of related elements
4) First 10 minutes prepared audience for the balance of the story
5) Character consistency after Introduction
6) Unique defiance of predictability
7) Opposition intensity increased
8) Character demonstration of profile history
9) Consequences of back-story
10) Identification of Character Arc
11) Use of Sex and Violence blatant or subtle
12) Demonstration of Anxiety Curve
13) Contrasting qualities of Antagonist to Protagonist
14) Consistently logical Scenes with smooth Transitions
15) Definitive build from Mid-Point on
16) Balance of Character story importance to role
17) Every Scene credible vs. melodrama
18) Smooth, unquestionable authenticity
19) Clean, credible adaptation
20) All questions answered in satisfying climax
21) Protagonist ultimately empowered

* * * * *

THE HUNT FOR RED OCTOBER

By Larry Ferguson, Donald Stewart from the novel by Tom Clancy
1990, Starring Sean Connery, Alec Baldwin, Scott Glen, James Earl Jones

Length: 133 minutes (with the credits flowing over the first 2 minutes of visual story time)

Log Line: Intending to defect to the U.S. with an innovative nuclear sub, a high-ranking Russian officer eludes those bent on the vessel's destruction.

Statement of Purpose: To prove wary adversaries can become allies when the goal is freedom

Intro Image: Computer words overlay a military map of the North Atlantic giving intro exposition.

First 11 minutes
Who:
RAMIUS, Respected, calculating Soviet sub commander
RYAN, Intellectual, principled CIA researcher
MANCUSO, Decisive, careful American sub commander
When: 1984 (height of the Cold War)
Where: Washington DC & North Atlantic
What: As sub sails, Ryan flies to CIA in Virginia to share disturbing analysis
Why: Intelligence community rattled by launch of silent-running, nuclear Russian sub

Four related subplots:
Ramius & his officers
U.S. Military & Intelligence treatment of *Red October*
Russian politics & naval treatment of *Red October*
Ryan's personal journey

Time Line: Approx. 1 week

Image repeats:
Underwater sub images
Cold North Atlantic ocean
Casual American vs. "controlled" Russian diplomacy
Questioning military
Decisive military
Life-threatening risks
Peaceful Past (fishing)
Ramius's intellectual wife
Maps
Sonar
Potential for war

Act I = Set-up of Ordinary World: Innovative *Red October's* maiden voyage triggers intelligence concerns and Russian retaliation
11 min **Intro:** *October* sails, Ryan reports to CIA, *Dallas* listening out in North Atlantic

18 min **Inciting Incident**: Ramius kills the Political Officer, burns orders & replaces with new
27 min **PP I:** Ramius addresses the crew & engages the caterpillar drive

Act II = Life 180 degrees: Ryan's quest to connect with *October* & Ramius's efforts to elude Soviets.
41 min **Pinch I:** Ryan believed but told expendable & Soviet Alpha ordered to "kill a friend"
63 min **Mid-Point:** Sabotage found on *October* (set-up for need for ASAP defection)
95 min **Pinch II**: Ryan convinces Mancuso of Ram. defection who orders "cavitate"/noise-announcement
102 min **PPII:** Faked radiation leak gets crew off the *October*.

Act III = Resolution: *October* boarded by U.S. & "rescued" from Soviet destruction
115 min **Climax:** Soviets attack the *October* and saboteur strikes
128 min **Commitment**: Mancuso calmly plays "chicken" with Tupolev since he now believes
After-story Conclusion: Ramius and *Red October* given refuge in U.S. river

Dialogue Notes:
Authoritative yet warm Adm. Greer
Accents of "Russians" when shifted to English
Southern drawl of Secretary of State Jeffrey Pelt
Ryan's mimicking of Adm. Painter on *Enterprise* and Ramius on *Red October*

Alpha Character posturing differences:
Ryan subtle change between Intro Beta into Alpha aboard *Red October*
Mancuso vs. his XO vs. Jonesy vs. the Chief
Enterprise's Adm. Painter & his XO (and that man's shift toward Ryan)
Ramius the Alpha vs. his XO (Visili) vs Dr. Petrov vs. Navigator
Sec. of State Pelt vs. Russian Ambassador Putin

Supporting cast Unique Character Gems:
Adm. Greer
Skip Tyler (Ryan's friend)
Visili
Sec. of State Pelt
Jonesy
Dallas XO
Tupolev

Background effects, the nuances of aura:
Underwater scenes of subs
Underwater canyons
CIA offices & meeting room
Red October (especially the "roomy" conn)
U.S.S. Dallas (especially its close-quarters)
U.S.S. Enterprise
Chopper in flight
Harsh North Atlantic ocean

Elements from Other Genres: Historical, Western, Mystery

Question: Did you "buy" Ryan's Beta persona AFTER learning of his Naval Academy history?

Appearance or reference to recurrence of Evil Theme in Min: All who are trying to block Ramius from completing his mission of handing over the *Red October*. This film/story is pure Action-Adventure on an international scale, though several of the scenes were blatantly personal. The scope was bigger than the players, thus the stakes were very high.

This was not a minute by minute analysis. Rather, you need to 1) read the novel then 2) print out the script (especially if you are considering adaptation of your own). When you read the book, look for the pacing in there and the subplots that were eliminated (or combined) in the film. You to "walk" through the script looking for the signposts and beats of the scenes. Remember: The Main Plot is about the *Red October*/Ramius defecting, both his desire to do it and Ryan's belief that is what he is doing. One of Ramius's major concerns was that he didn't want to bargain with some "buckaroo."

CONCEPTS DISCUSSION

By this time you are an expert at identifying elements and structure. Every book you read, every movie you see, even every TV episode should trigger your recognition of story pacing and characterization. You should continue to build your appreciation for the more advanced Progressive Concepts of good stories. And you should be able to apply those concepts to your own scripts.

CHOREOGRAPHY

It is well-known that Tom Clancy researched his novel thoroughly and sought the expertise of many people, inside and outside the government and military. The general public has opinions and imaginings of how the intelligence, political and diplomatic communities operate. That "fictionalization" is shrugged off. The military matters are a tad more restrictive, but this entire story relied heavily on "getting it right."

In the film industry, the branches of the military will provide advisers with the caveat that they can "nix" anything. (The 1992 A FEW GOOD MEN is one example where the Marine Corps pulled their advisers—and their elite drill team--because the story did not reflect well on the Corps. Oh, a university military drill team donned the Marine uniforms and did the fancy maneuvers that Jo passed on her way to talk to Caffey). The alternative is to employ ex-military to provide the uniform, protocol and procedural guidance. You should know this in case you want to write a military script . . .

Once again, you should track one character at a time throughout the film and pay attention to body language, habits and nuances of posturing. The majority of these are the actor's realm, but many instances prevail where the writer can describe those actions necessary to advance the story in that scene. Be succinct and be meaningful . . . then leave the rest up to the actor.

CINEMATIC VISUALS

The underwater clips "made" several of these scenes—the high tension scenes—credible. They were all special effects and done with models. That is an awesome thought. Consider the little rescue sub approaching the *Red October* and shining its light over that expanse. Did it not seem real, credible, exciting? Glossing over the technicalities of the DRV docking over the hatch of the *October* by staying inside the DRV was genius. That "arrival" was tense enough but the tension was ratcheted when Mancuso insisted Ryan take the handgun before even "knocking" on the hatch.

Some of the *USS Enterprise* shots (the footage of that plane crashing, in particular) were taken from film and news archives. Most of those are not free. You should never hesitate to include such images. Their inclusion and availability are up to the production staff. Your job is to framework the drama.

The more exotic, foreign or dangerous a local, the higher the budget. The more people who have to be involved for stunts or Special Effects, the higher the budget. (Ah, also the higher the insurance.) If you are writing a "simple" story, the only concern will be if the location scouts will be able to find a place that matches your vision or if it will have to be created and green-screened. Scott Free Pictures (Ridley & Tony Scott) simply contracted a lot of digital artwork in creating the Coliseum for GLADIATOR and Jerusalem for KINGDOM OF HEAVEN (next up, BTW).

Experienced screenwriters know you must think large . . . as in beyond big. Film tells stories through visuals. Go back through your most recent script and really, really consider how you can broaden or give more vivid imagery to your visuals. You do not want to write like a novelist, but you do want to give a scope with detail that will excite the imaginations of your collaborators.

Search out the scripts of movies that had visuals you vividly remember. Read how those scenes were written, then practice, practice, practice.

Progressive Concepts to Consider:

1) Appropriate Title
2) Types of Suspense utilized
3) Webbing of related elements
4) First 10 minutes prepared audience for the balance of the story
5) Character consistency after Introduction
6) Unique defiance of predictability
7) Opposition intensity increased
8) Character demonstration of profile history
9) Consequences of back-story
10) Identification of Character Arc
11) Use of Sex and Violence blatant or subtle
12) Demonstration of Anxiety Curve
13) Contrasting qualities of Antagonist to Protagonist
14) Consistently logical Scenes with smooth Transitions
15) Definitive build from Mid-Point on
16) Balance of Character story importance to role
17) Every Scene credible vs. melodrama
18) Smooth, unquestionable authenticity
19) Clean, credible adaptation
20) All questions answered in satisfying climax
21) Protagonist ultimately empowered

Almost at the end with 21 of 24 elements at your command. You are moving to that professional level that is no longer awed, but can evaluate and judge the positives and negatives of cinematic stories based on sound criteria.

* * * * *

GENRE FILM Chapter 12 Exercises

Exercise 12a. Write Pg 84-88 avoiding predictability with your "What if" list and looking back at Lesson Two-A list of ways to increase tension as you move toward your Climax.

Exercise 12b. Analyze these final scenes for micro-choreography and melodramatic dialogue, both to be avoided at all costs.

Exercise 12c. Write pg 89-94 into your Climax, playing off the tension of how both sides are fighting and "could" win.

Exercise 12d. How and where did you conclude all of your subplots? Is there the implication of "After-story life" to those agendas?

CHAPTER 13

Engaging Emotions, After-story, Revision, Marketing/Inspirational

EMOTIONAL WRITING

This component of screenwriting is here at the end of the book for one reason: Vulnerable humans tend to sublimate emotional elements that could put their inner being at risk. They don't want to be judged. Most creative writers who tackle screenwriting quickly discover how relevant the almighty dollar is to getting a film into production. They also find that many of the people involved in film-making are guarded and careful to offer opinions and criticisms in an industry based on illusion and imagination. No one wants to injure egos or burn bridges, so choose to "walk on eggs." Rarely is anyone 100% forthright. Wow, that all "seems' rather cynical, but it is not when you understand that everyone is in the same boat, whether that person is George Clooney, George Lucas or George Nobody. Everybody wants a break and nobody wants to be "used." So one and all are cautious.

How does this specifically apply to screenwriting? The majority of strug-gling–to-be-read writers tend to think in terms of "What will most likely sell?" Nothing wrong with that except that it is a barrier to writing the script "pulled from the burning asphalt of your life" as UCLA's Lew Hunter likes to call it. Raw "newbies" and tentative writers who want to make a living at their craft tend to write what they think is popular, trendy, or "mainstream." And their efforts sound flat simply because they lack passion for those stories. Stories wrenched from the soul, from the angst of living a trauma, from the horrors of a life on the edge deliver a depth of character, dialogue and events unmatched by "commercial efforts." Those are powerfully therapeutic stories no one else could tell.

Remember that Statement of Purpose you were asked to write early on? Were you 100% honest with yourself when you wrote that? Did you truly consider life issues that haunt and harass you? Do your "Ho-Hum" conventional characters struggle but cannot rise above a genre to be more because you feared being over-the-top "edgy" or even the dreaded melodramatic?

Pushing the envelope is risky business, especially if it is the male venturing into the world of "touchy-feely" stuff or the female wallowing in crude violence. We tend to play it safe in so many parts of our lives . . . so why can't you step to the edge of storytelling's cliff and take a leap of faith? Why can you not write gritty characters who sound like potty-mouthed sailors but take on the woes of the world like Mother Teresa? Why can't your characters defy peer pressure or the establishment? Why can't you be different?

WE TEND TO PLAY IT SAFE IN SO MANY PARTS OF OUR LIVES . . . SO WHY CAN'T YOU STEP TO THE EDGE OF STORYTELLING'S CLIFF AND TAKE A LEAP OF FAITH?

Challenge: Comb back through a recent script or a work-in-progress and identify one rebel, one iconic personality who can epitomize freedom to your inner "demons." Just to you. No one else matters. Evolve that person with passion and integrity, determination and the will to survive despite sacrifice. Give that person the ability to show soul-deep emotions and proudly proclaim them because he or she recognizes and accepts responsibility for living life on his or her terms. Have this character grab life by the throat and resolutely refuse to let go! Now, identify all the scenes that experience a ripple effect from the power of this emotional personality . . . and revise them.

A writer is not ready to try writing this kind of character until all the intellectualizing has been accomplished. Writers need to hone their craft well before being emotionally courageous. Once you have tried it you will continue to use this one highly emotional character tool again and again to enrich each of your stories.

A huge step in that direction would be to study *Writing for Emotional Impact by* Karl Iglesias. He preaches how to turn the emotional screws. As he professes: Anyone and everyone can write a story with the "proper" plot points in the prescribed number of pages and format with the expected dramatic characters speaking lines of succinct dialogue. Again, anyone can do that. Hundreds or even thousands of scripts out and about this moment have all that. Those fundamental qualities will not sell a script.

The writer whose script gets passed up the food chain for the decision-makers to evaluate writes sentences, scenes, and speeches that create an emotional response in the reader. Iglesias emphasizes the emotional content of each of the prescribed acts, plot points and signposts. If you do not inherently know what this means, then you need to read his book! He is not talking about the emotions of the characters, but the emotions you want to tweak in the Reader/Audience.

This kind of writer goes beyond his or her own passion, beyond focus on a vicarious cinematic experience to wrenching gut-deep emotions from every single person who reads the script. The story becomes a "wow" kind of inexplicable experience as the reader turns the pages. Some of that writing is a talent, a gift, but it can also be learned and enhanced, if the writer wants to achieve that level of writing. Iglesias's book explains how. Consider yourself just introduced to the concept with the prodding to wonder if you are ready for that advanced writing technique.

VALUE OF AFTER-STORY

Between the climax and THE END is the drift into possibilities of After-Story, all those lives continuing on when the theater lights come up. The "let-down" after the climax has a definitive purpose: to visually depict the characters putting all their lessons to use from this point forward. This is the "Commitment" or "Ah-h-h-h Scene" that implies the future. Alfred Hitchcock called it the "Refrigerator Talk Scene." He felt strongly that this final scene was what brought movie goers back to see another movie by a film-maker. People needed to be sent home to pull a snack from the refrigerator and talk about the story people as if those characters actually lived . . . and then to hypothesize about how they continued to live into their future. Hitchcock felt that was the proof of a good movie.

Haven't you ever discussed characters as if they were real or what their lives were like after a movie? Haven't you ever at least listened to others debate the principles of various film characters . . . as if they truly existed? Sure, sometimes you scratched your head and wondered what others are talking about and felt the need to say "Hey, get a life!" But you miss the valuable point that the film-maker created characters and life experiences that made people think. It's as simple as that.

REVISING A SCREENPLAY

Each person evolves their own revision technique. Here is one for your consideration.

Storytelling is a dynamic process meaning it changes and improves with practice. The better craftsman you become, the easier the first draft, BUT the more intense the revision!

Note this is a generalization: The majority of people just starting out in writing think the most difficult and time-consuming part is the first draft, getting those original words on paper. The qualifying "just starting out in writing" give it away. By the second or third project, the majority of writers have learned the revising and rewriting is much, much, much more demanding. Many writers spend triple the time on the final draft than on the original draft of anything, be it short story, magazine article, novel or screenplay. Never simply spew the words out then rush to submit anything. Why? Because you (and every other writer) are far from perfect.

One can experience the Zen-like state of initial creation. This can evolve into a euphoria the writer seeks to experience again and again. First drafts are never drudgery for this writer. At with the beginning or the end of the process, the creative "high" is indeed addictive. But, the astute writer must also evolve the practice of rereading and rereading as he or she is working. Some people adamantly avoid going back over their work feeling they begin to obsess and that stops the creative flow. The attitude is understand . . . but the brain can be trained to spew a fast flow of grammatically correct, vivid sentences by going back over the work as it is produced . . . without losing that creative high.

A SUCCINCT PROOFING TECHNIQUE

Note the title to this portion is "Proofing Technique" and not revising, rewriting, editing. This is merely one work technique. Is it how everyone should work? Definitely not. You need to find your own method that produces the cleanest, most error-free manuscript possible in the least amount of time for you. In other words, in this section and throughout the remainder of this revision discussion, choose and test suggestions until you achieve a logical, consistent process in your own writing! Copy and paste, rearrange and analyze until you find your process.

This method begins with rereading the previous day's pages to start the new day. Revision or proofing is done as the current day's words are flowing. At the end of each scene, the writer rereads to re-experience the flow and again at the end of each completed Act. This re-reading is focused on looking for misspelled words, typos, sentence variety. A writer using this process is not bogged down because a daily page-goal forces the writer to keep producing even as the proofing is done. The goal is like a nag that will not be ignored.

Once completed, the manuscript will be read eight more separate times looking for different "things" each time. Lew Hunter discussed these specific reads in his book *Screenwriting 434*.

1) First sentence of subsequent narrative paragraphs for variety,
2) Word "Search" for passive "to be" forms (is, was, were),
3) Read each main character from beginning to end (via "Search") looking for consistency of description & dialogue (read that aloud),
4) Look for story's signposts at reasonable intervals (going by Paradigm comparison to pages looking for timing and balance of parts of the story),
5) Skim for "white space" and look for an overall feel of balance of narrative density with dialogue,

6) Reread first & last scenes of Acts for hooks,
7) "Search: commas for proper use, overuse of ellipsis, proper use of dashes
8) Spell check and formatting errors.

Finally, identify three peers to read, people who are knowledgeable of the type of genre. DO NOT ask just anybody to read and analyze your script. English teachers, librarians, high school drama teachers and journalists who have never seen a screenplay before make lousy "critiquers" (vs. just being critics). You want to identify people who understand screenwriting and film, people who will not be confrontational with over-inflated egos who will be hyper-critical or people who will ask more questions than they will answer. You want confident, practiced screenwriters and film-makers to analyze your effort. How do you find them? That's why you network.

AGENT OR PRODUCER NOTES

Most writers sublimate their ego about the second or third year of serious writing. About that time they know what they can do and what they cannot. When they start submitting to professional film-makers they must acknowledge the experience and wisdom they are accessing. They need to accept the fact of life that there are a whole lot of people out there who know more about screenwriting and storytelling, especially those making a living at film-making like agents and producers. It is perfectly reasonable to carefully evaluate notes from these industry Pros to hone a script to marketable quality before it is sold.

If these people didn't think the script had a chance to sell, they wouldn't make the suggestions in the first place. Remember that when your feathers get ruffled. Secondly, remember that you are merely drawing a blue-print and this design will go through many revisions before it makes it to the screen. So be gracious and objective when the Pros ask for changes. Your story has given them a vision and they suggest changes to make that vision come to life. You always ask yourself who is in control, you or that Pro? Who is the one who can make it happen?

MARKETING

The *Learn Screenwriting* book provides a succinct explanation and how-to's of a synopsis, the one-pager marketing tool the busy people request.

SYNOPSIS

First, consider the "Log Line." The essence of marketing screenplays is to understand that everyone in the business is rushing to "make things happen."

They are multi-tasking and therefore have the attention span of a gnat. The search for that one block buster script is a disease that has infected everyone from the studio reader to the studio executive department head. It starts with a killer Log Line that is so intriguing that the person has to read the synopsis.

If you have never written a synopsis, you are about to learn that you need to. Rarely is a screenplay read in its entirety before a synopsis. That little gem is the "One-Pager" that tells the story in its most succinct yet complete form. It has prescribed structure that dictates summary of the premise and characters then Beginning-Middle-Ending. It is agony to condense the highlights of a 100-page screenplay into a 550-650-word, single-spaced page. Not a writer alive enjoys writing them. Professionals accept their necessity and simply "gird their loins" to produce one.

Synopses are torture to write, but you had better learn how to do them and do them well. Studio readers, producers and agents expect you to have one for every script you intend to market.

SYNOPSIS BASICS

1) The structure coincides with the paradigm
2) It relies on your ability to vividly summarize
3) It is written in present tense.
4) Single spaced with drop-downs between "Acts"

There's what you need to know to begin. After filling out the original paradigm, some writers create a "work-in-progress" synopsis and put it in the project's file folder with story research notes and Character Profiles. It need not be touched again until the screenplay is finish. Most paradigms (thus synopses) will probably change during the actual writing. Time can be wasted perpetually tweaking that original synopsis as the changes are incorporated to the script. Why do that? Wait until the end when you've made all the changes you are going to make to the script, then revise the synopsis to match your finished product.

Here's a start for you:

Signposts of Beginning:
Opening Scene.
Main Characters introduced with succinct characterization.
Summarize "ordinary life" and its trials.
Glimpse of pending threat.
Life-changing event forcing Protag ACTION

Middles's Paragraphs Two-Three-Four: Summaries of the key confrontations the Protag faces in the "New Life," that 1/2 middle portion of the story that has the reader on the edge of the seat. Main plot events are essential. Subplots and supporting characters are not necessary in these paragraphs, even though you see them adding depth and dimension. The only names you should mention are the leads, the characters the story is focused on, the hero-heroine-antagonist. Avoid exposition and explanation. A synopsis is telling of cause-effect events, not explaining the logic of why.

Paragraph Two will be a summary of complications confronting Protag in this new life, the main tests and the main players (referred to by role, not by name).

Paragraph Three will be the summary of the event that leads to another life-changing experience, the Mid-Point where the Protag is tested and recognizes the importance of the adventure, the moment when the Protag's motivation intensifies thus the stakes of the ultimate outcome are higher. Frequently, in a romance, that is when one of the lovers acknowledges love or the first time the pair make love.

Paragraph Four is the summary of the growing strength of the Antagonist (or antagonistic elements), the confident exertions of the Protag to be worthy, and the final sentence summary of the crushing moment when the Antagonist is at his strongest and has backed the Protag into a corner. The action of the final sentence implies the Protag could be defeated as a form of death and is at the lowest ebb of confidence, thus must surrender in defeat or or rise from the "death" like a Phoenix to fight. (This sentence summary is what forces the Protag to cause the Ending to happen as it does.)

Signposts of Middle, Paragraph Two:
Protag facing new life, new tests, new people
Antagonist inserting threat.
Protag's glimpse of "worst fear" becoming real
Protag trying new skills, taking risks

Signposts of Middle, Paragraph Three:
Protag chooses to assert "power"
Protag experiences internal "denouement"
Protag acts on awareness of exciting possibilities
Others shown as critical or puzzled observers of Protag

Signposts of Middle: Paragraph Four:
Protag proves worthiness to Observers
Antagonist demonstrates vivid growth in power
Protag experiences a moment of startling success
Antagonist's power evolves
Life changing moment of Antagonist cornering Protag in near-defeat/pseudo-death

ENDING'S Paragraph Five: Intense, high energy summary of Protag's preparations to fight as Antagonist blithely carries out plans. Succinct yet vivid fireworks of the "Climactic Battle" of wills or events where the Protagonist succeeds and Antagonist is defeated.

Signposts of Ending
Protag's reaction and preparation for battle
Antagonist's confident arrogance
Climactic Battle.
Defeat of Antagonist

FINAL SCENE's Paragraph Six: The one sentence summary of the rewarding results of the Resolution (that implies an "After-story").

Key: Force yourself to keep your paragraphs to 75-100 words and, yes, you count "the" and "a" or every word. The font is usually 12-pt, though writers have been known to "fudge" to 11-pt and tweak the margins to less than standard to get it to the one-page.

An example synopsis of an Academy of Motion Picture Arts & Sciences' Nicholl quarterfinalist script, THE LONELY MAN, can be found in Appendix K.

THE "FIVE SCRIPTS" RULE

Another Lew Hunter phrase can be recited by his students: "Practice, Perseverance and Patience will get you Produced." It's from his "P-ing all-over-Hollywood" lecture. He emphasizes to every new writer the importance of learning craft before marketing. Everybody has a screenplay idea then about 50% of those people have a screenplay either hidden somewhere on their person or lurking in their car. There is an essential wisdom in another of his principles: "Write five scripts before you even think of marketing one. By the time you get done with the fifth one, you will know what has to be revised in the other four." Lew has been in the trenches of writing and production for 50 years now, including working for every major studio of his time plus serving for seven years in the second-in-command position of Program Director at NBC. His advice is based on wisdom and experience.

First scripts are generally lousy. Don't obsess. Rarely does a first script show evidence of incredible genius. Nothing will train you as thoroughly as practice, practice, practice.

FIRST SCRIPTS ARE GENERALLY LOUSY. DON'T OBSESS.

PITCHING IS ITS OWN ART FORM

Whether via e-mail, hard-copy letter, phone or face-to-face, pitching requires its own mind-set. An absolute "have to memorize" book is Stephanie Palmer's *Good in a Room.* A Creative Director is one of the top four positions in a major studio. Stephanie held that title at MGM for six years. She then left the corporate madhouse to establish her own Public Relations firm and wrote that book. Though a bible for the film industry, the principles in it are also applicable to any "sales" situation. You will find the outline for the Pitching Process in Appendix L.

INDUSTRY ATTENTION THROUGH CONTESTS

Yes, producers and agents pay attention to established screenplay competitions. The most prestigious is the annual Nicholl (annual May 1 deadline) sponsored by the Academy of Motion Picture Arts and Sciences, the Oscar people. In 2018 they received close to 7,000 entries. The approximate 300 quarter-finalists are announced around July 1, the approximate 150 semi-finalists in August then the few finalists in September.

The fellowship winners receive their first portion of the hefty award money at the November banquet. Subsequent portions are doled out as they send in designated sections of a new screenplay written during their award year. Producers and agents read the Nicholl's posted lists of those writers and scripts culled out of the thousands, all the way from quarterfinalists through to the winners. Sometimes the winning scripts get contracted and sometimes a writer's script two to four years down the road gets to the screen. The point is the named contestants are in the limelight and the movers and shakers take note.

Other well-known, reputable contests include the Austin Film Festival and Sundance. Search on the Internet noting history, credentials, and entrance criteria. Investigate thoroughly the claims and successes of any advertised contest, as well as query who the judges are. It is a well-known fact that many a film festival designate judges who are merely people wanting to be involved in film but who have no formal training. They are reading and judging only on their gut instinct as an audience member.

If you submit to one that provides feedback (Blue Cat, for example) understand that you will get one person's opinion. Most contests do not give time-consuming feedback. Realistically, they just don't have time considering the number of submissions. They just take your money and run.

Look over the kind of Score Sheet used in some competitions provided in Appendix M. The example sheet asks some specific questions but still relies heavily on the judge's gut instinct and expertise.

HOW ARE SCREENPLAYS EVALUATED?

Coverage (evaluation) is provided by professional readers for both agencies and studios. There is even a union for Hollywood readers. Some employers provide forms to be completed by the reader. Most ask for the professional readers to write their own synopsis of the work with summaries of strengths and weaknesses. These evaluations provided to studios and agents are usually not available to the writer. However, a writer can pay for coverage. Fees vary according to the extent of the evaluation you want. Do an Internet search for "Screenplay Coverage Services." Two services I have used with feedback useful to revision and marketing are Story Sense and Coverage, Ink.

For a more thorough understanding of what a professional Reader does pick up this insightful book:

THE 1-3-5 STORY STRUCTURE SYSTEM, Donna Michelle Anderson
(A little handbook written by a Studio Reader applying BASICS)

Now a producer, Anderson explains how both the writer and the project are separately evaluated for Pass, Consider, or Recommend. A Pass-Pass means both are history for this script in its present state. A Consider for the script means the reader recognized potential that another writer could clean up if the studio executives think it viable. A Consider for the writer means the executives might want to think about asking for other scripts from this person. Of course, the most desirable outcome would be Recommend-Recommend where both writer and script are strongly suggested for a contract. Such a writer would be evaluated to join their list of "referrals" for rewrites on other scripts (which is the most viable route for a steady income).

QUERY LETTERS

Query letters are the first communication between a writer and potential agent or producer. You must always remember those letters are representative of you, your first impression on whoever you are submitting to. Secondly, never forget that concept of "the attention span of a gnat." Thirdly, you want to be succinctly businesslike but memorable. The format is the same whether you are submitting to a production company or an agency. They are business people with little time. Though anyone appreciates levity in the entertainment industry, a query letter is not the place to use it.

Paragraph One: Grab attention to focus or power of your project, give title, page length and that 25-word Log Line.

Paragraph Two: In 50-75 words, summarize the Beginning, Middle, Ending of the actual story. Think of this as comparable to the back-cover blurb on paperbacks. So, yes, this paragraph could be about the dynamics of the main character. "a one-page synopsis is included for more details."

Paragraph Three: Think appeal. Who would come to see this movie? This is where you "could" reference other movies similar to your theme or tone. "Fans of So-and-So would enjoy the complexity of my screenplay's romance." Or you could refer to your demographics (audience) research. such as "Romantic comedies maintain audience appeal in the U.S. and foreign market as evidenced by the most recent report of BRIDESMAIDS with 80-million earnings." (Current sales figures can be found on IMDb--Internet Movie Database).

Paragraph Four: This is the you paragraph where you summarize your credentials and credits pertinent to this project. If you have none then succinctly explain why you felt the need to write this story.

Paragraph Five: Closing of "Thank you for your consideration. I look forward to a response requesting the screenplay in either hard-copy or electronic file."

WRITERS GUILD OF AMERICA . . . and Elsewhere

Learn about the professional screenwriting organization relative to where YOU live. In the U.S., if you live east of the Mississippi, you head to the website of WGA-East http://www.wgaeast.org headquartered in New York City. If you live west of the Mississippi you refer to WGA-West http://www.wga.org/ and their offices in Los Angeles. Go to whatever site is appropriate and read everything you can about who they are and what they do. Bottom line: The guilds are unions formed to protect the rights of writers working in the film industry. You cannot just "join." You have to be eligible for membership.

Do you have to be a member of the WGA to sell a script in the U, S.? No. And if your goal is only to sell one script, you do not have to join the Guild and pay their initiation fee within 30 days of selling a script. That's if you sell the script outright. However, if you want to contract for any re-writes, you do have to join the WGA or there will be repercussions, as in you can't get the contract for your own re-write as it will go to a WGA member and you will have a next to impossible chance of selling a second script.

Understand this: The studio system is essentially "closed shop," meaning it uses and supports all the unions from the Directors Guild to the Screen Actors Guild to AFTRA (American Federation of Television and Radio Artists). The WGA is a union. I refer you to this website to learn more: http://www.filmmakers.com/links/member/unions.htm . The unions have a distinct purpose in the film industry and that is to give individuals the power of many to help them when they are treated unjustly. They are not "blood suckers."

There are about 13,000 members of WGA-West and only about 10% of them are employed at any one time. Reading the information on the WGA site you will discover that once you qualify for membership and pay your initiation fee you will owe them a percentage of your annual income from screenwriting or $200 minimum, whichever is greater.

There are also many foreign writing guilds, so if you live outside the U.S., do your homework. Understand that if you live in the U.S. but market to a foreign film company, those film-makers do not have to abide by the minimums or policies of the guilds in the U.S. It is your responsibility to clarify your rights and responsibilities before contracting.

Of course, the WGA has no jurisdiction over independent film makers, either. Once you become a WGA member, however, you are obligated to communicate with the Guild about any negotiations with independents and you will still owe the Guild a percentage of your income from that independent work.

GROWING YOUR NETWORK LOCALLY

The film industry is alive and procreating nicely thanks to the evolution of digital cameras. The 35mm cameras are expensive and do produce high quality. However, technology is racing forward. And that technology is becoming more accessible to the general public with high quality images and ease of editing capabilities, all at a relatively low cost.

Investigate independent film-making in your area. Find and associate yourself with your regional film organizations. Meet the young film-makers nearest you, especially in your local community college or university programs. Find out what they are doing and volunteer in whatever capacity you can. Free labor is always welcomed. In exchange you will be educated in titles and job descriptions as well as the drudgery and meticulous nature of "getting just the right shot." You will learn why film budgets are what they are (to pay all those people and services involved). You will discover that "Living the Film-Making Process" is important to all involved. Bonds and relationships will be formed, as well as a credit earned for your experience resume.

TAKE AN ACTING CLASS

Writers tend to be loners, especially when in the depths of their craft. The dramatic arts require interaction with all who collaborate to bring the story to the stage or the screen. To enhance your appreciation for the nuances of the dramatic process, take an acting class. You will discover the creation of a dramatic persona is NOT as easy or natural as really good actors make it look. You will gain a profound insight into characterization that will give you a mental eye for look and sound that mere reading of scripts and talking with other writers cannot give you.

GATHER WITH OTHER SCREENWRITERS

Spouses, significant others and friends may laud what you are doing, but nobody on this earth will understand you like another writer. In this instance, that refers to another screenwriter. Novelists, journalists, poets, even playwrights will not be able to give you the depth of feedback another screenwriter can.

Of course, you are going to find the insecure and the paranoid when you go in search of like-minded Creatives. But sincerity and integrity will win out. Committing all in the group to the concepts of giving honest feedback and not getting caught up in the comparison game, of evaluating the screenplay and not the writer, you can enjoy a highly beneficial network of comrades-in-arms who will help one another improve their craft. No one's going to steal your idea. Why? Because professionals know each person has more passion about their own story than anyone else's. The coming together will give you more than just by exchanging and marking up pages. Give table readings a go, with cohorts giving voice to assigned parts. The experience will become an invaluable benefit of the give-and-take of trust and respect no one else will understand.

Make a regular get-together a habit. Schedule a time and place that can be relied on, no matter what is going on other lives. That discipline of attendance because you rely on one another will become a motivation to write and polish the pages you are going to bring to the table. Guaranteed.

INSPIRATIONAL GENRE

Let's start with the explanation that this particular genre has a special meaning to many people. You would be surprised (or maybe not) to know that every single character birthed by some writer has a carefully considered spiritual status. The tenuous or staunch position of that character's spiritual awareness plays a major role in the story's journey. Such a writer believes that most of life's experiences are inter-related, thus our spiritual life and souls are impacted by our experiences. We just have to be paying attention to learn the lessons. It has been the experience of many in screenwriting that the stories of characters who arc deep within are those who inspire others . . . thus many just plain good stories are inspirational. Did the writer and film-makers intend for them to be inspirational in the sense of advancing the soul's growth and demonstrating a strong faith? Probably not. But, the writer attuned to the spiritual makes that a deliberate decision.

Consider the movie RUDY, for example. Rudy was a Roman Catholic, but the story was about his personal commitment to living the life of a football player at Norte Dame. His determination and work ethic inspired everyone else in the football program at that time. The film wasn't about his religion. It was about his personal integrity . . . which, in truth, grew out of his faith.

CLASSIFYING INSPIRATIONAL

Do not get caught in the thought association grinder that dictates "Inspirational" means "Christian." Christian literature has its own market and expectations. There are other religions and "positive stroke" stories out there, each with its own agenda and set of rules. Basically, however, all have a very narrow focus: triggering positive affirmations from the human soul. Remember, differentiating into genre storytelling categories is for marketing and bookstore shelving purposes . . . unless you are writing specifically to a readership/target audience. And some stories like KINGDOM OF HEAVEN analyzed for this genre, tells of how some men rationalize their actions quoting the dogma of their faith and others actually live the tenants of their faith.

Have you ever searched a library, bookstore or on the web for fiction told from the Jewish, Hindu, Muslim or Pagan perspective? Not a whole lot out there. Even "New Age" material could be considered among the subgenres of Inspirational, if you want to get very technical. The concept in this discussion is that the Main Plot of Inspirational fiction has to focus on the character's internalized questing for value and answers to questions of spiritual concepts, how to find self-worth on a plane beyond a pragmatic basis, how to live a satisfying life beyond self. **The Inspirational label means a values and faith-based story.**

Can you see how this kind of quest could be woven into the fabric of many other genre stories? But the intensity, the focus, the number of words spent on the spiritual growth of the Protagonist will take up a substantial portion of the story, not always in telling mode either. Inspirational stories show the character striving to be better, striving to prove the tenants of faith/principle/personal integrity in their actions, not just dialogue. That means you avoid long episodes of lecturing and explaining.

CHRISTIAN MARKET

Since Christian literature is the biggest, most dominate type of Inspirational story, it certainly warrants some separate attention.

Consider two pieces of very serious advice: 1) Research the producers' history, either previous productions or interviews for what is acceptable material for them (Example: Larry Levinson Productions for the Hallmark Channel or the film companies doing productions for various faiths) and 2) if you are going to write about a denomination you do not 100% understand or have an in-depth appreciation of, have the good manners to consult practitioners (even if you feel you will disagree).

Not paying attention to these two points will do one thing: Prove your ignorance. Just like relating historical accuracy in period writing, you have a responsibility to interpret religious tenants and practices with dispassionate accuracy. You may be a fictional liar, but have the Creative Conscience to be accurate in your details.

Christian publishers, producers, writers and consumer public have founded many organizations geared toward promoting and sustaining their interests. The American Christian Fiction Writers and the Christian Booksellers Association are two examples serious folks should check out. Why should screenwriters bother? Because there are also many faith-based companies networking with these organizations. The wise writer is the one who researches the market and understands the purveyors and the targeted audience.

FUNDAMENTAL CONCEPTS OF INSPIRATIONAL

1. Main Character's spiritual principles are challenged and proven true by overcoming circumstance/antagonist.
- Like in any other genre, inspirational audiences are NOT interested in the boring "Happy People of the Happy Village." They want to see how this character discovers and resolves their spiritual problems in a very realistic manner. Do not dwell on long dissertations of thought or dogma discussions. Hit-and-Run internalizations and even discussion summaries are much more effective because audience members seek principles put into action. If they want explanations, they will turn to nonfiction sources.

2. Write (and submit) material strictly consistent with publisher/producer's theology
- Your purpose is to get this material published thus you will not be read if you do not comply with the publisher's requirements. You want to make a friend of the editor, not challenge their faith beliefs. Evangelizing is not done through confrontation on the editor/publisher level. People who have attempted this experience the obvious results: Rejection.

3. Spiritual virtue always wins and the character always witnesses "why's" as fundamental to success.
- The main character's goal needs concrete proof of spiritual virtue whereas the internal angst can wander toward the abstract as an attitude. The explanations of the "why's" should be as succinct and simple as possible since the proof is visible. If you need an example, watch the old classic movie CHARIOTS OF FIRE. Though he recognized God's gift that made him a fast runner, he would not dishonor his faith practice of worshipping that God by racing on the Sabbath.

> MOST SPIRITUAL ISSUES ARE INTERNALIZED BUT ACT AS MOTIVATORS FOR ULTIMATE ACTION. THERE IS YOUR FOCUS.

4. Avoid preaching/lecturing through brief internalizations/reflections and even more abbreviated dialogue with detailed "faith in action."
- Most spiritual issues are internalized but act as motivators for ultimate action. There is your focus.

5. Understand the issues and language allowable or to be avoided.
- Most inspirational markets do not want overt sexuality, graphic violence and cursing or obscene language. Ascertain the euphemisms that can be allowed such as "He cursed." In the Christian market there can be admiration of "form" but no specific description, just as there can be a hand to neck (or above) and kissing with thoughts summarized but not detailed. The point of the story is not to titillate, merely to allude to the various issues, like the closed bedroom door. The point of the story is faith and life issues that complicate that, so you do not dwell on the sensuality or problems that will thought-associate away from faith issues. These are concepts of the market you either practice or don't submit to this market.

INSPIRATIONAL CHARACTER REQUIREMENTS

Characters who are in crisis or questing on a spiritual level are **complex, uncertain risk takers.** They cannot be weak or easily manipulated. Of course, not all us humans succeed in all endeavors or capture the ultimate prize because we are imperfect creatures. The interesting Inspirational Main Character is someone who is tenacious and willing to sacrifice to understand and live the professed tenants proven true.

The Inspirational Protagonist must face Antagonists that are **worldly and powerfully seductive with the very real possibility of turning sinister**. The Antagonist must be just as certain of right behavior and belief in opposition to the Protagonist and determined to prove the Protagonist wrong. Can you see how the Antagonist could be an entire culture or way of life?

INSPIRATIONAL PLOT TYPES

1. Religious Book (Bible/Koran) Parallel or Allegory
- The legends or stories of the holy book are lived again in a different, fictional circumstance such as in a fantasy world or among the Aztecs.

2. Evangelizing recruitment story
- A character is out to deliberately show others how right their faith and way of life is in comparison to the current status quo.

3. Testimonial Autobiography or Biography story
- I refer you to the movie RUDY for an example of faith-based self-awareness that drove that man to stay the course no matter what. And some life lessons that come off as self-righteous are more effective when disguised as fiction.

4. Corrupt Life Salvaged
- Nothing is as motivational or moving as a life spiraling toward total destruction that is turned around and set on a path of selfless action that helps others, especially when faith is the motivational element of the epiphany. The changes resulting are action proof to the audience.

5. Pastor/Practitioner Changing an Institution
- The leader who faces self-doubt in the midst of responsibility for many other lives can deliver a powerful message.

6. Prodigal Son
- The lost who is found and once again accepted and loved gives others the hope that anyone can be loved no matter what. When the experience revolves around faith-based issues the story becomes apocryphal or legend-like in its repetitive nature.

7. Crucial Test
- The story that pushes the main character to the ultimate make-or-break point where all is lost or all is gained. This story focuses on rising tension of how much is too much to that climactic battle point. Words are never enough in this story. Action proves faith.

8. Innocence Leads
- Simplistic thought is sometimes the straight arrow through the complex issues. Faith is bound to trust. Innocence (not ignorance) is total trust that goes so deep it cannot be destroyed.

9. Converted Savage
- Similar to #2 Evangelizing and #4 Corrupt Life, the writer has to weave a more careful path through the current belief system of the ignorant Savage to convince the character (and the audience) that the new belief system is better, more complete, more satisfying. The temptation is to preach but contemporary movie goers will not tolerate that for long. The focus here is on the changes in the Savage, not the righteousness of the messenger.

10. Ravaged Body
- This story will grow out of the Main Character's failed coping mechanisms and the exaggerated swing up either pathway of the Anxiety Curve toward

Apathy's withdrawal or Panic's anger. The messenger gradually convinces the Protagonist of how to cope more effectively through a change in faith.

11. Temptation
- In the Character Profile you will come to understand Motivation, Ambition and Goal concluding "How far would this character go to attain what he or she wants?" then you know where to insert the dilemma of temptation and how to attack and counter with a greater worthy goal that will be recognized. If you character has a closed mind, he or she will not be capable fo opening to possibility or change. You-the-Writer throw faith and values in to change the game and ultimate outcome.

12. Denominational story
- I am Episcopalian with a couple of Episcopalian novels. I understand MY denomination. There are publishing houses for specific denominations such as Methodist and Roman Catholic. They expect the stories submitted to them get the tenants, rituals and dogma correct. The denominational stories evolve out of that denomination's issues.

Inspirational storytelling is not everyone's preference. On the other hand, some writers may think "I want every story I write to be inspiring because I have a point to make." Inspirational and inspiring are NOT the same thing. By this point in this lesson you should understand that. The key point of this genre is **faith, an internal value system that guides all decision-making**.

INSPIRATIONAL FILM ANALYSIS

You are now mentally armed with many elements to look for. In these films you are focused on the sometimes subtle, sometimes blatant demonstrated spirituality of the characters and their experiences. Their values system dictates their action choices. The character's choices at signpost events reflect value motivation.

* * * * *

KINGDOM OF HEAVEN

By William Monahan
2005, Starring: Orlando Bloom, Liam Neeson, Eva Green, Jeremy Irons

Length: 135 Minutes

Log Line: A bastard blacksmith takes on his father's title and honorable legacy in 1184 Jerusalem, facing corrupt Christians and warring Saracens.

Statement of Purpose: To prove that honor comes from conscience and right action.

Intro Image: Medieval riders pass a cross marker on a country road.

First 10 minutes:
Who:
GODFREY, Knight and Baron of Ibelin
BAILIN, Godfrey's bastard son, village blacksmith by trade
HOSPITALER, cynical Templar knight of a medical order
When: 1184 Winter
Where: France, countryside village near a castle
What: Baron returns from the Crusades to claim his adult son
Why: Aging warrior has come to awareness of fragile life and value of legacy of honor and service he wants to continue.

Three related subplots:
Templars vs. King's men (in Jerusalem
Corrupt Christian Empire vs. Muslims
Sibylla & Bailin Love Affair

Time Line: One Year (Winter to following Spring)

Image repeats:
Cross
Redemption
Honor
"God wills it!"
Swords, arrows, spears
Water
Fire
Desert as threat
Battle Towers & Catapults
Beheadings

Act I = Set-up of Ordinary World: Godfrey passing inheritance to Bailin
10 min **Intro:** Godfrey introduces himself as father & invites Bailin to Jerusalem
14 min **Inciting Incident**: Fighting the men come for Bailin, Godfrey wounded
24 min **PP I:** Dying Godfrey knights his son charging him with honorable oath

Act II = Life 180 degrees: Bailin learns of legacy, intrigues, lands and love
45 min **Pinch I:** Guy publicly denounces Bailin as a bastard unfit for King's table
64 min **Mid-Point:** Bailin leads knights against Imad's forces at Kerak
77 min **Pinch II**: Jerusalem offers Bailin control of the army & Sibylla
98 min **PPII:** Bailin finds Saladin's carnage of the Christian knights at Hattin

Act III = Resolution: Bailin leads the defense then surrender of Jerusalem
106 (-123) min **Climax:** Epic Siege of Jerusalem
131 min **Commitment**: Bailin walks beside Sibylla in the dusty walk away from Jerusalem
After-story Conclusion: Bailin refuses acknowledge self to King Richard bound for Crusades with "I am a blacksmith."

Dialogue Notes:
Proper English of the nobility
Command of Arabic (Sibylla)
Cynical tones of Hospitaler, Tiberias & Reynald
Variations of Muslim accents (Imad, Saladin, Mullah)
Perpetual sneer in Guy's voice
Bailin almost reluctant to speak then only briefly (except for epic speech)

Alpha Character posturing differences:
Godfrey vs. Hospitaler & his other warriors vs. Guy
Bailin vs his cousin priest (in village) vs. Godfrey vs. Hospitaler
Bailin vs. Imad (on desert) vs. Ibelin's men vs. Tiberius vs. Sibylla & Jersualem
Bailin's watchfulness changing to confidence after Kerak
Jerusalem vs. Tiberius vs. Guy
Saladin vs. Imad vs. Mullah vs. Bailin

Supporting cast Unique Character Gems:
Hospitaler, Village Priest, Odo (Baron's German warrior),
Imad, Ibelin's men, Patriarch of Jerusalem, Raynald, Jerusalem (King)
Mullah

Background effects, the nuances of aura:
Crude wintry Medieval village & smithy
Camps in forest & at Medina
Chapel at Medina

High seas aboard ship with horses
Desert starkness & oasis
Spectacle of Jerusalem, marketplace, under seige
Jerusalem palace, many rooms, courtyard
Ibelin's pastoral quality
Stark Kerak
Killing fields, including grasses around Saladin's sister
Battle towers
Muslim tents

Elements from Other Genres: Historical, Action-Adventure, Romance

Question: In the theatrical release, did you question Bailin's initial competency with a sword and seeming innate knowledge of cavalry/knightly tactics and battle strategies? (Explanation was in the Director's Cut)

Appearance or reference to recurrence of RELIGIOUS Theme in Min: Both Christian and Muslim.

Act I = Set-up of Ordinary World: Godfrey passing inheritance to Bailin
1-2 Gravediggers working beside cross on country road, unprincipled priest takes ngold cross necklace from throat of shrouded dead beauty, then order them to chop off her head because she was a suicide
8-9 Same priest (Bailin's cousin) encourages he take the Crusade to help his wife move out of purgatory, "but what do without a head?" Bailin sees her cross on his neck & runs him through
10 **Intro:** Godfrey introduces himself as father & invites Bailin to Jerusalem
14 **Inciting Incident**: Fighting the men come for Bailin, Godfrey wounded
17 Hospitaler removes arrow & pronounces God's will if Godfrey lives
18 Priest on road to Medina pronounces Crusades "Path to Heaven."
20-21 Sick Godfrey talks to Bailin of opportunity in Jerusalem, serving the king who trying to make a Kingdom of Conscience, a Kingdom of Heaven.
22 Bailin observes Muslims at prayer on beach, "Sounds like ours."
23 Bailin at prayer beside fire when called to chapel
24-26 PP I: Dying Godfrey knights his son charging him with honorable oath, Hospitaler asks Godfrey if sorry for his sins, "Yes to all but one." Anointed, he dies.

Act II = Life 180 degrees: Bailin learns of legacy, intrigues, lands and love
36 After killing Muslim horseman, Bailin knocks Imad from his horse who proclaims "It was end of his time."

34-36 Gives Imad the horse & frees "Not own a slave" "Your quality will be known among your enemies wherever you meet." Bailin asks where Christ died, climbs hill, sits through night praying, buries her cross.

39-40 Hospitaler greets Bailin as dressing, "How find you out of God's grace?" "Lost my religion." "Holiness comes from right action for those who cannot. Godly desires here (heart).

41-42 Templar knights being hung, "Dying for what pope order but not this king or Christ"//Tiberius confronts Reynald hung for raid he ordered.

45 **Pinch I:** Guy publicly denounces Bailin as a bastard unfit for King's table

47-48 Masked King receives, tells of father's service & noticed Leperosy,"Saracens say hell is worse. If so, not fair." "A King may move man but your soul is your own."

55 Sybilla visits Ibelin & Bailin's new water wells, He says "What would I be if not to make my world better?"

58 Husband Guy (*Gee*) with Reynald & troop of Templars descend on Muslim caravan "God wills it!"

60 King's court with Patriarch, Guy & Templars vs. Tiberius before King, arguing war with Saracens, "Must, God wills it!"

64 **Mid-Point:** Bailin leads knights against Imad's forces at Kerak

68-70 Defeated Bailin before Imad who reminds of "Quality will be known" "What becomes?" "You must reap what you sow." My master here, stopps seeing dust & huge shining cross. "Jerusalem has come." Rhousands face thousands. "We have terms. Send you my physicians." Bows to King.

74 In Kerak, King calls Bailin to his litter: "I shall find a use for you." "God has none." "But I do."

75-76 Mullah confronts Saladin in tent, "Why retire?" "God determines." "How many battles won before I came, or God willed me to come?" "Thank you for your visit." "You promised Jerusalem."

77-78 Pinch II: King offers Bailin control of the army & Sibylla with Guy & his Templars execution. Bailin refuses reminding King he owns his own soul. Tiberius confronts & Bailin recites "Jerusalem is either a Kingdom of Conscience or it is nothing.

79-80 Sibylla confronts, "You would have me like Guy?" "One day you will wish you had done a little evil to do a greater good."

91-92 With King dead **&** Guy crowned, he seeks vote to go to war, battered Balin arrives to advise against, "God wills it," Tiberius says "Without my knights." Bailin greets Hospitaler "I shall tell your father what I have seen you become."

96 Defeated Guy insults Saladin giving cup of water to Reynald, Mullah offers Saladin sword for beheading. "A king does not kill a king." But he DOES behead Reynald.

97-98 PPII: Bailin finds Saladin's carnage of the Christian knights at Hattin, Tiberius tells first came to Jerusalem for God then wealth & land so ashamed. No more Jerusalem. Tells Bailin "God be with you,; he's no longer with me."

Act III = Resolution: Bailin leads the defense then surrender of Jerusalem

100-101 As Bailin surveys preparation in Jerusalem, Patriarch suggests they leave. "And the people?" "Unfortunate, but God's will."

102 Bailin addresses assembled people: All here not born when city lost. Fight when we did not offend. Jewish holy place over the Roman, Muslin over yours. Whose holier? The Wall, Mosque, Sepulcher? All have claim!" "Blasphemy!"

103-104 Bailin knights en masse & pronounces "Be brave that God may love you-Truth even in face of death-Protect the helpless!" Slap to remember. Rise a Knight!

105 That night, lone Muslim rider shouts "Victory except through God!"

106 **Climax:** Epic Seige of Jerusalem

109 Muslim prayer chants at sunrise. Saladin pronounces "No mercy."

117 At night, Saladin views massive number of bodies to be buried & prays

118 Outside walls, Bailin views pyre of corpses , Patriarch decries "If burn, they cannot be resurrected." "In 3 days disease will spread, If God does not understand then not God and not worry."

124 After stalemate at breech in wall, Patriarch suggest "Convert to Islam & repent later." Bailin tells him "You've taught me enough about religion." Bailin goes to Saladin for terms of surrender

126 After offered passage to the sea for everyone in the city**,** Bailin reminds Saladin that Christians butchered all Muslim when took the city. Saladin says "I am not those men."

127 As Bailin leaving, he asks "What is Jerusalem worth?" Saladin says "Nothing & everything."

128 Bailin announces surrender. "If this is the Kingdom of Heaven, let God do with it as he wants."

129 As Saladin walks into palace, finds cross on floor & sets on table.

130 Imad returns horse to Bailin & tells him "If God did not love you, how did you do all that you have done?" Saladin & Mullah look up to see the Muslim emblem returned to top of Masque.

131 **Commitment**: Bailin walks beside Sibylla on the dusty road away from Jerusalem

After-story Conclusion: Bailin looks over his old village smithy shop when Crusaders ride up.I am King Richard of England. We've come to find Bailin, defender of Jerusalem." "I am a blacksmith." Postscript: "Peace still elusive 1,000 years later."

DISCUSSION OF THIS FILM

Any of you who are history (or Christian history) buffs should purchase the DVD and watch the movie with the Historical notes. It was discussed as "History vs. Hollywood" on The History Channel and was the subject of many chat rooms/sites. Some are still out there on the Net, if you are interested.

Bailin's circumstance as depicted was essential accurate. In the Director's cut you find out he had been on many fighting campaigns with Godfrey's elder titled brother who owned the castle near the village. Thus Bailin learned swordsmanship, tactics & strategies and how to build the various war machines. He was more than a simple blacksmith.

Also the true story of the negotiations with Saladin was much more dramatic than this film depicted. Saladin originally asked to counsel with Bailin before the siege and offered him and his household passage to the coast (based on the debt of honor owed him). Bailin refused saying he could not in all conscience leave the city defenseless. Thus, he returned behind the walls and fought Saladin to a standstill. And the real surrender was not as "clean" because Saladin demanded payment for each person who left the city. Those who could not provide the "ransom" were slaughtered. Remember the barbaric times and the invading Christians had done worse o the Muslim residents when they took the city 100 years before.

WRITING EMOTIONS

The writing, directing and acting in this film provide a fascinating study of how a story can show actions, reaction, events that grip audience emotions. The character of Bailin is a fine example. Essentially he was a stoic male who said very little, but when he did speak what he had to say was powerful. Look back at Pinch II when the dying King offers Bailin command of the army. Bailin refuses when he finds out Guy and his knights would all be executed then defends his stance to Tiberius citing his conscience. His second powerful speech, of course, is when he addresses the citizens of Jerusalem about why they must fight, not for the holy shrines which belong to all . . . but for one another. Other than these times, Bailin was a man of few words. His actions spoke for him. He was vulnerable yet willing to fight for what he believed in. He took his knight's oath into his soul, even when he felt he had "lost his religion."

From the first scenes in the village blacksmith as Godfrey awkwardly asks for forgiveness . . . to Bailin riding to his father on that wintry road asking to join him in Jerusalem to seek his wife's redemption . . . to Bailin's knighting and the death scene in the chapel at Medina, the emotional roller coaster was perpetually up and down . . . just as it should be. His relief of waking up among the dead on the beach, losing the horse only to find it again then having to fight to keep him . . . Wow! And how does he act toward his enemy? He asks Idam to take him to Jerusalem then frees him gifting the horse to him. That Muslim in turn spares Bailin's life at Kerak and later has to defend that decision to Saladin when he identifies Bailin, Son of Godfrey, as the man leading the defense of Jerusalem. And what does he ultimately do? Idam gives back the horse so that Bailin the knight may ride instead of walk on his journey.

The ups and downs of Sibylla's position in the story was a play off sympathetic emotions from her husband's deliberate public ridicule at the formal dinner table . . . to her teasing of Bailin . . . to her attraction and seduction . . . to her painful parting from her beloved brother. The viewer has to shiver as she was cutting her hair and the mirror's distorted image showed her brother's face super-imposed. She was brought low, yet Bailin chose to walk by her side as they left the city. And of, course the very last scene is of them riding side-by-side away from the French crossroads where Bailin's wife is buried . . . into a future together, perhaps back in Ibelin?

And what emotions did you experience witnessing the not-so-pristine behaviors of the Christian Patriarch in Jerusalem being manipulated by Guy then being so self-serving during the siege, as well as the demanding, implacable Mullah insisting that Saladin provide what had been promised? And then there was the Hospitaler, an ordained priest-man of medicine-Templar warrior who demonstrated confidence in his own spirituality with a touch of cynicism about the world he lived in.

Practically every single scene in this movie evoked some kind of emotional response. May you write so powerfully!

REVISION vs. FILM EDITING

Story revision doesn't stop with just your spec script or the first re-write in development. The real art comes when the film editor and director apply their creativity and "camera eye" to the filmed scenes. For a broader appreciation of what kinds of scenes get cut out, you should buy the DVD of any film and compare the Director's cut to the theatrical release. The idea is not to frustrate you but to teach you what a story can do without. That is an invaluable concept when writing your spec script!

In the Director's cut of KINGDOM OF HEAVEN, not only will you find the explanation for how Bailin had the skills he used in Jerusalem, but you will also see about 12 minutes cut from the opening of the movie with more insights into Godfrey's familial relationships. More importantly, the Director's cut has an entire subplot sequence that was cut from the theatrical release. That sequence referred to Sibylla and Guy's young son who was the next male in line to her brother's throne. After her brother's death and her son's crowning, Sibylla discovers her little boy evidences the early stages of Hansen's disease or leprosy. She is so horrified by the memories of what her brother suffered that she makes the excruciating decision to poison her son so that he not live that agony. That loss and guilt were the reasons for her prolonged and profound grief there at the beginning the siege of Jerusalem. It was found in early test screenings that most of the audience lost sympathy for the character, even though the logic of her act was understandable. The whole sequence was edited out.

These are lessons any and every screenwriter can learn to identify any "extras" that the spine of the story can "survive." Yes, they add aura and nuance, even an additional emotional layer, but cutting those scenes in the front and that sequence in the middle carved almost 30 minutes of screen time and the story survived.

Progressive Concepts to Consider:

1) Appropriate Title
2) Types of Suspense utilized
3) Webbing of related elements
4) First 10 minutes prepared audience for the balance of the story
5) Character consistency after Introduction
6) Unique defiance of predictability
7) Opposition intensity increased
8) Character demonstration of profile history
9) Consequences of back-story
10) Identification of Character Arc
11) Use of Sex and Violence blatant or subtle
12) Demonstration of Anxiety Curve
13) Contrasting qualities of Antagonist to Protagonist
14) Consistently logical Scenes with smooth Transitions
15) Definitive build from Mid-Point on
16) Balance of Character story importance to role
17) Every Scene credible vs. melodrama
18) Smooth, unquestionable authenticity
19) Clean, credible adaptation
20) All questions answered in satisfying climax
21) Protagonist ultimately empowered
22) Statement of Purpose proven
23) Powerful story = Enthusiastic pitch
24) To write or not to write like this

* * * * *

SMOKE SIGNALS

By Sherman Alexie
1998, Starring Adam Beach, Evan Adams, Irene Bedard, Tantoo Cardinal

Length: 82 minutes

Log Line: Two Indian youths, one a cynic and the other a seer, travel to Arizona to recover a father's ashes and discover the meaning of forgiveness.

Statement of Purpose: To prove storytelling has the power to put the truths of life in perspective and help humans cope.

Intro Image: Stark vista of rural Idaho's Couer d'Alene Indian Reservation.

First 8 minutes
Who:
ARNOLD JOSPEH, tall, broad Indian with long hair and a drinking problem
ARLENE JOSEPH, slender, watchful wife of Arnold
GRANDMA BUILDS-A-FIRE, mourning though traditionally spiritual Indian woman left to raise infant grandson
VICTOR JOSEPH , 22-year old athletic, cynical Indian youth
THOMAS BUILDS-A-FIRE, 22-year-old nerdy, always smiling & storytelling Indian youth
When: July 4, 1976 to 1998
Where: Cour d'Alene Indian Reservation, Idaho
What: A drunken Arnold catches baby (Thomas) thrown from upstairs window of burning house.
Why: 4th of July house fire kills parents of Thomas and creates a lifetime of guilt for Arnold

Three related subplots:
Arnold's journey of guilt
Thomas-the-Storyteller's spiritual journey to help his friend
Thomas – Victor relationship

Time Line: Approximately one week (with flashbacks to 22 years and 10 years before)

Image repeats:
Fire
Native American song/chant
Isolation

Reservation life
Hair (braids, long, short)
Basketball
Storytelling

Act I = Set-up of Ordinary World: Victor's reservation life with drunken father who left & has died
8 min **Intro:** The house fire, baby Thomas's rescue, Arnold's apology, his leaving 12 years later
10 min **Inciting Incident**: Thomas offers to pay for Victor's trip to AZ if he can accompany
21 min **PP I:** Victor accepts the money & Thomas

Act II = Life 180 degrees: Victor & Thomas travel to AZ to check on what happened to Arnold
32 min **Pinch I:** Arnold abandoning his family in Idaho, Victor chasing, climbs in truck, Dad lifts out, hugs leaves.
41 min **Mid-Point:** Thomas tells stories as walk to trailer where Arnold's ashes are given to the two
54 min **Pinch II**: Victor hears his father's story of 12-yr-old son beating white men at basketball
64 min **PPII:** Victor & Thomas viciously argue & drive off the road.

Act III = Resolution: Victor's experience leads him to understanding Thomas & forgiving his dead father
76 min **Climax:** Victor pours half his father's ashes into Thomas's money jar for him to share
80 min **Commitment**: Grandma asks Thomas to tell what happened and "What will happen" (acknowledging his spiritual gift)
After-story Conclusion: At Spokane river, Victor dumps father's ashes and finally grieves.

Dialogue Notes: Classic Native American cadence, cynicism and humor

Alpha Character posturing differences:
Victor vs. Thomas, vs. Arlene
Victor vs. toughs on buss
Arnold vs. Arelene vs. Victor as boy
Thomas vs. Grandma

Supporting cast Unique Character Gems:
Arlene
Arnold (especially older version)

NA traffic commentator
Girls in backwards car
Grandma

Background effects, the nuances of aura:
Stark reservation
Arnold's isolated AZ trailer
Contrast of Thomas's braids and black-rimmed glasses
Contrast of Thomas's rigid suite/vest/button-up shirt to Victor's casual style
NA male long hair vs. short hair
V.O. of Thomas's storytelling emphasis

Elements from Other Genres: Western, Humor, Juvenile

Questions: 1) Did you feel this was a classic native American coming-of-age story or could the circumstance be apocryphal and lifted to any time-period, any culture? 2) Did you feel a sense of authenticity of culture since it was written, produced, acted by Native Americans?

Appearance or reference to recurrence of Spiritual Theme in Min: Thomas's "storytelling (usually with his eyes closed) has part of his sharing of his spiritual view of the world.

Act I = Set-up of Ordinary World: Victor's reservation life with drunken father who left & has died

3 V.O. about "some children of pillar of flames and some of ashe>'

4 Grandma: "You did a good thing." Arnold: "I didn't mean to." V.O. Cut his hair, practice vanishing (see his drinking)

7-8 Thomas bugs Victor about memories of fire & Dad in Phoenix, Victor: Mine left me and yours burned up. Shut up, Thomas. Thomas talks of Geronimo, Apache too short to be Great. Great day to die or play basketball.

9 Thomas: "Sorry about your dad." "How hear?" "From the birds . . . Your mother just here."

10 **Inciting Incident**: Thomas offers to pay for Victor's trip to AZ if he can accompany

12 FB: Arnold talks of drunks & "Make myself disappear."

14 Grandma & Thomas praying at table, knock on door, they grin expectantly at each other

16 Victor "No stupid stories."

18 Girls in car will give lift but barter: Thomas tells story of Arnold. Victor tells "full of shit." Grinning girls "Example fire oral tradition."

21 **PP I:** Victor accepts the money & Thomas

Act II = Life 180 degrees: Victor & Thomas travel to AZ to check on what happened to Arnold

28-30 Thomas tells of Arnold finding him at age 12 on Spokane River bridge "waiting for a sign." "While waiting for a vision, you'll get mugged." Took to breakfast. "Sometimes a good day to die; sometimes a good day for breakfast."

32 **Pinch I:** Arnold abandoning his family in Idaho, Victor chasing, climbs in truck, Dad lifts out, hugs leaves.

33-34 **FB:** 12-yr-old Thomas sees Victor turning porch light on-off, "I felt you (needed me). Why did you dad leave you? Does he hate you?" Victor pounds on Thomas.

35-36 What you remember of my dad? Victor tells story of him eating 15 pieces of fry bread , Victor denounces with "You think you're some medicine man like Dances with Wolves? And quit grinning!" Stoic or whites walk all over you. "Our people were fishermen. You want to be Dances with Salmon?"

39-40 On bus mention of John Wayne who never smiles then chant "John Wayne's teeth"

41 Mid-Point: Thomas tells stories as walk to trailer where Arnold's ashes are given to the two Thomas takes when Victor freezes.

47 After compliment Susie's Fry bread, Thomas launches into story of Arlene's dilemma of 100 Indians but only 50 pieces of bread until she tore in half.

52 As Susie telling Victor of Arnold's stories, Arnold "faraway expression" as talked of son

54 Pinch II: Victor hears his father's story of 12-yr-old son beating white men at basketball. Amazed that he remembered it like that because he DIDN'T beat them.

58 Maybe the stories not true, but Susie says she knows more than Victor

61 Victor enters malodorous trailer with flashlight, finds father's wallet with family pic, takes out pocket knife & cuts his own long hair.

64 **PPII:** Victor & Thomas viciously argue & drive off the road.

Act III = Resolution: Victor's experience leads him to understanding Thomas & forgiving his dead father

67-68 After accident caused by drunk, Victor says he'll run 20 mile for help, while running he hears chanting & sees visions, V.O. Thomas talks of Magic and Fire. Victor collapses & thinks sees his father pulling him to his feet (really a road construction guy).

76 min **Climax:** Victor pours half his father's ashes into Thomas's money jar for him to share, Thomas says he'll take to Spokane River to toss them in and let his father rise in a Salmon." Victor says "I never thought of my father as a Salmon." (reference back to the essence of their people and Dances with Salmons)

79 Arlene receives canister of Arnold's ashes & hold high.

80 min **Commitment**: Grandma asks Thomas to tell what happened and "What will happen" (acknowledging his spiritual gift)

After-story Conclusion: At Spokane river, Victor dumps father's ashes and finally grieves.

CONCEPTS DISCUSSION

Here is a fine example of the subtle undertones of Native American spirituality and concepts of morality and familial-tribal responsibility. Though the westernization of many customs has created diversity and doubts, the spirituality of the indigenous peoples can be seen blatantly demonstrated in the choices they make.

Another point in this particular story is the recurrent thread of humor. Think about the natural set-up, expectation and reversal pay-off Thomas repeatedly delivers. Consider the sophistication of the storytelling elements in this story, as well as the 24 points so eloquently depicted.

AFTER-STORY

Any inspirational story is ripe for imaging the after-story. In SMOKE SIGNALS (adapted by Alexie from one of his short stories), we are given insights into the emotions of both Victor and Thomas. Where Victor hardened his heart as he lost respect for his drunken, abusive father, Thomas innately knew Arnold was a good man with an emotional burden he was trying to escape through alcohol and leaving. Where Arnold had been a touch possessive and demanding of his own son, he had been tolerant and gentle with Thomas . . . because of his burden of guilt for drunkenly setting the fire that killed the boy's parents.

So, we go on this journey witnessing Victor's cynicism for the world in general and Thomas's appreciation of everything . . . because he closes his eyes and sees the stories from people's hearts. It didn't matter if the incidents really happened. He saw the potential in each person's heart. No matter how rude or denigrating Victor is, Thomas hangs in there until he feels Victor giving up. At that point the accusations and cruel remarks fly. Ultimately, Victor "mans up" and takes the run for help listening to his memories. He accepts his father for who he was and that's enough. Thomas is overjoyed to return to his grandma to tell her what happened and "what will happen." He has freed his friend to forgive the father and grieve at last instead of holding on to his anger.

And in the After-Story? Do you not see Thomas continuing to grow his spiritual gifts and soothing the pains and frustrations of reservation life for his people with his stories? Do you not see a now-whole Victor leaving the "Res" for an education, perhaps even becoming a teacher so he can return and motivate other Couer d'Alene young people?

That's the magic of really good film-making, folks!

Progressive Concepts to Consider:

1) Appropriate Title
2) Types of Suspense utilized
3) Webbing of related elements
4) First 10 minutes prepared audience for the balance of the story
5) Character consistency after Introduction
6) Unique defiance of predictability
7) Opposition intensity increased
8) Character demonstration of profile history
9) Consequences of back-story
10) Identification of Character Arc
11) Use of Sex and Violence blatant or subtle
12) Demonstration of Anxiety Curve
13) Contrasting qualities of Antagonist to Protagonist
14) Consistently logical Scenes with smooth Transitions
15) Definitive build from Mid-Point on
16) Balance of Character story importance to role
17) Every Scene credible vs. melodrama
18) Smooth, unquestionable authenticity
19) Clean, credible adaptation
20) All questions answered in satisfying climax
21) Protagonist ultimately empowered
22) Statement of Purpose proven
23) Powerful story = Enthusiastic pitch
24) To write or not to write like this

Give yourself a pat on the back or celebrate however you can. You are now empowered to assess, compare and contrast and create your own screenplays. You have all 24 film concepts committed to memory. Anything is possible when tackled a little at a time.

* * * * *

GENRE FILM Chapter 13 Exercises

Exercise 13a. Write Pg 95-THE END paying attention to VISUAL closure on all points and providing the innuendo of that rich After-Story.

Exercise 13b. Analyze your script for the specific emotion you sense at the following points and list them in ONE WORD . . . Look for primary "in your face" emotional impact:
Act I:
Act II:
Act III:
Plot Point I:
Mid-Point:
Plot Point II:
Climax:
Conclusion:

Exercise 13c. Consider your final visual image as a variation on the very first visual image you wrote in the script. This is called "Bookend Imagery" that suggests a roundness of life's full circle.

Exercise 13d. Write one short, simple sentence stating each of these points in your script. Forget being all-inclusive. Think succinct and specific.

Signposts of Beginning:
Opening Scene.
Main Characters introduced with succinct characterization.
Summarize "ordinary life" and its trials.
Glimpse of pending threat.
Life-changing event forcing Protag Action

Signposts of Middle, Paragraph Two:
Protag facing new life, new tests, new people
Antagonist inserting threat.
Protag's glimpse of "worst fear" becoming real
Protag trying new skills, taking risks

Signposts of Middle, Paragraph Three:
Protag chooses to assert "power"
Protag experiences internal "denouement"
Protag acts on awareness of exciting possibilities
Others shown as critical or puzzled observers of Protag

Signposts of Middle: Paragraph Four:
Protag proves worthiness to Observers
Antagonist demonstrates vivid growth in power
Protag experiences a moment of startling success
Antagonist's power evolves
Life changing moment of Antagonist cornering Protag in near-defeat

Signposts of Ending
Protag's reaction and preparation for battle
Antagonist's confident arrogance
Climactic Battle.
Defeat of Antagonist

Closing Image

. . . Now connect these sentences into one kick-ass great synopsis of your script!!!!

CHAPTER 14

Writing a Script in Twelve Weeks

Learning is absorbed best and knowledge retained when carefully considered in small increments. Of course, some people will come to a book like this to look for specific information about a concept or a genre. However, if this book is approached in increments of Chapters 1-2 in one week then subsequent chapters taken one a week with the Exercises accomplished as explained (thus writing 10 pages a week—5 pages on Monday and 5 pages on Thursday), an entire screenplay can be carefully crafted in 12 weeks. Yes, screenplays can be written in less time, just as some people can take much longer. As was pointed out at the conclusion of each chapter, a list of Progressive Concepts was delivered a little at a time and continuously reinforced. Just as those concepts wee absorbed a little at a time, a screenplay can be written a little at a time.

YOUR SCRIPT WRITING PROGRESS in Weeks 1, 2, 3

For those of you who have taken the challenge of actually writing a script during the reading of this book (wherein you actually apply the concepts explained), you should complete your fundamental planning and begin writing actual pages.

From Week One, you should have:
1) Paradigm outline of high-points/signpost events in your story
2) Protag-Antag Casting with their Character Profiles clarified
3) Log Line to keep you focused on this story

From Week Two, you should have:
1) Subplots sketched for grasp of contributing material
2) Time Line so you have the story's "real time" in your head
3) Statement of Purpose to keep you focused on inclusion & exclusion

In Week Three you should have:
1) Mon-Wed: Writing the first five pages of your Intro Image & 5 W's
2) Thurs-Sat: Writing next 5 pages of continuing Act I "Set-Up"

Anything is possible when tackled a little at a time . . . If you haven't laid your foundation, "Get with it!" and focus your creativity.

YOUR SCRIPT WRITING PROGRESS in Weeks 4, 5, 6

These weeks you are delving more deeply into cause-effect series of events and introducing more characters.

From Week Four, you should have:
1) Written Pg 11-20 through Inciting Incident of Act I
2) ID'd archetypal characters and their role-influence on one another
3) ID'd Major and Minor Antagonists
4) Solidly set your story's POV

From Week Five, you should have:
1) Written Pg 21-30 past PPI & into Act II's "New Life"
2) Established Main Character's consistent mode of reacting to "New Life"
3) Established Subplots & impact on Main Plot
4) Depicted solid understanding of Major Antagonist
5) Woven in back-story elements to create credibility

From Week Six, you should have:
1) Writing Pg 31-41 thru Pinch I (greatest fear)
2) Sense of pacing your Jeopardy
3) Established characters' unique dialogue voices
4) Demonstrating understanding of other genres contributing to main genre expectations

If you haven't laid your foundation and gotten the flow of your story into Act II, "Get with it!" and focus your creativity.

YOUR SCRIPT WRITING PROGRESS in Weeks 7, 8, 9

By this time you are invigorated by the lives of your characters and should be emotionally involved in the experiences of your characters. You will be moving through the middle of the script and into the dramatic "Dark Moment" of reckoning for your Main Character. This the part of the script where you truly have your Audience sitting on the edge of their seats worried about the outcome.

From Week Seven, you should have:
1) Written Pg. 42-52 through Mid-Point's Epiphany
2) Understand subplot influences & evolution, especially anxiety-causing
3) Choreographed the POV Character learning & reacting to the New World
4) Referenced Antagonist's evolution in ebb-and-flow manner

From Week Eight, you should have:
1) Written Pg 53-62 to Pinch II reward event
2) Formulated habit of succinct narrative without micro-choreography
3) Demonstrated how POV Main Character being confident & assertive
4) Reviewed Paradigm & subplots for Scene-Sequel units of logic
5) Shown Antagonist gaining focus

From Week Nine, you should have:
1) Writing Pg 63-72 up to Plot Point II's Dark Moment
2) Demonstrate # of pages/speeches of cast = importance to story
3) Achieve balance of ebb-and-flow tension & anticipation
4) Definitely trying to weave in elements from other genres

If you haven't laid your foundation and gotten the flow of your story almost to Act III, "Get with it!" and focus your creativity.

YOUR SCRIPT WRITING PROGRESS in Weeks 10, 11, 12

Your responsibility as a storyteller is at its apex. You are charged with the need to satisfy your audience. You want them in knots of anticipation and cheering for your embattled Main Character. Once you have polished this sucker, you must then go back to your fundamental outline and reduce the approximate 25,000 words down to around 500 for a synopsis that will sell your project. Is that All? Are you done? No, you have just begun your journey.

From Week Ten, you should have:
1) Written Pg. 74-83 through PP II into "Phoenix Rising"
2) Carefully, dramatically depicted Antagonist as his/her strongest & Protagonist at his/her worst
3) Woven in the subplots evolving toward their resolutions

From Week Eleven, you should have:
1) Written Pg 84-94 into Climax
2) Created tension and intensity of enthralling preparation for Climax
3) Analyzed out micro-choreography & melodrama

From Week Twelve, you should have:
1) Writing to THE END and Fade Out
2) Compared final visual to Intro Image
3) Clearly painted a lead-in to the audience's imagining of After-Story
4) Outlined a succinct Synopsis

THE ONLY WAY TO GET YOUR STORY INTO THE WORLD IS FOR YOU TO WRITE IT.

The only way to get your story into the world is for you to write it. If you do not, the characters will never exist and the world will never share their journey. Their existence is up to your willingness to take the risk of Creation . . . then market it to the world.

POINT & PASSION

People who survive and excel in any competitive profession are capable of learning how fundamentals can evolve into something greater. Their discovery results in a passion that pushes each forward to conquer life's problems. Every single story you sit down to write absolutely MUST demonstrate two things: Your point and your passion. If either of those is lacking the writing will be dull, unappealing, predictable. Your vehicle for point is the action of the story and your vehicle for passion is your cast of characters. A final Lew Hunter phrase: "Give your characters passion and they will give you plot. Write on!"

Hopefully, you now have all that you need and more than you expected so you can achieve your dreams and more!

LEARN GENRE FILM SECRETS

PART TWO

ROMANTIC SCREENPLAYS 101

ROMANCE CHAPTER 1

My Waltz with Romantic Cinema

You have come here to read about how cinematic romantic stories work. Long ago I researched those very concepts so I could write those kinds of scripts. However, I had learned many insights over a long period. I did not encounter them all at once. Now, I want to share them with you.

ROMANTIC SCREENPLAYS 101 grew out of my many on-site and on-line classes by that title, material arranged in logical progression for the seminar attendees. After teaching "Intro to Screenwriting" in so many one-day seminars, I discovered many people did not understand the many romance audience expectations. I knew I had to dig deep into all my resources of romance fiction to meld that genre's story and character concepts into a cohesive discussion suitable for screenplay translation. I had been applying my knowledge of romance for some time without specific step-by-step awareness. I helped myself as I constructed the romance course. Bottom line: I wanted to explain for myself what works and what doesn't then spread the word to people trying to write romantic cinematic stories.

ROMANCE WRITERS OF AMERICA

Truthfully, no people are as obsessive about the elements of romance as the members of Romance Writers of America. RWA is comprised of the published and hoping-to-publish writers producing stories for devout aficionados of the "happily-ever-after" crowd. Those readers pushed romance sales to greater than 50% of the mass paperback market year after year. The members of RWA evolved seminars and programs to explain how the relationship game works, or, rather, how to describe its many intricacies and nuances. Since the early 1990's thousands upon thousands have flocked to the conferences and attended chapter meetings all over the country to listen and learn. For eighteen years I was one of the hopeful then published writers of that organization. I am profoundly grateful for all the information I absorbed.

MALE vs. FEMALE APPRECIATION OF ROMANCE

I found it particularly fascinating to learn the psychology and subtle details of fictional romance. As a female health care professional (Critical Care/ER R.N.) the body language lessons and rationale RWA folks presented made total sense. Here's a generalization: I also soon learned most males didn't "get it." (There are always exceptions.) Many males and uneducated females denigrated the romance genre for a variety of reasons. I perceived this as another example of psychologist John Grey's "Men are from Mars, Women are from Venus." Most women didn't care because they did "get it." Those females wrote, bought, read, clamored for more and continue to do so. The demographics spread to all levels of education, professions, ages and, yes, genders. Relationship stories evolved in every other genre/category of fiction, creating unique concepts of expectations in those romance "sub-genres."

RESEARCHING ROMANCE WRITING

People who have analyzed all the aspects of romance from primal sexuality to the life-cycle roller coaster have provided a mountain of material one can study. I wallowed in it. I became an avid fan, appreciating the skills of those RWA authors who titillate at various descriptive levels and continue to attract readers. Writing both novels and screenplays, I considered how movie goers might explain what they understand to those who don't. Melding my print and cinematic areas of knowledge just made sense.

There are many courses and materials about writing romantic fiction by people experienced in that genre. Here I present my take on how those print concepts work on screen.

I am *not* an instructor who "talks the talk, but can't walk the walk." I can't be described as someone who teaches because I can't do whatever. I *use* the principles I am about to explain to you every time I sit down to write a romantic screenplay, every time I want to portray a cinematic relationship story. Fundamentals never get outdated. They are what they are: essential to the storytelling process.

As you accumulate information about romantic screenplays and consider how to apply it, I urge you to read through each chapter's initial review material then think hard about the suggested exercises. Review deepens the neurological grooves of a thought making it easier to recall and connect faster than if you do not concentrate and merely skim instead. When you apply the concepts in the exercises, you are making even more complex connections thus reinforcing the knowledge into skills.

That "Read-Review-Apply" process is a well-proven learning theory in the discipline of education.

Do not assume just because you can watch a romantic film that you can write a screenplay for one. The first directive is: "Learn your craft."

> THE FIRST DIRECTIVE IS: "LEARN YOUR CRAFT."

If you are totally new to screenwriting, you may find some of my romantic screenplay terminology similar to a foreign language. Do not be frustrated. Simply invest in some of the fundamental screenwriting textbooks from this list . . .

Book Recommendations

LEARN SCREENWRITING, From start to Adaptation to Pro Advice, Sally J. Walker
(A succinct, fundamental walk-through of the basics, adaptation process, and commentary on comparison-contrast of the wisdom of Christopher Vogler and Blake Snyder.)

THE IDIOT'S GUIDE TO SCREENWRITING, Skip Press
(A fundamentals-type text with lots of insider questions answered)

THE WRITER'S JOURNEY, Christopher Vogler
(A storytelling construct applying Joseph Campbell's concepts)

SCREENPLAY, FOUNDATIONS OF SCREENWRITING, Syd Field
(Another fundamentals-type textbook)

THE SCREENWRITER'S WORKBOOK, Syd Field
(An applications-type textbook)

THE ART OF DRAMATIC WRITING, Lajos Egri
(A fundamentals concept book for stage & film writers)

THE 1-3-5 STORY STRUCTURE SYSTEM, Donna Michelle Anderson
(A little handbook written by a Studio Reader/Producer applying BASICS)

Others (in progressively more complex-concept order):
SCREENWRITING 434, Lew Hunter
SAVE THE CAT, Blake Snyder
MAKING THE GOOD SCRIPT GREAT, Linda Seger (And any other Seger books...)
STEALING FIRE FROM THE GODS, James Bonnet
WRITING SCREENPLAYS THAT SELL, Michael Hauge
STORY, Robert McKee
THE ANATOMY OF STORY, John Truby
WRITING FOR EMOTIONAL IMPACT, Karl Iglesias

LEARN GENRE FILM SECRETS

SCREENWRITING SECRETS IN GENRE FILM, Sally J. Walker
WHICH LIE DID I TELL? William Goldman
SCREENWRITING IS REWRITING, Jack Epps, Jr.
YOUR SCREENPLAY SUCKS, William M. Akers

ROMANCE CHAPTER 2

Fundamental Concepts

Tackling the specialized genre of romance in the discipline of film implies that you come already versed in writing screenplays. You know the craft, jargon, and format of screenwriting.

If not, then you need to back-track to the essentials of Character Profiling (available in Appendix C, explained in Appendix D) and plotting with a Story Paradigm (available in Appendix A with its terminology explained in Appendix B). Romantic characters will be addressed in Romance Chapter 5 and plotting a romance in Romance Chapter 7. The fundamentals of both subjects are explained in my book, *LEARN SCREENWRITING, from Start to Adaptation to Pro Advice.* The requirements of Character Profiling along with Paradigm planning and pacing in cinema are different from novel writing. You cannot craft a cinematic story in the proper format without understanding what the professional film-makers expect of the screenwriter to provide.

PLOT PARADIGM

Read the many recommended resources on the craft of screenwriting listed in Romance Chapter 1. Commit story-building concepts to your soul as explained by Syd Field, Chris Vogler, John Truby, Michael Hauge, Lew Hunter and so on. Understand the basic Paradigm outline that is detailed because this book will build on that fundamental, indicating the pacing or story structure you must use. Study and understand the 3-Act structure before imagining your characters establishing a relationship within that structure and time line.

At first the 3-Act Plot Paradigm may seem cumbersome, asking for many things at once, but the more you work with it in all of your storytelling, the easier it will become. All of the referenced books look at the screen-time page limits and elements needed for cinematic storytelling, some merely using their own terminology but maintaining a classic 3-Act structure. In reality, the progression of the signpost events proposed by the various experts creates a simple, logical process for your outline of the growth of a relationship amidst life's complications. You don't have to reinvent the wheel. The outline and the screenplay format have been used by the industry for over 100 years. Whether the romance is the Main Plot or a complicating subplot, the beats of your imagined relationship can have a logically pacing in the dictated, underlying pattern.

Do not be intimidated by the "vastness" of the various approaches. In truth, they are the same concept with a variety of semantics. They all deal with "how to tell a satisfying story in a confined time limit."

The key concept is to incorporate what works for you into your story organization. Some people have enlarged the Paradigm to poster size and laminated it to use like a wet board. Others have created programs that have pages for each portion of the Paradigm. In both Final Cut and Screenwriting's Movie Magic professional software programs you will find the 3-Act structure embedded with "Scene Cards" you can use as you spew your script. Some writers feel overwhelmed by the visual of the entire Plot Paradigm and work better in increments, such as one act at a time.

Some storytellers have a file folder full of printed copies of the Plot Paradigm. A copy is taken out for each story, be it a short story, a children's book, a novel, or a screenplay. These writers use itty-bitty pencil print to gradually fill it in once the over-all structure or sign-posts of the plot are figured out. They like to keep the whole evolving story in front of them as they write. Those who prefer to write in scenes on index cards or the software's Scene Cards they can shift around and even color code according to character or subplot sequencing.

The point is not to get scattered, confused or overwhelmed. Try one process, work with it then maybe incorporate something else . . . until you find the match to your creativity. There is no right or wrong beyond the screenplay page limits and making every word contribute to the story logic. You may find new awareness at any point in your writing journey. Any of the above approaches simply allow you to identify when something is or isn't working and exactly where, so you can revise better, stay on track, or identify when you've missed something.

SPECIFICALLY ROMANCE

Both fiction and the film industry categorize the subject matter of their products for one reason: **consumer expectations**. So, what does an audience expect of a romantic screenplay? Both male and female audience members expect **a relationship story**. In my opinion, the difference is that **men expect physical responses** between the couple

> MEN EXPECT PHYSICAL RESPONSES BETWEEN THE COUPLE AND FEMALES EXPECT AN EMOTIONAL COMMITMENT.

and **females expect an emotional commitment**. Tongue-in-cheek, I simplify this to "Men just need a place; women need a reason."

The bottom line is both sides of the equation want to see a story about a satisfying relationship. The term "satisfying" initially has different levels of meaning for the two genders in this context. Yes, males like to see a story that has one woman committed to her man, but they are more interested in his demonstration of his manliness and sexual prowess than in all the "touchy-feely" softening of the male beast to the feminine wiles of the female. Men want to see the action of the man proving himself worthy.

Women want to see the gradual evolution of the male surrendering to his emotional need for this one woman. From the woman's point-of-view I define this as "The male-female unit struggles through life's changing saga until the female (intentionally or unintentionally) transforms the male's awareness of her value to him." Women identify with the element of female empowerment. The evolution of the relationship makes the woman more than she was before. As was said in JERRY MAGUIRE "You complete me." A guy in the audience may have groaned when Jerry (Tom Cruise) said this but every woman sitting there got it! With that line, the woman won! She was complete because he needed her!

Note to any groaning males: Here's the generalization. Women are inherently nest builders seeking a mate to create family, whereas males may desire the security of a relationship but are more concerned about the world, not the nest. They seek the challenge of "spreading it around," attracting as many females as possible . . . as a side-line hobby, not as a vocation. The human male is about survival (jeopardy), whereas the female is about assuring the continuation of the species (consequences of sex). That's the lowest common denominator in our biology, not a stereotyping, merely a biological imperative.

THE HUMAN MALE IS ABOUT SURVIVAL (JEOPARDY), WHEREAS THE FEMALE IS ABOUT ASSURING THE CONTINUATION OF THE SPECIES (CONSEQUENCES OF SEX).

IS CONFLICT IN ROMANCE A BATTLE OF THE SEXES?

The simple answer is "No" for more often the characters are experiencing an internal battle of what each wants to do within the framework of their circumstance. Each is resisting the change demanded by the attraction. There has to be resistance or angst by one or both parties or there is no conflict. No conflict means there is no story. The internalization can be explained in a novel but in cinema it has to be demonstrated by facial expressions, body language and dialogue's diction (inflection) and syntax (choice of words). The internal struggle has to bleed over into the choices and consequences the audience sees.

Additionally, you want the kind of conflict that will throw the two parties together and make the unseen pheromones fly as they struggle with the everyday life demands. Plot out the evolution of the relationship and their acting upon the attraction then curl the controversy and opposition around their attraction and awareness of one another.

Look at SLEEPLESS IN SEATTLE. Both Tom Hanks in Seattle and Meg Ryan in Baltimore were constantly "thinking" about one another! The promise of a relationship came back again and again until they had to meet and know the other was their life partner. This was inferred, certainly not acted upon at the top of the Empire State Building, just as happened in AN AFFAIR TO REMEMBER, the model for the ending.

A ROMANCE CHALLENGE

Many who want to write romantic screenplays are already "addicted" to the romance genre via novels. Romance readers are credited with being voracious readers. You, in turn, need to be an obsessive student of romantic films.

Watch as many films with a primary or secondary romance as possible. After finishing this book, go back and watch each a second time to see if you "missed" anything. You should "see" nuances and signals you were not aware of the first time around. (Note: There is a list in Appendix M that will continue to grow as the film industry continues to release them.)

Remember, a film need not be a story with the main plot focused on the romantic relationship. The romance could be a subplot contributing to the complications of the main plot. The two requirements are that 1) the relationship evolves because of the main plot and 2) the couple needs to advance through the various stages toward commitment in the end. Whether the relationship is the main plot or the subplot, the key is that the pair will be a committed couple in the end.

REQUIRED ELEMENTS OF A ROMANCE

1. Motivated character-driven, not complex plot-driven story . . . A highly motivated character is an intense character, a role that appeals to the really talented, dynamic actors. These characters are the ones who do not just let life happen to them; they make it happen. They are inherently dramatic from the beginning. That means they are not watchers but doers. Every scene they appear in, the audience expects them to make things happen.

One of the major characters will arc or change internally in the course of a character-driven movie. In a romance this can be either the male or the female and the change will be because of the relationship! (This will be explained more when the cast itself is addressed in Romance Chapter 5.)

Character-driven stories are perpetually focused on the words of the dialogue and the consequences demanded from those speeches. The dialogue of character-driven stories is compact, multi-layered, and demands gut-deep intensity from the actor. The dialogue of a good character-driven plot enthralls the director so much that he/she naturally focuses on motivating the actor's facial expressions and body language. The only time a screenwriter needs to describe either facial expression or body language/positioning is if a contrast is intended rather than the natural nuance of the dialogue. A screenwriter's job is to write dynamite dialogue that motivates the actor and the director to live their jobs with concentrated excitement.

Plot-driven stories are based on events and how the characters react to them. Think of historical renderings, police procedurals, or James Bond movies. Yes, characters can cause events to happen, but the events themselves are the focus of the story. A romance is about the emotions of the people, not the events they experience.

2. Predictable structure of meeting, misunderstanding, separation, commitment

. . . Several of the UCLA Film Department faculty often quote: "No one wants to see the story of the happy people in the happy village." In a romance that translates to 1) introducing the characters to establish the attraction, 2) creating an opposition which can be either external or internal but plays off character history and personality and sets them at odds, 3) pushing the couple apart despite the attraction with the implication that they are overwhelmed by circumstance to make the relationship work, 4) then forcing them back together with the realization that satisfaction in life can only be achieved with this mate.

"NO ONE WANTS TO SEE THE STORY OF THE HAPPY PEOPLE IN THE HAPPY VILLAGE."

It doesn't matter that this structure is predictable! That is the required expectation of the genre or category of storytelling. If this structure is violated in a supposed romantic screenplay, it is reduced to merely a love or lust story like SOMERSBY or THE BRIDGES OF MADISON COUNTY. A successful chick-flick romance ends with the couple living together into the "happily ever after." Knowing that will be the ending means the audience watches wanting to know *how* they overcome the misunderstanding and separation to achieve that commitment.

Some people have a difficult time grasping what separation means in the couple's experience. Separation has to be an element that threatens the relationship. It is a "torn asunder" wrenching that discomfits the audience and hurts the two parties . . . even if only for a moment. That threat creates the angst however it is played. Think of SOMEWHERE IN TIME, OUT OF AFRICA, AN AFFAIR TO REMEMBER and on and on. The audience has to care about the division as much as the two lovers. What moment creates the greatest angst of never seeing one another again for your two people? Answer that and you have your moment of separation.

This "Relationship Plane" and its accompany Definitions can be found in Appendix N.

3. Consistent expression of emotional impact and angst . . . This element of romance in screenplays takes quite a bit of work because the screenwriter cannot describe every nuance. That interpretation is the realm of the actor and the director. So, you must carefully write dialogue that demonstrates the emotions and angst of the characters without being melodramatic or maudlin. Visual subtext or signaling and verbal "codes," such as the couple used "See you soon, then." in DEAR JOHN, are key techniques in cinematic romance.

Every speech must be absolutely essential to moving the story forward, yet not explain everything. If story progression can be accomplished by the narrative's action, that will create the preferable "movie, not a talkie." Is that contradictory to the importance of dialogue? No. Your economy of dialogue in each and every speech must use words that depict character mindset and purpose with word choices and phrasing unique to this character's history, education, training. Angry speeches are not verbose or detailed whereas seductive speeches are slow and sensually suggestive. Males tend to speak succinctly, whereas females explain the setup to the point (unless they are trying to be secretive and manipulative). Fear produces tentative questions or statements. Demands are abrupt and confrontational. Education may have sublimated regional or "class" idioms (like favored obscenities), but intense anxiety can pop them out of a character's mouth.

Actors (and their agents) will highlight just one character's dialogue throughout a script. That practice has a two-fold purpose: 1) So they can practice the speeches and see if they "connect" with the part and 2) to evaluate how many scenes or how much of the story they appear in (which will translate to the amount they expect to be paid for the part). As a screenwriter, you need to be aware of this and do the same thing for each character. This is the easy way to analyze the consistency of the speech patterns, word choices and evolution of the emotional character you created.

4. Balance of time/pages between male and female leads . . . Every page of a standard formatted script equals one minute of screen time. As just stated, actors highlight their speeches to calculate how much screen time they will get. At this time in the 21st Century it is expected that the male and the female leads will get a fairly equal amount of screen time in any romantic film. So, yes, you need to evaluate the logical back-and-forth scenes between what is happening in the separate lives of the main characters. You will not maintain audience interest if you abandon one too long. You want to hold the interest and concerned anxiety of the audience in their vicarious experience with the characters.

5. ALL subplots/minor characters/environment must impact the relationship . . . In a character-driven screenplay about a relationship it should be relatively simple to exclude the inconsequential and include the relative. Yes, the male lead may have a large family of dictatorial females but if that family dynamic is not going to create a scene in this story, forget it. Yes, the female may have suffered one job loss after another and is financially strapped, but it is not necessary to specifically mention that unless it impacts the relationship. Is the season of the year or the specific locale of the story relevant to the relationship? Think about SLEEPLESS IN SEATTLE. Sometimes writers get so caught up in the profiles or extensive histories they created for their characters that they forget to be exclusive. The economy of a screenplay demands that you be exclusive. Yes, you have to establish logical motivation but concentrate only on those people, those elements that will impact the relationship!

6. Feature film and TV movies require LOVE scenes, not SEX scenes . . . First, the level of titillation in skin-to-skin scenes is dictated by the market you are writing to. Secondly, you can summarize and leave the ultimate "choreography" to the director and the actors. The one thing you have to do is set-up, set-up, set-up. People do not randomly throw themselves at one another in current storytelling, unless the film is intended for the erotic X-rated adult film industry.

Physical commitment is an evolutionary consequence of visual communication. The couple has to maintain eye contact and "read" the invitation and acceptance. The primping and posturing can be subtle or blatant. The gradual invasion of personal space has to be "allowed." And so on. Screenwriters can choreograph this build up to contact. They can even spread out the signaling through several scenes to add to the character (and audience) tension and anticipation. The caring, not the lust, between the partners is the primary consideration. And the consequence of the mating is the commitment, whether immediately or in the end. Thus the sex scene is translated into a love scene. A contrast example of this happened in the two separate hotel rooms in FRENCH KISS. Culmination of the sex act was not possible because neither of the couples truly cared about their partner. Their love and commitment was invested elsewhere.

WRITING TO THE STUDIO READER OR THE AUDIENCE?

Writing "Spec Scripts" (written on speculation that have not been contracted but are going to be pitched to people who can get them produced) means you are initially writing to prove yourself to these buyers. You have to get by a studio/agency reader before it will ever make it to an agent-producer-director-actor-or-paying audience. Like novel writing, you have to write to entertain that reader . . . but you have to write to the format, the medium and the budget that the highly respected reader understands and is looking for.

Format = Standard Screenplay Format

Medium = Feature film of 90-120 pages OR TV exactly 108 pages written in "segments" of 7-8 minute breaks (for commercials EVEN if written as a cable movie since they think re-distribution in the future).

Budget = Low (limited cast, limited & easily accessible locations, few to no special effects or stunts, WGA-designated of less than 1Million and common TV movie), Medium (requiring 1-2 investors usually for location, costuming, props, minimal special effects, CGI substitution), High (requiring 3-10 investors including a major studio with multiple locations & complex special effects as well as high-end/A-List actors)

And, yes, you can be asked to place your movie in these categories. On a typical reader's evaluation form they have boxes to check covering these considerations. If that reader is not entertained and intrigued you will get a "Pass-Pass." That means pass on the script and pass on the writer. BTW, that *The 1-3-5 Story Structure* by Donna Michelle Anderson (available on Amazon) carefully explains exactly what a studio reader looks for.

So, how much should these concepts impact your writing? First and foremost, just like when writing a book, get it written then revise with these concepts in mind. You market to those studios or agencies known for your type of story with the understanding that it is a crap shoot!

Writing screenplays must be a joy, not torture. Some people find it very easy because they write visually to begin with. Others struggle. That kind of resistance will be reflected in the power of the script, the nuance of the writer's excitement and energy. The enjoyment of the writing is a contagious abstraction that subtly flows into the screenplay or novel. The structure, the format, the entire process must translate to and stimulate the reader, especially in screenwriting! You don't entrance that reader, that script will never make it into production.

So do you write to deliberately entice and entertain the industry reader? Of course! Write to entertain whoever is reading it. That screenplay is only a blue print that must be so good it excites the imagination of so many other film disciplines . . . after the reader gives it a "Recommend-Recommend" so it will be passed on for further evaluation. One reader of a screenplay does not a sale make!

* * * * *

ROMANCE Chapter 2 Exercises

Note: If you are thinking of adapting your romance novel to the screen, you can begin honing in on essential elements with these exercises. And you will find more "how-to's" in *Learn Screenwriting's* Part Two on Adaptation.

Exercise R2a: Answer these questions . . .

1) What is the female's Tangible Objective in your story? What concrete, realistic thing does she want that is driving her at the outset of the story?

Note: The word "tangible" means something that can be evaluated via the senses. Not abstract, not a value or concept, but real. "Purpose for being alive" is a concept though it could be measured in tangibles. Think about it. Think about your character. What thing would make her feel alive, the verifiable proven thing that could be experienced and described through the five senses?

2) What is the male's Tangible Objective?

3) List minimum of five ways these two objectives could create conflict between the two.

Exercise R2b: List ten (minimum) obstacles these two people could encounter in the evolution of their relationship, then pick the one antagonistic element that is as strong as if not stronger than either or both of the main characters.

Exercise R2c: List the female lead's influential friends and subplots or various life agendas that could be "going on" throughout this story. (We will use these in Romance Chapter 5). Now, do the same for the male lead.

ROMANCE CHAPTER 3

A Romantic Log Line

Using the logic of starting simple, you must look to your Log Line first. This is the sentence that focuses your attention and introduces others to your story. That one sentence of 25 words or less tells the story is essential to both the mental and the written process. Why?

Saying the story in one sentence focuses the writer on the bare bones framework of this story, thus automatically eliminating other concepts. The Log Line identifies the main character, the story's driving force and the main obstacle (or antagonist) to be overcome. This is simply "What" the story is about, cut and dried, to the point. However, it cannot be a boring sentence. You want nouns, qualifiers and action verbs that deliver layers of potential action, a cascade of thought-associated images. It must explode with powerful innuendo that will suck the reader/audience in and make them want to know exactly what goes on in the story, what happens to the characters, how they live the adventure.

Essentially, a Log Line delivers the outline of the story's essence. When someone asks you "What is your book (screenplay) about?" this is the succinct sentence you tell them. The majority of the people who will ask you are merely being polite, so here's a key point: If the listener is intrigued or curious, they will ask you for more information. If not, either your story holds no appeal or they aren't really interested anyway.

Let's assume your single sentence told of a story that does not appeal to this person. Is it the story itself or the person's tastes? If it is the story itself then you need to rethink your sentence.

Always ask yourself how your story is different from others "in the same category." You can practice by writing a Log Line for five or more stories of one type such as "military romantic suspense" or "Regency marriage of convenience" or "Scottish bridal kidnapping" or "serial murderer defying police" or "rich man-poor girl rescues" or . . . You get the idea. Pick several books or movies of the same type and write a Log Line for each. Don't dwell on the words you choose. Write the Log Lines quickly. How similar are they? Why? Because they deal with similar or stereotypical characterizations or plot lines?

Now, think about your story. You have to make your story different, fresh, enthralling. If you don't feel that way about your story, how will you get someone else to want to read it? Your difference will begin with a powerful Log Line.

STEP ONE: IDENTIFY CHARACTER ROLE/IDENTITY

Names of characters do not create images in the reader's mind, but roles do. Think of a name as the identity of the character to the rest of the world, but the underlying power of the character is what he or she is doing in the world. Names can be changed, but that innate power demanded by various roles will not change.

All of us have many roles in our lives: Child, Sibling, Spouse, Parent, Friend, Employee, Professional Engineer, Home Owner, Church Member, Writer, Poet, Screenwriter, Dancer, Gym Member, Horse Owner, on and on with each of us obviously making different lists. Each of those roles has its own agenda or tasks, concerns, "business" that is important only to that role. In reality, each role is its own "life." Of course, some bleed over into other roles, influencing actions and choices–like becoming a parent influences spousal expectations or a boss's demands of over-time makes our bowling team mad or paying for a hospital bill means not repainting the house this year which could in turn send our neighbor into an angry out-burst--but our daily lives are moments lived in each of these roles. A story grows out of the drama of those moments.

What is the dominant role in your Main Character's life that is "in the camera's eye" for the majority of the story? What is the role central to this story with all other roles subordinate or influenced by the demands of that role? Is it a working mom, a deployed Marine, an accountant?

STEP TWO: DOMINANT PERSONALITY FACTOR

The underlying, driving force of a personality is what allows each of us to tackle the big challenges of our lives. And sometimes only our internalized self is aware of that power lurking within. Only when we are forced will that deep characteristic evolve to its fullest. That is what You-the-Writer need to yank out of a character and put to work to meet the life-changing challenge in your story. That is the characteristic you will plug into your Log Line.

Like multiple life-roles, each of us has an array of personality traits, sometimes relevant only to particular roles, some hidden deep in the essence of our mental lives and others shown every day by our actions, choices, words. All of those traits are essential to who we are as individuals. They categorize our "personality type" to psychologists. Storytellers evolve into amateur psychologists as we analyze and depict make-believe characters. You-the-Writer must carefully consider your Character Profile and select the dominant characteristic that will energize the Main Character throughout your story.

Pick that one personality factor that will be vital to the character enduring and succeeding, even if it is something to be overcome. Create a Log Line using that characterization qualifying trait and life role to evoke images.

"A callous Southern playboy....."
"A haunted, introverted librarian...."
"A brilliant but ignored daughter..."
"A frigid female heart surgeon..."
"A ridiculously happy family man..."

Still not sure of how to describe your Main Character? Make a list of five positive and five negative personality characteristics you have. Now, pick one that your family will agree on and another that your close friends will agree on. How many of your mere acquaintances are aware of both of these? Which "face" do you show the real world? What "secret" personality trait do you harbor, waiting for the right moment, the right opportunity to use? Consider the power within your Main Character that will be called up throughout the story.

Avoid using more than one trait in your Log Line. One is usually enough. Choose the one that will visually communicate the power that will drive the story.

STEP THREE: IDENTIFY MOTIVATING CIRCUMSTANCE /ADVENTURE

What is the situation or "New Life" the character is thrown into? In the Hero's Journey construct this is something not normally sought. It is a change that demands more effort, a challenge to who this person is.

In category or genre fiction a writer is tempted to insert the situation common to the genre or sub genre. Resist the urge. Instead, identify what makes your story circumstance unique from every other romance or fantasy or mystery. This implies that you have read a lot in your genre and know common storylines.

Yes, it is essential to create a Log Line in the spirit of your genre. But, in the same vein, be absolutely 100% certain yours is unique to your story and not a "cookie cutter" that could be applied to any other Regency, any other paranormal, any other Navy SEAL romantic suspense . . . You get the idea.

Also, when the romance is the Main Plot fearlessly use phrases like "While falling in love," "Fighting their attraction," ". . . discover love while . . .," to focus the studio reader on the relationship. If you do not reference the relationship in the Log Line, the reader may truly miss how the relationship is vital to your story. So, it is not a mystery but a romantic suspense or not merely a horror story but a romantic paranormal. If your relationship is a subplot complicating the main events, don't muddy the waters for the reader. Add the romance to the Log Line.

In fact, blatantly wave the romance flag. A *brand* identifies the kind of stories you write as the basis for your reputation as a writer. Originally, I listed my screenplay log lines on my website according to the subject genre, such as Mystery/Suspense/Thriller, Western, Inspirational. Once a writing guru identified my brand as Dramatic Romance (rather than Romantic Comedy which I don't write), she had me rewrite all my log lines to reflect the focus on romance so my agent would know what market to focus on. Before that rewriting, I had a producer option one of my mystery scripts then give me notes to revise out material I knew contributed to "showing" the essence of the two leads that he saw as irrelevant. He totally missed how those "irrelevant" scenes contributed to the evolution of the relationship. He had focused on the mystery and the identity roles of the two leads working together to solve the mystery. When I pointed out the deliberate need of the essence scenes and rewrote the log line using the "fall in love" phrase, he "got it."

STEP FOUR: OPPOSITION TO OVERCOME/ CHALLENGE/IRONIC COMPLICATION

Here is the point you introduce the truly unexpected twist or irony contrasting with personality trait and role. Of course, it must be logical to the circumstance and genre. Primarily it has to be wildly evocative. You-the-Writer must propose a story with any number of possibilities that can be guessed or not. They must so enthrall or intrigue the reader that more detail is demanded! You want the reader/listener to ask for the synopsis or entire manuscript.

Look over these examples of one character's story possibilities in many genres:

Romance
"A callous Southern playboy cannot inherit until he convinces the attractive new female pastor that he's worthy."

Mystery
"A callous Southern playboy uses his prison time to network favors and find who ruined his family."

Fantasy
"A callous Southern playboy defies a curse and is whisked into a swampland world where he is the servant."

Western
"A callous Southern playboy wins a whorehouse filled with underage orphans and an outraged madam."

Log Lines are not meant to be simple; they are meant to be powerful. Think of the imagery of poetry: Every word should be evocative of a cascade of images. Remember, this must be an intriguing, defining sentence about both character and story. It is the hook that will demand your story be read. A Log Line is your introductory sales pitch. It is the line you use in your query or cover letters.

LOG LINE POINTERS

Read your sentence aloud in one breath. If you have to take a breath or hesitate, it's too long. That's why the 25 words. Again, remember that agents/editors/producers have the attention span of a gnat. So keep the sentence tight and pertinent. Do not try to cram it with an overwhelming amount of information. You want their imagination set on fire with a cascade of images and possibilities, not flooded with so much they feel like they are drowning. Focus on primary traits, primary trials, primary goals. Not all traits, trials, goals. Primary means the most important to the entire story.

Watch out for passives. Any "is" verbs or use of vague, genre-specific wording like "gets saddled" which is 1) passive, 2) cliché and 3) a "western" connotation. It's not "meant" to be any of those but when writing a log line for a unique genre, do not "mix your metaphors."

* * * * *

ROMANCE Chapter 3 Exercises

Exercise R3a. List the internal and external/role characteristics of your main character. Carefully choose your qualifiers for edginess, qualities that can either be positive or negative.

Exercise R3b. What is the character's main goal that makes him or her continue to strive?

Exercise R3c. List all the possible obstacles to achieving that goal.

Exercise R3d. Now formulate your "Log Line"....in 25 words or less.

Key Points:

1) Pick your "role" noun, identify your most tantalizing and pertinent qualifiers, then put that noun in action with the most vivid verb you can come up with. Power words with lots of levels that demand to be explained. Can you make a list of more action-packed verbs that imply the action of the story?

2) Look at your qualifying clauses and your verbs. Does the agent/producer get lost between the subject (the main character noun) and the verb?

Exercise R3e. Explain to yourself how your story is different from all the others in that story "category."

Exercise R3f. Is the potential for a romance inherent in the Log Line? If it is not lurking or blatant, then rewrite until it is!

Exercise R3g. Pick apart these four romantic Log Lines for the four elements and *look for the implied romance.* Do you see the romance as a Main Plot or a Subplot?

Temperance: In 1875 West Texas, an enigmatic saloon owner and a strong-willed young woman find unlikely love as they join forces when accused of murdering her father, a New York banker-turned-fire-breathing-temperance leader.

Chaco: A virile Hispanic nurse and a cynical California female doctor are drawn together as they encounter tri-cultural trials in the struggle to build a medical clinic in the rural canyon country of northwestern New Mexico.

Shooting A world-renowned fashion model defies her grasping agent and encounters love when she takes responsibility for the cop disabled by her stalker's bullet.

The Gift Exchange An enigmatic stock broker/ SCA enthusiast falls in love with the family-challenged computer whiz he hires to help him find who is manipulating accounts in the brokerage.

ROMANCE CHAPTER 4

Four Approaches to Romantic Screenplays

Review

- As a category or genre, a Romance is expected to be a relationship story.
- Men expect to see physical responses, women expect to see commitment.
- Cinematic romances must....
  1) Be character-driven, not plot driven stories
  2) Have structure of meeting, misunderstanding, separation, commitment
  3) Present consistent expression of emotional impact & angst
  4) Balance screen time between male & female leads
  5) Incorporate subplots/minor characters/environment only impacting couple
  6) Depict love scenes, not sex scenes

APPROACH ONE: "TWELVE STEPS OF INTIMACY"

As a significant approach to cinematic romance, I want to present an overview of best-selling romance author **Linda Howard's "Twelve Steps of Intimacy"** wherein she explains how to demonstrate the physical progression of the sex drive from recognition to the act itself. Here's the outline:

1. Eye to Body
2. Eye to Eye
3. Voice to Voice
4. Hand to Hand

* * *

5. Arm to Shoulder
6. Arm to Waist
7. Mouth to Mouth

8. Hand to Head
9. Hand to Body

* * *

10. Mouth to Breast
11. Hand to Genitals
12. Genitals to Genitals

The logic of this progression lies in **trust, acceptance** and **permission.** The more one trusts, the more access to the body will be wanted and allowed. On a primal level, each step makes the person more vulnerable to a lethal attack. Think about that as you again look down the list. Each move actually invades another's space more. Each exposes the body to attack or allows total control of a body part that could have been protected or defended previously. Hand holding keeps one from running and each subsequent movement pulls the body closer, making the person vulnerable. Mouth and head are where breath moves in and out and where one exposes the fragile spine and vital blood vessels. Each step allowed gives freer access to vulnerable body parts and surrenders control by responding, becoming more stimulated and willing.

Yes, medical science has told us the pheromones should be signaling the attraction and desire, but those libido-freeing buggers are not visible on the screen. So, as a cinematic storyteller, you have to show your characters losing self-control and becoming more vulnerable, more trusting, whether hurriedly or in progressively more sensual signaling throughout the entire script. Romance moves through these 12 Steps. Rape goes from Step 1 abruptly to anything beyond Step 9 because it is meant to be a violent violation, domination, a destruction of trust. It is a crime, not the foundation for a relationship.

Another key point is that Steps 1 through 9 are acceptable as public displays of affection in our modern age, whereas in ancient through the Victorian era only Steps 1 through 4 were tolerated. In some cultures such as Chinese nobility and strict Islamic practices, not even eye contact was or is allowed. Most of society expects greater intimacy to be moved to private quarters because it is meant to be actions between just these two people. Think about the "naughtiness" or voyeurism of the adult porn industry in relation to these 12 Steps, titillation and trust vs. professional promiscuity. Think of actual "public display" laws in conservative communities or countries.

Now, with the above choreography in mind, we will move into some concepts of building the cinematic romance.

APPROACH TWO: IDENTITY AND ESSENCE

Michael Hauge is a Story Consultant in the film industry. He evaluates scripts for actors, agents, producers and directors, studio executives, TV networks and even evolving script writers. Based on his experience, he has developed some concepts helpful to romance. (His seminar is available on a DVD on his website www.ScreenplayMastery.com).

He talks of two facets of personality: **Outer Identity** and **Inner Essence**. Most humans operate by showing the external world that Outer Identity with skills, knowledge, habitual coping mechanisms, speech patterns, body language. It is who the world thinks that person is, the role assumed by that person. But, deep in the psyche throbs the Inner Essence, that soul that harbors aspirations, deep desires for what that person really wants to do and be in this life. Only a select few are allowed to "see" that Inner Essence. The Soul Mate, the sexual match meant to cherish and appreciate good and bad, sees beyond the Outer Identity to that Inner Essence.

Hauge solved a story problem for one script writer with this concept when he explained how a love triangle proves who should be the lover who wins. Of the two vying for the third's affections, one is attuned only to Identity of the apex person while the true soul mate (who should win) recognizes and plays to the Essence of the beloved.

APPROACH THREE: THE RELATIONSHIP PLANE

This approach to a relationship's evolution fits well into the structure of Syd Field and those suggested by various other Hollywood gurus.

Start with the idea of a stair step of complications encountered, blocking life moving forward and forcing consideration of other options, a choice of action moving forward until another event forces consideration of new action. The result is ever-worsening circumstances, the climb up the staircase of dramatic action thus creating "Rising Tension" and sucking the audience along with empathetic concern.

The formula of meeting-misunderstanding-separation-commitment is a solidly accepted trope (storytelling tool) in romance. The aficionados come to the story *expecting* those stages to play out. They look for them in the Beginning-Middle-Ending of the 3-Act plot. Romance writers have the opportunity to weave an even more complex evolution of the journey toward final commitment.

Any romantic attraction that is resisted provides a powerful story, no matter the complicating circumstance or varied personalities involved. RWA's extensive research over three decades has identified a viable, recognizable pattern beyond the four stages woven into the 3-Act Structure in the gradual increase of tension called the **Relationship Plane**. The schematic of this pattern and its accompanying terminology definition and discussion is provided in Appendix N.

Does this all sound too prescribed, too predictable? That is the fun part in the process: You-the-Writer get to insert and rearrange all your complications and unique personalities as they meet the audience expectations.

Anything can be analyzed to the "nth" degree. The point is to understand the analysis then twist and turn it to work for your story and your lovers.

APPROACH FOUR: CLUSTERING OF STEPS

The joy of experiencing a cinematic romance is in the anticipation, the pacing of your "reveals" of the Pull-Push (Pull of attraction but the Push of denial) emotions. If you cram everything into one meeting, you are "cheating" your audience of that element that keeps them focused, hoping what will come next. Now, the males in the audience prefer everything as a "reveal" at once. They tend to say "Cut to the chase. Don't give me all that touchy-feely stuff." So, yes, you could condense but, unless the female is desperate (which is a tad pathetic), aren't you rushing?

A movie-going audience likes to see the characters work for whatever. Make them contemplate one another in the Pull-Push game. Engagement is the tantalizing tease of saying "Yes, I am available to *you*!" The permission is succumbing to the desire. Create your relationship in droplets, not one bucketful splash scene. Those kinds of scenes are thrown into action-adventure movies and come off gratuitous. The finesse of light brush strokes that build and focus is much more tantalizing in a cinematic romance. Example: YOU'VE GOT MAIL

BRAINSTORMING POSSIBILITIES

"Brainstorming" is the creative process of letting your imagination run wild and thinking of any possibility that could happen. It is like "free writing" where you make lists. Those lists give you options to consider. Two things to remember: Do not go for the most obvious or most convenient and do not make anything a coincidence. The choices made and the actions taken must be deliberate choices. Yes, two people can be in the bank at the same time it is held up and they are taken as hostages, but that they "just happened" to have gone to school together and had a high school affair is too much of a convenience. At that point the "What if" becomes contrived and melodramatic.

You bring them together and have then interact out of their natural, normal routine and the meeting will come off as "of course it was meant to happen" serendipity.

By the time you get to the last scene before "The End," think about how you want your couple feeling after the climax of the story, after they have come into their powers to overcome the antagonist and have recognized they need one another to go forward into life as a unit. How do you want them showing their commitment to each other?

* * * * *

ROMANCE Chapter 4 Exercises

Exercise R4a: State four possible situations or events for your story's four major relationship points:

1) Meeting
2) Misunderstanding
3) Separation
4) Commitment

Note: This is an exercise in making "What if" lists, of many possibilities of actions and reactions you could use.

Exercise R4b: What are three Major roles in your female lead's life that create her Identity? Now, the three major roles in your male lead's life?

Exercise R4c: What is your female's Essence (what does she want more than anything else, but keeps locked within)? The Essence of your male lead?

Exercise R4d: How do you want these two complex people to celebrate their victory over life's assault on their tenuous relationship after the Climax of your story? What "Happily Ever After" images will your audience take home to translate into their own imaginings of the couple's future?

(**Note:** If you can imagine the histories of these two characters then how they meet at the beginning of your story . . . and you know how you want to conclude the story, it becomes much "easier" to construct the middle . . .)

ROMANCE CHAPTER 5

Unique but Universal Hero & Heroine and Cast

Review

- (Yes, I DO intend for you to re-read these to commit them to your mental arsenal)
- As a category or genre, a Romance is expected to be a relationship story.
- Men expect to see physical responses, women expect to see commitment.
- Cinematic romances must....
  1) Be character-driven, not plot driven stories
  2) Have structure of meeting, misunderstanding, separation, commitment
  3) Present consistent expression of emotional impact & angst
  4) Balance screen time between male & female leads
  5) Incorporate subplots/minor characters/environment only impacting couple
  6) Depict love scenes, not sex scenes
- On screen lovers must be seen moving through the "Twelve Steps of Intimacy" visually demonstrating trust, acceptance and permission the audience believes.
- The physical signaling in the romance will be true to values of the culture and era.
- Both Hero and Heroine will visually depict both "Outer Identity" of roles seen by the world and "Inner Essence" of precious internal desires shown only in private and the true lover will want the beloved because of the Essence, not the Identity.
- When the Romance is the central plot, the visualization of the relationship moves up the rising tension of the Relationship Plane with crucial moments pacing the story.
- Controlled pacing demands awareness of how close together you depict your "Pull-Push reveals."

FUNDAMENTAL CINEMATIC CHARACTER CONCEPTS

Because a romance is character-driven, it is absolutely essential that you totally understand your Hero and Heroine through in-depth Character Profiling before you write the script. Character makes the events happen; the events do not happen then the character reacts. So, to control your story from the get-go, you have to understand character history, influences, motivations. Many novelists "like" to get to know their characters as they set them in motion and the length of the medium gives them that luxury. Screenplays demand succinct depiction of character and, to do that, you must figure out character beforehand. Period, end of the discussion of the need for Character Profiling.

You will find a **36-Step Character Profile** in Appendix C with an explanation of how to use the Profile in Appendix D. There are many Profile forms out there that others may like better, but this contains the essential information for you to understand your Character. It is divided into three main sections.

First is the **General** data that deals with fundamentals like appearance, birth, education, home environment, etc. Despite the fact that you may be writing a character with a specific actor in mind, you still need to document your visualization. However, the only words you will use when the character first appears will be age (26), physical attributes, costuming choice pertinent to this story at the beginning and a phrase alluding to attitude or bearing pertinent to this story at the beginning.

The middle section is **Personal** information that reveals the many layers of influence and preference, even the "Typical Day." Each item can provide a glimpse of the person that moves this character from stereotypical to unique. Most of the items also provide a common link that audience members can identify with. Never, ever feel you have to use everything, but when you know this much about a person you will see where you can threaten for the most dramatic impact. Of course, #17 "Greatest Fear" is a prime target . . . and in the case of a romance you want to consider both "Greatest Fear" from point-of-view of Identity and from the point-of-view of "Essence." That is tweaked/depicted at Pinch II around Page 37 in the first half of Act II.

The final section of the Character Profile deals with the **Story** itself. When you think through these you begin to grasp the possibilities for the Cause-and-Effect waterfall of events you have to depict and those you can simply infer (such as the passage of time or the consequences say of cars headed to same intersection then chaotic and panic-filled scene in the Emergency Room).

Appendix E is a Cinematic Character Worksheet specifically aimed at the inherently dramatic characters one needs in the lead roles of screenplay. Be vigilant about one major factor: Cinematic lead characters are inherently dramatic rather than "evolving" as they do in a novel. When they appear on camera the audience knows something is going to happen. Think of the "class clown." Everyone knew this guy was going to do something silly to call attention to him. He couldn't help himself. It inevitably, consistently just happened. That is how you must think of a lead character in your screenplay. Pulling from the Character Profile, create personality elements that will make things happen because of this character in your screenplay.

ESSENTIALS OF THE ROMANTIC HERO

Each of the genres has its own fundamental requirements of attributes the audience expects the lead character to possess and develop in the course of the story. Romantic heroes must demonstrate primary attributes of the "Alpha Male" in Identity but evolve into capability to explore the "Beta Male" lingering in his Essence. Re-read that sentence. The Hero's Outer Identity--his role to the world--and the events he faces will call upon that character's dominant traits to result in success in the world . . . but the inner Essence of his Beta side will dictate his success in the romance.

> ROMANTIC HEROES MUST DEMONSTRATE PRIMARY ATTRIBUTES OF THE "ALPHA MALE" IN IDENTITY BUT EVOLVE INTO CAPABILITY TO EXPLORE THE "BETA MALE" LINGERING IN HIS ESSENCE.

The concept of Alpha vs. Beta refers to humanity's primal origins.

> THE INNER ESSENCE OF HIS BETA SIDE WILL DICTATE HIS SUCCESS IN THE ROMANCE.

The **Alpha Male** is the dominant provider, protector, progenitor. He thinks in compartmentalized, hierarchal terms to conquer one thing at a time. He is action-oriented and relies heavily on habit. The "Big Man" typical of the Alpha Male is a cross-cultural phenomena.

The **Beta Male** is the intellectually evolved survivor because he is an adaptable problem- solver. He is careful to act and relies heavily on data and the evaluation of sensation. He is highly attentive and is actually perceived cross-culturally as potentially more dangerous than the Alpha Male. The Alpha Male may be powerful, but the exercise of that power is predictable. The Beta Male's thought associations cannot be predicted.

Here's a "comparison" of behaviors or how each is perceived:

Alpha Male	Beta Male
1. Gains resources..................	Shares willingly
2. Physically attractive.............	Willingly sensitive
3. Seeks sexual intimacy...........	Emotionally attentive
4. Child proves prowess...........	Sincerely wants to nurture
5. Focused on value for time.......	Sees relationship as exchange

Remember: **"The most dangerous animal on earth is the human male."**

The simple summary of all this for the romantic hero is he needs to be **Alpha-Beta, motivated and confident yet vulnerable.**

ESSENTIALS OF THE ROMANTIC HEROINE

When characterizing the female lead in a romantic screenplay do not confuse the terminology I use with the "primal origins" in the discussion of the male. Women are considered according to their dominant intellectual traits thus motivational forces symbolic of "archetypes." Yep, women truly are much simpler . . . as "types."

The **Alpha Female** is assertive, confident, athletic, tough. The Warrior Woman is willing to attack and defend. The Whore is sexually aggressive and adept. The Crone personifies the controlling matriarchal power.

The **Beta Female** is perceptive, emotional, maternal and soft. The Madonna is the attentive and vulnerable mother. The Priestess is the knowledgeable guide and communicator. The Healer is the nurturing problem-solver.

Fascinating contrasts can be created by mixing demanding traits from an unfamiliar yet logically inherent role such as the fragile Madonna girds herself as a Warrior Woman to defend her children then must become the Priestess teaching them to survive. Or think of the slut seen as the Whore who nurses the epidemic's victims in the saloon and converts the townspeople to accepting her as a Madonna figure.

Here is a more in-depth look at cinematic examples of Pinkola-Estes's concepts of female characters she explained in *Women Who Run with the Wolves*, a thick tome written in PhD-eze to be read and digested in bits and pieces. Think more intensely about your heroine.

PRETTY WOMAN: Whore to Priestess to Madonna (his choice for a mate and softer in the end)
LAST OF THE MOHICANS (Cora): Madonna to Priestess to Whore to Warrior Woman
QUIGLEY DOWN UNDER: Whore to Madonna to Warrior Woman to Priestess
LITTLE WOMEN (Jo): Crone (over her sisters) to Priestess to Healer (wasn't she meeker in the end?)
DANCES WITH WOLVES: Priestess to Whore to Madonna to Healer (See that she was predominantly Beta?)
THE BIG EASY (Ann): Crone (power position) to Whore to Priestess to Healer to, finally, Madonna

These are opinions based on logical analysis. You might see vacillation many times in a movie depending on the skills that are called upon in order to cope. "Weaker" roles are the Beta roles whether male or female and "forceful" roles call for Alpha traits. Always ask yourself who instigates or initiates whatever action in a scene to identify what roles are needed at that time.

A person's role in a single scene will not change. The role shift comes in the subsequent scene. In the first scene Ann in THE BIG EASY is the attorney from the D.A.'s office investigating police corruption. She is in the power position. Try as he might Remy (Dennis Quaid) cannot rattle her until he manipulates her into a dependent position and fires up her hormones to respond to him sexually. However, she still has control of herself as he works his wiles and she allows herself to enjoy his seduction. But the evolution of the investigation throws her back into Crone role. Then she's dependent and a whore again and then she's the Crone charging Remy with taking a bribe. She shifts into Priestess mode (with Remy becoming more powerful as gains her access to the police department). Remy makes himself vulnerable and she is briefly the Healer to his tears. But as Remy takes charge in full Warrior mode, she then is Priestess and in the final scene his bride, his Madonna.

It is impossible to have two characters dominant at the same time. Story tension will not logically allow that. From their history, you can tell who is going to be the player in control of the scene, each demonstrating how he or she is coping at the moment

And here is an applicable quote about women: **"The most unpredictable animal on earth is the human female."**

The summary of this for the romantic heroine is she needs to be **Beta-Alpha, motivated toward pride and empowerment.**

OTHER CAST MEMBERS

Look to your lead Character Profiles to identify who you absolutely need in your story. Pay attention to two factors: 1) What is this non-lead character's role in life and impact on the romantic relationship? 2) Amount of space/word/page count equals importance to the story as a whole.

ANTAGONISTS who are the major obstacle to the relationship's success are present throughout the story. They must be as strong as the leads or stronger if they are to threaten, recover, subvert, attack again and again! Their power to threaten must be visual. Don't forget the Minor Antagonists, those irritants that annoy everyone, the audience included, just don't belabor or repeat to the point of "boo's."

SUPPORTING Characters are the "Second Bananas" and are most commonly used as contrasts to the leads either in appearance or abilities. They can also provide the psychological balance the leads need and can be the "point makers." Use only those that will specifically enhance or complicate the relationship in a succinct manner. Remember a screenplay is more like a short story than a novel. Limited pages, limited cast.

WALK-ONS can be your **GEMS** for both the actors and the audience. Each character who has dialogue deserves a name and identity that any actor would be proud to do. Do not make these valuable personas merely numbers, as in Policeman #1 or Lady in Line. Think about movies that etched themselves into your memory and you will recall vivid characterizations of bit players. They provide the subtle background in brilliant paint strokes.

CHILDREN should be used in action and speech appropriate to their stage of Growth & Development. Don't use your own childhood as a guide because your memories are skewed. Rely on medical and social science for guidance. Carefully maintain appropriate maturity level of the child. Look at the Growth & Development Guidelines in Appendix G as a basic reference.

ANIMALS have personalities, too, but never, ever choreograph unnatural behavior for an animal. Animal trainers can ONLY do so much. You want the animal action to be authentic, not contrived--unless you are writing a version of DR DOLITTLE.

COMIC characters are meant to provide comedic relief to the drama. They set-up an expectation then credibly respond in an opposite manner. Their practical jokes can teach a subtle lesson, like Mrs. Doubtfire's "run-by fruiting" scene.

COMPLEX COWARDS are effective point-makers. They usually begin as stereotyped negative "fluff," disdained and discounted by other characters. In their "moment of glory" they do one right thing that balances everything else. The repulsed coward has a moment of vindication and worth. The best example ever depicted in film was in SAVING PRIVATE RYAN.

* * * * *

ROMANCE Chapter 5 Exercises

Exercise R5a: Complete a Character Profile for your Hero. Now complete one for your Heroine. Don't leave any number blank because you don't think it will be important or even used in your screenplay! When you know the character this thoroughly they come alive and you can both hear their dialogue and see them move. You can predict how they will respond!

Exercise R5b: Look back at your notes for Exercises R2b and R2c from Romance Chapter 2 regarding the female and male leads' influential friends and subplots. Revise them according to your just completed Character Profiles.

Exercise R5c: Always complete a Profile on your **Major Antagonist** as well. Giving that person depth prevents stereotyping. Remember an Antagonist is anyone who opposes the Protagonist. An Antagonist is not necessarily a repulsive Villain (like a well-meaning but overly strict parent), but **a Villain is always an Antagonist**.

ROMANCE CHAPTER 6

Hollywood's Need for Sex and Violence

Review

(Yes, I DO intend for you to re-read these to commit them to your mental arsenal)

- As a category or genre, a Romance is expected to be a relationship story.
- Men expect to see physical responses, women expect to see commitment.
- Cinematic romances must . . .
  1) Be character-driven, not plot driven stories
  2) Have structure of meeting, misunderstanding, separation, commitment
  3) Present consistent expression of emotional impact & angst
  4) Balance screen time between male & female leads
  5) Incorporate subplots/minor characters/environment only impacting couple
  6) Depict love scenes, not sex scenes
- On screen lovers must be seen moving through the "Twelve Steps of Intimacy" visually demonstrating trust, acceptance and permission the audience believes.
- The physical signaling in the romance will be true to values of the culture and era.
- Both Hero and Heroine will visually depict both "Outer Identity" of roles seen by the world and "Inner Essence" of precious internal desires shown only in private and the true lover will want the beloved because of the Essence, not the Identity.
- When the Romance is the central plot, the visualization of the relationship moves up the rising tension of the Relationship Plane with crucial moments pacing the story.
- Controlled pacing demands awareness of how close together you depict your "Pull-Push reveals."

- Character Profiling allows you to flesh out, understand and orchestrate your characters.
- Character Profiles need to cover general history/background, personal preferences/influences, and forces driving the character in the current story.
- Romantic Heroes need to be Alpha-Beta, motivated and confident yet vulnerable.
- Romantic Heroines need to be Beta-Alpha, motivated toward pride and empowerment.
- Every other cast member has to have a direct influence on the Hero-Heroine relationship in a romance.

FUNDAMENTAL CONCEPTS OF SEX & VIOLENCE

Hollywood is fickle and there s no such thing as a "trend." Why? Every power figure in the industry has his or her own preferences and absolutely no one can predict what will click with the ticket-buying public. There will be a lot of "copy cat" projects, however, after a successful film. But, think about it. How long does it take for a script to go from concept to financing to development to production to the screen? The public could move on to some other "flavor-of-the-month" by the time your rendition of a similar story makes it into the theaters.

The only constant in film making is no one wants to read/see the story of "the happy people in the happy village." That means dramatic conflict is essential in every genre. The most basic definition of conflict is "want is blocked by a powerful obstacle" and the two basic human wants are the perpetuation of the species and the continuation of life . . . thus sex and violence are common elements in every kind of genre. It doesn't get any simpler than that.

Definitions for this discussion:

Sex: Chemistry of physical attraction vital to establishing a loving, trusting relationship that will lead to sexual intercourse, whether visualized or inferred.

Violence: The threat or actual physical jeopardizing of human life, be it disruption of status quo or actual death.

SEXUAL CONTEXT IN VARIOUS GENRES

To begin with, we are not talking about sexual intercourse on screen here. We are talking about Linda Howard's Twelve Steps of Intimacy, the titillation of inference, the unspoken assumptions. If you haven't got those down then refer back to Romance Chapter 4's discussion of those steps.

What does someone mean when they say "That couple has great chemistry" or "I don't believe the attraction because the on-screen chemistry is just not there"??? Yes, actors who possess that sexual charisma and great acting ability can turn a simple conversation into a raging seduction scene. But, screenwriters have to create the characters, the fundamental choreography, the subtle dialogue that gives the actors the tools to work with. Visuals, visuals, visuals at all three levels of 10 characterization, 2) movement, and 3) dialogue.

Time and again you will hear some industry people say "The barest hint of what is going on or closing the door will create greater titillation for the audience than if you film an R or X-rated sex scene." Some call these scenes "tasteful illusion" and others roll their eyes and say "That's a director cheating to get by the censors." Both are right. However, an artful screenwriter can heat up the screen with the characterization, movement, and dialogue to the point the audience members are squirming in their seats because their vivid imaginations are racing.

Probably the most common tool of playing off sexual assumption is the touching or partnering of spouses, parenting referrals, pregnancy or the presence of children, even the image of a double bed. Small children will not even think about the underlying assumption that sexual congress is implied in all of that. Cartoon guys getting "bug-eyed" when a curvaceous cartoon gal walks by swinging her hips is humorous, but for different reasons to different levels of maturity. So the teen films that show skin and hormonal boys are alluding to the assumption of sex. An elderly couple holding hands are at what stage in Howard's Twelve Steps of Intimacy? Is the contrast between those two examples in the assumption of vigorous activity for the purpose of procreation or pleasuring a partner? What exactly is the implied difference? What is normal and what is "pushing the envelope" of the observer's imagination?

Here is where you, the romantic script writer, have to very deliberately plan the sex you will use in your story by specific visuals of the Twelve Steps, the titillation of inference, or the unspoken assumptions.

Keep a list of the visuals that will depict thoughts and emotions, such as his hand sliding around her bare, sweaty midriff and her gasp and shiver then verbal denial as "What? No, nothing's wrong. You just startled me." He frowns then pinches his eyes to concentrate harder. Movie-making is about the visuals you give the actor and director to tell the story. The physical "signaling" is how the audience connects with the character's thoughts. This is a matter of delivery by the actors and reception by he audience.

Here's an interesting exercise to get you in that visual mode: Put in your favorite movie that you watch over and over . . . sans the volume. Watch how the body language and facial expression show the story.

Of course, as a writer you will not depict every nuance, just insinuate what a good actor can latch onto. To describe every expression, every physical move is called "micro-choreography" and will get your script promptly sent back to you or thrown in the recycle bin. Imagine yourself as an artistic actor who wants to recreate a memorable character on camera. As an actor do you want somebody who wrote the thing three years ago dictating to you how to do your job? Instead, think Macro-managing

Did you know that in live theater the playwright's words are sacred? Not one line or one word can be changed without the playwright's authorization. It ain't that way in film-making. Everybody and their mom can come on the set or to rehearsals and suggest changes. All you the screenwriter can do is to write out the best story you can at the outset . . . then let go of that baby you have birthed and let it learn and grow into that incredible on-screen adult the rest of the film-making world has advised and fashioned into being.

VIOLENCE DOES NOT MEAN BLOOD & EXPLOSIONS

Think of violence as "increments of jeopardy." Crewella Deville in 101 DALMATIANS was a violent woman who wanted those puppies to die. The horrors visualized as Omaha Beach on D-Day in SAVING PRIVATE RYAN was as visually accurate as cinema could get. At the other end of the spectrum you have the mother warning her misbehaving son with "The Look." No violence is committed, just the threat of something the boy would not like. The same thing could be said about gunfighter opponents and the stare-down scene where one relaxes and looks away, unwilling to act. No violence evolved, merely a threat resulting in the response of allowing the Alpha Male to reign supreme.

So here's the basic storytelling formula:

M + G + O = Dramatic Conflict
(Main character) + (Goal) + (Opposition) = Dramatic Conflict

And here's the VIOLENCE formula:

W. M. + W.G. + THREAT = Jeopardy
(Willing Main Character) + (Worthy-of-Risk Goal) + THREAT = Jeopardy

Examine each of those components in your story and you will discover the level of violence you must have in your story.

Highly motivated people are logically more willing to take risks. The more confident and skilled the person, the greater the risk they will be willing to take. At the other end of the spectrum is the innocent, ignorant character who makes assumptions and takes risks without awareness of the consequences. So, you must examine Character in each scene for these two extremes.

Cinematic stories are about exaggerated circumstances, so goals have to be BIG. The more important the goal, the greater risks the motivated character will be willing to take to achieve that goal . . . within the parameters of their personality. Think back to the innate personality traits talked about in Romance Chapter 5. What would motivate a devoutly religious character to respond violently and take a human life? The most decorated soldier of WW I, Sgt. York was a registered conscientious objector with Quaker roots, yet when he committed himself to defending the rights of people to live freely rather than under tyranny, he killed and captured more German soldiers than any other one man in the history of that war. He committed to both his willingness and a worthy-of-risk goal that motivated him to the ultimate of violent acts, taking other human life. By instinct, animals are willing to do whatever it takes to survive. Consider that in your formula.

The greater the threat, the greater the level of jeopardy, as well. Think about how stalking can escalate, yet every level is frightening to the victim. Every level is an invasion of territory, a disruption in the continuum of a safe, secure life. Practical jokes are a threat. Holding a door closed, forcing someone to eat something, putting a bug or snake into someone's backpack or bed . . . all of these disrupt and threaten the security of the moment. Restraining someone whether body-to-body or with some sort of tie-down is a threat to physical freedom for the person being restrained. In hospitals, law enforcement or military actions this act may be necessary for the safety of the majority . . but it is still a threat to the one restrained.

Some people have personal difficulty identifying the entertainment value of the violence of multiple car wrecks like in THE BLUES BROTHERS or in the gore and terror of "slasher" movies. Emergency personnel see the reality of human suffering, so the on-screen pain and suffering is definitely not entertaining. Many ex-military had a tough time sitting through the battle scenes of SAVING PRIVATE RYAN and even such epics as BRAVEHEART. The cinematic drama of the violence in those films ripped right to the soul, which was appropriate for each story. The battle scenes were there for more than entertainment value . . . which cannot be said of the gratuitous scenes in THE BLUES BROTHERS and various "slasher" movies.

JEOPARDY IN ROMANCE

All of that said, let us go back to the concept of jeopardy in romantic movies. The Main Character or Hero and Heroine must be willing to risk their personal well-being for the ultimate sake of the relationship. That is what makes O. Henry's Christmas story "The Gift of the Magi" so intensely meaningful: the husband and the wife loved one another so much they were willing to give up the one thing they treasured most to make the other happy. They jeopardized their personal want to make the other feel cherished.

How to consider jeopardy is simply a matter of identifying what the character values most then listing the many different ways that "thing" could be diminished, tarnished, or destroyed completely. Some assaults merely undermine the value whereas other actions can malign and destroy the essence of character values.

Every single character should have their own set of "golden idols," those things that are sacred to them. Of course, as human beings we will share some common values . . . but most of us hide and protect those "things" that are the most sacred to each of us alone. Those sacred things are what make each of us vulnerable for nothing, not one thing, not one institution, belief, or physical possession, not one relationship, one human ability is above attack or beyond destruction. Stephen Hawkins is the most brilliant man of our world but he is trapped in a deteriorating body and must rely on machines to communicate his brilliance. Our human shells are fragile. Our belief systems are certainly even more fragile. Who is right and who is wrong? When will the truth be known for certain? One man's truth is another man's abhorrent way of life.

So each writer must create each character with his or her own set of values and personal idols then create a story experience that will assault those values. You-the-Writer have to suck the audience in to care about that character's values in Act I then depict all the trials and stressors that strain and jeopardize those valued ways of life in Act II and finally force the character to defend the well-being of that character's values in Act III.

Here's an important concept when trying to identify what is jeopardized: Intense drama results when the person has two choices and both are horrific, both will hurt or destroy something of value to the character, such as in SOPHIE'S CHOICE. That is called a "dramatic dilemma." Story is predictable when the choices are merely between right and wrong or between two rights. But when the choice is between two wrongs or two definite losses, the tension becomes glaring anxiety. Dilemma creates even a greater sense of jeopardy for the character who must act! In romance you will have every opportunity to use both sex and violence because you have a basic story of conflict in these two elements from the beginning. They want what they can not have . . . without earning it. So you put them in jeopardy and make them earn it.

REVISING OUT MELODRAMA

Many, many even experienced romance novelists (let alone screenwriters) fall victim to melodrama. They are not aware of it because they sincerely think "that's the way the story should go." They are affronted when the melodrama is pointed out. If there is one thing editing and screenwriting should teach you it is "Get over yourself!" Nothing is carved in stone. And if anyone tells you something even hints of melodrama, you better damn well examine that scene or story line from every angle possible.

Any storyteller knows that a motivated character encountering forceful opposition will act out dramatic conflict. Drama is defined as "any series of events having vivid, emotional, conflicting or striking interest or results." Melodrama goes one step further as "a form that does not observe cause and effect and that intensifies sentiment and exaggerates emotion." The difference between the two is **illogical intensity** and **exaggerated emotion**. A dramatic scene delivers credible insight to the audience; melodrama delivers laughs, groans, and even squirming discomfort. Drama builds illusion, whereas melodrama destroys it. Yes, you want "bigger-than-life" characters, empowered people who create change. What you do not want is a story, an event, a character that is unbelievable for even one moment.

You must examine each scene and each line of dialogue for excess, not just to save the cost of production that any good film editor will leave on the cutting room floor, but to hone your story to the barest essence of its own power, its own reality.

Even solid comedies avoid melodrama by being reality-based. They propose the reality then turn around the audience expectation. Think of CLUELESS, MRS. DOUBTFIRE, THE FULL MONTY. Each had moments of silliness and immaturity that were balanced with moments of pathos and potential. Melodrama does not provide balance because it goes that one step too far. The audience cannot believe the inappropriate illusion.

The essence of powerful storytelling vs. melodrama is covered by "The Three R's: Real, Relevant, Riveting."

IS IT REAL?

The story events must be logically aligned. Even the convoluted MEMENTO was meticulously set up in retrospect. It was a journey constructed of piece-by-piece memory fragments. It was credible because it delivered the tension of mounting discovery. No one's memory is perfect. Ask any police officer taking statements from multiple witnesses or the author of anecdotal history whose view is skewed from lack of knowledge of all contributing factors. The audience bought into the illusion and lived it with the story characters.

Credible stories are logical stories. Logical, not predictable. Logical means the events are presented in cause-and-effect order. The effect, the result of a cause or motivation can be bizarre. What it cannot be is illogical.

You are responsible for establishing reality through blatant imagery or exposition. Of course, in the film industry imagery is preferable. The subtle or inner workings of a character are the exposition. For this exposition to be real and not melodramatic, the timing must be perfect to the story line, the words and delivery succinct and pointed. If a character belabors a point, that is melodrama. Too much. Audience overload. The same goes for imagery. When the image has made the point of Arctic cold or Stock Exchange chaos, move on to the next logical thought association for the audience.

Give your audience (and studio reader) credit for a degree of intelligence. Our Information/Technological Age has developed a taste for intriguing entertainment. Not lecture, but guessing games about the actions of characters we care about. Develop the characters and the story with drama's vivid events to the point of memorable impact then move on. The result will be fast-paced, credible story reality, be it a children's story or a sedate romance.

IS IT RELEVANT?

Tension builds with relevance, with the audience mentally asking the question "What does it mean to the rest of the story?" Melodrama prolongs the moment until the audience can predict the effect and loses respect for the character. They don't believe the character would say something so inane nor do something so illogical. "Stupid is as stupid does."

Every scene, every piece of dialogue needs to be 1) the result of what came before in the story line known to the audience (or what they will find out), 2) consistent with the character's motivation, and 3) necessary to the logical flow of story events to follow.

Again, melodrama will result when the audience is overloaded with more intensity and emotional display than the story event and characterization warrants.

Whenever there is any sort of emotional outburst (or visible control of emotion) in your story, ask yourself why it is necessary to depict. What will happen later in the story where you can use this? In A LEAGUE OF THEIR OWN, the alcoholic Peaches coach (Tom Hanks) rips into one of his fielders and makes her cry then rants "There's no crying in baseball!" This is a set-up for when that player repeats the mistake in the crucial game and he quivers with exaggerated control, merely telling her "We'll have to work on that." In THE COWBOYS, we watch two bulls going head-to-head as the herd is rounded up for the trail drive. Will Anderson (John Wayne) explains to his crew of youngsters how sometimes the young bull wins because he's stronger, quicker, but this time the old bull won because he has the experience. This was a succinct set-up for Plot Point II when Anderson wins a fist fight against the younger Bruce Dern character then endures being shot piece by piece to let Dern expend his vicious temper on him rather than the boys. No melodrama of excess and both examples totally logical to story and characters, interesting, even riveting.

IS IT RIVETING?

Good storytelling operates in an ebb-and-flow of tension. The audience must always be in the story vicarious living it with the characters. For the illusion's reality to be maintained the audience must see, feel, hear all the relevant data as the character is aware. Keeping the rubber band of mental tension pulled taut is as dangerous a form of melodrama as is clichéd characterizations.

Riveting story means credibly enthralling. The audience forgets the theatre and life beyond. They live the story with the characters.

It would be wonderfully gratifying if this level of storytelling happened every time you sat down to write. It's not going to happen. However, you can work at it with awareness of how to control your own form of exaggeration, how to pace the revelation of character motivation, where to allow the audience glimpses and where to let them wallow in the forces driving your characters. Riveting doesn't mean physical tension. It means mentally focused.

You can achieve this in one word: Planning. Consider what you want each character to depict. What will be subtle and what will be intense about each one's demeanor? How will each character's personal agenda impact the main plot line or the main characters? What plants can you logically set-up early on then pay-off? Example: Remember early on in GLADIATOR when Maximus briefly watched the sword "exercises" of the man he ultimately faced in the Coliseum.

Every scene, every piece of dialogue must be real, relevant, and riveting. No excessive sentiment or emotion. Let your audience live with your characters.

* * * * *

ROMANCE Chapter 6 Exercises

Exercise R6a: What is your Hero willing to sacrifice or endure for his beloved's happiness? What empowerment will the Heroine demonstrate, what risks will she take for her lover's well-being?

Exercise R6b: What level of violence is inherent in your story? What level are your main characters capable of (hero, heroine, antagonist)?

Exercise R6c: Rate your current screenplay plot events on a scale of 1 (Total disregard of sexual signaling) to 10 (Graphic Sexual Activity). Do you perceive any "moral issue" in the level of sexuality of your story? (And, yes, editing out of love-making scenes is sometimes done to get a "better" or more general audience rating from the censors to improve box office income.)

Exercise R6d: List five behaviors the male will use in the story's "courting ritual." Now, list five of the heroine's behaviors. Do you see any as "stereo-typical" or even "melodramatic"??? Do you perceive the male or the female as the sexual "instigator" or "seducer"?

ROMANCE CHAPTER 7

Sexual Tension vs. Plot complications

Review

(Yes, I DO intend for you to re-read these to commit them to your mental arsenal)

- As a category or genre, a Romance is expected to be a relationship story.
- Men expect to see physical responses, women expect to see commitment.
- Cinematic romances must . . .
  1) Be character-driven, not plot driven stories
  2) Have structure of meeting, misunderstanding, separation, commitment
  3) Present consistent expression of emotional impact & angst
  4) Balance screen time between male & female leads
  5) Incorporate subplots/minor characters/environment only impacting couple
  6) Depict LOVE scenes, not sex scenes
- On screen lovers must be seen moving through the "Twelve Steps of Intimacy" visually demonstrating trust, acceptance and permission the audience believes.
- The physical signaling in the romance will be true to values of the culture and era.
- Both Hero and Heroine will visually depict both "Outer Identity" of roles seen by the world and "Inner Essence" of precious internal desires shown only in private and the true lover will want the beloved because of the Essence, not the Identity.
- When the Romance is the central plot, the visualization of the relationship moves up the rising tension of the Relationship Plane with crucial moments pacing the story.
- Controlled pacing demands awareness of how close together you depict your "Pull-Push reveals."

- Character Profiling allows you to flesh out, understand and orchestrate your characters.
- Character Profiles need to cover general history/background, personal preferences/influences, and forces driving the character in the current story.
- Romantic Heroes need to be Alpha-Beta, motivated and confident yet vulnerable.
- Romantic Heroines need to be Beta-Alpha, motivated toward pride and empowerment.
- Every other cast member has to have a direct influence on the Hero-Heroine relationship in a romance.
- A romantic screenplay needs to deliver sex in the Twelve Steps of Intimacy, the titillation of inference, the unspoken assumptions.
- Violence in a romantic screenplay should be delivered in "increments of jeopardy" pitting a willing main character with a worthy-of-risk goal against a high stakes threat resulting in the inference or actual harm to character well-being.

IN THE BEGINNING

If a couple is happily united at the outset of a romantic story where can the story go? The relationship would have to be torn asunder and rebuilt or other relationships with other partners evolve. Of course, those are possibilities. However, screenplays, like short stories, need to grab the reader by the throat and involve them immediately in character dilemma and desire. There is no time to leisurely reveal the dark undertow of problems for these "happy people in the happy village." Some novelists prefer to build interest in the character before tackling what is challenging them and their real story doesn't begin until Chapter Two. Most editors will tell them to delete Chapter One and get to the meat of the story, dropping in the set-up characterization as the story progresses and that information about the character is needed.

Screenplays are even more demanding. Put the characters at risk of high stakes gain or loss within the first 10 minutes/10 pages of the script. Reveal the strengths and flaws of the main character and that soul-deep goal that drives him or her to take the risks, to charge ahead into life-changing actions. It does not have to do with the male and female meeting but has to do with sucking in the audience to care enough about the Main Character that they will want him or her to meet the match.

Since this is a romance and Hollywood wants sex and violence, how do you insert budding awareness from the introductory scene on? Visually hint at the internal **Essence** of the main character who will be the one who changes internally, the one who arcs because of the events of the story. You also have to depict the external **Identity** or role of this character, the "who" they are in the world. The audience/reader has to be sucked into the demands and problems of that role from the moment the character shows up. Chaos, turmoil, crisis have to depict this character in action. Yet you want to deliver a glimpse of the essence yearning for fulfillment. From squeaky clean, fun teen movies through intensely emotional and dark adult thrillers, you must show the main character noticing, wanting, needing a mate.

WHEN THE TWO MEET

Re-examine Howard's Twelve Steps. With those in mind, consider what you want to see happen when the male and female encounter one another the first time. Of course, you will not move from Step One to Twelve within two scenes . . . . if your story is to be built on more than acting on physical attraction, the lust-of-the-moment. FOOLS RUSH IN was about the consequences of that experience which in turn caused the ultimate commitment and the ending when the two welcomed their child into the world and accepted their need and love for one another. As a rule, most relationships are the more common, cautionary exploration.

Even the inverted relationship story in FOOLS demonstrated what is called the **"Pull-Push" of sexual tension**, the recognition of attraction followed immediately by the rejection of willingness to act upon it. "I want her, but I don't want to be trapped."

The key here is to show both parties 1) feeling that pull, 2) wanting the partner, but 3) rejecting/pushing away involvement by focusing on other story complications (out of the sub-plots). That process puts the caring audience into the anticipation mode. They know the couple will get together but the wondering about "how" that will happen keeps them questing with the lovers.

CONCEPTS OF BODY LANGUAGE

No discussion of describing meetings and signaling can avoid the intricate world of body language. This is a tight wire for the screenwriter to walk.

Two people make the ultimate decision about characterization on screen: the actor and the director. However, the insightful screenwriter can provide a distinct framework by choreographing specific body language that translates a message. Ever heard the adage "We want movies, not talkies" and wondered what that meant? It boils down to "Replace intent and content of dialogue with a visual or a character movement wherever possible."

Some body language is subtle and taken for granted, but others are blatant. A father-son argument erupts. The son steps close to the father (aggressive invasion of personal space, a subtlety) and the father starts to slap the kid but stops, his hand shaking in mid-air (a blatant depiction of anger controlled). The actors and director might add the father's eyes tearing and the boy's grunt of disgust as he turns away . . . or the screenwriter could write that in if the purpose of the scene was to depict how the mature man reins in his temper and how little the son understands the father's motivation.

DELIVERY AND RECEPTION

Motivation is the "why" of a person's action and is the key concept of a character's mannerisms and **delivery** of movement. The writer must decide what motivates movement in each scene then choreograph only what is important. Never, ever micro-manage, micro-choreograph everything. Obviously actors and directors do not need that and it ultimately is viewed as the sign of an amateur writer.

Motivation of delivery results in intent as known to the character moving.

The second component in the use of body language is **reception** or how it is perceived. In the example scene the arrogant son had been deliberately baiting the father, pushing him toward a physical response, something he has never seen from the man. He receives the man's control instead of violence and perceives it as weakness or cowardice.

The motivation of reception's expectation results in content as perceived by the observer of the action.

As the writer you must be aware of both the party **delivery** and the party **reception,** the motivation-reaction, the cause-effect flow.

BASICS OF OBSERVATION

Some "Primary Affect" facial expressions are cross-cultural such as joy, fear, anger, pain. Body language allows the actor and director to delve deeper into the psyche of the story character.

When creating character profiles, the writer begins to envision this living, breathing person. From that character's history the writer grows an understanding of what motivates the character. Thus the writer can predict response and choreograph movement.

When will the character's stance appear dominant (subtlety of confident strength) and when will it become submissive (subtlety of trusting, accepting, or fearful)? When would the character make offensive/aggressive moves or how would he look when defensive? Is the body movement instinctive (such as jumping when startled or chugging water when dying of thirst) or learned (stoic tolerance of pain or embarrassment)? Does the character's innate personality make them impetuous/thoughtless of consequences or does the young warrior remember boot camp drilling and move deliberately?

Carefully examine the character's history in your profile to identify triggers that could change the inner character's willingness to move differently. In the concept of the Anxiety Curve, blank apathy exists at one end and thoughtless panic at the other. Most of us function at the apex between the two, swinging a little in each direction according to how we cope with daily stresses. With this in mind, think of a young woman who was gang raped as a vibrant, cheerful teenager. The traumatic experience has mentally beaten her self-concept so that she rarely maintains eye contact with anyone, her head is always down, her shoulders slumped, her hands either limp or fidgeting. But, her car has broken down, a drunken man stops to check it out, and puts her up against the car. Two options: surrender or attack. How do you visually depict the change in her demeanor? Eyes focused, teeth clenched as she juts out her chin, shoulders up and back as she takes a deep breath in preparation for battle, and hands clawed. The apathetic wimp has become an aggressive tigress. Is this not better visual film technique than having her scream "I *will not* be raped again!"

HEAD-TO-TOE MANTRA

Law enforcement training teaches officers to observe body language for survival's sake. The writer can use the same lessons, not in micro-choreography but when delivery is important to make a story point about a character.

Eyes-Body-Head-Hands. That's the litany you want to recite. Officers are trained to take in the picture all at once to sense the person's intent in the first crucial moments of the confrontation. Their lives depend on it.

EYES-BODY-HEAD-HANDS.

"Eyes are the windows to the soul." Well, that's debatable. Some say they are simply instruments of sight surrounded by highly sensitive nerves and muscles that can "frame" the eyes with expression. The one concrete is "Where is the person looking?" Eye-to-eye contact? Glancing nervously about? Deliberately avoiding something? **Eyes deliver intent.**

Is the body positioning offensive? Knees bent ready to move, arms controlled vs. relaxed. Or is the wife hunched, as if guarding from future assault? **Positioning signals offensive or defensive movement.**

Is the head positioning casual, relaxed or up and arrogant, challenging? Think about military training. Attention! Stand tall, shoulders back, head up. Be proud, be ready, be focused. **The head position is the indicator of self-awareness** in this circumstance.

To an officer, the eyes, body, and head won't kill you . . . but the hands will. So what about your character's hands? How do they habitually use them? Confident movement? Hesitant? Gentle, always willing to stroke? What subtle message is depicted from the character to the audience's mind? **Hands are the "receptors" to the encounter.**

PERSONAL TERRITORY

Dr. Edward Hall coined the term "Proxemics" to describe our perceptions of personal space and territorial zoning. Each of the spaces or zones has limits of "close" and "far" which are quite logical. The four zone Proxemics classifications are 1) Intimate, 2) Personal, 3) Social, and 4) Public. Surprisingly the limits of our own self-awareness are taken for granted, unless invaded. Now you need to translate your character's reaction into a visual message of his perceptions.

THE FOUR ZONE PROXEMICS CLASSIFICATIONS ARE 1) INTIMATE, 2) PERSONAL, 3) SOCIAL, AND 4) PUBLIC.

Moving from far to close, the **Intimate Zone** means touching of skin, invasion (medical procedures), and insinuation (possession of kissing and sex). The **Personal Zone** is a step or two back where one can maintain eye contact and carry on a conversation. Close can be an aggressive police interrogation and far could be possession of a corner of an elevator. The **Social Zone** is the next step back where we can conduct a business exchange and where we find the most frequent examples of dominance (big executive desk) vs protection (dependence). The broadest zone is the **Public Zone** of cultural bonding and group identity. When discussing crowd control, law enforcement prefers a "loose crowd" (thus the concept of "safe capacity" in public buildings). Compact crowding frequently leads to tension and the ripple contagion of mob mentality. Thus how does the writer describe the movement of the background crowd, Social or Public Proximity? What happens to the crowd on a beach when there is a drowning victim brought to shore?

Stepping back to character motivation, think about how your character appears in moments of aggression or dominance as the zones are progressively invaded. What mannerisms change when the character is showing vulnerability or submissiveness to a higher authority? What is the body language of the "Big Man," be he taller and more physically fit or higher in the hierarchy of power at the moment? What personality type is this character, thus what is the predictable body language?

FIVE STEPS OF SEXUAL SIGNALING

This is the ultimate example of Delivery-Reception and it is played out in every singles bar or any other male-female environment you can imagine. It can be instinctive and it can be deliberate, but it is predictable and consistent.

First comes the "**Preparation Phase**" where body tension shifts to some habitual "preening," maybe the female fluffing the hair or the male rubbing his jaw. The protective side-view (least body visible) shifts to frontal view (subtle demonstration of vulnerability and willingness to be evaluated).

Secondly, the two parties **maintain eye contact longer than 30 seconds**. That's a long time, relatively speaking. Assessment and acceptance are being translated here.

Thirdly, one party makes an **invitational gesture or movement**, such as cocking the head, arching the eyebrows, or laugh. Next, upon approach the two parties exchange some verbal responses to pacify the other party and confirm that "I'm okay to talk to."

Finally, the two **move closer into the Personal Zone to exclude others**.

An important concept to keep in mind here is that whenever either party stops or omits a step, the flirtation stops, the "Sexual Connection" is broken, be it in the corporate world, at an elegant dinner, or on the bar scene. Be aware of how to choreograph the intrusion or attempts of others into your Main Characters awareness.

All of this analysis agrees with some of Linda Howard's Steps, yet it is a much more "entertaining" and educational exercise when people-watching at a crowded bar or a party where there are a lot of singles circulating or trolling.

THE ROLE OF KISSING AS TITILATION

Little has been written on kissing for romance writers to reference, but we frequently use this sensual tool. Why? Because Kissing is titillating without being biologically threatening. Sexual intercourse IS threatening because its fundamental purpose is change, to turn courtship into parenthood. Kissing merely tests the senses and readiness of the partners. It is a vital romantic element for screenwriters because it is visual.

> KISSING IS TITILLATING WITHOUT BEING BIOLOGICALLY THREATENING.

How do we use the act of kissing in romance? Of course, we can describe the choreographed components with physical sensations of sight, sound, smell, taste, touch. In a screenplay however, the "turn-on" of innuendo and the near-miss intention then reaction of the characters can make for a highly sensual scene both males and females in the audience will automatically "get."

The cerebral processing after the action becomes the internalization of the characters' immediate responses. On screen that inner turmoil must be related in subtle body language and facial expression. The question for the screenwriter is then "How much so I choreograph in the script and how much do I leave to the actors?" This has to come from how significant the response is to the evolution of the relationship. If it is important then the writer must briefly mention response. Otherwise, leave it up to the "chemistry" of the actors the director can see in the camera's eye.

Normally, the attracted people begin to analyze the emotional impact within and ultimately display of a logical or illogical exaggerated physical reaction. They note facial expression and body language in the other person, looking for signs of arousal. If those kinds of messages are pivotal to the forward movement of the relationship in the story, then brief depiction of each catalogued visual is warranted in the script for the audience's sake. The female looks at the male's lips or reaching hands that hesitate in uncertainty yet wanting to touch. The male looking at how her fast breathing lifts her breasts, the rapid pulse in her throat, her quivering sigh before she gains control. The writer is telling the director and actors this is important and must be seen by the audience.

And finally, the writer must use this "event" to move the story forward as a complication or to create a relationship question the audience wants answered. Will it lead to more "foreplay" or will both characters continue their denial? Episodic TV that has a floundering relationship as a hook for viewers plays off these titillating scenes all the time for a reason. They keep the audience involved and caring what happens as a consequence to that kiss.

STAGING THE KISS

Kissing implies acceptance, the primitive concept of physical vulnerability exposed to assault. The mouth with feral teeth gains access to another's body, be it lips, throat, or downward. Our job in romance is not to ravage as if the two participants are out of control, but to titillate and arouse by recreating the giving and the taking. We can do a better job when the picture is painted in stages. "Show, don't tell." And use all four steps of description, internalization, emotional impact, and story complication at each of the four stages!

"**Anticipation**" is the first stage when the partners become aware of the physical attraction of the other. Pheromones scent the air and nerve endings tingle. They catalog what they want from the other and look at what they want. That is where the screenwriting can focus the visuals for the collaborative director and actors. The characters must visual demonstrate either an emotional resistance or surrender. Either reaction will create a rise in story tension. The audience will live the anticipation phase with the characters.

"**Teasing**" begins stage two wherein the two participants actually invade one another's personal territory, collecting data with the senses, mentally testing their own readiness and the willingness of the partner, outwardly demonstrating desire, and moving the romance forward. Here is another opportunity for pacing the build to the kiss. The confident screenwriter does not belabor the visuals or the choreography. Describe those glimpses of character actions that will set the stage and create the on screen chemistry.

The third stage is the "**Act Itself**" and herein the romance writer's imagination takes flight and is guided solely by the characters motivation, history, and potential. The pacing of the physical choreography this stage, with the camera's eye cataloging snippets, the rapid fire play of emotional facial expressions, and the story demanding ultimate lip to lip hungry commitment, sometimes followed by mouths opening and the invasion of the tongues. Always? Ah, innuendo can do as much for story tension as blatant clasping of body to body and dialogue stating need. And must it be fast and hot? Of course not. A brush of lips or tender movement back and forth can create as much sensuality and be just as soul-shattering as uninhibited abandonment, depending on the storyteller's characters. Think of the comparison between a young couple's first tentative acceptance and the "consuming" kiss between Lancelot and Guinevere in FIRST KNIGHT.

Finally, in the "**After-Glow**" stage, the characters relive the choreography, demonstrating wonder, fear, the shiver of emotion, the anticipation of how this will affect the future and thus the story.

The fine art of choreographing the essence of kissing in a screenplay can create incredible motivation for the chemistry between two actors. They must see the sizzle on the page they can ignite into a memorable, iconic love scene of innuendo, not intercourse. Hot on-screen kissing and titillation of the camera's perception can infer consummation. Bottom line: Your careful, succinct description and purposeful placement should enhance both the characters' and audience's experience!

PAY ATTENTION

Now that you have all these Body Language tools, try this exercise: Rent your favorite movie. Turn off the volume and describe the major story elements and character emotions you see delivered through body language.

Remember, "Write movies, not talkies." The only way to do that is to consider what dialogue is absolutely vital and what dialogue can be delivered instead through body language. Know your characters well enough to use their body language to deliver their vital emotions visually, but never to the point of micro-choreography. Play around with the juxtaposition of "Primary Affect" facial expressions and the character's actual body language.

COORDINATING THE SIGNALING AND THE 12-STEPS

Though the assumption is that any screenwriter reading this book is familiar with the structure of a screenplay, now is the time to review the use of the use of the Paradigm Form and the Definitions of its parts. You will do an "overlay" of the steps of a romance onto this basic framework.

USE OF THE PARADIGM

After you are comfortable with the form, look at the Subplots section. See how the lines go entirely across the story? ONE of these subplots (possibly the first line) should be labeled "Love Story." Every time either the hero or heroine encounters the other, you will place a dot (.) for that scene. When the encounter **heightens** the sexual tension between them, you place a "T" representing the THREAT/SEXUAL TENSION the characters visually demonstrate in that scene. Do you see how you can create a visual tool for pacing the evolution of the romance? Too many dots with T's too close together and you have clumps of scene sequences without forward story movement as a whole. Too many long blank spaces (while other subplots are being seen) mean you have gone too long without calling the audience's attention to the romance!

Which of Howard's Steps are subtle, quick movements in your story, thus just dots and which Steps are blatant, sensual scenes filled with Sexual Tension of signaling thus a "T"on your form?

As you think about how you want your romance to unfold and the timing of the couple's interaction, look up at the main points or sign-posts of the linear story. Have you paced the relationship scenes or do you envision the timing of the story events to align with the life-changing Plot Point I at the end of Act I . . . the "New Life" of Act II being keyed to the exploration of the new relationship or the questing for the relationship . . . the Mid-Point Epiphany (where awareness and focus changes) as crucial to the relationship exploding into something more powerful . . . the heart-crushing Plot II where failure threatens but motivates the action of Act III . . . and there the Climactic events creating the survival of the male-female unit. . . and, finally, the Commitment Scene where the two actually become the committed unit to the world facing the future together.

If you find yourself edging toward predictability, ratchet up the stress in the characters because that will also be experienced by the audience. For example: Remember that the build to the Dark Moment has to be mounting tension and risk, mounting jeopardy . . . then the tension becomes even worse until the release-valve of the Climax in Act III. The audience has to be constantly worried about not only the lives of the main characters but the "torn asunder" aspect of the relationship. Will they survive to become a unit? And never write this all in an over-the-top melodramatic manner but focus on the risky events the characters endure. Do not ever describe or choreograph the emotional displays the actors can deduce on their own throughout this process. You are the explaining writer and they are the performing actors.

GENERAL CONSIDERATIONS IN SEXUAL PLOTTING

No one but no one wants the romance evolution to be predictable or "cookie cutter" perfect, yet you have all these prescribed "timed events" that must be created. You can **avoid predictability by careful consideration of:**

1. Giving glimpses and hints,
2. Varying the revelation of one character's awareness in comparison to the other's,
3. Providing the perspective of the subplot/supporting character cast as they view the two interacting,
4. Creating "kinky" or unexpected sexual triggers (every time the heroine sees ice cream melting down a cone, she gets turned on or any time she innocently brushes his skin with a fingertip, he has to head for a cold shower) and
5. Don't forget the concept of Repeat Images (daisies in YOU'VE GOT MAIL, crowds & watchers in CHASING LIBERTY, political campaigns in FIRST DAUGHTER, ice skating lifts in THE CUTTING EDGE).

From your Character Profiles you know the value system and personal philosophies of the hero and heroine. Of course, you know your own. As you write--and especially when you revise--pay careful attention to the **consistency of those values**. If virginity is important (for any number of reasons) to the character at the beginning, a sudden decision to accept a sexual partner would be a major scripting flaw. Motivation-Reaction. Set up your inherent values and re-examine how you either uphold those values or the characters gradually change.

Another hint for achieving reality is simply to **be realistic**. I'm not addressing graphic pornography here. I mean as you research your character types and roles and the background of your story do not make the mistake of depicting behavior that would violate any of those roles in real life. We live in an age of lots and lots of STD's, but so did the Victorians and the Romans. Has the presence of STD's ever prevented promiscuity? Nope. Sexual desire with pheromones saturating the air and exchanged "do-me" looks is as old as our species. But, the comfort level of your characters needs to be consistent with their personalities, histories and motivation to take risks.

There's one more factor: fantasies, a huge game a storyteller gets to play. When you are creating your characters and creating your plot, when you are thinking about how you want their relationship to evolve, **fantasize** to the "nth" degree. You can always ratchet things back a bit in the revision process, but you owe it to yourself to have fun with the "What if's" on that first draft!

A MOVIE ANALYSIS

The Romance Genre section of this book's Part One provides the analysis of the Action-Adventure/Fantasy Romance AVATAR (Page 182). Though it was not James Cameron's specific intent to write to the Relationship Plane and Signaling of a romance, he did it quite well. You will also find the analysis of ROMANCING THE STONE (Page 192). Under the Western Genre the romance is noted in THE MAN FOM SNOWY RIVER (Page 215) and a solid romance is charted in the Historical Genre 's analysis of THE LAST OF THE MOHICANS (Page 235).

* * * * *

ROMANCE Chapter 7 Exercises

Exercise R7a: Look at your Main Plot and Subplot progressions. Where could you insert sexually tense scenes to complicate the relationship evolution and create natural challenges that must be overcome by the two characters? Would this feel contrived or logical to you?

Exercise R7b: Re-examine the Relationship Plane. How have you woven looking-touching-kissing into the pacing of your envisioned Love Story? Have you got a "What If" list of other possibilities?

Exercise R7c: Where do your lead couple actually recognize they are courting and want "Forever"??? Do you intend to write a specific seduction scene and, if so, where do you think it will satisfy the audience's questing? Will it be predictable or surprise even the two characters? Note: Do not rush or summarize what the audience wants to experience more slowly and pay attention to the signpost events as pivotal changes in what is demanded of the characters.

Exercise R7d: What do you still see as the appropriate "showing" of the relationship in Climax and Commitment for your story?

Exercise R7e: Make a "Fantasy List" of what you would "like" to see happen between these two. Now, pick one or two things that you can use in the script.

ROMANCE CHAPTER 8

Considerations: Time-Place and Theme

Review

(Yes, I DO intend for you to re-read these to commit them to your mental arsenal)

- As a category or genre, a Romance is expected to be a relationship story.
- Men expect to see physical responses, women expect to see commitment.
- Cinematic romances must. . . .
  1) Be character-driven, not plot driven stories
  2) Have structure of meeting, misunderstanding, separation, commitment
  3) Present consistent expression of emotional impact & angst
  4) Balance screen time between male & female leads
  5) Incorporate subplots/minor characters/environment only impacting couple
  6) Depict love scenes, not sex scenes
- On screen lovers must be seen moving through the "Twelve Steps of Intimacy" visually demonstrating trust, acceptance and permission the audience believes.
- The physical signaling in the romance will be true to values of the culture and era.
- Both Hero and Heroine will visually depict both "Outer Identity" of roles seen by the world and "Inner Essence" of precious internal desires shown only in private and the true lover will want the beloved because of the Essence, not the Identity.
- When the Romance is the central plot, the visualization of the relationship moves up the rising tension of the Relationship Plane with crucial moments pacing the story.
- Controlled pacing demands awareness of how close together you depict your "Pull-Push reveals."

- Character Profiling allows you to flesh out, understand and orchestrate your characters.
- Character Profiles need to cover general history/background, personal preferences/influences, and forces driving the character in the current story.
- Romantic Heroes need to be Alpha-Beta, motivated and confident yet vulnerable.
- Romantic Heroines need to be Beta-Alpha, motivated toward pride and empowerment.
- Every other cast member has to have a direct influence on the Hero-Heroine relationship in a romance.
- A romantic screenplay needs to deliver sex in the Twelve Steps of Intimacy, the titillation of inference, the unspoken assumptions.
- Violence in a romantic screenplay should be delivered in "increments of jeopardy" pitting a willing main character with a worthy-of-risk goal against a high stakes threat resulting in the inference or actual harm to character well-being.
- Consistently utilize the "Pull-Push" of sexual tension, the recognition of attraction followed immediately by the rejection of willingness to act upon it.
- Pay attention to the pacing and timing of the Sexual Signaling throughout the romantic screenplay.
- Avoid predictability, be consistent in character values, and be realistic WHILE playing out your own fantasies.

FUNDAMENTALS OF TIME-PLACE AND ROMANTIC THEME

Two concepts need to be carefully considered when in the planning stage of a romantic screenplay, whether it is intended to be "sweet" inference or erotically sensual. They will dictate the story setting and the thrust of the story. Here are their definitions:

Story Time-Place: The **where** and **when** of a story stages or "frames" the characters and their plot with reader/audience immediately thinking "environment."

Romantic Theme: The classification of the "kind" of relationship story also stages the characters and their plot providing another reader/audience expectation element.

Both of these concepts have been the fodder for many critics of the romance genre, yet they continue to attract an avid audience. I will agree that they suggest some predictability. On the other hand, they also challenge the writer to reveal unique and fresh circumstances within those parameters. It is that challenge to tweak and twist predictability that gives me a smug smile when I discuss the topic with literary or cinematic elitists.

SETTING'S TIME-PLACE CONSIDERATION

A common division of romantic stories is:

1. Contemporary: Occurs within past 20 years up until present
2. Historical: Within documented past events
3. Regional: Specific to a particular place, country, culture
4. Western: Setting in frontier, frequently Old West
5. Medieval: Middle Ages feudal period with castles, knights, serfs
6. Regency: Early 1800's England and Europe
7. Scottish: Scotland & Scots from ancient times to present
8. Paranormal: Ghost/Vampire/Werewolf/Time-Travel
9. Futuristic: Sci-Fi/Fantasy quality of future projection

Obviously, your descriptions of place, props and costuming, the mores and values of your characters, dialogue and characterization back story will all require careful research and meticulous rendering. Do not fall into the trap of thinking that you do not have to do this because you are merely providing the blueprint and the studio will have researchers, prop masters, costumers who must uncover authentic details. Of course, you will not be describing in as much detail as a novelist, but if you have to name something or use a prop, do so with researched authority.

> IN THE BEGINNING WAS THE WORD AND THE WORD WAS . . . WRITTEN BY THE SCREENWRITER.

In the beginning was the Word and the Word was . . . written by the screenwriter. All of the details inherent to Time-Place are your responsibilities. Do not be so arrogant to think you can get away with vague wording. The quality of your story will rest in the authenticity of your detail . . . as well as the depth of your characterizations.

THE LITERARY ESSENCE OF THEME

On the Paradigm just below Story Line (Log Line) is "Statement of Purpose." When writing it you will include the phrase "I want to prove . . . ." In any story this is the "point" you are trying to prove through the experiences of your characters and it will provide your thematic spine. It will be the star that guides every scene, the inclusion and exclusion of cast members, the glimpses vs. depth of character, back story, subplot. It can be simple or complex, but it must be the one single concept your story impresses on your reader/audience.

THE DIFFERENCE OF "ROMANTIC THEME"

Harking back to predictability of the romance genre that you must grapple with and defy, here is one list of the "kinds" of romantic stories in our culture:

1. Innocent being initiated
2. Cynical, hardened becoming vulnerable
3. Marriage of convenience
4. Forced marriage
5. May-December Story
6. Social/Cultural/Professional barriers
7. Shared adventure
8. Rediscovery of an old love

Various movies had to have flashed through your mind as you read this list. And you should be asking, "How can it be that simplified?" Well, long before our time, an astute Frenchman named Polti analyzed Greek and Shakespearian stories and concluded that there are only 36 basic stories that can be told. Many have challenged his assertion but have not yet identified a short story, novel, stage play or film that could not be found on his list. In fact, many sophisticated stories even include more than one with a main plot and an influential subplot. You will find the original list in Appendix F.

"There are no new stories." So, how can Hollywood keep saying they want "fresh" stories? One element that you can give them: unique characters living those stories, responding to circumstances in heart-rending, courageous ways that take the reader/audience along on their adventure.

Remember, in romance the audience knows how the story will end. They want to go along on the ride of **how the couple gets there**!

Again, look over the analysis of AVATAR in Part One's Chapter 9 (Page __) and apply the above concepts.

BEING UNIQUE

Producers like known entities that have been box office hits and at least earned out the investment of the production. However, they want "fresh" takes and are always looking for a trend-setter, not a copy cat script.

You avoid any trend in Hollywood by writing the story of your soul, one with a broader appeal. For example: Tweaking a limited appeal paranormal love story into a kick-ass credible action story that makes the hero and heroine stretch beyond the predictable. Broad-appeal spec scripts have a better chance of getting read and passed up the food chain. The key is to know exactly where your story concept is unique from everyone else's and where it can stand toe-to-toe with other Action-Fantasy stories. Think of romance scenes from LORD OF THE RINGS.

That comparison-contrast is the reason to scan the http://www.IMDb.com website (Internet Movie Database) to gather information about other movies in production or even produced in the past in your "theme" area or that utilized any of the elements you incorporate into your script. This will give you the specific ammunition the answer when somebody asks "Would you say this is similar in any way to TWILIGHT or any other vampire movie?" . . . or "Are these fantasy threads like the fairy stuff in LORD OF THE RINGS or HARRY POTTER?" As the creator, you want to demonstrate that you understand the market, as well as your script.

Let's say you find the people who like the kind of stuff you write. All of the elements being given to you here will prepare you to discuss your movie and characters in the comparison-contrast game.

When doing your analysis think in details. The location, characterizations and roles of the characters are unique. Think whatever is different about your story, not in the general terms. It's a romance. The females dragging their males to this know it will end up in a successful commitment in the end. In the atmosphere of our modern culture, we know the female will be independent and no one's doormat. Yadda, yadda. Yes, those are the generalities that are predictable . . . so what are the differences in your story? How is this genre of story different from STAR WARS? How is your heroine different from other heroines? How is your story not melodramatic?

* * * * *

ROMANCE Chapter 8 Exercises

Exercise R8a: State your Time-Place by specifically.

1) List the locations you will need to describe
2) What props will be pertinent to this Time-Place?
3) Costuming considerations unique here?

Exercise R8b: Summarize research already done or make a list of topics you still need to research. (And, yes, authenticity is your job, especially in a spec script).

Exercise R8c: Write your "Statement of Purpose." Look at your romance Log Line and post both above your computer for duration of this script writing.

Exercise R8d: State your Polti theme and your romantic theme. Now, list five ways your story will vary this theme to make your script unique!

Note: The point of analysis is to make you think and make deliberate choices. When you understand the intellectual nuances of your writing, you are in control. Then you can intelligently and confidently explain the underlying power and meaning of your story to the potential agent or producer.

ROMANCE CHAPTER 9

THE Romance as Main Plot or Subplot

Review

(Yes, I DO intend for you to re-read these to commit them to your mental arsenal)

- As a category or genre, a Romance is expected to be a relationship story.
- Men expect to see physical responses, women expect to see commitment.
- Cinematic romances must . . .
  1) Be character-driven, not plot driven stories
  2) Have structure of meeting, misunderstanding, separation, commitment
  3) Present consistent expression of emotional impact & angst
  4) Balance screen time between male & female leads
  5) Incorporate subplots/minor characters/environment only impacting couple
  6) Depict love scenes, not sex scenes
- On screen lovers must be seen moving through the "Twelve Steps of Intimacy" visually demonstrating trust, acceptance and permission the audience believes.
- The physical signaling in the romance will be true to values of the culture and era.
- Both Hero and Heroine will visually depict both "Outer Identity" of roles seen by the world and "Inner Essence" of precious internal desires shown only in private and the true lover will want the beloved because of the Essence, not the Identity.
- When the Romance is the central plot, the visualization of the relationship moves up the rising tension of the Relationship Plane with crucial moments pacing the story.
- Controlled pacing demands awareness of how close together you depict your "Pull-Push reveals."

- Character Profiling allows you to flesh out, understand and orchestrate your characters.
- Character Profiles need to cover general history/background, personal preferences/influences, and forces driving the character in the current story.
- Romantic Heroes need to be Alpha-Beta, motivated and confident yet vulnerable.
- Romantic Heroines need to be Beta-Alpha, motivated toward pride and empowerment.
- Every other cast member has to have a direct influence on the Hero-Heroine relationship in a romance.
- A romantic screenplay needs to deliver sex in the Twelve Steps of Intimacy, the titillation of inference, the unspoken assumptions.
- Violence in a romantic screenplay should be delivered in "increments of jeopardy" pitting a willing main character with a worthy-of-risk goal against a high stakes threat resulting in the inference or actual harm to character well-being.
- Consistently utilize the "Pull-Push" of sexual tension, the recognition of attraction followed immediately by the rejection of willingness to act upon it.
- Pay attention to the pacing and timing of the Sexual Signaling throughout the romantic screenplay.
- Avoid predictability, be consistent in character values, and be realistic while laying out your own fantasies.
- Carefully consider Story Time-Place and the Romantic Theme to be sure you are writing to the expectations of your audience.
- A Statement of Purpose will provide you a solid guideline for writing every scene, every character, every speech as providing evidence for the point your story is trying to prove.

INCORPORATING ROMANTIC ELEMENTS

Quite simply, some stories must focus on a series of events, a main plot, that is not a romance and the relationship story you want to unfold will function as a complication to that series of events. The romance becomes one of the lesser subplots. That's okay.

However, if you intend to write a strictly relationship story as the main plot then you must understand the expectations of the film industry. Here's the Review's second point: "Men expect to see physical responses, women expect to see commitment." So, you must ask yourself if your main plot and genre writing are essentially targeted at the male audience or at the female audience. The next "genre" consideration draws from Point 13 and its "titillation of inference" and "unspoken assumptions." So, do you want this to be a sweet G-rated film? And, finally, how does a romance play in a high-concept (intense) "Box-Office Hit?"

Each of these four genre categories has different plot progression expectations for romance as a main plot and romance as a subplot.

A Man's Movie . . .wherein audience expects to see physical responses

1. Main Plot: Male action, power, image (TRUE LIES)
2. Subplot: Sexual attraction, compliment, need (SPEED)

A Woman's "Chick Flick Movie . . . wherein audience expects to see commitment

1. Main Plot: Meet, misunderstand, separate, commitment (PRETTY WOMAN)
2. Subplot: Impacts main plot, sexual tension, commitment (TEA WITH MUSSOLINI)

A "G-Rated" Family Movie . . .wherein sexuality is only inferred and assumed

1. Main Plot: Communication, values, child/family commitment (SOUND OF MUSIC)
2. Subplot: Complication to main plot, nuance, family commitment (POLLYANNA)

A Box Office HIT . . . wherein intense, high concept story has universal appeal

1. Main Plot: Interwoven/Interdependent Action & Conditional Commitment (TITANIC)
2. Subplot: Impacts main, sexual tension, commitment (STAR WARS)

Did you note that in the "Man's Movie" the relationship did not necessarily end in commitment and in the Main Plot of the Box Office Hit the commitment was conditional? These play to male desire for ambiguity, that playboy fantasy of "having it all." Not for a minute am I saying that males in the real world do not want hearth and the one woman at his side into the "golden years." But the primal instinct of the male animal is "spread it around" to assure the continuation of the species. That has nothing to do with the more civilized awareness of conscience, values, selectivity. It just is the "nature of the Alpha beast." You need to be aware of the story elements that play to that primal male fantasy. This is another "That's okay" concept, if that is the story your heart of heart tells you to write!

RESEARCHING YOUR DEMOGRAPHICS (When you are ready)

Discovering the demographics of who would come to see your film is a matter of researching the entertainment industry on a regular basis (which few people have the time to do) and understanding exactly who your appeal would reach. You get a feel for "who" goes to see CARZ 2, TRANSFORMERS, HANGOVER, etc. etc. You get a feel for who is most likely to NOT see particular movies. In general, the 18-25 yr old males would see a romance film because their dates want to see it. Just consider if someone would go by themselves to see something. Realistically, not "hopefully." There's your demographics.

Studio personnel and agency personnel are paid to keep on top of this information and all the surrounding stats. So, there is no one place you can go to as a measuring stick. You have to rely on your gut. Of course, you won't need to do that until you are ready to pitch the movie. Per the urging of UCLA Film Department professors like Lew Hunter, you will not want to do any pitching until you have written five scripts. Five scripts will have given you the practical skills to understand the craft. One script does not a screenwriter make. When you have five and have gone back and polished each to diamond brightness, you start worrying about your demographics for your pitch to an agent or a production studio . . .

HOLLYWOOD'S FAVORITE: THE ROMANTIC COMEDY

There can be humor sprinkled throughout a drama, but in the end it is focused on tension and jeopardy to life and limb. Comedy, on the other hand, relies on 1) set-up, 2) expectation, and 3) reversal. The chain of events makes you smile and feel light-hearted. The circumstances can be serious, but the events flow with the anticipation of warm fuzzies, non-life-threatening confrontations and upbeat resolutions.

Here are explanations of two approaches to the Romantic Comedy, "The 7 Beats for Romantic Comedy" and "Writing the Romantic Comedy," both from Billy Mernit in *Writing the Romantic Comedy*.

Billy Mernit's first book is an in-depth look at that type of cinematic story. His approach to the Romantic Comedy in the "The 7 Beats for Romantic Comedy" aligns perfectly with the Plot Paradigm (and Romance's Relationship Plane, Appendix N). Here is my interpretation/explanation of his approach:

The 7 Beats for Romantic Comedy by Billy Mernit

(Note: This concept builds around the Three-Act structure, simply shifting the main points to fit a romantic comedy and Mernit's terminology/semantics.)

1. Set-up (the chemical equation)
2. Catalyst (the cute meet)
3. First Turning Point (a sexy complication)
4. Mid-Point (the hook)
5. Second Turning Point (the swivel)
6. Climax (the relationships' dark moment)
7. Resolution (joyful defeat)

1. Set-up's chemical equation: Scene sequence of events identifying both the exterior Identity and interior Essence conflicts. After the opening scene it tells the audience about the lead character and what is lacking in that character's life.

2. Catalyst's cute meet: Event that brings the man-and-woman together AND into conflict, irrevocably changing both their lives. A "good" romantic comedy makes the meeting genially meaningful. It resonates and sets the hook in the audience's imagination.

3. Turning Point's sexy complication: The ending of Act One event that has male and female "thinking" of the other, thus the balance of the story is their new life together. This event is a startling development that defines the character goal, making the internal conflict of the two people drive their external actions. Think of this Plot Point II as a kind of explosion forcing awareness and changing the two people.

4. Mid-Point's hook: An intense heightening of sexual tension and emotional involvement, implicating the relationship's outcome and creating higher stakes awareness of what is to be lost or gained. Blatant depiction of story theme.

5. Second Turning Point's swivel: At the end of Act II, this is the event that jeopardizes the protagonist's chance to succeed at his/her goal and is the main character's "point of no return" in the internal conflict, the character arc. The only option is for the character to take action to either a) choose love over his/her original goal or b) sacrifice love to get the goal. There's the dilemma, but, of course, since this is a romance, the choice will be to choose love).

6. Climax's dark moment: The consequences of the "swivel" decision create an intense confrontation where private motivations are revealed and relationship as well as worthy goals are on the verge of being lost.

7. Resolution's joyful defeat: The Relationship wins with the reconciliation and re-affirmation of the primal importance of the two-as-one, sometimes with the personal sacrifice of the main character's external goal.

Walk this 7-Beat Structure through any of your favorite romantic comedies. By about the fifth film you will begin "seeing" the concepts without list in hand. Your mind will look for them.

DISCUSSION OF *WRITING THE ROMANTIC COMEDY* BY BILLY MERNIT

Mernit points out "In romantic comedy, the 'A' story or main focus of the movie is the relationship between its romantic protagonists and the 'B' story won't be obtained without that romance's existence. Ex: Every subplot in SHAKESPEARE IN LOVE stems from the love affair between Will and Viola. The show goes on only because they go on; passion fuels every conflict. The couple is at the core of this comedic story, so we call it a romantic comedy.

"The classic three-act structure is usually defined in terms of a single protagonist who is trying to obtain a goal. In ANALYZE THIS, the shrink helps the gangster overcome a phobia, but the shrink's romance (while a catalyst for conflict) is ultimately not an essential story element.

1. CONFLICT: The hero takes on a problem
2. CRISIS: The hero can't solve the problem
3. RESOLUTION: The hero solves the problem.

In a romantic comedy, the three-act structure is revised as a meet-lose-get formula involving two protagonists.

1. MEET: Girl and Boy have significant encounters.
2. LOSE: Girl and Boy are separated.
3. GET: Girl and Boy reunite

In romantic comedies, the real subject matter is the power of love. Love is not merely the catalyst for action in a romantic comedy; it's the shaper of the story arc. And in most cases, love itself is the antagonist. It's the force that the story's characters have to reckon with; they either succumb to love's power or reject it. Wrestling with love can force a character to grow or resist growth, but either way, love's effect on the central character is what drives the story.

Such complications in a romantic comedy, a series of stake-raising problems, arise from the characters' internal issues confronting the external obstacles. It's the thing that pushes the protagonist from the end-of-second-act turning point into the third act's resolution.

In a sense, one could restate the paradigm for a three-act structure in a romantic comedy:

1. CONFLICT: Love challenges the characters
2. CRISIS: The characters accept or deny love.
3. RESOLUTION: Love transforms the characters"

On Mernit's Blog at http://www.livingromcom.typepad.com/ he lists his favorite romantic comedy films from the distant past and from the modern era. Go there and see if you agree with his choices. And, while you are there, drink in some of his fantastic insights. Better yet, buy his book to dig more in depth.

* * * * *

ROMANCE Chapter 9 Exercises

Exercise R9a: To get ready for the final exercises in plotting your own screenplay (or rethinking your current WIP), identify:

1) the major classification (from the four provided) for your story
2) If your romance is Main Plot or Subplot in that classification

Exercise R9b: Is yours a drama or a romantic comedy? What makes it that?

Exercise R9c: Re-examine your concept of Character Arc. Who is your audience cheering for? Is this character the one who is the focus of your story? Does this person arc because of the relationship or despite it?

Exercise R9d: Write a list of five questions you still need answered to feel you understand writing the romantic screenplay!

ROMANCE CHAPTER 10

Plotting YOUR Romantic Screenplay

This entire chapter is going to be a kind of application-review-analysis challenge.

From the Fundamentals and Log Line . . .

- As a category or genre, a Romance is expected to be a relationship story.
- Men expect to see physical responses, women expect to see commitment.
- Cinematic romances must . . .
  1) Be character-driven, not plot driven stories
  2) Have structure of meeting, misunderstanding, separation, commitment
  3) Present consistent expression of emotional impact & angst
  4) Balance screen time between male & female leads
  5) Incorporate subplots/minor characters/environment only impacting couple
  6) Depict love scenes, not sex scenes

The most important focus at the start is to write a clarifying "Log Line." At this point you should be able to analyze your log line and anyone else's for the elements stated above. Coldly, clinically ask yourself "Would anyone reading this log line know it is a romance?' A Log Line is not meant to puzzle the reader, but to intrigue the reader and motivate that person to read the script (or watch the ultimate film).

From the Four Approaches . . .

- On screen lovers must be seen moving through the "Twelve Steps of Intimacy" visually demonstrating trust, acceptance and permission the audience believes.

- The physical signaling in the romance will be true to values of the culture and era.
- Both Hero and Heroine will visually depict both "Outer Identity" of roles seen by the world and "Inner Essence" of precious internal desires shown only in private and the true lover will want the beloved because of the Essence, not the Identity.
- When the Romance is the central plot, the visualization of the relationship moves up the rising tension of the Relationship Plane with crucial moments pacing the story.
- Controlled pacing demands awareness of how close together you depict your "Pull-Push reveals."

The primary point of a screenplay is to deliver a story in visuals. A screen writer must smoothly carry the reader/audience along on the journey of the two people, logically and unobtrusively 1) choreographing the 12 Steps of Intimacy and 2) depicting visual evidence of "Inner Essence" and "Outer Identity." When deciding the romance will be the Main Plot, the major points of the story progression will also be the major events in the couple's relationship. Quite simply, the relationship is the story.

QUITE SIMPLY, THE RELATIONSHIP IS THE STORY.

From Characterization . . .

- Character Profiling allows you to flesh out, understand and orchestrate your characters.
- Character Profiles need to cover general history/background, personal preferences/influences, and forces driving the character in the current story.
- Romantic Heroes need to be Alpha-Beta, motivated and confident yet vulnerable.
- Romantic Heroines need to be Beta-Alpha, motivated toward pride and empowerment.
- Every other cast member has to have a direct influence on the Hero-Heroine relationship in a romance.

Since romances are character-driven stories, profiling is a "necessary evil." When approached as an exercise in discovery, profiling characters can give you insights into the motivation of subsequent logical reactions to one another. Lew Hunter likes to lecture "Give your characters passion and they will give you plot!" So once you have established your strong, thoughtful hero and your questing-toward-empowerment heroine in the circumstance of your "Log Line" you will logically be able to identify the cast needed to contribute to and support your story.

From "Hollywood wants Sex and Violence" & Sexual Tension in Plotting . . .

- A romantic screenplay needs to deliver sex in the Twelve Steps of Intimacy, the titillation of inference, the unspoken assumptions.
- Violence in a romantic screenplay should be delivered in "increments of jeopardy" pitting a willing main character with a worthy-of-risk goal against a high stakes threat resulting in the inference or actual harm to character well-being.
- Consistently utilize the "Pull-Push" of sexual tension, the recognition of attraction followed immediately by the rejection of willingness to act upon it.
- Pay attention to the pacing and timing of the Sexual Signaling throughout the romantic screenplay.
- Avoid predictability, be consistent in character values, and be realistic while playing out your own fantasies.

By now you should have a definitive handle on how you want these two people to interact as the audience feels the pull of their attraction and the discomforts of the complications that push them apart. Your writing, your words on the page must deliver the cinematic Pull-and-Push of the relationship. Think significant jeopardy, worthy-of-risk goal, and sexual tension to prevent any possibility of encountering "the happy people of the happy village." Yeah, you should be sick of hearing that phrase enough to avoid it at all costs! Yet, you want your characters to be empathetic enough for the reader/audience to care and unique enough keep the interest high is "how" they will resolve their dilemmas.

From Time-Pace, Theme & Main Plot or Subplot . . .

- Carefully consider Story Time-Place and the Romantic Theme to be sure you are writing to the expectations of your audience.
- A Statement of Purpose will provide you a solid guideline for writing every scene, every character, every speech as providing evidence for the point your story is trying to prove.
- The four "kinds" of movies will dictate the amount of space and the elements of the romance you will depict: Man's Movie, Chick Flick, G-Rated Family Fare and Box Office Hit.
- The four "kinds" of movies require different sexual intensity and relationship focus in the romantic plot as either Main Plot or as Subplot and all are based on reader/targeted audience expectation.

The evolving romance industry has grown the various subgenre following who come to the stories of choice with definitive expectations. A writer has to understand those expectations and meet them or fail to capture the discerning audience. Once the core story elements are clarified, the writer can formulate a Statement of Purpose that will provide the depth and diversity of human experience good writing, good storytelling requires. This is the point when a mature writer examines a gut-deep attitude about a subject and plots a story to make a point based on that attitude! The writer's passion then overflows into the vivid writing, action, dialogue of the story's characters. The romantic passion of the relationship story then is carefully choreographed to meet all the expectations of the "kind" of story that evolves.

Do you see how all of the information must be woven in to create a dynamic story, your unique story? Yes, there are basic story lines and the predictable "meeting, misunderstanding, separation, commitment" structure to a romance. But your how and the uniqueness that you instill into your characters will create a vivid cinematic template for all the other film industry professionals to build on!

HOW TO CLARIFIFY YOUR THEMATIC POINT

Never forget the concepts beyond fundamentals, some concepts that will truly give you powerful characters living memorable stories! In "Hollywood-speak" theme translates into the "spine" of your story. So, pull out your Statement of Purpose. Are you still having difficulty identifying the core theme driving your story?

IN "HOLLYWOOD-SPEAK" THEME TRANSLATES INTO THE "SPINE" OF YOUR STORY.

Here's a section from the 1-3-5 Concept of DMA (Donna Michelle Anderson, www.movieinabox.com) in her *The 1-3-5 Story Structure.* She is a "story analyst" or "reader" for the CEO's of several well known Hollywood production companies. In other words, she writes the make-or- break coverage on submissions. Her concept is:

Insert the **one word, one issue** (the same word for all three sentences) driving the theme of the screenplay, the one word completing these statements about what is experienced by the Main Character (thus identifying that character's internal Character Arc):

REJECT: I don't want ____________
EMBRACE: I do want ____________
SACRIFICE: I reluctantly give up ________ to make myself a better person and the world a better place.

Examples:
Tom Hanks in BIG. That character says:

I don't want "adulthood."
I do want "adulthood."
I will sacrifice "adulthood" so I can be a better person and the world a better place.

Any "Jay-Lo" Movie . . .

I don't want "intimacy."
I do want "intimacy."
I will sacrifice "intimacy" so I can be a better person and the world a better place.

Story consultant Michael Hauge recommends you complete one sentence to further clarify the driving concept behind your character's motivation, thus your story. Complete his suggested sentence to help focus your plotting and Character Arc, wherein the Main Character/Protagonist says:

I'll do whatever it takes to ____________, but don't ask me to ____________ because that's not me.

Do you see the correlation of theme driving the story and Character Arc that happens because of the story? Does it make you think of plot twists and turns you can create to "test" your Main Character's resolve? Does it give you ideas of where to make your character question their own motivation and perhaps change priorities?

A "typical" western hero statement (LAST OF THE MOHICANS), Nathanial says:

I'll do anything it takes to save Cora, but not become a helpless prisoner because that's not me.

Nathaniel's Character Arc becomes:

I don't want cultured society's mores. (Rejects militia recruitment)

I do want cultured society's mores. (Embraces Ft. William battle to be with Cora)

I will sacrifice cultured society's mores to make me a better person and the world a better place. (Sacrifices his Alpha Male persona by tolerating label of "coward" for leaving Cora to Magua's capture)

FROM PLANNING TO WRITING

The concept driving this book was to give you the fundamental tools for thinking through and planning your story. Not for a minute should you ever think that any romance writer will produce a mirror image of someone else's story . . . if they truly allow themselves to create. Yes, we as human beings have some fundamental similarities, but each of us is unique in our experiences, in the details we have encountered. That means each of us has assimilated details that color our preferences and decisions. In that uniqueness you have an obligation to take the fundamentals found in this book and write your own very unique story.

Brainstorm your "What if's" in both your Character Profiles and your Paradigm. With an understanding of audience expectations, push the envelope.. Analyze your passion for the point you want to make then go the extreme (not the predictable) route to prove that point. Yes, in a romance the couple will end up together as a committed unit, but what a challenge to get them to that point in a memorable story!

ROMANCE CHAPTER 11

Concluding Remarks

Anyone entering the creative writing game with illusions of immediate, frequent, big-money sales is delusional and wrong-minded. The more reasonable and sane goal is to learn and practice one's craft then complete every project to best of one's own ability for the sole purpose of getting it out of one's mind and into the validating form of the written word. You document your imaginings for you, no one else. Then you let others read it and finally you research the how's of marketing. While marketing you continue to write. That is your immediate positive reinforcement of why you are alive with this talent to tell stories. What if you never sell? Doesn't make any difference. You have gotten the abstract images from your mind into the concrete form of written words.

WHAT IF YOU NEVER SELL?

If the Fates smile and all things come together—right project at the right time for the right agent or producer—then you can wallow in the glory of having someone else believe in your story, your characters. Maybe you never sell another script or story. Does that matter? Not to the focused and confident Creative.

So, crawl through the preparation/planning stage then stand-up and toddle through the first draft stage, then stride into the marketing stage and, hopefully one day jump up-and-down enjoying the sale stage. But do so humbly understanding that stage may only come once or twice. Like all writers, you had to crawl before you could stand and walk. You "simply" have to want to go through the process with the determination to thoroughly enjoy each phase.

No one but you can tell your story. Make it the best you can write and prepare yourself for the marathon journey of a lifetime!

So, go forth and write an iconic Romantic Screenplay!

APPENDIX A

Plot Paradigm Form

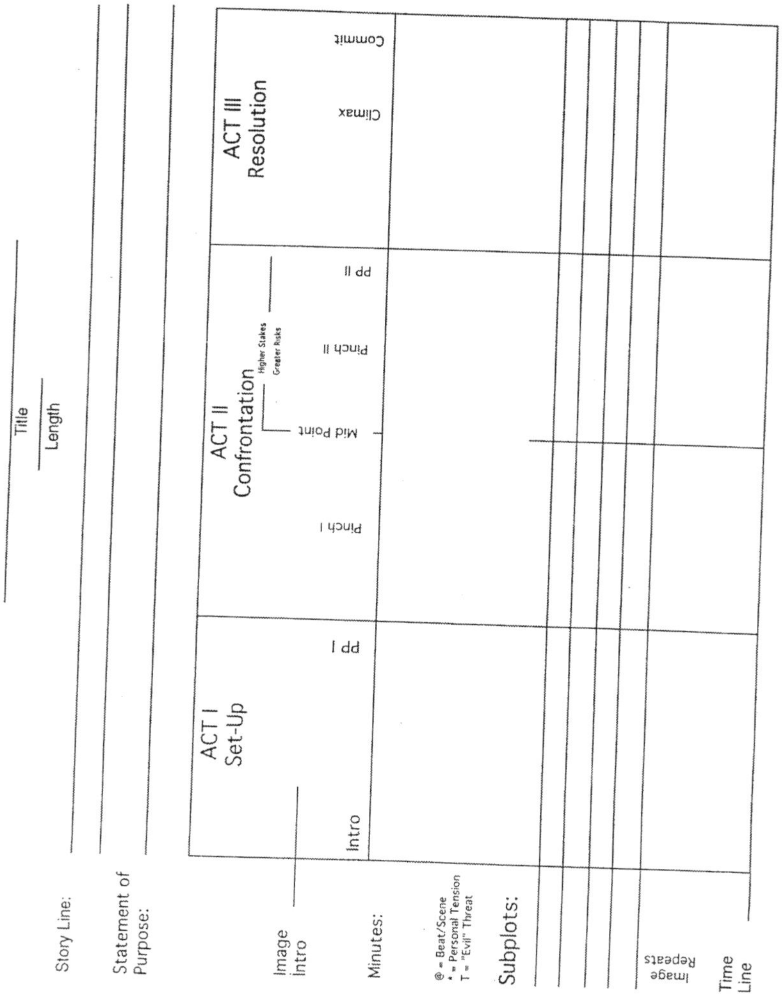
Title
Length
Story Line:
Statement of Purpose:
Image Intro
Minutes:
@ = Beat/Scene
* = Personal Tension
T = "Evil" Threat
Subplots:
Image Repeats
Time Line
ACT I
Set-Up
Intro
PP I
ACT II
Confrontation
Pinch I
Mid Point
Higher Stakes
Greater Risks
Pinch II
PP II
ACT III
Resolution
Climax
Commit

APPENDIX B

DEFINITIONS for accompanying PARADIGM:

(NOTE: Useful in ANY storytelling but vital to Screenplays, so many references to "minutes" and pages in screenplay context. Just translate to X-many pages & chapters of a novel.)

PARADIGM: A model, pattern, or conceptual scheme of a screenplay / plot line, as explained by Syd Field.

SCREENPLAY: A linear story told in pictures, ranging in length from 90 to 144 pages (each page equal to one minute of screen-time) with current spec length expected to be 100 pages, arranged in three Acts, with an approximate length division of Act I 1/4, Act II 1/2, and Act III 1/4. The writer may originate the script, however, the ultimate product is a revised and refined collaborative effort dependent on performance, production, and technical staff. (A novel is between writer-editor-reader, long, complex with multiple subplots, exposition and internalization *not* present in a Screenplay).

TITLE: Announcement of the story's content, impact, or image, a succinct and memorable audience grabber. Title is the hook that must be powerfully intriguing but not on-the-nose.

STORY LINE / LOG LINE: One line statement (25 words or less) of what the story is about, a simplified attention-getter that will attract viewers. It must be unique to this story, this Protagonist, delivering dominant character trait and "job" role in the story, the change or challenge faced and the jeopardy or powerful obstacle the Protagonist must overcome.

STATEMENT OF PURPOSE: The intellectual point or moral of the story, frequently the lesson learned by the characters and demonstrated in the action experienced by the characters.

BACKSTORY: The history of the characters and events preceding this story, creating the situation and / or motivating the characters that will be implied or used as droplet flavoring.

ACT I: Approximately 1/4 of the script, THE SET-UP where the audience is introduced to characters and their problems. The audience begins to ask questions they want answered for the characters. Act ends when an event happens that disrupts life and forces everyone to deal with situations they would rather avoid and the Protagonist is forced into a "New Life" or way of living.

IMAGE INTRO: Audience's first sensual experience of the story which establishes mood and expectation. It can set scene, introduce character, create immediate tension, but it must be visually sensational. It should reflect the theme / purpose of the story and can act as a "bookend" or quotation mark to the story that follows.

INTRODUCTION: First ten pages / minutes when audience experiences the 5W's of 1) Who the story is about, 2) Where the story is happening, 3) When the story is happening, 4) What events are happening in the life of the characters, and 5) Why these events are disturbing / motivational to the characters. In these ten minutes the audience will decide if they like the story and care about the characters. (Not a Prologue in a novel, but Chapter One)

INCITING INCIDENT: Event happening at 10-17 pg / min which causes Plot Point I. (About Chapter Three of novel)

PLOT POINT I: The event approximately at 23-25 pg / min which totally disrupts the characters' lives and forces them to deal with situations they would rather avoid, told in approximately 3-5 pages of action and ends Act I. (Chapter Five-Six of a novel)

ACT II: Approximately 1/2 of the script, THE CONFRONTATION where events, choices, and reactions become increasingly more difficult. The audience questions become more intense with the rising tension of the story's action. Subplots contribute the complications the linear story must deal with and depict character motivation at PINCHES I and II. Herein, the Protagonist is initially learning about / reacting to the new world. Between 48-52 pg / min, an emotional MID-POINT epiphany, an intellectual "Aha," divides Act II and from that point on the characters are more focused but under greater stress, driven to CAUSE events / consequences. ACT II ends with a vividly dramatic event which forces the characters to take the ultimate action.

PINCHES: Subplot events which depict character motivation / insight and affect the story line. PINCH I occurs approximately 1/4 into ACT II or approximately 35-37 pg / min and is a glimpse of Protagonist's greatest fear / greatest weakness and PINCH II is a tense highlight approximately 3/4 through ACT II at about 65-67 pg / min that depicts acknowledgement / sense of confidence / impending reward for the Protagonist.

PLOT POINT II: The event at approximately 72-77 pg / min which attacks the Protagonist's sense of well-being, backs that person into a corner, and forces a decision to take control by confronting the threat and performing the ultimate action that will resolve the situation. It is the Antagonist's greatest moment when victory / satisfaction is at hand because the Protagonist is beaten. (In a novel this happens approximately at 75-80% point of the book's length.)

ACT III: Approximately 1/4 of the script, THE RESOLUTION where the characters are at their finest hour, whether the negative Antagonist or the positive Protagonist, the STATEMENT OF PURPOSE is defined, and the linear story is satisfactorily concluded. All audience questions are answered, including SUBPLOT complexities. Suspense / tension builds quickly to culminate in the action climax then falls / mellows with character commitment to some purpose.

CLIMAX (GREAT BATTLE): The dramatic highpoint of the storyline where the audience sees forceful characters pushed to their limits and someone conquers the problems and attains their goal. The Protagonist "barely" wins *or* discovers something greater to achieve and cherish.

COMMITMENT: The concluding scene sequence where the characters commit to some purpose that will carry them forward beyond the end of the story. This is the audience's "Ah-h-h," the falling action or release of tension created in the Climax.

AFTER-STORY: The imaginings of the audience of what the characters do after the cinematic story concludes.

SUBPLOTS: The storylines, each with its own agenda, surrounding the linear / main story of a script which are going on simultaneously and have an effect on the main story, frequently involving supporting cast or the elements that pre-existed and will probably continue after this story is concluded. Where a novel may have numerous subplots, a screenplay must be confined to three to four subplots and only depict those vital to the main story movement. The amount of space (Number of words or pages) given to a subplot equates its importance to the main plot.

IMAGE REPEATS: Images, actions, or dialogue that reappear later in the story for emphasis and impact on the memory of the audience. The dramatic arts rely upon this economical tool to create a sense of unity and purpose in depicting this particular series of events in such a condensed form. In a novel it translates into repeat symbols to subtly deliver the same subtext.

TIME LINE: The passage of time in the linear / main story. Screenplays depict the passage of time through dialogue, costume changes, daily routine actions, time of day or season changes, and character or scene aging, as a few examples.

BEAT / SCENE: Screenplays are built in units called scenes, each comprising a BEAT in the action, each with its own beginning, middle and ending and frequently linked together in scene sequences (subplot events going on simultaneously, for example) to depict many facets of the story within a limited time period in the story.

PERSONAL / SEXUAL TENSION: Subtle element of frustration experienced by the main characters which motivates them to seek resolution. A satisfying story is written in ebb-and-flow with a build of tension, a release of goal attainment or confrontation then a slowing or "down-time" for audience or reader to absorb / appreciate evolution of story and character. Sustained tension (such as a battle scene) that goes on too long will cause impact to be lost. If too brief the importance may be missed or ignored.

THREAT: The negative or evil elements which touch the lives of the characters, intending to thwart achievement of some goal. The dramatic arts utilize this emotional tool to heighten suspense / tension and enhance audience empathy. The intensity of the threat needs to climb as the story progresses with the Protagonist made aware of more to gain or lose by confronting the threat. Threat can be subtle or blatantly violent. It has to reappear at intervals to remind the audience / reader and keep them in their seats / turning pages.

APPENDIX C

36-POINT CHARACTER CHART

General

1. Name:
2. Age:
3. Height & Weight:
4. Hair:
5. Eyes:
6. Scars/Handicaps:
7. Birthdate & Zodiac:
8. Birthplace:
9. Parents & Childhood:
10. Education:
11. Work Experience:
12. Home & its Physical Atmosphere:

Personal

13. Best Friend:
14. Men/Women Friends:
15. Enemies & Why:
16. Strongest/Weakest Characteristics:
17. Greatest Fear:
18. Sees self as...
19. Is seen by others as...
20. Sense of humor about...
21. Basic Nature:
22. Ambitions:
23. Philosophy of Life:
24. Hobbies:
25. Music, art, reading preferences:
26. Dress & Grooming Habits:
27. Favorite Colors:
28. Typical Day:

Story

29. Present Problem:
30. How will it get worse?
31. What is the best that can happen?
32. What is the worst that can happen?
33. What trait will be dominate thus be vital to story?
34. Why is this character worth writing about?
35. Do I like/dislike this person? Why?
36. Why will this character be remembered?

Fundamental to Story
What is Character's TANGIBLE OBJECTIVE/Heart's Desire/Goal?

APPENDIX D

ON CHARACTER PROFILING

(From Chapter 3 of *LEARN SCREENWRITING From Start to Adaptation to Pro Advice)*

To create any credible, come-to-life, well-rounded fictional character you need to start with a Character Profile that outlines each primary and secondary character's essential background and current status. This is a viable tool for fleshing out every fictional character needed for short stories, novels of any genre or length, stage plays and screenplays.

Some Seat-of-the-Pants writers do not think profiling is necessary. They may even proclaim profiling stifles their creativity. For the majority of prolific and selling writers profiling is absolutely essential for credible storytelling. Whether prose or cinema, stories are about people. Those people deserve to be "birthed" as complex, fascinating entities who enter into dramatic challenges that provide experiences they can live through to become better human beings. Since no storyteller has the luxury of a time-consuming flow-of-consciousness depiction from birth to the current story, profiling allows the writer to paint character history and motivation before writing their current situation. Yes, most writers learn more about the cast members in the creating of their dialogue and actions. Sometimes a writer may even find secrets erupting that deepen or change the initial Character Profile. If that's so, why go to all the trouble of documenting a "Character Profile" in the first place?

A written profile provides four things:

1) Consistency that allows me to predict reactions and puts me in control thus preventing writer's block, a wandering storyline, and inconsistent details,
2) Complexity that allows me to provide meaningful motivation, avoid stereotyping, and create audience questions
3) Individuality that allows me to demonstrate unique characteristics relevant to this story from unseen past to quirks or habits,
4) Exaggeration that is credible, interesting, powerful, yet arouses audience concern.

KINDS OF PROFILES

A variety of profile methods and forms exist. Some evolve only family and home life based on the principle that humans act and think based on their history. Others go in-depth into the psychology and internal life of characters. One writer copies any profile method she encounters into a single, massive 100+-page program. Preparing for a project, she wanders through the various elements, filling in what comes to mind about the fictional person living in her mind. She then prints out just what she has completed. While she is writing the project, if she uncovers an area not explored, she goes back and fills in that portion of the profile.

The 36-Step Character Profile here has proven to be enough for the majority of writers. This succinct Profile creates a clearer, more vivid awareness of this person just as if You-the-Writer are talking to him or her. In turn, that awareness gives the character access to your imagination and he or she talks to you. One popular exercise in film schools is to write an interview or conversation with this fictional character.

THE THREE-PART PROFILE

Note the divisions of this form: Personal History, Psychological Profile, and Roles in Story's Conflict. Let's begin with Personal History.

BIRTHING CHARACTERS

Writers give birth the easy way because they imagine these humans into the world. And they can change the characters to fit the story. Book editors and studio executives generously apply that concept. Don't cringe. Not all changes in fundamental characterizations are bad. Consider how a truly good actor's research can change his character's affect.

Remember two things about profiles: First, every facet can contribute a possible conflict and/or subliminal characterization. Second, every facet does not need to be used in the story, however much you researched it. The writer should only use those elements that impact the story. More is audience overload, less is audience ignorance.

GENERAL BACKGROUND DATA

As you fill in the blanks, remember everything delivers subliminal thought associations to the audience and, most importantly, expectations. . . .

1. **Name:** Evokes images, cultures, ancient meanings, as in "A Boy Named Sue" or a recognizable Russian first name and an Irish last name, a child repeatedly being told to live up to his name which means "Warrior."
2. **Age:** Life stage evokes expectations
3. **Height & Weight:** Again cultural expectations, voluptuous versus starvation-thin, tall & muscular versus small & wiry.
4. **Hair:** Color, style, especially if it characterizes as in U.S. Marine cut or matted & filthy.
5. **Eyes:** Unusual coloring, telling characteristic, or expressive habits

6. **Scars/Handicaps**: History of incident or development creates expectations
7. **Birth date:** Era or circumstance can impact or typify social status as in "Far and Away."
8. **Birthplace**: Again reflective of social status in the eyes of audience as in the each of the players in the original "Highlander" movie.
9. **Parents & Childhood**: Foundation of character's life expectations either as exemplary or defiance.
10. **Education:** Forced feeding of information and social interactions, as in royal guard of Montezuma versus contemporary, orphanage-reared U.S. Navy SEAL.
11. **Work Experience**: Similar to Education category in impacting social and cultural expectations and attitudes.
12. **Home & its physical environment:** A reflection of personal priorities and opportunities

Out of this basic information, the character begins to take on a personality in your mind. Why? Because You-the-Writer, the creator, begin to understand how that personality developed and what provided the major influences. You consciously choose what internally motivates that character's choices as you write.

IN-DEPTH PERSONAL DATA

Now that you know where the character came from, you can move into where the character is at the moment of the story. You flesh out personal data with the kind of information your closest confidants know about you!

13. **Best Friend:** Who and why? "You are known by the company you keep."
14. **Male and/or Female Friends**: Again the choices reflect needs met and subliminal reasons
15. **Enemies & Why:** From frivolous to vicious, no one relates positively to everyone else.
16. **Hobbies:** What entertains, distracts, attracts, challenges, and why? Even ancient peoples carved, painted pottery, told stories. Why?
17. **Music, art, reading preferences:** Tastes reflect satisfaction of needs, even if peer or social pressures, but what if the preference is an oddity or adversity?
18. **Dress & Grooming Habits:** Direct correlation to self-image and preferences.
19. **Typical Day:** From beginning of wake-up ritual through the mundane meals and work routine to night's sleep patterns, every moment of the "typical day" presents an opportunity for something to go awry, to frustrate and rattle the character...forcing a change that will become the story.

UNDERSTANDING EQUALS MOTIVATION

The essence of "Character Profiling" is creating a realistic, credible fictional character . . . or making fictional suppositions about a real-life person. The only person you can truly "Profile" is yourself. Even then you probably will not be 100% truthful or totally knowledgeable. After all, don't we learn more about ourselves every day we live?

Documenting the back-story and personal data of a character can certainly be as flexible as our own self-awareness. Watching TOP GUN we understood a boy's dream to be a fighter pilot like his old man. But why did he have to overcome the bad reputation? How crucial was that back-story to the character's motivation? Aw, therein is the subtle need of both character and writer to overcome stereotyping. That one element gave the character consistency, complexity, individuality, and exaggeration that carried the story forward.

PSYCHOLOGICAL PROFILING

An in-depth Psychological Profile can take the creator and the audience into the realm of multidimensional characterization. It is not a difficult process and can be downright fascinating for one simple reason: Curious human beings want to know why people do what they do! They want to understand themselves, family members, co-workers, criminals, politicians, friends, and enemies. As the creator of characters, you get to answer those questions... for your story!

You made a start with the Character's History. The Psychological Profile builds on this, and goes one step further, actually delving into three key areas for storytellers: 1) Self-awareness, 2) Social Status, and 3) Motivation.

You expected a mention of "Normal" and "Abnormal." However, each of the three profile areas can have both these elements pulling the character this way and that. The fun of characterization is choosing what is going to dominate in any given situation. Drama results when the choice raises the stakes in the story and creates more audience questions they just have to have answered! They go questing with the characters!

SELF-AWARENESS

Psychologists tell us it is normal to have conversations with ourselves, whether within our thought processes or right out loud. This is a part of self-perception. Sometimes we're mad or ashamed, sometimes proud or righteous and the list could go on and on. When you are writing a character, you need to go inside the mind, the emotions, the soul of that human being and figure out that self-image. Then you write the actions and dialogue consistent with that perception. You consider the character's history then add the salt and pepper of normal and abnormal self-'concept. This singular approach to characterization will prevent you from writing stereotypes. So, you ask yourself "This characters sees himself as...."

The next powerful element is "What is his greatest fear?" Indiana Jones in RAIDERS OF THE LOST ARK? Snakes! That fear was introduced in the first five minutes of the movie and used as his greatest challenge when he was thrown into the pit. Of course, it doesn't always have to be that blatant, but certainly can tighten the tension in any story if the character is forced to face that darkest nightmare!

Life is not painted in black and white, but has varying shades of gray. That's an old platitude, but very applicable to creating multi-dimensional characters. So, don't forget what makes the character laugh, smile tenderly, feel euphoric or invincible. A kill-hardened Navy SEAL who pauses to stick a wild flower in his pocket and momentarily remembers his ex-wife creates more audience questions than the womanizing James Bond.

Another aspect of this gray concept is the Male-Female or Yin-Yang attributes within us all. Some have explained this as Alpha Warrior and Beta Thinker, whether a male or female was being discussed. Again, play with the character's self-perceptions of who they are at any given time and what they are capable of feeling and demonstrating in a given situation.

From these basics you can state "philosophy of life" and ambition or dreams.

SOCIAL STATUS

Here is the question "How do others see this person?" Again, the history profile provides a lot of "status" information, but as a writer you can twist this in so many directions, positive and negative. Why is a once happily married professor of philosophy from an Ivy League college now a pool-hustling drunk in the slums of Miami?

Ask yourself "Who are his enemies and why?" "Who is his best friend and why?" Think of the Morgan Freeman character in SEVEN. What about the relationship between Thelma and Louise? What about the personality dynamics of the whole cast of LADYHAWKE?

A classic storytelling device is the creation of a "comfortable" or, more appropriately, familiar environment the character exists in. Her social status is established then--BAM!--all hell breaks loose! This quiet little woman is suddenly widowed and forced to defy the expectations of her community and work side by side with a black man in the cotton fields to maintain her independence and dignity. The disruption of social status that assaults the self-concept! Powerful stuff!

MOTIVATION

Ultimately, the writer is led to this driving force of all things in this world. Motivation is the reason for action. You are hungry, so you search for food. It doesn't matter that you are only three years old and alone in the alleys of Saigon or the only survivor of a plane crash in the Canadian north woods.

If you have written a complete history of your character then profiled the self-awareness aspects of that personality, and have clearly placed them in their social environment, motivation becomes logical. You will not experience "Writer's Block" simply because your characters want to get on with the story. They have things to do. You motivated them!

NORMAL

Writers who require more help than these basics have many resources available, such as the Myers-Briggs, the Enneagram, and the NEO-PI personality tests. For a little fun, even the signs of the Zodiac can help you create your character's personality.

ABNORMAL

Ah, yes, the fascinating part of humanity. You will encounter many definitions or philosophies of what is considered normal and abnormal behaviors, coping mechanisms, or thought processes. As far as You-the-Writer is concerned, you establish the definitions for your story. What was normal treatment of servants and animals in medieval Europe would be abuse today. So when and where is your story set? What are the norms of that culture, that time period? Who was "normal" in ONE FLEW OVER THE CUCKOO'S NEST?

Every fiction writer should own a textbook on abnormal psychology to get into the true problems of abnormal thought processes and sociopathic behavior. One succinct resource is the *MASSACHUSETTS GENERAL HOSPITAL HANDBOOK OF GENERAL HOSPITAL PSYCHIATRY.* It gives brief overviews of normal and abnormal manifestations of the wondrous conditions of the human mind. Many a mystery writer uses information from the book *MINDHUNTER: INSIDE THE FBI'S ELITE SERIAL CRIME UNIT* by Douglas and Olshaker, the renowned FBI profilers. .

In conclusion, Character Profiling is an exciting part of story planning. You create characters who never existed before. Oh, you may have patterned this one after someone you worked with or that one after another character from a favorite movie, but in the end you have created a new fictional person. "There are no new stories, just new people."

CHARACTER-DRIVEN VS. PLOT-DRIVEN

Many facets of the film industry like to classify a script as either plot-driven or character driven. The plot-driven movie focuses on the events forcing reactions from the characters. Examples would be Action-Adventure like THE FIFTH ELEMENT or historical sagas such as THE LAST OF THE MOHICANS. When powerful personalities enthrall the audience in their choices and the events that result, the character is said to dictate plot as in TERMS OF ENDEARMENT. Sometimes it is difficult to distinguish which came first, plot event or character choice. Just ask yourself if events or characters cause the plot to unfold. Especially telling are the turning points in the plot.

The impact of a Character Profile on the plot can aid the writer in focusing the script on either events or character choices. Some questions might be "How much of the Character's Personal History will come into play in the story? How deeply must the writer delve into the Character's psyche to demonstrate motivation, option awareness, coping mechanisms?" This is not rocket science-difficult here, just common sense. Yes, characters must move through the plot, but is the character causing or reacting to the plot events? Cinematic characters must be inherently dramatic, not wimpy watchers. They throw themselves into the story events. So inherent personality does not differentiate between character-driven stories and plot-driven.

Commonly, if the narrative or camera's eye is more often on the events rather than on the character responses, that will be a plot-driven script. If the majority of the narrative refers to the expressions, reactions and choreography of the characters, that script usually has a character-driven focus.

PUTTING A PROFILE TO WORK

Once a Character Profile is completed with that Personal History and a Psychological assessment as just discussed, you should begin to think through how this character (yes, one character at a time) will participate in the story you want to tell. Usually, this preplanning focuses the writer on whether is creating a plot-driven or a character driven story.

The process goes through three stages:

1) I identify (and highlight) interesting quirks, strengths, weaknesses in the Character Profiles of all Major Players that you want to tweak and explore in the story.
2) Consider where each of the Major Players is at the beginning of the story and where you want that person to be by the end. For the lead roles this may be the classic Character Arc or for supporting characters it may be simple resolution or contribution.
3) Finally, identify the skeletal plot points of the story you want to tell . . . then consider the logic of "Did the characters cause these pivotal events . . . or are they reacting to the events?"

EXPLORING CHARACTERS IN STORY

As a Character Profile is completed, you should find yourself intrigued by how this personality evolved to the point where your story begins. This is a fictional person, yet he/she begins to "live" in your imagination. The more complete the Profile, the more vivid the personality. You should begin to understand what makes this character "tick," identifying what kinds of things will stress this person and cause a reaction. The more threatening or more important the stressor, the more dramatic the reaction. VIOLA! Story begins to emerge or you at least begin to see logical direction of "this could lead to this."

Lists of possible character stressors lead to these "What If" lists. Out of those ideas can identify a pattern that you can use and build on in the story. The more important the person obviously the more extensive the Profile, as well as the "What If" lists. Compare and contrast the characters and how they will interact. The story should take shape as you see if character is dictating plot or if plot is going to drive character.

CHARACTER ARC: INTERNAL IMPACTING EXTERNAL

Most writer really do like people. Personalities and the why's of actions intrigue writers. Storytelling allows us the luxury of manipulation. You can make your characters do what you want. You can create the endings you want. Of course, in the collaborative effort of movie-making, your visions and intentions can be twisted and subverted . . . but your foundation script must be true to your vision of these characters or you have failed the most important critic, yourself.

That critic dictates that your Major Players must demonstrate some point, some lesson about their life as they experience the story. Because you should be driven to understand why your characters are motivated, start from both the Personal History and the Psychological Profile to identify where these people are in their lives when this story begins. What does this character want out of life in general? Then what does he/she want at this very moment? What options does this character perceive that will allow the achievement of these goals? These are "Internal Motivators."

Taking it one step further, the writer is also able to identify what could provide the most dramatic "External" opposition to achieving those goals. VOILA! The writer has a logical basis for where and how to challenge the character in the story!

A cinematic story is not a boring status quo. It moves the characters through a life-changing experience. The Major Players to grow and change. For the most part, the Protagonists grows in a positive direction, while the majority of the Antagonists suffer defeat. Good over Evil, you might say. Therefore, you need to identify how you want to demonstrate the **internal** change. That internal Character Arc or shift in awareness must impact the Character's external action choices, thus the events in a visual, active demonstration of the change. That active demonstration must be integral to the Main Plot of the story! How did Dustin Hoffman's character in TOOTSIE change and demonstrate that change? And wasn't that demonstration also the Climax of the story? In this instance, the movie was character-driven.

The character makes a conscious choice and proceeds to act in a different manner. The change doesn't work if it is sudden, unpredictable, coincidental.

The challenges of the stressors in the plot and the character's subsequent actions or reactions must set-up the internal growth. Blatant hints don't work either. That's over-the-top, on-the-nose melodrama. Paying attention to the character's Psychological Profile will prevent that mistake. Adage: People don't change overnight.

Does a Character Arc work in an Action-Adventure plot-driven script? It does if the Arc is integral to the plot. Sometimes the reluctant warrior merely proves his metal as in Ryan coldly shooting the cook in HUNT FOR RED OCTOBER. Before that, the audience saw an intellectual man who willingly took on challenges inherent to circumstances. We learned his personal history of surviving a helicopter crash yet graduating from the Naval Academy. When he came face to face with the enemy, he did the deed and slept on the plane ride home. The audience saw that subtle evidence of his internal motivation grown to the point of calmly accepting the personal consequences of a life-and-death decision. Bart Mancuso, commander of the Dallas, changed from distrust to acceptance of Sean Connery's character, Ramius, and willingly played submarine "chicken." Oversimplification perhaps, but both demonstrate subtle Character Arcs all the same.

PLOTTING CHARACTER

Students and practitioners of screenwriting quickly become very familiar with the skeletal points every script must have to prevent expensive, boring, wandering story lines. These are plot points that maintain and build the suspense, whether the story is plot-driven or character-driven.

Complete Character Profiles ease the process of creating these plot points. The writing goes faster when a writer understands and can predict the actions and reactions of the script's people. The Profile identifies prime dramatic material in those personalities. The writer knows what they want, what will logically block their achievement, and how they should change. The tool provides the elements to build a powerful story in the experiences of those characters.

The Main Plot is the linear story line. By stating that in the log line, a writer can easily eliminate images and events that may create milieu or aura, but in reality would not move the story forward. What characters do you need to introduce in Act I when you set up present circumstance and identify these people to the audience? Then what singular event will CHANGE the direction of those characters' lives and force them in a new direction? What needs to happen to the Protagonist/Lead at Mid-Point to raise the stakes and seriously focus that person on a new goal? What would push this character into a corner to the point of "Fight" rather than "Flight?" How can this character's dramatic potential explode into dramatic action at the Climax?

Do not overlook the story's Time Line and how time, seasons, routine life, if you will, impact the characters' actions and choices. Notations prevent overlooking the subtlety of these influences. Sometimes, you can discover even more potential stressors in the time line and can toy with "What If" lists for those.

Next, consider each Major Player's personal agenda, routine, and those notes on where the character is at the beginning and where you want them by the end. What mundane material can be skipped? What hints are needed for audience empathy or understanding of an important point and what would be overload? This exercise allows you to identify essential material and sometimes even pacing.

Those personal agendas frequently develop into Subplots essential to the Main Plot line. You can see where the major characters' agendas will intersect with the Main Plot and with one another. This is where you control screen time of the supporting cast as their subplots impact the main plot. This is the creative time to identify holes in story logic where set-up or foreshadowing was missed or where extraneous material can be eliminated.

SCREENPLAY CHARACTERS ARE DIFFERENT

Many new screenwriters get caught in the mental hassle of letting go of character detail in a screenplay. Here is a dramatic character worksheet that will help you shift from a novelist's mindset to a screenwriting view of what characters need to people a film's cast. It is essential that you understand that those characters you want up on that screen must be inherently dramatic. Their attitude, tone, habits, demeanor creates a change when they walk into a room. They are the Alpah people of the world who make things happen by reacting visually and powerfully to the circumstance, dialogue, people they encounter. Cinematic characters are never boring or common. The audience expects them to be vividly interesting.

PROFILING CONCLUSION

A Character Profile empowers the writer with consistency, complexity, individuality, and the ability to credibly exaggerate. Such documentation provides a reference of background and personal data that allows the audience to empathize with the character's motivation. Delving into the character's psychological realms of self-awareness and normal vs. abnormal responses gives the writer a dimension that defies stereo-typing. Transferring this data into character action and dialogue as a story unfolds is the ultimate in writing ecstasy! The result of creating such well-thought out fictional characters will be a script that has to be read because these people are so dynamic, so fascinating, they have to be brought to life on the screen.

The writer's Character Profile has zero relationship to an Actor's profiling that character. Good, trained actors need to evolve their own insights so they can "feel" a character and get "into the skin" of the character. If you mention you have a completed Profile, they may ask for it, but most rely on their own gut instincts. That's why they are actors. Actors act, writers write.

APPENDIX E

A CINEMATIC CHARACTERIZATION WORKSHEET

Note: Stories are about conflict. Interesting characters are those who INVOLVE themselves in conflict and strive toward some resolution. BUT, there is a difference between the power of an interesting Protagonist in a novel and one in a screenplay.

Overall Dramatic Characterization:

- Emotionally conflicted
- Physical demonstration
- Paradoxes of internal conflicts
- Hero hides in neutrality though tested & eventually caves
- Lives in serious emotional dilemma
- ANTAGONIST: 1) outsmart protagonist, 2) scheme to ID weakness, 3) possess unique morality

A novelist shoves a character against opposition, forcing conflict, creating reader tension, demonstrating growth. Ordinary people in novels create expectation of dramatic scenes to follow.	* * * *	A screenwriter uses an inherently dramatic character to evolve tension in EVERY scene. Character causes story tension & keeps audience involved.

FUNDAMENTALS OF PERSONALITY

CORE TRAITS (Overall Generalizations)

*
*
*
*

FLAW (Constant Internal War, Vulnerability)

*
*
*
*

DILEMMA (Want vs. Need vs. Expectation)

*
*
*
*

SUBTEXT (Coping & Covering Truth)

*
*
*
*

SPECIAL (Unique Aspiration or Talent)

*
*
*
*

APPENDIX F

POLTI'S 36 DRAMATIC SITUATIONS

1. Supplication: Persecutor, Suppliant, Authority Figure
2. Deliverance: Unfortunate, Threatener, Rescuer
3. Crime Pursued by Vengeance: Criminal, Avenger
4. Vengeance taken for Kindred upon Kindred: Avenger, Guilty Remembrance, a Relative of Both
5. Pursuit: Punishment and Fugitive
6. Disaster: Vanquished Power, Victorious Enemy, Messenger
7. Falling Prey to Cruelty or Misfortune: Unfortunate, Master
8. Revolt: Tyrant, Conspirator
9. Daring Enterprise: Bold Leader, Object, Adversary
10. Abduction: Abductor, the Abducted, Guardian
11. Enigma: Interrogator, Seeker, Problem
12. Obtaining: Solicitor, Adversary or Arbitrator & Opposing
13. Enmity of Kinsmen: Malevolent Kinsmen, Reciprocally Hated Kin
14. Rivalry of Kinsmen: Preferred Kinsman, Rejected Kin, Object
15. Murderous Adultery: Two Adulterers, Murdered Spouse
16. Madness: Madman, Victim
17. Fatal Imprudence: Imprudent, Victim, Object Lost
18. Involuntary Crimes of Love: Lover, Beloved, Revealer
19. Slaying of Kinsman Unrecognized: Slayer, Unrecognized Victim
20. Self-Sacrificing for an Ideal: Hero, Ideal, Creditor, Sacrifice
21. Self-Sacrificing for Kindred: Hero, Kinsman, Creditor, Sacrifice
22. All Sacrificed for Passion: Lover, Object of Passion, Sacrifice
23. Necessity of Sacrificing Loved Ones: Hero, Beloved, Necessity
24. Rivalry of Superior & Inferior: Superior, Inferior, Object
25. Adultery: Two Adulterers, Betrayed Spouse
26. Crimes of Love: Lover, Beloved, Social Norms
27. Discovery of Dishonor of Beloved: Discovered, Guilty
28. Obstacles to Love: Two Lovers, Obstacles
29. An Enemy Loved: Beloved Enemy, Lover, Hater
30. Ambition: Ambitious Person, Thing Coveted, Adversary
31. Conflict with (a) God: A Mortal, an Immortal or Principle
32. Mistaken Jealousy: Jealous, Object, Accomplice, Perpetrator
33. Erroneous Judgment: Mistaken One, Victim, Cause, Guilty
34. Remorse: Culprit, Victim or Sin, Interrogator
35. Recovery of Lost One: Seeker, One Found
36. Murder of Loved One: Slain Kinsman, Spectator, Executioner

APPENDIX G

GROWTH & DEVELOPMENT GUIDELINES

*Note: These are generalities from psychology studies & medicine. Every human is unique.

Infancy to 1 year/Period of TRUST:
Emotional: Meet needs. Minimal frustration.
Social: Self-centered. Identify/bond with parents/care-givers.
Physical: Rapid growth.
Spiritual: Parental centered.
Play: Motor, sensory.
Books: Sounds & simple, uncluttered, colorful pictures.

Toddler ages 1-3/Period of AUTONOMY:
Emotional: Limited attention span. Testing of limits.
Social: Extended awareness. Family circle.
Physical: Slower. Dexterity. Heightened sensory association.
Spiritual: Can recognize death, separation, guilt.
Play: Can identify parallel/comparison. Motor. Spontaneous.
Books: Simple, syllabic words. Sentences with pictures.

Pre-School ages 3-5/Period of INITIATIVE:
Emotional: Curiosity at work. "Why?" and testing results.
Social: Cooperative. Interactive. Relating wanting and acceptance.
Physical: Steady growth. Initiate physical-mental coordination
Spiritual: Develops conscience and self-esteem.
Play: Cooperative. Action. Expressive.
Books: More complex stories. Identifies morals & characters.

School- Age ages 6-10/Period of INDUSTRY:
Emotional: Performance. Accomplishment. Competitive.
Social: Identifies own sexuality, peer groups, emotions of others.
Physical: Steady, Accident-prone.
Spiritual: Personification of external applied internally.
Play: Dramatization, collections, formal games & competitions.
Books: Peer-oriented. Broaden environment. Positive/Good triumphant.

Pubescent/Pre-Teen ages 10-12/Period of IDENTITY:
Emotional: Capable of independent responsibility. Conflict of worth.
Social: Sexuality comparison & discomfort/uncertainty. Awareness of attraction.

Physical: Rapid growth. Reproductive development.
Spiritual: Internalization and questing of "Why?"
Play: Serious competition testing personal abilities. Romantic/Idealistic & Fantasy.
Books: Heroes/Heroines 2-4 years older. Seeking role models.

Adolescent/Young Adult ages 13-21/Period of INTIMACY:
Emotional: Introspective. Self-doubt. Fears of adulthood responsibilities.
Social: Sexual intimacy. Seeking independence from authority.
Physical: Level off, but "body type" established, as well as health habits.
Spiritual: Begins to develop personal philosophy & to apply to situations.
Play: Vocational. Creative. Talent development/interests.
Books: Older heroes/heroines. True life. Credibility of fiction.

APPENDIX H

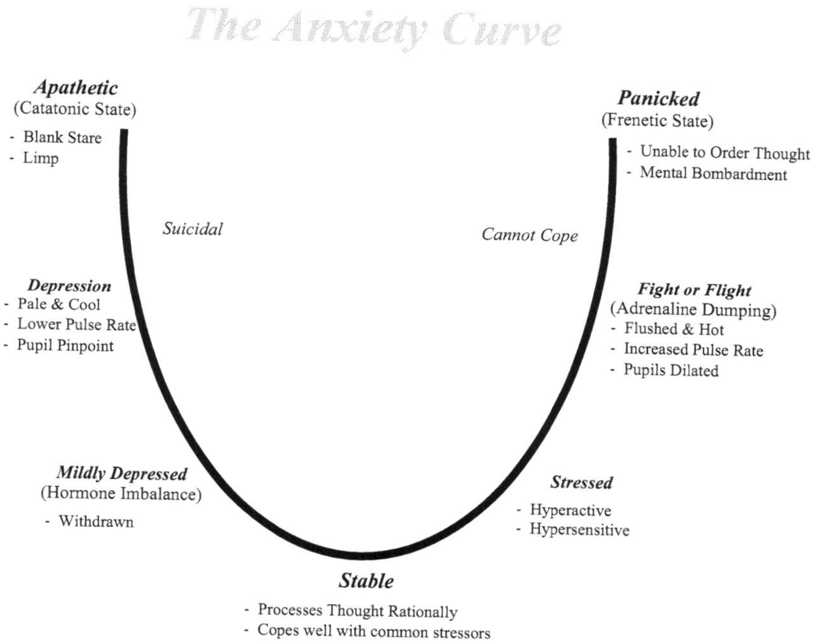
The Anxiety Curve
Apathetic
(Catatonic State)
- Blank Stare
- Limp
Panicked
(Frenetic State)
- Unable to Order Thought
- Mental Bombardment
Suicidal
Cannot Cope
Depression
- Pale & Cool
- Lower Pulse Rate
- Pupil Pinpoint
Fight or Flight
(Adrenaline Dumping)
- Flushed & Hot
- Increased Pulse Rate
- Pupils Dilated
Mildly Depressed
(Hormone Imbalance)
- Withdrawn
Stressed
- Hyperactive
- Hypersensitive
Stable
- Processes Thought Rationally
- Copes well with common stressors

APPENDIX I

FADE IN:	**Scene-Sequel Analysis**
EXT. WYOMING MOUNTAIN MEADOW - DAY	
CAT'S POV, IN BLACK & WHITE: (Cat Subplot)	**SCENE: Cat hunt**
Watching a lone sheep graze in the snow-edged pristine meadow, slinking forward, breath clouds in the cold air.	Goal: I.D. prey Conf: Imply cold
The snarling unseen cat lunges onto the sheep's back. Bone crunches as the SHEEP CRIES OUT.	Dis: Kill sheep

---

INT. CHICAGO ARCHITECT OFFICE - DAY	**SCENE: Plans awry** (Main Plot)
MATT PRICE (30), athletic, confident architect, works at a large screen, CAD display computer.	
The door behind quietly opens and LISSA (27), elegantly dressed, bubbly artist, slips in.	Goal:Confront groom

She tip-toes forward, startling him as she pushes against his back, her hands seductively sliding around his waist.

Matt savors her position then turns and pulls her into his arms for a hot kiss.

LISSA
Do you have any idea how much I love you? Everything about you. You are--necessary.

MATT
I could lock the door.

LISSA
Tempted. But . . . I need to pack for the honeymoon. Time's running out. Conf: Time crunch

She steps back to pull two brochures from her purse.

LISSA
Is it Rome or Hawaii?

MATT
Neither. Dis: Groom's plan

Lissa scowls.

SEQUEL: Persuasion
React: Upset

MATT
I'm reminding you what you just said when you tried to seduce me.

Dil: Manipulate

.2

LISSA
What?

MATT
How much you love me. Love me, love my family. Right?

Dil:Reflect back

She looks wary.

MATT (CONT'D)
My brothers paid for the honeymoon, but the artist in you will love it! Guaranteed.

Dil: Bros paid

He abruptly pulls her back into his arms.

MATT (CONT'D)
I have this fantasy. Making love in the out-of-doors under the stars, listening to a mountain stream.

Dil: HIS want

He nuzzles her neck. She stiffens and draws back.

LISSA
Are you talking Wyoming, like your annual male bonding trip? Not going to happen.

Dil: Her refusal

MATT
You showed your mom's horses for how many years? — Dil: Remind history

She pushes him away.

LISSA
I quit in high school and went to live with Dad. I haven't been back to Kentucky since then. No horses. Period.
(Picks up brochures)
You can't afford it, I'll pay for the honeymoon. — Dil: Her alternative

MATT
Don't pull the heiress bullshit. There's a reason for Wyoming. — Dil: His reasoning

LISSA
Not important enough for me.

MATT
Patty Callahan needs the business. Desperately. And the money's already been paid.

.3

LISSA
Playing a guilt card? What an asshole! Okay, here's the deal.
(Eyes tear up.)
No horses. Hikes. Camping out. You fish while I paint. — Dec: Accept, limits

She whirls away to look out a window and regain her composure. Matt frowns with concern and peeks around her.

MATT
It'll be memorable. I promise.

EXT. WYOMING MOUNTAIN MEADOW - DAY — **SEQUEL: Kill response** (Cat Subplot)

RAUL CORTINA (38)a lean, dark-visaged, nasty-tempered Basque sheepherder in a heavy, distinctive coat of dirty white with horizontal slashes of color woven into it, stares down at the mauled sheep.

He kicks the carcass in frustration then, viciously angered, fires his rifle into it. — React: Cort's anger

He drops to his haunches, his gaze raking the surrounding ground. He reaches out to part the grass with dirt-encrusted fingers bared in his half gloves.

A huge cougar print indents the wet soil. Cortina's hand splays atop the print, comparing size. Dil: Finds trail

He sits back on his heels, looks around, wipes a nervous hand over his lips.

CORTINA

Sonofabitch!

He stands to search for a trail, sites it, lines up with the mountain valley behind, then starts tracking the cat.

EXT. SMALL MOUNTAIN CAVE - DAY

In the late afternoon light, Cortina stops climbing the rocky hillside to catch his breath.

He looks around cautiously then crouches to listen.

COURGAR CUBS MEWING AND HISSING. Dil: Finds cubs
Cortina squints.

He then slings his rifle onto his back and pulls out his Dec: Retaliation big hunting knife. Sneering, he enters the cave.

CUBS SCREECH.

APPENDIX J

"Eyes" Step Outline/Beat Sheet by S. J. Walker

ACT I

1. **(Intro)** In Wyoming Cortina finds sheep carcass and follows cougar tracks back to den where he kills the cubs. In Chicago architect Matt hedges to artist bride Lissa that his brothers paid for their honeymoon and it is not a cruise. Introduce Lissa's experience with horses but adamant refusal to be exposed to them again.

2. An elderly Basque sheepherder wears Cortina's coat to take a sunrise piss and is Cougar's first victim. Cortina is disgusted by third sheepherder's superstition and tells him to take the body down the mountain. He throws him the heavy, discarded coat to keep him warm in the approaching spring snow.

3. Matt & Lissa arrive at Wyoming airport bickering over the wilderness honeymoon in the early spring before the normal tourist. Matt has brought fishing gear, Lissa her art supplies. Night at town's luxury hotel depicts Matt's proprietary temper and their passion.

4. Arrival at lodge/working ranch where Matt & brothers visited for 15 years. Hard-nosed ranch owner Patty Callahan chides Matt over expectations of citified Lissa. Matt reveals she had been avid horsewoman so he made assumptions.

5. Matt commiserates with Blaine, macho ranch foreman. Allude both ranch troubled finances & difficult women. Blaine required to check on Spring cattle roundup & sheep move down for sheering. Lissa furious that Matt wants to go and refuses to accompany. **(Inciting Incident)**They leave without her.

6. Lissa watches a barn cat stocking a mouse and is sickened at its feral instincts. She shows worry about Matt's safety, remembers trauma on mother's stud farm.

7. Young cowboy helping with spring cattle roundup finds downed packhorse with wrapped body of cougar's first victim then the ravaged remains of sheepherder. Just as he picks up Cortina's coat, the Cougar attacks.

8. Matt and Blaine arrive at campfire tended by three nervous cowboys. Blaine examines bodies of two sheepherders and young cowboy. Pronounces kills by cougar totally absurd. He will take three bodies down to the ranch. None of

cowboys volunteer to check on sheep being brought down for sheering. Not intimidated, Matt volunteers. Blaine insists he take the heavy coat because of pending snow.

9. Blaine arrives at ranch with the three bodies. Patty must report deaths to sheriff and U.S. Fish & Wildlife. **(Plot Point I)** Lissa is horrified her new husband has gone off by himself to check on the sheep herd. Defiant & controlling fear, she gears up to accompany Blaine on ride back up the mountain.

APPENDIX K

THE LONELY MAN

by S. J. Walker

Can an honorable man like Nolan Marks ignore bull-headed ignorance and the abuse it spawns? The war gave him debilitating images of his men dying, then smallpox took the last of his family, his three-year-old daughter. The guilt-ridden Nolan burns his wagon of household goods, buries his daughter, and finds an isolated valley where he can lose himself in the books intended for the school he was to open in a nearby town. Night Watcher, an ostracized Cheyenne, joins him in the alcohol-numbed companionship of lost warriors.

In the frontier spirit of minding one's own business, the townspeople tolerate a crude mountain man, Roman Stalarski, and shun his three young children and older, mute daughter Kathy. Nolan finds ten-year-old Tom and five-year-old Sammy Stalarski in his cabin. They had expected to discover guns in his crates instead of the strange books. Their lack of education motivates the lonely man to take on the manipulative town, praying he can control his flashbacks.

Nolan watches Roman deliver stolen Army horses to the Cheyenne, but stops him from bartering Kathy. Giving in to his pent up frustrations, he beats the repulsive man before turning him over to the Army. Feeling responsible for the Stalarski brood, Nolan privately tutors the two boys and eight-year-old Carrie. Mute Kathy's inability to communicate prompts him to ask the Cheyenne Night Watcher to teach her sign language. When the commercially-minded town wants Nolan as the main attraction at a picnic, he agrees if the Stalarskis can attend. A thunderstorm and a Walt Whitman reading bring on one of Nolan's flashbacks. The crowd gapes as he shouts to the dead men of Gettysburg.

Roman exonerates himself to the Army by naming Nolan as a Cheyenne conspirator. Finding Kathy communicating with Night Watcher, the incensed father attacks her. The Indian steps in and takes a fatal knife wound. As Kathy runs to Nolan for help, Roman suffers one of his epileptic seizures. The little ones hide their unconscious father from Nolan's anger. He takes the dying Night Watcher to his people, unwittingly providing an easy trail for the Army. The Cheyenne hear from Night Watcher how the teacher-warrior restored the former Dog Soldier's lost dignity.

Awakening, Roman wanders off mumbling he'll make Nolan pay for interfering in another man's family. The children prepare to escape from their abusive father. Carrie insists she must collect a cherished book from her hidey-hole in Nolan's valley. Nolan arrives at his bloodied cabin, just before Kathy and the boys come looking for Carrie. They follow a trail of book pages to the child's mutilated body. The town accuses their crazy teacher. Horrified that he had not prevented the tragedy by eliminating Roman when he had the opportunity, the crushed Nolan stoically accepts responsibility.

Fear prompts Roman to reinforce rumors Nolan hid another murdered child in the cemetery. As one drunken bunch digs up that grave, a second group drags Nolan to the hilltop hanging tree. Kathy frantically chases after her father, but cannot stop him from setting fire to Nolan's schoolhouse and his "evil books." She faces the Dog Soldiers who have come for revenge upon Roman and courageously convinces them to stop Nolan's execution.

The Cheyenne leader speaks for Kathy as she signs about Nolan's character to the vigilantes. She then accuses Roman of little Carrie's murder. Weeping that he couldn't stop himself, the father admits it. As Nolan refills his daughter's grave, little Tom Stalarski denounces the people for caring only for themselves. Nolan and his new family leave the townspeople watching flames consume the school.

APPENDIX L

THE ART OF PITCHING

By Sally J. Walker

I. Develop a Mindset . . . Beforehand

Evaluate your ability to create . . .

1. Likeability: Allow yourself to care & be curious about this stranger
2. Common Ground: Requires honest interest, cannot be faked
3. Connection: Genuine warmth about being in this person's presence
4. "Being in Sync" : Pacing, changing "depths" and "tone"
5. Outward Focus: ON the buyer's body language, speech patterns, eye, contact

II. Prepare for THIS Person/Organization . . . How Professional are YOU?

A. Know the CANON of your industry, current trends, daily updates
B. Research the person/organization, role in the company, credits
C. General knowledge needed beyond narrow focus, current affairs, experts

III. Understand the Purpose of this Event, Your Square One

A. "What do I want?"
   1. To learn (about this person, this organization, how I "fit")
   2. To build rapport (with this person as one more "Link in Life")
   3. To get ONLY ONE request met (because I have shown my worth)

B. "What do they want?"
   1. They want to find that one "special" project for the world
   2. Be ready to adjust as you discover new information

C. "What do they expect?"
   1. What did your competitors propose?
      a. How was it presented?
      b. What materials did they use?
      c. What was their "Core" message?
      d. How did they "Position" themselves . . . How are you different?
   2. EXCEED expectations in your own UNIQUE way

IV. Make the Process EASY on your Buyer

A. Understand YOURSELF, if you want EITHER . . .
   1. Success . . . of having ONE request fulfilled
   2. Respect . . . a superior position to the buyer (intellectual, creative, etc.)

B. So, make it EASY by . . .
  1. Work around their schedule, not yours
  2. Starting by stating your purpose in being there
  3. Again, make ONLY one request
  4. Have materials prepared, in the order needed
  5. Provide context of "You already know this, but . . ."
  6. Be able to summarize previous points if interrupted at any point
  7. Be ready for MORE (if asked "Do you have anything else?")
  8. Offer to handle follow up contact
  9. Offer to supply written synopsis/notes on the meeting
  10. Arrive early & plan to end EARLY

V. Self-confidence is necessary

A. Be aware of yourself & your success patterns
B. Define your realistic concept of success

C. Tense on the inside, calm outside . . . takes practice
  1. Talk less (with leading statements to the buyer for feedback)
  2. Use short sentences (conversational with natural gestures)
  3. Pause (Beat) when buyer done speaking (as if absorbing thoughts)
  4. Breathe deeply, maintain relaxed appearance

D. Remember: "If you are willing to die, its easier to live."
- Appreciate the moment!

VI. The Preparation

A. Anticipate questions
  1. "What do you do?" (Name, home, occupation, interest) BE BRIEF!
  2. "What's your project about?" (Logline, Characters, Theme)
  3. "What EXACTLY do you propose?" (Target audience, length)

B. A moment's access is NOT an opportunity
  1. Be considerate of appropriateness
  2. The "NEVERS"
    a. Someone you don't know
    b. Without prior customizing your pitch to their needs
    c. Deliver pitch like an intimate "First Kiss"

C. Title your project . . . S.M.A.R.T.
Short
Memorable
Accurate
Repeatable
Tonally appropriate

D. Develop a Teaser . . . Logline (and in-hand Synopsis)
   1. Provide statistics, catch phrases, comparisons, long-term effects/benefits
   2. Test/Practice, elsewhere, conversational, present then stop talking

VII. The Presentation . . in Stages (One step at a time)

A. Avoid "Deal Breakers," anything that stops (apology, flamboyance)
   Problem: Lack of focus on buyers signals & common sense

B. Rapport's connection
   Problem: Talking the pitch before comfortable with one another

C. Info Gathering
   Problem: Pitching before knowledge of buyer's state-of-mind

D. Actual Pitch (simple, Enthusiastic, Key Words = Conversational)
   Problem: Boring, weak or strained, missing the buyer's target

E. Closing (Ask for ONE thing only & offer the follow-up)
   Problem: Too aggressive/presumptuous, impatient, immature

VIII. Practice, Practice, Practice

A. Write it out, read aloud in a mirror & time it
   1. Have notes on characters, research
   2. Focus on the drama of the story, the power of the characters
B. ID comfort level = Recite until conversational
C. Focus: Logline, Characters, The Point/Theme (Memorable)

APPENDIX M

SCREENPLAY Score Sheet

Score ______

Title of Manuscript ________________________________

Genre:			
	Film Noir	Contemporary	Period
	Adaptation	Action-Adventure	Comedy
	Mystery	Family/Juvenile	Fantasy
	Science Fiction	Horror	Romance/Love Story
	Western	Inspirational	

SCORING: 5 = Outstanding 4 = Above Average 3 = Average 2 = Below Average 1 = Poor

CHARACTERIZATION

____ Are the Main Characters easily identified & succinctly described?
____ Is the Antagonist (person/element) identified & as strong/stronger than Protagonist?
____ Are character actions believable & visually motivated?
____ Are Supporting & Ancillary Cast used appropriately?
____ Do you CARE what happens to the Main Characters?

DIALOGUE

____ Is the majority of the speeches succinct & true to character?
____ Does the dialogue strengthen character & motivation?
____ Are the speeches free of dialect & overabundance of parentheticals?
____ Does the dialogue consistently move the story forward?
____ Does action-narrative play well off dialogue (more showing vs. telling)?

STORY DEVELOPMENT

____ Does the Opening Scene have a strong hook?
____ Is the STORY QUESTION proposed in the first 10 pages & ultimately answered?
____ Are the elements of time, place, tone sufficiently established & consistent?

____ Is the story well-paced, smoothly structured with rising tension & in the appropriate length?
____ Is the story original & strongly representative of its genre without stereotyping?

OVERALL IMPRESSION
____ Is the writing fresh & free of clichés?
____ Does the writing & story as a whole hold your interest throughout?
____ Does each scene serve a purpose? Are scene & transitions handled well?
____ Is narrative visual yet not over-loaded with extraneous detail & in appropriate length?
____ Is there a story/character ARC that you CARE about?

MECHANICS
____ Is the script presented in appropriate spec script format & length?
____ Is the script free of spelling & grammatical errors?

STUDIO EVALUATION
____ Writer: Pass= 0 Consider= 3 Recommend= 5
____ Script: Pass= 0 Consider= 3 Recommend= 5

APPENDIX N

The Relationship Plane

The Relationship Plane is the overview of the entire flight of stairs, so to speak.

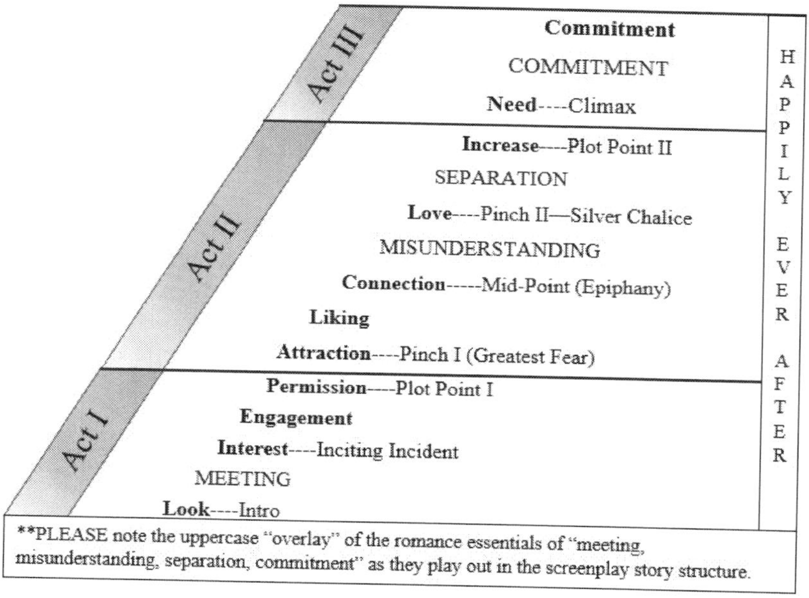

FIGURE 1.2 The Relationship Plane

Your narrative introduction of the dynamics within the three acts of storytelling.

Relationship Plane Definitions . . . as related to Screenplays:

Look: Initial encounter where Linda Howard's Step 1 happens . . . but characters are going about their business. Though other person is noted and that event is seen by the audience, the two characters are not instantaneously turned on!

Interest: Howard's Steps 2 . . . This contact can illicit an awareness of pheromones prompting the body language of opening toward this other person, watching and listening for what makes this person so intriguing. This event must happen to move the relationship forward, to make them memorable to one another when they are apart. This event will have a direct link with the "Permission" of Plot Point I that ends the set-up and launches the couple into actually investigating the totally new world of this relationship.

Engagement: Howard's Step 3 . . . Where the two people seek a mental commonality and acknowledge the "Pull Factor" of the pheromones-physical attraction. But the tentative nature of cautious humans maintains the distance with the "Push Factor."

Permission: Howard's Step 4 . . . The two have moved close enough to physically touch hand-to-hand and maintain that contact. Trust blossoms and in the awareness of accepting, the two step across the social barrier from acquaintances to curious investigators. They allow themselves to intellectually open to this other person.

Attraction: Howard's Step 5-6 . . . Acknowledging that this "might" be an important person is admitting one may not be complete and independent, may need someone else to make life a happy experience. How does one happily survive incomplete? That can create insecurity and fear of loneliness heretofore not recognized. The need to step close and hold this other person can be a driving force.

Liking: Not related to any of Howard's Steps but a definite element in relationships is liking one another, a visual element vitally important to the longevity of the relationship. In the build up of physical attraction and the signaling of all that chemistry, a writer has to demonstrate these two people **respect** one another then they begin to see glimpses of Essence. Those inner qualities make them feel so comfortable they want to be around that other person more. They want to share some of their own Essence to see if they are compatible. Are their values the same?

Connection: Howard's Steps 5-9 . . . At the Mid-Point of a story an "epiphany" happens, a culminating event that shocks the characters into an awareness of the high stakes of both failure and success. I propose merely heightening the physical tension, but it could be taking the couple all the way through Step 12, *if* your plot events will now rip them apart in the second half of the story. Otherwise, you have just completed "The happy story of the happy people in the happy village" and now who wants to see the rest of the movie? No! This physical epiphany has to really complicate the evolution of the relationship. It has to result in questions and consequences that drive through the rest of the story.

Love: Characters remembering Howard's Steps . . . These two people privately recognize Essence and each is changed forever because of the other person. They accept they are in love with one another, but are not ready to announce it. The visual evidence of this awareness, this cherishing of new emotional depths is the "False Reward of the Silver Chalice" wherein the two people so badly want to love and be loved. They falsely believe they can win the heart and devotion of the other person.

Increase: Risk of losing intimacy forever . . . When the antagonist or the world beats the lead characters into a corner. All of their skills and knowledge are proven inadequate. What is the one thing they want above all else in a romance? To be a whole unit with the beloved. The bond forged now may never reach its fullest potential. This increased risk of loss so assaults the Essence that the characters have no choice but to come up fighting for the very survival of who they are.

Need: In the climactic "battle" for survival, both parties recognize and accept that they are not whole without the other, Essence to Essence. Words are not enough. Visuals, visuals, visuals. Body language, eye contact, a race through Howard's 12 Steps. The couple joyously succumbs to the "Pull Factor."

Commitment: This is the visual evidence that the two have become one, not skin-to-skin, but as a united couple ready to face the world. This provides the logical consequences the audience can imagine as the After-Story.

Happily Ever After: The relationship goes on with the two united and making a happy life together. They can cope with anything life throws at them because they are together. That ain't SOMERSBY where he chooses an honorable death over the relationship or LOVE STORY where she dies and he lives alone. Or OUT OF AFRICA where he dies and she lives the rest of her life alone.

APPENDIX O

List of Primary Romance Films and List of Love Story Films

NOTE: I am not standing in judgment of how strong or weak any of these are, just saying they have a relationship story that evolves into a romance with the couple as a committed unit by the end.

PRIMARY ROMANCE FILMS

27 Dresses
Accidental Tourist
Alex & Emma
An Affair to Remember
Angel Eyes
Australia
AVATAR
Breakfast at Tiffany's
Charade
Chasing Liberty
Claudine
Down with Love
Ever After
Far & Away
For Love of Ivy
French Kiss
Garden State
Ghost and Mrs. Muir (if commitment after death counts)
Giant
Gilda
Hitch
How Stella Got Her Groove Back
Il Postino
I.Q.
Jane Eyre (Joan Fontaine/Orson Welles)
Jerry Maguire
Jewel of the Nile
Jezebel
Juno

Kate & Leopold
Kingdom of Heaven
Ladyhawk
Lethal Weapon IV
Letters to Juliet
Love Actually
Love in the Afternoon
Maid in Manhattan
Maurice
Meet Joe Black
My Big Fat Greek Wedding
Never Been Kissed
Ninotchka
North by Northwest
Notorious
Now Voyager
Original Sin
Possession
Pride and Prejudice (Laurence Olivier/Greer Garson)
Pretty Woman
Raiders of the Lost Ark
Return to Me
Riders of the Purple Sage (starring Ed Harris for Turner
Romancing the Stone
(A) Room with a View
Sabrina (Humphrey Bogart/Audrey Hepburn)
Shakespeare in Love
Sideways
Six Days, Seven Nights
Sense and Sensibility
Sleepless in Seattle
Some Like It Hot
Some One Like You
Something's Gotta Give
Somewhere in Time
Splash
Stargate
Star Wars II, III, V, VI
Story of Three Loves (Equilibrium)
Sweet Home Alabama
The Adjustment Bureau
The African Queen
The American President

The Best Years of Our Lives
The Big Easy
The Devil Wears Prada
The Family Stone
The Fifth Element
The Holiday
The Lady Eve
The Lake House
The Last of the Mohicans
The Man from Snowy River
The Notebook
The Proposal
The Quiet Man
The Wedding Date
The Wedding Planner
The Young Victoria
Top Gun
Two Weeks Notice
Valentine's Day
(A) Walk in the Clouds
When Harry Met Sally
While You Were Sleeping
Working Girl
Wrangler
You've Got Mail (The Shop Around the Corner)

LOVE STORY FILMS
(Where the couple did not end up with a commitment into the future at the end)

A Stranger Among Us
Braveheart
Bridges of Madison County
Brokeback Mountain
Casablanca
City of Angels
Duel in the Sun
Gone with the Wind
Legends of the Fall
Mr. Jones
Out of Africa
Portrait of Jenny
Roman Holiday

Somersby
Story of Three Loves (The Jealous Lover, Mademoiselle)
Sunset Boulevard
The Heiress
The Horsewhisperer
The Wings of the Dove
Titanic
Witness

* * * * * * * * * *

ABOUT THE AUTHOR

Omaha resident Sally J. Walker's published credits include literary, romance, and western novels, two essay collections, several creative writing textbooks, children's books, stage plays, poetry, and many magazine articles on the craft of writing, including staff contributions to two international film magazines for 10 years. Under the mentorship of UCLA's renowned film industry icon Lew Hunter, Sally has written over 30 screenplays with Hollywood representation and is active in the Nebraska Film Association. Even with her strenuous writing schedule, Sally found time to be Editorial Director for a small publishing company for 18 years and teach creative writing, both on-line and in the classroom. For updated information, go to her website at http://www.sallyjwalker.com